# The Cambridge Companion to Thomas Mann

Key dimensions of Thomas Mann's writing and life are explored in this collection of specially commissioned essays. In addition to introductory chapters on all the main works of fiction, the essays and diaries, there are four chapters examining Mann's oeuvre in relation to major themes. These thematic explorations include his position as a realistic writer concerned with the history of his own times and as a commentator on German and American politics; his controversial reputation as an intellectual novelist; the literary techniques that enabled his challenging fictions to appeal to a wide audience; and the homosexual subtext running through his fiction and diaries. A final chapter looks at the pitfalls of translating Mann into English. The essays are well supported by supplementary material including a chronology of the period and detailed guides to further reading. Altogether the volume provides an invaluable resource for scholars and students.

RITCHIE ROBERTSON is Professor of German at Oxford University and Fellow and Tutor of St John's College, Oxford. He is the author of *Kafka: Judaism, Politics, and Literature* (1985) and *Heine* (1988), which have also been published in German translation, and *The 'Jewish Question' in German Literature, 1749–1939* (1999). He has also published numerous translations from German, including works by Heine and Hoffmann. He is an editor of *The Modern Language Review.*

THE CAMBRIDGE
COMPANION TO THE

# THOMAS MANN

# CAMBRIDGE COMPANIONS TO LITERATURE

*The Cambridge Companion to Greek Tragedy*
edited by P. E. Easterling

*The Cambridge Companion to Old English
Literature*
edited by Malcolm Godden and
Michael Lapidge

*The Cambridge Companion to Medieval
Romance*
edited by Roberta L. Kreuger

*The Cambridge Companion to Medieval English
Theatre*
edited by Richard Beadle

*The Cambridge Companion to English
Renaissance Drama*
edited by A. R. Braunmuller and
Michael Hattaway

*The Cambridge Companion to Renaissance
Humanism*
edited by Jill Kraye

*The Cambridge Companion to English Poetry,
Donne to Marvell*
edited by Thomas N. Corns

*The Cambridge Companion to English
Literature, 1500–1600*
edited by Arthur F. Kinney

*The Cambridge Companion to English
Literature, 1650–1740*
edited by Steven N. Zwicker

*The Cambridge Companion to Writing of the
English Revolution*
edited by N. H. Keeble

*The Cambridge Companion to English
Restoration Theatre*
edited by Deborah C. Payne Fisk

*The Cambridge Companion to British
Romanticism*
edited by Stuart Curran

*The Cambridge Companion to
Eighteenth-Century Poetry*
edited by John Sitter

*The Cambridge Companion to the
Eighteenth-Century Novel*
edited by John Richetti

*The Cambridge Companion to Victorian Poetry*
edited by Joseph Bristow

*The Cambridge Companion to the
Victorian Novel*
edited by Deirdre David

*The Cambridge Companion to American
Realism and Naturalism*
edited by Donald Pizer

*The Cambridge Companion to
Nineteenth-Century American
Women's Writing*
edited by Dale M. Bauer and Philip Gould

*The Cambridge Companion to the Classic
Russian Novel*
edited by Malcolm V. Jones and
Robin Feuer Miller

*The Cambridge Companion to the French
Novel: from 1800 to the present*
edited by Timothy Unwin

*The Cambridge Companion to Modernism*
edited by Michael Levenson

*The Cambridge Companion to Australian
Literature*
edited by Elizabeth Webby

*The Cambridge Companion to American
Women Playwrights*
edited by Brenda Murphy

*The Cambridge Companion to Modern British
Women Playwrights*
edited by Elaine Aston and Janelle Reinelt

*The Cambridge Companion to Virgil*
edited by Charles Martindale

*The Cambridge Companion to Dante*
edited by Rachel Jacoff

*The Cambridge Companion to Proust*
edited by Richard Bales

*The Cambridge Companion to Thomas Mann*
edited by Ritchie Robertson

*The Cambridge Companion to Chekhov*
edited by Vera Gottlieb and Paul Allain

*The Cambridge Companion to Ibsen*
edited by James McFarlane

*The Cambridge Companion to Brecht*
edited by Peter Thomson and
Glendyr Sacks

*The Cambridge Chaucer Companion*
edited by Piero Boitani and Jill Mann

*The Cambridge Companion to Shakespeare*
edited by Margareta de Grazia and
Stanley Wells

*The Cambridge Companion to Shakespeare
on Film*
edited by Russell Jackson

*The Cambridge Companion to Shakespeare
Comedy*
edited by Alexander Leggatt

*The Cambridge Companion to Spenser*
edited by Andrew Hadfield

*The Cambridge Companion to Ben Jonson*
edited by Richard Harp and Stanley Stewart

*The Cambridge Companion to Milton*
edited by Dennis Danielson

*The Cambridge Companion to Samuel Johnson*
edited by Greg Clingham

*The Cambridge Companion to Keats*
edited by Susan J. Wolfson

## CAMBRIDGE COMPANIONS TO CULTURE

# THE CAMBRIDGE
## COMPANION TO
# THOMAS MANN

EDITED BY
## RITCHIE ROBERTSON

**CAMBRIDGE**
UNIVERSITY PRESS

PUBLISHED BY THE PRESS SYNDICATE OF THE UNIVERSITY OF CAMBRIDGE
The Pitt Building, Trumpington Street, Cambridge, United Kingdom

CAMBRIDGE UNIVERSITY PRESS
The Edinburgh Building, Cambridge CB2 2RU, UK
40 West 20th Street, New York, NY 10011-4211, USA
477 Williamstown Road, Port Melbourne, VIC 3207, Australia
Ruiz de Alarcón 13, 28014 Madrid, Spain
Dock House, The Waterfront, Cape Town 8001, South Africa

http://www.cambridge.org

First published 2002

Printed in the United Kingdom at the University Press, Cambridge

*Typeface* Sabon 10/13 pt.    *System* LATEX 2$_\varepsilon$   [TB]

*A catalogue record for this book is available from the British Library*

*Library of Congress Cataloguing in Publication Data*
The Cambridge companion to Thomas Mann / edited by Ritchie Robertson.
p.   cm. – (Cambridge companions to literature)
Includes bibliographical references and index.
ISBN 0 521 65310 X – ISBN 0 521 65370 3 (pbk.)
1. Mann, Thomas, 1875–1955 – Criticism and interpretation – Handbooks,
manuals, etc.   I. Robertson, Ritchie.   II. Series.
PT2625.A44 Z54385   2002
833'.912–dc21                                    2001035306

ISBN 0 521 65310 X hardback
ISBN 0 521 65370 3 paperback

# CONTENTS

# NOTES ON THE CONTRIBUTORS

MARK M. ANDERSON is Professor of German at Columbia University and author of *Kafka's Clothes: Ornament and Aestheticism in the Habsburg Fin de Siècle* (1992).

ALAN BANCE is Professor of German at the University of Southampton. His publications include *Theodor Fontane: The Major Novels* (1982) and many studies of Thomas Mann and other modern German prose writers.

MICHAEL BEDDOW has recently retired as Professor of German at Leeds University. His publications include *The Fiction of Humanity: Studies in the Bildungsroman from Wieland to Thomas Mann* (1982) and studies of Goethe's *Faust I* and Mann's *Doctor Faustus*, the latter in the series 'Landmarks in World Literature' (1994).

PAUL BISHOP is Professor of German at Glasgow University. His publications include *The Dionysian Self: C. G. Jung's Reception of Friedrich Nietzsche* (1995) and many studies in literary and intellectual history from Goethe onwards.

TIMOTHY BUCK has recently retired as Lecturer in German at Edinburgh University. He has published numerous studies of German linguistic history and medieval literature.

YAHYA ELSAGHE is Professor of German at the University of Berne. He has published numerous studies of Hölderlin, Goethe and Thomas Mann, most recently *Die imaginäre Nation: Thomas Mann und das 'Deutsche'* (2000).

WOLF-DANIEL HARTWICH teaches German literature at Heidelberg University. His publications include *Die Sendung Moses: Von der Aufklärung bis Thomas Mann* (1997).

FREDERICK A. LUBICH is Professor of German at Old Dominion University, Norfolk, Virginia. He has published *Die Dialektik von Logos und Eros im Werk von Thomas Mann* (1986) and two studies of Max Frisch. He is currently working on two books: *Mann-Mosaik: Studien zum Werk von Thomas Mann* and *The Return of the Great Mother: The Discourse of Matriarchy in 20th-Century German Literary and Cultural History*.

MICHAEL MINDEN is Lecturer in German at Cambridge University and a Fellow of Jesus College. He has published *Arno Schmidt: A Critical Study of his Prose* (1982) and *The German Bildungsroman: Incest and Inheritance* (1997), and edited *Thomas Mann* in the series 'Modern Literatures in Perspective' (1995).

T. J. REED is Taylor Professor of German at Oxford University and a Fellow of the Queen's College. His books include *Thomas Mann: The Uses of Tradition* (1974; enlarged edition 1996), *The Classical Centre: Goethe and Weimar* (2nd edition, 1986), and several studies and editions of *Death in Venice*. He is one of the editors of the forthcoming annotated edition of Mann's complete works.

RITCHIE ROBERTSON is Professor of German at Oxford and a Fellow of St John's College. His books include *Kafka: Judaism, Politics, and Literature* (1985) and *The 'Jewish Question' in German Literature, 1749–1939* (1999).

JUDITH RYAN is Harvard College Professor and Robert K. and Dale J. Weary Professor of German and Comparative Literature at Harvard University. Her books include *The Uncompleted Past: Postwar German Novels and the Third Reich* (1983), *The Vanishing Subject: Early Psychology and Literary Modernism* (1991) and *Rilke, Modernism and Poetic Tradition* (1999).

SUSAN VON ROHR SCAFF is Professor of German at San José State University in California, and author of *History, Myth and Music: Thomas Mann's Timely Fiction* (1998).

HINRICH SIEFKEN has recently retired as Professor of German at Nottingham University. Besides studies of medieval literature, Kafka, Broch and Theodor Haecker, he has published *Thomas Mann: Goethe – 'Ideal der Deutschheit': Wiederholte Spiegelungen* (1981).

ANDREW J. WEBBER is Lecturer in German at Cambridge University and a Fellow of Churchill College. He is the author of *Sexuality and the Sense of Self in the Works of Georg Trakl and Robert Musil* (1990) and *The Doppelgänger: Double Visions in German Literature* (1996).

Thomas Mann continues to have the widest appeal of all German novelists. Although he identified profoundly with various conceptions of Germany and Germanness, he sought during most of his literary career to build bridges between German culture and a succession of wider worlds. His first masterpiece, *Buddenbrooks*, the unrivalled bestseller in twentieth-century German fiction, adopts techniques from French, Russian, and Scandinavian realism to chronicle the lives of a family in a North German backwater. *The Magic Mountain*, though set in the confines of a Swiss sanatorium, takes its setting as a stage where debates about the shape of European culture can be dramatised. The huge tetralogy *Joseph and his Brothers* explores the cultures of the ancient Near East, the origins of religion and culture, and the foundations of a Judaeo-Christian humanism that, as Mann wrote, was under threat from Hitler's Third Reich. And in *Doctor Faustus* Mann revived a German myth, with its theological underpinnings, to present the fictional biography of a quintessential German artist whose tragedy lay not least in cutting himself off from European culture.

Mann's mission to explain Germany to the wider world was made more urgent by his own exile from Germany. Having been an outspoken opponent of the reactionary Right and of the National Socialists from 1922 onwards, he moved, after Hitler's accession to power, to France, Switzerland, and eventually the United States. Deprived of his German citizenship, he became a citizen first of Czechoslovakia and later of the United States. In America, where the translations of his fiction already had a large readership, he enjoyed more prominence than almost any other émigré, and used it to become a spokesman for humanism and a cultural mediator.

During Mann's lifetime, his public persona inevitably coloured the reception of his novels. They were often understood with dutiful awe as intellectual fiction of a high order, top-heavy with German philosophy and history. Over-attention to this aspect of Mann's fiction often distracted readers, especially those reliant on imperfect translations, from the light and polished irony, apparent even in the short stories with which Mann entered the literary scene in the 1890s, and from the practically Dickensian humour governing the characterisation in the major novels. In the 1970s scholars drew attention to Mann's career as a politically engaged intellectual and to the close links between his political stances and his writing, especially *The Magic Mountain*, the short fiction of the 1920s, and the large body of reflective and thought-provoking essays that Mann produced for many public occasions. It was also in the 1970s that Mann's surviving diaries began to be published, not only proving an invaluable biographical source and a major addition to the canon of literary journals, but also disclosing much about his lifelong homosexuality. Although *Death in Venice* and some published correspondence were frank enough, the insights provided by the diaries coincided with the new perspectives of gender-oriented criticism to open up additional layers of meaning in large areas of Mann's fiction.

Like any classic, therefore, Mann has continued to be reread in new ways, and part of the purpose of this collection of introductory essays is to offer a variety of approaches to his work. The first four contributions are thematic. They consider Mann in the light of his engagement with German history; as an intellectual novelist; as a supremely skilful practitioner of the novel, both heightening his readers' moral awareness and providing them with gratification; and using these techniques to explore forms and categories of masculinity. There follow three essays on the shorter fiction, six on the major novels (other fictional works, including *Royal Highness*, are dealt with in passing), and appreciations of Mann the essayist and the diarist. Finally, there is a critical examination of the translations of Mann currently available in English, reminding us that despite his popularity in the English-speaking world, part of his claim to fame lies in his uniquely skilful and untranslatable use of the German language. The essays are intended to be useful both to readers who have access to the original, and readers who know Mann in English translation. Each chapter concludes with a list of further reading relevant to the subject of the chapter; the selected bibliography at the end of the book gives information about German and English editions of Mann's works and includes a wide selection of criticism written in both languages.

I should like to thank all the contributors to this book for their enthusiastic and good-natured co-operation; the four anonymous readers enlisted by Cambridge University Press for their detailed, supportive and constructive comments; and Linda Bree for her invariable helpfulness and patience as editor.

Ritchie Robertson

1875   6 June: birth of Paul Thomas Mann to Julia (née da Silva Bruhns, born 1851) and Thomas Johann Heinrich Mann (1840), the second of five children. Paul Thomas's siblings are Luiz Heinrich (born 1871), Julia (1877), Carla (1881) and Viktor (1890).

1877   Mann's father is elected to the Lübeck senate.

1891   Mann's father dies on 13 October; the family firm (Johann Siegmund Mann Corn Merchants, Commission and Transport Agents) is liquidated and the family house sold, leaving Heinrich and Thomas with independent means sufficient to establish themselves as writers.

1893   Frau Mann moves to Munich with the three younger children (Julia, Carla, and Viktor); Thomas stays at school in Lübeck.

1894   Thomas leaves school and joins his mother in Munich, where he starts working for an insurance company, but leaves it after four months in the hope of a career as a journalist. His first story, 'Gefallen' [Fallen], is published in the Naturalist journal *Die Gesellschaft* [Society]. In the next few years he gradually publishes short stories in the periodical edited by his brother Heinrich, *Das Zwanzigste Jahrhundert* [The Twentieth Century]. The two brothers also work and travel together.

1898   *Der kleine Herr Friedemann* [*Little Herr Friedemann*], a collection of short stories, Mann's first book, is published.

1899   beginning of friendship with Paul Ehrenberg

1900   Mann completes the novel *Buddenbrooks* in May. Called up for military service, beginning on 1 October, but thanks to an inflamed tendon in his right foot he is confined to bed and given leave in December.

1901   *Buddenbrooks* published in two volumes. This novel was the foundation for Mann's reputation and success: it sold a million copies in just over a year, and continued to have a steady sale.

1903    Another collection of short stories, *Tristan*, appears (including 'Tonio Kröger').

1905    11 February: Mann marries Katia Pringsheim (born 1883), daughter of a wealthy Munich mathematics professor of Jewish descent.

       9 November: birth of their first child, Erika Mann

1906    18 November: birth of Klaus Mann

1909    27 March: birth of Gottfried ('Golo') Mann. Mann publishes the novel *Königliche Hoheit* [*Royal Highness*], which is judged lightweight by comparison with *Buddenbrooks*.

1910    Mann begins work on *Felix Krull*, only to abandon it in 1911.

       7 June: birth of Monika Mann

       30 July: suicide of Mann's sister Carla

1911    May: feeling ill and depressed, Mann visits the Adriatic island of Brioni and Venice with his wife; they stay (26 May to 2 June) in the Hôtel des Bains on the Lido at Venice.

1912    *Death in Venice* completed in June, published in a journal in October and November. 15 May to 12 June: Mann visits Katia, who is staying in a sanatorium in Davos in Switzerland.

1913    Mann begins work on *The Magic Mountain*, planning it as a novella similar in length to *Death in Venice*.

1914    August: outbreak of war. Mann shares the widespread patriotic euphoria.

1915    November: Heinrich Mann's essay on Zola is published, with a hostile reference to Thomas Mann, who is inspired to start work on the *Reflections of an Unpolitical Man*.

1918    24 April: birth of Elisabeth Mann

       9 November: proclamation of a German Republic

       Just before the war ends, Mann publishes *Reflections of an Unpolitical Man*.

1919    7 April: a Soviet Republic is declared in Munich; it is overthrown by government and paramilitary troops on 1–3 May.

       21 April: birth of Michael Mann

       Mann resumes work on *The Magic Mountain*.

1922    24 June: assassination of the Foreign Minister, Walther Rathenau

       15 October: Mann delivers his address 'Von deutscher Republik' ('On the German Republic') in the Beethovensaal in Berlin; ostensibly a celebration of the dramatist Gerhart Hauptmann's sixtieth birthday, it is recognised as Mann's public avowal of support for the Weimar Republic.

1926    31 August to 13 September: the Manns take a holiday at Forte di

Marmi in Italy, where the events inspire *Mario and the Magician* (published 1930).

1927   10 May: suicide of Mann's sister Julia

1929   Mann is awarded the Nobel Prize for Literature, explicitly for *Buddenbrooks*.

His speech on Lessing, at the bicentenary of the latter's birth, marks an important attempt to reconcile myth with reason in the struggle against fascism.

1930   February to April: travels in Egypt and Palestine

1932   The centenary of Goethe's death brings forth important lectures and essays.

1933   30 January: Hitler becomes Chancellor of Germany.

10 February: Mann delivers lecture on Wagner at Munich University.

11 February: Mann leaves Germany with his wife, initially to lecture in Holland and Belgium, then to visit Switzerland; while there, his children Klaus and Erika warn him not to return. After spending the summer on the French Riviera, the Manns settle at Küsnacht outside Zürich in Switzerland.

October: publication of *The Tales of Jacob* (first volume of *Joseph and his Brothers*)

1934   April: publication of *The Young Joseph*

May–June: Mann pays his first visit to the United States; lectures on Goethe at Yale University.

1935   June–July: Mann revisits the United States and receives an honorary doctorate from Harvard.

1936   Mann is deprived of German citizenship; becomes a Czech citizen. Also deprived of his honorary doctorate from Bonn University.

*Joseph in Egypt* is published in Vienna by Bermann-Fischer, Mann's publisher, now also in exile.

8 May: lecture on 'Freud and the Future' delivered in Vienna to celebrate Freud's eightieth birthday.

1937   April: Mann revisits US at invitation of the New School for Social Research in New York.

1938   February: returns to US for long visit; news of Hitler's annexation of Austria encourages Mann to settle in US; accepts a chair at Princeton University.

1 October: German invasion of Czechoslovakia

9 November: 'Kristallnacht': attacks on Jewish homes and synagogues throughout Germany

1939 3 September: Britain and France declare war on Germany after Germany invades Poland.

1941 April: the Manns move to Pacific Palisades, Los Angeles.

December: US declares war on Japan after its attack on Pearl Harbor; Germany and Italy declare war on the US.

1943 *Joseph the Provider* published by Bermann-Fischer, now in Stockholm.

23 May: Mann begins work on *Doctor Faustus*.

'The Tables of the Law', Mann's story about Moses, is published in a book entitled *The Ten Commandments: Ten Short Novels of Hitler's War against the Moral Code*.

1944 Thomas and Katia Mann become American citizens.

1945 12 April: death of Roosevelt

7 May: Germany's unconditional surrender

29 May: lecture, 'Germany and the Germans', delivered at Library of Congress: it is Mann's major statement on the German catastrophe, closely linked to *Doctor Faustus*.

1947 May to August: Thomas and Katia visit Europe, including Britain, Switzerland, Italy and Holland, but not Germany.

1949 21 May: suicide of Klaus Mann

Mann revisits Germany (Frankfurt, Munich, Weimar) in connection with celebrations of Goethe bicentenary.

12 October: founding of German Democratic Republic in Soviet zone of occupation

Beginning of anti-Communist hysteria in US, stirred up by Senator Joseph McCarthy

1950 2 March: death of Heinrich Mann

1951 Mann resumes work on *Felix Krull*.

1952 Alarmed by McCarthyism, Mann moves to Switzerland; he and Katia rent house at Erlenbach near Zürich.

1954 The Manns buy a house at Kilchberg on Lake Zürich.

1955 12 August: Thomas Mann dies in Zürich of arteriosclerosis.

# LIST OF THOMAS MANN'S WORKS

English titles given here in square brackets are not published titles.

| | | |
|---|---|---|
| 1894 | 'Gefallen' | 'Fallen' |
| 1896 | 'Enttäuschung' | 'Disillusionment' |
| 1897 | 'Der kleine Herr Friedemann' | 'Little Herr Friedemann' |
| | 'Der Bajazzo' | 'The Joker' |
| 1898 | *Der kleine Herr Friedemann* | |
| 1901 | *Buddenbrooks* | *Buddenbrooks* |
| 1902 | 'Gladius Dei' | 'Gladius Dei' |
| 1903 | *Tonio Kröger* | *Tonio Kröger* |
| | 'Tristan' | 'Tristan' |
| 1905 | 'Schwere Stunde' | 'A Weary Hour' |
| | *Fiorenza* | *Fiorenza* |
| 1909 | *Königliche Hoheit* | *Royal Highness* |
| | 'Süßer Schlaf' | 'Sweet Sleep' |
| 1910 | 'Der alte Fontane' | 'The Old Fontane' |
| 1911 | 'Über die Kunst Richard Wagners' | [On the Art of Richard Wagner] |
| 1912 | *Der Tod in Venedig* | *Death in Venice* |
| 1914 | 'Gedanken im Krieg' | [Thoughts in War] |
| 1915 | *Friedrich und die große Koalition* | [Frederick and the Grand Coalition] |
| 1918 | *Betrachtungen eines Unpolitischen* | [Reflections of an Unpolitical Man] |
| 1919 | *Herr und Hund* | *Master and Dog* |
| | *Gesang vom Kindchen* | *A Birth and a Christening* (literally, 'Song of the Baby') |
| 1921 | 'Goethe und Tolstoi' | [Goethe and Tolstoy] |
| 1922 | *Rede und Antwort* | [Address and Reply] (a collection of essays) |

| 1924 | *Der Zauberberg* | *The Magic Mountain* |
| | 'Vorspruch zu einer musikalischen Nietzsche-Feier' | [Opening Words to a Musical Celebration of Nietzsche] |
| 1925 | *Unordnung und frühes Leid* | *Disorder and Early Sorrow* |
| | *Bemühungen* | [Endeavours] (a collection of essays) |
| | 'Deutschland und die Demokratie' | [Germany and Democracy] |
| 1928 | 'Kultur und Sozialismus' | [Culture and Socialism] |
| | 'Dürer' | 'Dürer' |
| 1929 | 'Die Stellung Freuds in der modernen Geistesgeschichte' | 'Freud's Position in the History of Modern Thought' |
| | 'Rede über Lessing' | [Speech on Lessing] |
| 1930 | *Mario und der Zauberer* | *Mario and the Magician* |
| | *Die Forderung des Tages* | [The Day's Demand] (a collection of essays) |
| | 'Deutsche Ansprache. Ein Appell an die Vernunft' | [German Address: An Appeal to Reason] |
| | 'Lebensabriss' | [A Sketch of my Life] |
| 1931 | 'Die Wiedergeburt der Anständigkeit' | [The Rebirth of Decency] |
| 1932 | 'Goethe als Repräsentant des bürgerlichen Zeitalters' | 'Goethe as Representative of the Bourgeois Age' |
| | 'Goethes Laufbahn als Schriftsteller' | [Goethe's Career as a Writer] |
| | 'Die Bäume im Garten. Rede für Pan-Europa' | [The Trees in the Garden. A Speech for Pan-Europe] |
| 1933 | *Die Geschichten Jaakobs* | *The Tales of Jacob* |
| 1934 | *Der junge Joseph* | *The Young Joseph* |
| 1936 | *Joseph in Ägypten* | *Joseph in Egypt* |
| | 'Freud und die Zukunft' | 'Freud and the Future' |
| 1938 | 'Schopenhauer' | |
| 1939 | *Lotte in Weimar* | *The Beloved Returns/Lotte in Weimar* |
| | 'Bruder Hitler' | [Brother Hitler] |
| 1940 | *Die vertauschten Köpfe* | *The Transposed Heads* |
| | 'On Myself' | |
| 1941 | 'Goethe's "Werther"' | |

| 1943 | *Joseph der Ernährer* | *Joseph the Provider* |
| | 'Das Gesetz' | 'The Tables of the Law' |
| 1945 | *Adel des Geistes* | *Nobility of the Spirit* |
| | 'Deutschland und die Deutschen' | [Germany and the Germans] |
| 1947 | *Doktor Faustus* | *Doctor Faustus* |
| | 'Nietzsches Philosophie im Licht unserer Erfahrung' | 'Nietzsche's Philosophy in the Light of our Experience' |
| | 'Die Aufgabe des Schriftstellers' | [The Task of the Writer] |
| 1948 | 'Phantasie über Goethe' | [Goethe: An Imaginative Portrait] |
| 1949 | 'Goethe und die Demokratie' | [Goethe and Democracy] |
| 1951 | *Der Erwählte* | *The Holy Sinner* |
| 1953 | *Die Betrogene* | *The Black Swan* (literally, 'The Deceived Woman') |
| 1954 | *Bekenntnisse des Hochstaplers Felix Krull* | *Confessions of Felix Krull, Confidence Man* |
| 1955 | 'Schiller' | |

# A NOTE ON REFERENCES AND ABBREVIATIONS

Unless otherwise stated, translations of German works are the chapter author's own.

References to Thomas Mann's essays and literary works are to *Gesammelte Werke*, 13 vols. (Frankfurt: Fischer, 1974), cited by volume and page number.

This edition is supplemented where necessary by Thomas Mann, *Essays*, ed. Hermann Kurzke and S. Stachorski, 6 vols. (Frankfurt am Main: Fischer, 1993–1997), referred to as *Essays*.

Diary entries are cited by date from *Tagebücher*, 10 vols., ed. Peter de Mendelssohn (vols. I–V) and Inge Jens (vols. VI–X) (Frankfurt am Main: Fischer, 1979–95)

Letters are cited by date and correspondent, from the following volumes:
Thomas Mann, *Briefe*, ed. Erika Mann, 3 vols. (Frankfurt am Main: Fischer, 1962–5)
Thomas Mann and Karl Kerényi, *Gespräch in Briefen* (Zürich: Rhein-Verlag, 1960)
Thomas Mann, *Briefe an Ernst Bertram aus den Jahren 1910–1955*, ed. Inge Jens (Pfullingen: Neske, 1960)
Thomas Mann, *Briefe an Otto Grautoff 1894–1901 und Ida Boy-Ed 1903–1928*, ed. Peter de Mendelssohn (Frankfurt am Main: Fischer, 1975)
Thomas Mann, Heinrich Mann, *Briefwechsel 1900–1949*, ed. Hans Wysling (Frankfurt am Main: Fischer, 1984)

Some personal statements are quoted from *Dichter über ihre Dichtungen: Thomas Mann*, ed. Hans Wysling (Munich: Heimeran, 1975–82), abbreviated as *DD*.

*Other authors*

Unless otherwise stated, Goethe is quoted from Johann Wolfgang Goethe, *Werke*, Hamburger Ausgabe, ed. Erich Trunz, 14 vols. (Hamburg: Wegner, 1949–60), abbreviated as G with volume and page number.

Freud is quoted from *The Standard Edition of the Complete Psychological Works of Sigmund Freud*, ed. James Strachey, 24 vols. (London: Hogarth Press, 1953–74), abbreviated as *SE*.

Nietzsche is quoted from Friedrich Nietzsche, *Werke*, ed. Giorgio Colli and Mazzino Montinari, 8 vols. (Berlin and New York, 1972–), abbreviated as *Werke*. References to Nietzsche's works are by abbreviated title, with roman numerals for 'book' and arabic for 'section': e.g. *GM* III, §13. Abbreviations used are:

GM   *The Genealogy of Morals*
A   *The Antichrist*
BT   *The Birth of Tragedy*
CW   *The Case of Wagner*
D   *Daybreak*
EH   *Ecce Homo*
GS   *The Gay Science* (also known as *The Joyful Wisdom*)
TI   *The Twilight of the Idols*
WP   *The Will to Power*

# I

# Mann and history

It is paradoxical that a body of work which begins by being so narrowly preoccupied with problems of the writer's self, and which to the end centres on characters expressing his intimate and unchanged concerns, should also contain so much history. Partly it is a matter of natural growth, the widening range of experience in increasingly turbulent times, which a novelist of all people could hardly ignore; but it also sprang from a remarkable congruence between Thomas Mann's themes and the patterns of twentieth-century German history. His work, with all the traditions, ambitions and temptations that lay behind it, was representative of fundamental German situations and responses before he set out consciously to represent them in fiction. When awareness dawned and representation became deliberate analysis, he was able to represent those phenomena with such depth of insight because he had been so deeply part of them and they of him. We can read him for pleasure, but also for understanding. *Crede experto*: believe the man who has gone through it himself. He can offer, in a word that is central to both Mann's art and his ethics, *Erkenntnis* (a complex concept which embraces knowledge, insight, analysis, understanding). Two of Mann's novels in particular are impressive reports – they are a great deal more than that, but they are that too – on crises of modern history: *The Magic Mountain* of 1924 on pre-1914 Europe and on the conflicts, especially acute in Germany, which were left unresolved by the First World War; and *Doctor Faustus* of 1947 on the long roots of Nazism in German culture and society.

There is already history of a kind in Mann's precocious first masterpiece, the family saga *Buddenbrooks* (1901). The novel preserves in amber the commercial and private lives and attitudes of a German nineteenth-century city state (plainly Lübeck, though only its streets and landmarks are ever mentioned, not its name) and displays them in their full dignity, idiosyncrasy and sometimes tragedy. From the grand scenic opening where the city's merchant class and their professional friends gather for a lavish Buddenbrook house-warming, down through four generations of the family and all their vicissitudes to a final bleak scene where only spinsters, divorcees and a widow are left, everything Mann narrates and describes is concretely characteristic of its time and place: the place he knew as the scene of his early years, and the times he had heard tell of or could be informed about by his older relatives.

Recording history was not, however, Mann's aim. He drew on the rich materials to hand for quite different purposes. *Buddenbrooks* is a history of decline and rise: the decline of the family's old vitality and outward standing (the 'Verfall' of the subtitle), and the rise (nowhere so precisely labelled) of inward qualities – intellect, artistic sensibility, creative potential. These new and subtler strengths did not necessarily follow from the waning of vitality, but it seemed in some mysterious way to be their cause when they did arise. That, at any rate, was a common perception of the period; in the wake of Darwin and Nietzsche and their popularisers, heredity and decadence were common coin in the cultural debates of the 1890s. Nietzsche gave the terms a deeply ambivalent sense, decrying mankind's loss of healthy primitive instincts, yet at the same time recognising that the human animal only became 'interesting' when 'sick', that is to say, when instinct had been tamed and transformed into spiritual systems, however perverse.[1] So the thesis of decline and its problematic compensation is itself a piece of history that Mann's first novel enshrines. If the idea was not original, it certainly seemed to fit his own case as an artist sprung from an old merchant line. In *Buddenbrooks*, under the narrative's social surface, he was writing the history of his own talent. The novel grew indeed from the idea for a novella wholly devoted to a sensitive latecomer, a last-generation figure. This would not have been very different from other early stories of Mann's about suffering outsiders. They are all set in the present, with no space for more than a gesture towards causal explanation – accident, illness, mixed parentage. The novel form, in contrast, gave Mann room to show how this human type gradually came about. But the family's genetic history inheres in and interacts with social history. Tracing that inner history down through time by subtle hints and touches, the novel also registers external changes as it goes along, not least the hardening of an older commercial tradition into more hard-nosed business practice. These things compose a varied historical reality which is part of the novel's triumph and a large part of its readers' pleasure. This was not, for Thomas Mann, its point. It is symptomatic that as significant an event as Europe's 1848 revolutions is treated in an offhand, if beguilingly humorous way (I, 181–94; Part 4, Chapter 3).

*Buddenbrooks* remains Mann's one large social canvas. Though his interest in society and the political forces that shape it later became intense, he never again treated social reality head-on on such a scale. That approach belonged to a nineteenth-century realist tradition he had left behind, having just this once used its means for his own ends. It is ironic that his fullest portrayal of society was achieved, and in masterly fashion, when he was least concerned with it for its own sake.

Elsewhere in Mann's early work up to 1914, society is presented unambiguously as the outsider's antithesis and sometimes his antagonist. Society and its members have something he lacks: an unthinking normality and order, what in *Tonio Kröger* (1903) is called a 'seductive banality' (VIII, 302). For the excluded or self-excluding outsider, the 'joys of ordinariness' (ibid.) become an object of yearning. Mann, like Kröger, idealises its fair-haired, blue-eyed representatives. In another mood he pillories its less ideal embodiments, like Herr Klöterjahn and his alarmingly robust baby son in 'Tristan' (also 1903). Yet whether it is soft-focus idealisation or the sharp outlines of satire, these emblematic figures are ultimately biological rather than social types, animals living out their unimpaired vitality, as the figure of the infant Klöterjahn makes clear. Behind ideal and satire is a single reality; they are the contrasting faces of the life-force. As Mann later half-ruefully said, the leitmotif of blondness in his ideal figures was a harmless remnant of the 'blond beast', the vitality-symbol Nietzsche had set against modern decadence (XI, 110). Nietzschean vitalism is constantly present behind the young Thomas Mann's judgements and self-judgements.

Both the finished works and the unfinished projects of the years between *Buddenbrooks* and the First World War show the same inward-looking focus that scarcely engages the outside world. On the face of it, Mann's second novel, *Royal Highness* (1909), is a romantic comedy in which the prince of a small Ruritanian state saves its fortunes by marrying one. Mann had just consolidated his own fortunes by a good marriage. Private reference does not stop there. The tale's point is the allegorical equation of prince and artist: both are purely 'formal' existences, with no real function in society. Ruritania likewise has no real history. This slight idea is worked out over some 350 pages, a mass that did not prevent critics finding it too light from the author of *Buddenbrooks*. Mann did soon afterwards plan a novel about a prince of quite another calibre, Frederick the Great, which would have offered real historical substance and demanded a quite different treatment, but it came to nothing. The writer's points of contact with the subject were too limited and self-referential: the King's ascetic self-discipline and heroic 'ethos of achievement' (i.e. yet more of the prince–writer parallel), and perhaps the homosexuality common to them both.

A second project that seemed to promise and demand substance was the novel 'Maya', conceived as a tapestry of Munich society, a kind of Bavarian *Buddenbrooks*, though with a more calculated philosophical theme:

social 'reality' as a veil of illusion, for which 'maya' is the Buddhist and Schopenhauerian term. Moreover, the central interest, as the surviving work-notes show, is the fictional projection of Mann's intense relationship with his painter friend Paul Ehrenberg, to which society functions as an episodic background. This plan too came to nothing, though four decades later Mann set some of its episodes, with their now historical patina, in the narrative of *Doctor Faustus*.

One aspect of Munich did achieve brief but brilliant realisation in a finished work. The short story 'Gladius Dei' (1902) satirises the Bavarian capital as a reproduction Renaissance Florence: it too is devoted to a cult of visual art that refuses to look into the depths of suffering beneath life's beautiful surface. To complete the parallel, a monkishly costumed outsider rails against the city's wicked sensuality like some grotesque latter-day Savonarola. These echoes from the past serve the very specific protest of a displaced person from Lübeck whose own more probing and compassionate literary art is neglected by Munich in favour of the fashionable visual genre. Mann also treated the theme in its original period in a costume-drama, *Fiorenza* (1905). Despite the added historical distance, the message sounds more vehement, the identification with Savonarola's vengeful will to power is more patent, when narrative detachment is replaced by direct dialogue. The bite of the short story is lost in wordiness; what is left, as the theatre critic Alfred Kerr cuttingly wrote, is so much dutifully read-up Renaissance.[2]

The satire on modern Munich is linked with Mann's other main uncompleted project of these doldrum years, the essay 'Intellect and Art'. As the extensive work-notes show, this was to be a major treatise taking issue with the state of German culture around 1910: literature, theatre, music, art, crafts; trends and attitudes, fads, fashions and influences; major figures of the present (Max Reinhardt, Stefan George, Richard Strauss) and of the recent past (Nietzsche, Wagner); and some ancestral voices (Lessing, Goethe, Schiller, the Romantics) prophesying modernity.[3] The tone is critical, at times polemical, for in all the observed phenomena Mann made out something deeply inimical to his own art: a new wave of taste for the unproblematic beauty of modern (but not too modern!) visual art and music, and a rejection of analysis, social criticism, pathology and decadence – in short, of everything the writers of his generation had concentrated on.[4] The anti-literary trend he had first spotted in Munich now seemed to him an anti-intellectualism pervading German culture. As he was very much an intellectual writer, the new spirit was a threat to his values, hence to his popularity and so in the most practical sense to his career. Personal concerns again, then – but through the lens of the private he was at least starting to perceive external change. If he had completed the essay, it would have been a historical document (even the work-notes, in their rough form, are that) and perhaps a compelling historical diagnosis of society and culture around 1910.

The trouble was, where did he really stand? Was he committed to being only ever the cool analytic mind, the intellectual writer? Other kinds of literature were possible, and rising – writing that aimed to be fresh and unproblematic, healthy and poetic, 'Plastik' rather than 'Kritik', celebrating life in the way visual art was currently assumed to do. New writers were coming along to challenge the old. Some of his own generation – Gerhart Hauptmann, Hugo von Hofmannsthal – seemed to be adapting so as not to miss the bus. Should he polemicise against all this, and thereby publicly set himself against his times? Or should he follow suit and emphasise anything in his own work that was healthy? It was a classic case of beat them or join them. Mann was torn. The self-concern that was too narrow to base substantial novels on was also too uncertain of its direction to allow a clear public statement. The essay too was duly aborted.

Working on this project had involved looking in breadth at current social phenomena, and looking back in time at their historical roots. This was of course only literary and cultural history. Only? There is no clear dividing line between the merely cultural and the allegedly more real forces that make history. It was to be a key element of Mann's later *Erkenntnis* that every cultural or intellectual attitude is latently political: 'in jeder geistigen Haltung ist das Politische latent' (X, 267). Certainly in Germany, so he would write after the German catastrophe, 'das Seelische' – spiritual, cultural, emotional impulse – was the prime moving force, and political action only came after, as its expression and instrument (VI, 408).[5] These were truths derived from his own past, as well as from wider experience.

*Death in Venice* (1912) has a place in history in two distinct ways. In social terms, as a classic of homosexual passion which yet makes enough show of moral judgement not to seem a direct plea or cause a public scandal, and which has been made into a film and an opera with a prestige of their own, it has probably done more to edge homosexuality into the common culture than any other single work of art. The remark of Mann's old enemy Alfred Kerr, that the story 'made pederasty acceptable to the cultivated middle classes', was meant to be sarcastic but has proved prophetic.[6]

The novella has, secondly, something to say about political history, even though the sole mention of the public sphere is the threat of war in its opening sentence – the truncated date '19..' could refer to any one of several pre-1914 crises. Otherwise the themes are internal, first artistic, then emotional, and the hidden depths are moral and psychological. With his artistic discipline collapsing, Aschenbach travels to refresh his creative system, but instinctively is seeking a deeper release (as witness the alarming jungle vision of

Chapter 1). In Nietzschean terms, Dionysus is reasserting his power against too harsh a rule of Apollo; in Freudian terms, it is a revolt against repression. Mann was consciously using Nietzsche, but probably did not yet know Freud; on this his own accounts vary. The Polish boy's beauty does, briefly, inspire new writing, but then becomes an obsession overcoming all rational self-control (as witness Aschenbach's dream-vision of a Dionysian orgy in Chapter 5).

The issues become political only if the collapse of a disciplined individual life is read as a symbol of forces waiting to be unleashed in society. Georg Lukács was the first to see this angle, albeit by trial and error, first stressing Aschenbach's Prussian discipline. 'Prussianism' is an old bogeyman for historians of Germany, not because of any breakdown, however, but because of its ruthless persistence: Wilhelm II's provocation of crises until one of them led to war; the increasing Prussian military control of policy during 1914–18; Hindenburg's selling out of the fragile Weimar democracy to Hitler in 1933; the Wehrmacht general staff holding the candle to the devil of Nazism through the thirties and forties, until the belated conspiracy of a group of officers which nearly killed Hitler. What really matters, as Lukács eventually sees, is not the old Prussian discipline, but the emotional and social forces whose tool it increasingly became, the 'barbaric underworld' which the Venice novella suggests is lurking under the surface of an ordered life or, by implication, of an ordered society.[7] Even that stops short of Mann's own later insight. The solutions to his artistic difficulties that Aschenbach casts around for – rejecting the psychological analysis and understanding he practised in his early work, simplifying morality, abandoning himself to the dark emotions he no longer even wants to control – these things would later strike Thomas Mann, in exile from Nazi Germany, as a clear proto-fascist syndrome. The emotional nexus had taken on political form in the Nazis' violent attacks on reason and intellect, the whipping up of atavistic mass feeling, the collective unreason of enthusiasm for Hitler. Insofar as Aschenbach's problems and temptations had been Mann's own – 'I had these things in me as much as anyone', he wrote to his American patroness Agnes E. Meyer on 30 May 1938 – he shuddered to think he had embodied the coming politics of the age.

The 'socially responsible Apolline narrative'[8] that eventually takes over *Death in Venice* and consigns Aschenbach to a tragic death had not disposed of the potential for atavistic feeling in Mann himself. Within two years, the war that looms in that opening sentence had broken out and Mann was carried away, like most intellectuals in the combatant nations, by the nationalistic emotions of August 1914. Where Mann-Aschenbach's Venetian 'visitation' ('Heimsuchung') by homoerotic passion had been kept in moral check, this new and larger one could be welcomed and embraced. Mann uses the word 'visitation' again prominently in 'Thoughts in War', the article with which in 1914 he leaped to defend his country against the accusations of Entente propaganda: that Germany had provoked and begun hostilities, had flouted morality and broken international law by invading France via neutral Belgium, and was now committing atrocities. Such charges made much of the contrast between the true Germany of culture (Beethoven, Kant, Goethe) and the new Germany of ruthless *Realpolitik* (Nietzsche, Treitschke, the politicians and generals round Kaiser Wilhelm). Mann denied this distinction: true culture was compatible with and in touch with the terrible realities of life; all else was shallow or feigned, mere Western 'civilisation'. In *Frederick and the Grand Coalition* (1915) he drew a parallel with Prussian history: however 'enlightened' the philosopher-prince had been before acceding, the soldier-king was right to be ruthless once he was on the throne. Prussia's destiny was at stake, the outcome justified him. The same applied to Germany now – or, come to think of it (and he clearly did), to Thomas Mann's own transformation.

With these two pieces early in the war, Mann might have shot his political bolt, if his brother Heinrich – an increasingly radical left-wing writer, and now an outspoken critic of German actions – had not countered with his own historical parallel. Heinrich's essay 'Zola' celebrates the French novelist's political commitment, especially to the anti-militarist cause in the notorious Dreyfus affair. More generally, it is about the moral demands on writers in a sabre-rattling society like the French Third Republic and then, back to specifics, it uses personal allusions nobody else would recognise to condemn Thomas's own moral failure and corruption as a writer who has gone along with the sabre-rattlers of the Wilhelmine Second Empire. A long-smouldering conflict between the brothers was now flaring openly.

There were, however, no more exchanges of public rhetoric. Instead, deeply wounded, Thomas withdrew into a long, brooding examination of the essential, 'unpolitical' Germany and its necessary conflict with the political West; also of himself as a writer who, for all his intellectuality and enlightened modern views, had secret roots in that German essence. In a clear-sighted retrospect, he reads Tonio Kröger's nostalgic wish to preserve the innocent world of Hans Hansen against the influence of literature and intellect (i.e. against himself) as instinctive political conservatism (XII, 586, quoting VIII, 303). Yet the title of the enormous book that came out of these broodings was *Reflections of an Unpolitical Man*. The title was both accurate and inaccurate. On the one hand, Mann's image of Wilhelmine Germany, of how it got into the war and of what was at stake, was seriously out of touch with realities, as he later acknowledged. His antithesis of Germany and

'Western' civilisation was old polemical stock stretching back to the German Romantics, born of the humiliating defeat by Napoleon in 1806 and of the long frustration of German hopes to become a nation-state and not just a 'cultural nation'. The book was also unpolitical in being too long and too late to affect any debate that now mattered: much of its content had been overtaken by events, the war was already lost when it was published. Not for nothing did nineteenth-century laws dispense books over twenty printer's sheets in length from censorship: anything that long must have fallen behind the burning issues of the day. On the other hand, Mann's position was deeply political in two senses: first, any defence of the status quo, however allegedly unpolitical, is in practice political conservatism, as he recognised by quoting that *Tonio Kröger* passage; secondly, if enough people hold a view, however out of touch with realities, it becomes itself a political factor. Mann was far from alone in his kind of conservatism. It was to be a major factor in the politics of the Weimar Republic.

In 1918 Thomas Mann found himself among the losers, the more embittered because he saw his brother among the winners. Heinrich denied any triumphalism, but his satirical novel *Der Untertan* [The (Kaiser's) Subject], blocked by censorship in 1914, could now be published and widely acclaimed as the historical truth about Wilhelmine Germany: that it had been a society of conformists replicating from top to bottom the Kaiser's arrogant attitudes. Now the Kaiser had gone and a democratic republic had come – just the development the unpolitical Mann had feared. Faced with historical change on that scale, he retired hurt and wrote two idylls, both published in 1919. *Master and Dog*, begun in the last weeks of the war, was a prose sketch of the relationship with Mann's best friend; there followed, of all things, a poem in hexameters, *A Birth and a Christening*, about his new baby daughter. These minor pieces were a strange response to events: walks with his dog Bauschan on the banks of the Isar were no distance from political upheaval, and hexameters made an odd counterpoint to the machine-gun fire audible across Munich as a Soviet-style *Räterepublik* was first established and then overthrown. Mann was taking refuge in the small area of everyday stability the times had left.

He emerged from this spiritual retreat in 1920 to take up the fiction abandoned under the stress of war in 1915, *The Magic Mountain*. He had begun it in 1912 as a novella, a companion-piece to *Death in Venice*: after the tragic destruction of a great writer's ordered life, the comic break-up of a banal bourgeois existence – this time the central figure was one of those normal blond-haired young northerners. For was there really such a thing as normality? Hans Castorp was to be disoriented and undone, like Aschenbach, by the forces of Eros and illness. The setting was a Swiss tuberculosis sanatorium full of characters and caricatures from almost every European nation, where Castorp only ever meant to visit his cousin but stays on as a patient. High on the Mountain, he would learn deeper truths than are dreamt of in the Flatland's philosophy. The coming of war in 1914 force-fed the planned short work with topical meanings. Those deeper truths would now be the ones Germany was, in Mann's view, fighting for. The Mountain would be the moral and cultural high ground where the views of an Italian liberal, akin to brother Heinrich's 'Western' views, would be answered by a German pastor. Clearly the ending must now be the outbreak of war. Since Germany at that early stage seemed to be winning, this would have been historic confirmation of the rightness of the Mountain and its lessons.

But Germany had now lost the war, leaving the Mountain's lessons no longer backed by history. Or had history made a mistake? Either way, the novel's conception seemed hopelessly dated. Mann began to write again with no clear sense of direction. His political attitudes were meantime as much in turmoil as the politics of post-1918 Europe. His diary shows him toying with everything from a dissolution of the present German state and an eventual new Pan-Germany, to a communist Danube federation of Bavaria, Austria and Hungary. In practice he cast his vote for the conservative Bavarian Deutsche Volkspartei (diary, 12 January 1919); and he was openly relieved when the anti-revolutionary forces of General Epp put a violent end to the Munich republican experiment (diary, 7 May 1919).

Violence of a different kind broke into Mann's post-war waverings and resentments almost as dramatically as 1914 had activated his latent nationalism. Political opposition in the Weimar Republic early took the extreme form of political assassination. The murder of the Foreign Minister Walther Rathenau in 1922 was not the first such act, but it was what changed Mann's allegiance.[9] He now concluded that the Republic, however 'un-German' in origin (it was widely felt to have been imposed by the victors, and its constitution had been drawn up by a Jewish jurist), must be supported against subversion and filled as far as possible with German cultural values, so that Germans would willingly embrace it. Mann took that unpopular stand in a Munich speech of the same year, 'On the German Republic'. It was a startling change. If his wartime stand had come as a shock to those who thought him a liberal intellectual, his new position was an equal shock to those who had come to rely on him as a conservative nationalist. He was back roughly where he had started.

Mann's changed political position inevitably began to reshape the novel – its inner meaning, that is, for the outward narrative shape stayed as it was: the Mountain, the hero's educative disorientation through disease and love, the arguments between a liberal and a conservative, the outbreak of war in 1914 as the end of the story. But the point of the education was now to inculcate the balance and tolerance needed in a new political world; the arguments would point in a different direction; the war's end would open, not foreclose the large questions. The novel also began to grow inordinately. Back in 1917 Mann had said that writing the *Reflections* was vital if the novel was not to be overloaded (to Paul Amann, 25 March 1917). Now that the issues argued out in the *Reflections* were being rethought, he brought back his more extreme wartime and post-war notions and put them in the mouth of the conservative debater, no longer the German Pastor Bunge but a more disturbingly extreme figure, a Jesuit with leanings towards communism. In this bizarre mixture (gratuitously complicated by Naphta's Jewish descent) the common factor is a fiercely anti-humanist view of society and politics that links the pre-individualistic Christian Middle Ages with the post-individualist dogmas of totalitarianism. The individual counts for nothing, the impersonal collective is all; ruthlessness, whether revolutionary or reactionary, is the only realistic or desirable policy. Leo Naphta would be a caricature if it were not for the fact that such ideologues have been real in our century. Over against him stands, still, the old-fashioned Italian liberal, Lodovico Settembrini. First conceived as decidedly a caricature of Heinrich Mann's politics, he is one no longer. Though intellectually less sharp than Naphta and more often the loser in their convoluted debates, Settembrini is the more sympathetic figure, for Hans Castorp and probably for most readers. Since Castorp is anything but an intellectual, and the debates are often way above his head, he is left deciding the issues less on clear-cut contest points than by gut feeling – not altogether misguidedly either, since intellectual constructs normally have an emotional commitment as their unspoken premiss. Castorp is also shrewd enough to notice how both debaters get tangled in their own concepts, so that their positions are not simply opposed but seem at times internally inconsistent. It all seems to him a grand confusion. Perhaps political issues can never be fully resolved in the abstract? Yet Naphta and Settembrini stand for a real and fundamental antithesis which has underlain much of twentieth-century history. Could there be a humane politics in modern mass societies? Was there any future left in Enlightenment humanism, liberalism and democracy? Or was Naphta's ruthlessness, that is to say totalitarianism of the right or the left, the inevitable shape of things to come?

These were issues of the twenties, far more than of the war years in which the novel first took a political turn. So although it still evokes pre-war European society and ends in 1914, the book published in 1924 resonates with the crisis of the post-war years, the first third of the twentieth century, as Mann later said (XI, 602). No wonder the 'debate' sections stretch

to what many readers find an inordinate length. It is of course a principle of the German 'novel of education', the *Bildungsroman*, that what the
educable hero goes through has to be gone through in some detail by the
reader too. There is consequently no such thing as a short *Bildungsroman*.
In this late essay in the genre, moreover, no detail is gratuitous: any word,
idea or motif may recur somewhere in Mann's immense weave bearing a
new significance, linked to a new topic, integrated in a larger vision. This is
the serious and demanding sense of that seemingly tongue-in-cheek declaration in the novel's preface, that only what is thorough is truly entertaining
(III, 10).

That larger vision and the novel's positive answer are contained in Hans
Castorp's visionary glimpse of idyllic social harmony. Caught in a snowstorm when out skiing, dazed by the white-out, befuddled by unwise swigs
of port and nearly asleep on his feet in an opportune shelter, Castorp 'sees'
a sunlit Mediterranean landscape where a community lives in mutual consideration and kindness, but near to a temple where witch-like figures perform a horrific blood-sacrifice. The images are transformations of what Hans
Castorp has been hearing debated: Settembrini's life-affirming Enlightenment
activism and Naphta's ruthlessness that embraces darkness and death. The
'sun people' (III, 684) in Castorp's vision are living out a balance: neither
sunny optimism nor defeatist pessimism, but a humane solidarity informed
by their knowledge of the worst, the darkness that always presses us round.
The allegory is almost too general to speak to the concerns of any particular
time. But behind it is a more topical equation of the 'dominance of death'
and the dead hand of the past, the grip of outdated attitudes and allegiances
on what should be a responsive living community. When Hans Castorp concludes that he will 'keep faith with death in his heart, but be always aware
that allegiance to death and what is past is only evil and misanthropy and a
revelling in darkness if it controls our thinking' (III, 686), he is talking about
post-war German impulses to live in the past, resentments over lost glories
and status, nostalgia for past social forms – attitudes that were blocking
acceptance of the new democracy and had somehow to be accommodated if
the Republic was to survive.

Given that *The Magic Mountain* is itself a large-scale allegory, and
Castorp's snow vision therefore an allegory within an allegory, the reference to current politics may not have been immediately obvious.[10] It was
made clearer by Mann's actions and speeches outside the novel's pages, beginning with the pro-Republic speech of 1922 in which he tried to reconcile
past German values with the new democratic principle, invoking somewhat
incongruously the German Romantic poet and conservative thinker Novalis
alongside the American democrat Walt Whitman. More implausibly still,

Mann claimed that the essential beginnings of the present new German state lay in the enthusiasms of August 1914. Even with apter evidence and less far-fetched argument, the whole idea of continuity or reconciliation between old and new, tradition and change, was doomed to failure. Democrats might be prepared to accommodate the German past, but devotees of the past were not prepared to tolerate democracy. Nor, incidentally, were those at the other extreme of the political spectrum, the communists, for whom the new state had not rejected the past enough. The Weimar Republic was thus never an accepted forum for all parties to compete within, but an object of hatred, rejection and subversion to at least two large and hyperactive groups. Politics became ever more polarised, with democracy not even one of the poles but a vulnerable mid-point between them. In 1927 Mann wrote that Western ideas only seemed to have won the war, for there was currently more Naphta about than Settembrini (to Hanns Kreuz, 18 April 1927); and on 1 January 1933 he told another correspondent, Erich Ziebarth, that the Naphtas were now on top. Neither time does he mean the communists; the second occasion, indeed, was the eve of Hitler's coming to power. But the real point about Naphta was never just his communist sympathies; it was the totalitarian essence common to extreme left and right alike, what in *The Magic Mountain* is called 'iron allegiance, discipline, denial of the individual, violation of the personality' and 'the revolution of antihumane backlash' (III, 554, 636).

But we are anticipating. Between Mann's political turn in 1922 and Hitler's accession to power in 1933, Mann was deeply engaged in the unfolding history of his times and in resisting its ever clearer direction towards disaster. The bibliographical record shows for this period 375 items that have direct or indirect political bearing. Very little that Mann wrote at this time did not. Once he had seen that politics was latent in all cultural phenomena, no topic within his range of interests could well lack it. But he also saw the converse, which is a much less commonplace perception: that culture was latent in political phenomena, i.e. that the artistic, psychological, intellectual (or in Weimar Germany's case, *anti*-intellectual, irrationalist) movements within a society were powerful driving forces in politics. With culture and politics both moving to wild extremes, Mann turned to the writers of an earlier, saner German tradition for aid and authority. His literary essays – on Lessing in 1929, on Goethe in the high-profile anniversary year 1932 – draw on historical allies in the struggles of the present. The celebration of Lessing's robust rationality is an implied attack on the 'völkisch' (Nazi fellow-traveller) faction in literary life. The Goethe speeches try to rescue Germany's greatest poet from being exploited by those same people for irrational and nationalistic ends, and to show him instead as a representative of the liberal bourgeois European civilisation that was now embattled on all sides. Identifying with the great figures of the past was a conscious strategy, and it could be used with conviction because it fitted the conception of myth Mann was developing in *Joseph and his Brothers*: the latecomer consciously repeats the patterns of tribal lore and legend. Like Joseph in his times of tribulation, Mann re-enacted the roles of his great predecessors and felt strengthened by their example.

The intertwining of politics with culture meant that Mann was largely putting his ideas to a bourgeois readership, via themes not overtly political; but increasingly there were overt political occasions too. He became a speaker on Social Democratic platforms and even addressed gatherings of workers (XI, 890–910), which for someone of his background would at that time have been seen as a dramatic descent from the social heights. If he spoke to uneducated audiences in intellectual terms that may have passed them by, he was also capable of calling a political spade a spade. His 'German Address: An Appeal to Reason' of 1930 ranged over the material factors of a worsening situation as well as over its cultural-cum-psychological elements. He spoke out directly and forcefully against the rising tide of Nazism, for example in this statement in a Berlin newspaper at the eleventh hour of the crisis in August 1932: 'The Germany worthy of that name is sick, finally sick of the way, day in, day out, the air we breathe is poisoned by the braggings and threats of the National Socialist press and the half-crazed foamings at the mouth of a so-called Führer screaming for beheadings and hangings, food for crows and nights of long knives' (XIII, 624). As this protest against a poisoned atmosphere suggests, Mann's political activity was not divorced from the basic necessities of his work as an artist, which had in any case come increasingly to explore the relations between external and internal world, and especially the dangers to society lurking deep in the individual and communal psyche. Of the pro-Republic speech that started his new direction in 1922, he said quite specifically that it was written 'from the standpoint of the novel' ('aus dem Roman heraus': to Josef Ponten, 5 February 1925). That is to say, what he later (XI, 423–4) frankly called the 'result' of *The Magic Mountain* – purer aesthetes commonly disclaim anything so explicit – was the underlying principle of his politics.

It is important to see this connection, for there has been much facile criticism that Mann was not 'really' interested in politics, that it was all an unreal act. On the contrary, it was a real and urgently necessary act. As German politics staggered towards the abyss of the Third Reich, resistance became an increasingly desperate defence of ever more basic values, down to that free atmosphere which literature is not alone in needing. What cannot be argued away, politically or historically, is the fact and force of Mann's commitment.

He met the obligations that went with being a writer 'who deserves this name not merely for his talent',[11] consciously using the high public profile which his art and his very different first political involvement had given him. He demonstrably did more, spoke up earlier and saw things truer than any other German writer. Inevitably that later rankled with the rest – no one likes to hear 'I told you so' – and German attitudes to Mann's politics ever since have signally failed to do him justice.[12]

All of this does not mean he was a natural politician, and he never claimed to be.[13] In normal times he would have preferred to go on quietly writing novels; but these were not normal times, they were abnormal to the point where the very idea of social normality was threatened with destruction, and with it the possibility of humane literature. The proper distinction is thus not between 'real' literary and 'unreal' political activity, but between a natural inclination and an imperative duty. 'Real', in politics, is what someone publicly says and does; and what Mann said and did was certainly real enough to make exile his only guarantee of safety in 1933. Yet throughout he remained an artist too. It is cause for wonder that he was able to keep up such a rate of writing for a political emergency and also find time and energy – to say nothing of the calm of mind – for literature of the scope and quality of *The Magic Mountain*, or of the *Joseph* sequence that was begun hard on its heels and would later be a vital remnant of his old existence to offset the disorientation of exile.

The unease of living amid Weimar's social turmoil is the subject of a paradoxically relaxed and good-humoured novella, *Disorder and Early Sorrow* (1925), which comes so close to the realities of the Mann family in the twenties as to be almost straight autobiography. Mann makes the father into a professor of history, not a far cry from a novelist who was now consciously analysing the historical process. The past of academic history, though, is a safe haven, especially if the subject is a distant period. Abel Cornelius is an expert on the Spain of Philip II (there are echoes of *Tonio Kröger* here) and for him there is something reassuringly fixed in its pastness. It has finished happening, in contrast to the uneasy present of social change and galloping inflation. Tellingly, the story uses the present tense throughout, which is normally a narrative trick to make us feel that a climactic event is happening before our very eyes. In this case it suggests rather that too much is uncontrollably happening here and now; everything is in flux, there are no longer links with the past that hold.[14] Surrounding turmoil only adds to the usual problems of the generation gap, the bizarre dress-codes and manners and musical fashions of the young. Thus the problem over which *The Magic Mountain* had brooded is translated in this unpretentious vignette to an everyday setting and scale. At that level, it sees things through mildly conservative eyes.

Cornelius, while having (so to speak) Thomas Mann's children, is also partly modelled on Mann's then friend the literary historian Ernst Bertram, an unreconstructed conservative and later a committed Nazi. That, however, still lay in the future. The story stops short of being historically ominous. It offers a slice of life in which no catastrophe happens, except that the Professor's tiny daughter suffers a crush on one of the young-adult party guests. It is an early trauma for her, and a mild one for her father; for what seemed a settled corner of the world, another idyllic retreat (biographically speaking this is the same daughter whose birth was recorded in *A Birth and a Christening*), is on the hazard of history too.

Another family anecdote five years later ends in a real catastrophe. Where *Disorder* sketched a present with roots trailing back into the past, *Mario and the Magician* (1930) describes a present containing seeds of a dark future. It is one of Mann's finest narrative performances, moving deftly from the domestic and trivial to the demonic and tragic, from the heat of an Italian seaside resort to a chilling end where a hypnotist is shot by the young man his performance has humiliated. The story moves just as deftly from the literal to the allegorical, capturing first the beach-level nationalism of an Italy puffed up with fascist pride, then Cipolla's brutal mastery over his audience, a mastery which already exploits the techniques of charismatic control used in larger tyrannies. The story's lessons are political at both levels, right down to the final words with their dual sense: the killing of this violator of human dignity is 'an ending with terror, a most dreadful end. And yet a liberating end – I could not and cannot feel otherwise' (VIII, 711). 'Liberating' ('befreiend') suggests the relief of psychic tension, but its political sense is unmissable. If the linking of literal and allegorical levels anticipates *Doctor Faustus*, that concluding sentence with its reluctant decisiveness points forward to a passage in Mann's post-war diaries where he wishes that some 'fine young man' would shoot the anti-communist witch-hunter and underminer of American democratic freedoms, Senator Joseph McCarthy (2 March 1954). The writer whose position had been reversed in 1922 by violence against democratic politicians could clearly envisage violence as a last resort against tyrants.

Mann sometimes played down the political meaning of *Mario*, perhaps for fear that a piece of creative writing might be thought *merely* political, addressing only the issues of the day with no lasting value beyond.[15] If so, he seriously underrated the story's depth, for it analyses with a light touch fields of force that are permanencies of human nature and society. Yet the thirties did pose a dilemma: was it the writer's prime business to produce polemic born of hatred, or to create art born of understanding? History in the making demanded the first, to help stop civilisation sliding into the fascist abyss. History as record and interpretation demanded the second, at the latest once fascism was defeated. Indeed, long before then *Mario* was already meeting that demand. The story breathes revulsion, but also fascination. If the audience is in thrall to Cipolla, the narrator is in thrall to his subject, the psychology of demagogic power. Twice he wonders whether he should not have taken his family off when things turned unpleasant, first after the banal incidents at the hotel and on the beach, then in the interval of the fateful performance (VIII, 669, 695). He answers with a rhetorical question: 'Is it right to "up and leave" when life turns alarming and sinister?' And he makes the implied answer explicit: No, you should stay on, for 'that is precisely when there's something to be learned' (669). As the quotation marks make plain, to 'up and leave' means more than just literal departure, and 'staying on' is an ethos, an openness to events in the cause of understanding. There are echoes here of Hans Castorp's Mountain motto, 'placet experiri', which states a positive commitment to experience and experiment. The same idea is central to the essay 'Brother Hitler' of 1939, where to the disquiet of his friends Mann, the leading exile opponent of Nazism, probes the psychology of the failed artist Hitler for common ground between them, and sets the complex motive of analytical 'interest' above the simple emotion of hatred (XII, 846). Beneath these changing formulations, the pursuit of *Erkenntnis* remains the overriding concern.

For although Hitler 'had the great advantage of simplifying the emotions' down to a 'plain and mortal hatred', which meant that 'the years of struggle against him were a morally good time' (XI, 253–4), the hated phenomenon and its causes were not themselves simple. Even while Mann was throwing himself into the struggle, making a long series of broadcasts to Germany for the BBC and criss-crossing the American continent to persuade isolationist audiences that a war against fascism was their business too, he was also pursuing the analysis begun in *Mario*. The Hitler essay picks up very precisely the story's themes. It compares the collective fanaticism of Nazi rallies with the trances and convulsions of primitive tribal dance, which recall the hypnotic states and 'dance orgy' (VIII, 701) induced by Cipolla. The relapse into the primitive is one constant in Mann's account of Nazism. The other is the disquieting neighbourhood of demagogy and art: Cipolla is a kind of artist; Hitler was a failed one; Hitler's fanatical onslaught on civilised society is compared with Savonarola's (XII, 850), whose vehement will to power expressed Mann's own. Only a radical enquirer and self-critic could have drawn historical and allegorical parallels that were so uncomfortably close to home.

But Mann was not looking for easy comfort. His reckoning with German history became increasingly a reckoning with his own past. The insight that political developments have roots in culture – that what happens on the largest scale in politics will have been felt however obscurely in the inclinations and temptations of individual artists – made it possible to get a purchase on the German catastrophe by writing yet again about an artist, and one with whom, though Adrian Leverkühn is a composer, there are obvious autobiographical links. This, to superficial observers, seemed one more instance of Mann's endless self-absorption. In fact he was uncovering, under the issues that had absorbed him and been the substance of his work, the ominous tendencies of his age; he was now consciously writing what he called the 'novel of my epoch' (XI, 169). His hero, a highly cerebral artist at the end of intellect's tether and desperate to break through to a new creativity, deliberately infects himself with syphilis. The disease is a legendary heightener of genius (in Maupassant, Hugo Wolf, Nietzsche and others) though at the price of eventual collapse into madness and death. To this modern pathology Mann adds the second meaning of a pact with the devil (hence the novel's title, *Doctor Faustus*). By much the same technique that had half-hidden myth under a realistic surface in *Death in Venice*, he gives the diabolical elements an always plausible garb: the devil may be no more than a figment of the hero's mind, the traditional twenty-four years of the pact are the natural term of the disease. An evil more fundamental than streptococci is nonetheless powerfully suggested.

The combination of disease and devilry was not thought up for the purposes of the 1940s. It went back to an idea from 1904 for a story or an episode in a novel: 'Figure of the syphilitic artist: as Dr Faust who has sold himself to the Devil. The effect of the virus is intoxication, stimulus, inspiration...works of genius, the Devil guides his hand. But in the end *the Devil carries him off*: paralysis.' This extreme anecdote – crass in its use of disease, dated in its diabolism, arbitrary in its linkage of the two – got no further at the time. Yet history in the most chilling way had since given substance to those distant beginnings. It was now hardly an exaggerated metaphor to say Germany had sold her soul to an evil power, or that Nazism had been a kind of intoxication and, in the phrase used of the Italians in *Mario*, a 'national disease' (VIII, 667). Beside the extremes of German history, no fiction was any longer extreme. The novel includes within the allegorical structure, where the artist and his Faustian fate stand for Germany, straightforwardly realistic sketches of individuals and social circles whose thinking prefigured Nazism and prepared the climate for its acceptance. Some of these, like the Faustian seed-idea itself, also date back to the first decade of the century: they were materials gathered for Mann's never-written Munich novel 'Maya'. Now at last they could find their place and their point in a larger and more significant scheme than he ever dreamt of.

That is a typical pattern: things that Mann recorded early are seen in their full significance later. History as unintended document becomes history as considered record. *Tonio Kröger* in 1903 has a political meaning not perceived until the *Reflections* of 1918; the political commitment of 1914 is understood and revised in *The Magic Mountain* of 1924; aspirations captured in *Death in Venice* in 1912 appear from the standpoint of the late thirties as a proto-fascist syndrome; Leverkühn's career in 1947 is indeed a remake of Aschenbach's in 1912, seen now with a fuller consciousness of the problem and shown as a more conscious pursuit of Dionysian release at any price; overall, *Doctor Faustus* gives a clear meaning to the obscure impulses of Mann's self and his society in the early years of the century. At every point the past as he experienced it becomes material for historical judgement, the more authentic because recorded at the time with no set purpose.

Mann's judgements are both subtle and bold. They would not be accepted by all historians, but that is because for conventional history the cultural and psycho-social factors crucial for Mann are intangible and not ultimately demonstrable. That does not mean they were not real. Mann's sense of what was causally significant, the coherence of his overall picture, and its slow growth from experience mean that his analysis stands up well beside what other writers and historians of his time had to say when confronted by the enormity of the Third Reich.[16]

The year 1945 was not an end to history and its discomforts. For a German, relief at the defeat of Nazism was mixed with horror at the German atrocities that now came fully to light. For Mann the exile writer, there was immediate friction and conflict with Germans who rationalised their own self-serving conformism in the twelve-year Reich, begrudged him his exile as if it had been a luxury, and demanded that he now return to Germany to 'help heal wounds', as if nothing but geographical distance separated him from the land and people that had cast him out. Understandably he preferred to stay in California, where he had built a new life as a US citizen. From that vantage-point he looked on dismayed as old patterns seemed to be repeated, denazification was cut short under Adenauer's Restoration, West Germany was re-armed as the front line against the Eastern bloc, and a third world war seemed ever more likely. The passionate anti-fascist could not become a Cold Warrior. He had few illusions about communism, more than once interceding on behalf of victims of communist courts;[17] but he was more deeply disillusioned by the way his new country was betraying its own democratic principles, supporting reactionary regimes abroad and harassing its own citizens at home. That made Mann an anti-anti-communist. In matters German, he expressly recognised no zones (XI, 488). He had thrown the whole weight of his literary prestige into the struggle against Nazism; now he had to balance it on a fine line. At grand anniversaries – Goethe's in 1949, Schiller's in 1955 – he gave his lecture in both Germanies. Such even-handedness meant Mann was denounced in the United States as a communist, had an FBI file opened on him, and expected at any moment to be summoned before the House Committee on Un-American Activities. (He was probably only saved by his connection with Agnes Meyer, the influential wife of the editor of the *Washington Post*.) As the rabid tendency in the United States grew, he felt strongly drawn back to Europe. Germany remained an impossibility, but Switzerland had been a pre-war haven and was willing to have him back. For the last three years of his life he withdrew to Zürich and, as far as the world would let him, from history.

The Cold War was the last lesson in a lifetime whose engagement with history began late but was then as intensive as any modern writer's has been. Mann never gloried in that engagement or made grand claims for its effectiveness, much less for its profundity. Indeed, his politics was avowedly not a matter of being profound, but of defending the most basic rights and humane decencies by a practical rationality. Even that had been learned the hard way. In 1944 an American correspondent belatedly raked over Mann's aberrations of 1914–18, which were after all, he gibed, the work of a mature man of forty. Mann replied that they had sprung nevertheless from 'total political innocence and ignorance' (draft letter to C. B. Boutell, 21 January 1944). As for maturity, that was 'a very relative concept, and a man who has a long road ahead of him and much still to go through is perhaps not wholly mature at forty.' Was he mature even now, at nearly seventy? 'Perhaps maturity takes a whole lifetime, perhaps maturity is ripeness for death.' And he ends with a modest statement about his view of politics, his experience of history: 'I had simply learned something.' It was perhaps not that simple an achievement.

## NOTES

1 Man as '*the* sick animal': *GM* III, §13; as 'the animal that has turned out worst, the sickest, the one that has strayed most dangerously from its instincts, yet with all that the *most interesting* animal': *A* 14.

2 Alfred Kerr, *Die Welt in Drama*, vol. III: *Das neue Drama* (Berlin, 1917), p. 96.

3 The notes are included in Hans Wysling and Paul Scherrer (eds.), *Quellenkritische Studien zum Werk Thomas Manns* (Berne and Munich: Francke, 1967), pp. 123–233.

4 That music and painting could be thought of, in 1910, as 'unproblematic' shows how out of touch Thomas Mann was at this stage with the avant-garde. Modernity in music for him still meant Wagner, even Pfitzner, at the extreme Richard Strauss; painting meant the artists who had made socially successful careers in Munich – Stuck, Lenbach – and at the extreme the 'Blaue Reiter'.

5 This is the view taken in *Doctor Faustus* by Serenus Zeitblom, who in such judgements on German history is Mann's mouthpiece. The full passage reads: 'Bei einem Volk von der Art des unsrigen ist das Seelische immer das Primäre

und eigentlich Motivierende; die politische Aktion ist zweiter Ordnung, Reflex, Ausdruck, Instrument.'

6  In *Pan* 3 (1913), p. 640.

7  Georg Lukács, *Deutsche Literatur im Zeitalter des Imperialismus* (Berlin: Aufbau, 1945), p. 223.

8  Mann's own phrase for the force that took over from the 'Dionysian overflowing individualistic lyricism' to which the beauty of a Polish boy in Venice first inspired him (letter to Carl Maria Weber, 4 July 1920).

9  The murders of politicians like Rathenau and Matthias Erzberger were only the most high-profile crimes. Between 1919 and 1922, 354 political murders were perpetrated by the Right, and 22 by the Left. See Ian Kershaw, *Hitler 1889–1936: Hubris* (London: Penguin, 1998), pp. 171, 654.

10  Interestingly, Mann's political drift was clear enough to the highly conservative king-maker on the Nobel Prize Committee, Frederik Böök, who made sure that the award to Thomas Mann in 1929 was expressly for *Buddenbrooks* of 1901, not *The Magic Mountain* of 1924.

11  Unpublished review of a Swiss journal ('Anlässlich einer Zeitschrift') in *Essays*, VI, 151.

12  For a critical survey of recent scholarly arguments, see the chapter 'The Real Mann?' in my *Thomas Mann: The Uses of Tradition*, revised and augmented edition (Oxford: Clarendon Press, 1996), pp. 432–43. For the persistence of the cliché 'not really political' at a more popular level, see Joachim Fest's essay 'Thomas Mann: Politik als Selbstentfremdung', in his *Die unwissenden Magier* (Frankfurt am Main: Fischer, 1993), pp. 11–69. Fest rehearses the standard prejudice without providing relevant evidence. He argues the thesis of Mann's ironic non-involvement wholly from his fiction, which begs the question of the nature of his politics. The claim that Mann remained 'essentially' uncommitted is not supported by quotation, much less analysis, of the obvious texts, the speeches and essays – with reason, since any representative quotation from these sources would have proved the contrary. Apart from one vague reference (p. 11) to 'economic and social interests' that Mann was allegedly unaware of (which is also demonstrably untrue) Fest formulates no alternative view on any political subject so as to show where Mann erred. In fact Mann had a sharp eye and sound, principled judgement, as is further shown in his diaries (also ignored by Fest). Mann was not obviously wrong on German irrationalism in the thirties, on the follies of appeasing Hitler after 1933, on the blindness of American isolationism, on the destruction of American values by anti-communism, on the failure of denazification in the Federal Republic; and he spoke clearly and unambiguously on all these things. Fest may seem to carry weight, as a former editor of the *Frankfurter Allgemeine Zeitung* and author of political biographies (Hitler, Albert Speer); but his charge that Mann was 'ill-informed and out of touch with reality' (p. 14) visibly rebounds on him.

13  Mann makes the distinction himself in the essay *Culture and Socialism* of 1928: he is a politician 'if not in essence, then by an act of will' – 'wenn nicht wesentlich, so doch willentlich' (XII, 640).

14  See Lionel Trilling, 'Disorder and Early Sorrow', in his *Prefaces to the Experience of Literature* (Oxford: Oxford University Press, 1981), pp. 131–5.

15 See letter to Bedřich Fučík, 15 April 1932, in *DD* II, 370. Other letters reprinted there somewhat restore the balance.

16 For a comparison of Mann's account of German twentieth-century history with the views of influential contemporaries – Bertolt Brecht and the historian Friedrich Meinecke – see my 'Thomas Mann: The Writer as Historian of his Time', *Modern Language Review* 71 (1976), 82–96.

17 See 'Briefe in die DDR', in *Fragile Republik. Thomas Mann und Nachkriegsdeutschland*, ed. Stefan Stachorski (Frankfurt am Main: Fischer, 1999), pp. 162–73.

## FURTHER READING

Bergsten, Gunilla, *Thomas Mann's 'Doctor Faustus': The Sources and Structure of the Novel*, trans. Krishna Winston (Chicago: University of Chicago Press, 1969)

Reed, T. J., 'Thomas Mann: the Writer as Historian of his Time', *Modern Language Review* 71 (1976), 82–96

Scaff, Susan von Rohr, *History, Myth and Music: Thomas Mann's Timely Fiction* (Columbia, SC: Camden House, 1998)

Swales, Martin, 'In Defence of Weimar: Thomas Mann and the Politics of Republicanism', in Alan Bance (ed.), *Weimar Germany: Writers and Politics* (Edinburgh: Scottish Academic Press, 1982), pp. 1–13

Vaget, Hans Rudolf, 'Hoover's Mann: Gleanings from the FBI's Secret File on Thomas Mann', in Wolfgang Elfe, James Hardin and Gunther Holst (eds.), *The Fortunes of German Writers in America: Studies in Literary Reception* (Columbia, SC: University of South Carolina Press, 1992), pp. 131–44

'The Steadfast Tin Soldier: Thomas Mann in World Wars I and II', in Reinhold Grimm and Jost Hermand (eds.), *German Reflections of the Two World Wars* (Madison, WI: University of Wisconsin Press, 1992), pp. 3–21

# 2

## PAUL BISHOP

# The intellectual world of Thomas Mann

It has become a commonplace of criticism to refer to Mann as an 'intellectual novelist', and certainly Mann himself did nothing to discourage the view that he was a philosophical novelist whose works incorporate a vast body of German thought. In the first of his 'Letters from Germany' published in *The Dial* in November 1922, he spoke of the rise of a type of book he dubbed the 'intellectual novel', but the examples he cited were not exactly works of fiction: Count Hermann Keyserling's *Travel Diary of a Philosopher* (1919), Ernst Bertram's philosophical study, *Friedrich Nietzsche: An Attempt at a Mythology* (1918), and Friedrich Gundolf's monumental biography of Goethe (1916), not to mention Spengler's *Decline of the West* (1918–22) (XIII, 265). Clearly, Mann's novels belong to a rather different category from these texts (although they all have one thing in common – length). This chapter examines Mann's knowledge of major German thinkers and writers, his use of those figures in his novels and essays, and the way their ideas form part of his 'intellectual world'. Beginning with Mann's early fascination with Schopenhauer, Nietzsche, and Wagner, I go on to investigate his reinterpretation of Romanticism in the 1920s and his engagement with psychoanalysis in the 1930s. Throughout his writings, however, Mann's continuing preoccupation with Weimar Classicism enables us to reread the development of other aspects of his thought as an attempt in dark times to preserve and develop a tradition of humanism that is distinctively German as well as European. In 'On the German Republic' (1922), Mann defined his conservatism as standing 'not in the service of the past and of reaction, but in the service of the future' (IX, 829); as he termed it in 1926, it was a 'Zukunftskonservatismus' (conservatism of the future), 'serene, removed from all crude, sentimental atavism', and a conservatism 'which, its eye fixed on the new, plays with old cultural forms, in order to rescue them from oblivion' (IX, 189).

On several occasions, Mann drew attention to the thinkers who were most important to him, and he liked to list their names. In *Reflections of an Unpolitical Man* he spoke of Schopenhauer, Nietzsche and Wagner as 'a triad of eternally united spirits' (XII, 79; cf. 319); in an essay written in 1925 he included Goethe, Lichtenberg, Schopenhauer, Nietzsche and Wagner in his list of significant writers who had introduced him to the concept of cosmopolitanism (X, 191); in 'Goethe as Representative of the Bourgeois Age' (1932) he called Goethe, Schopenhauer, Wagner and Nietzsche 'the fixed stars of the firmament of our youth, Germany and Europe – all at once' (IX, 329); while in 'Dürer' (1928) he wrote of the painter, together with Goethe, Schopenhauer, Nietzsche and Wagner, as revealing 'the entire complex of fate and the galaxy, a world, a German world with its own ambitious self-dramatisation' (X, 231). And one could give many more examples of such roll-calls. But it is not just the listing of names that remains characteristic of Mann: throughout the years, the names themselves hardly changed. And surrounding each 'big name', others also gathered. For instance, in the case of Goethe, Mann compares him with such other great figures as Tolstoy, Rousseau and Schiller, as well as Luther, Erasmus and Bismarck (IX, 134–5; 300). And far from being mere intellectual counters that he manipulated in a glass bead game, Mann's intellectual heroes signal his attempt to make fruitful the awareness of a continuity in the theory and practice of art, which Mann called 'Kultur' but which some critics have unhelpfully hypostatised as 'Tradition'. Indeed, an interest in Mann's thought offers the reader rewarding access to much of what might otherwise not be understood in his fiction.

A clue as to how Mann regarded his use of famous thinkers can be found in his essay on Schopenhauer, published in 1938. Discussing Wagner's use of the philosopher, Mann spoke of all artists as 'betrayers' of a philosophy:

> I hold that a philosophy is effective not only – sometimes least of all – by reason of its ethical teaching, by the doctrine which it links to its interpretation of the world and its experience of it; but also and especially through this very experience itself . . . A philosophy is often influential less through its morality or its theory of knowledge, the intellectual bloom of its vitality, than by this vitality itself, its essential and personal character – more, in short, through its passion than its wisdom. (IX, 535, 561)

In fact, it is unclear what real influence Schopenhauer exercised on Wagner, although we know that Wagner read *The World as Will and Representation* when composing *Tristan and Isolde* and claimed it as a source of inspiration.[1] (For his part, Schopenhauer had little interest in Wagner's operas, and even less in Wagner's attempts at personal contact.) Famously, it was Nietzsche who drew attention to Wagner's alleged Schopenhauerianism. In *The Case of Wagner* (§4) he remarked that, in the *Ring*, Brünnhilde has to study Schopenhauer and transpose the fourth book of *The World as Will and Representation* into verse. So Mann's point about Wagner's use of

Schopenhauer is just as much a Nietzschean one. The triad of spirits is indeed eternally united.

## Schopenhauer and Nietzsche

Schopenhauer offers a good starting-point for investigating Mann's reading of German philosophy and his use of philosophical material in his fiction. Writing in 1938, Mann declared that Schopenhauer's philosophy constituted an 'artist-philosophy' (*Künstlerphilosophie*), not simply because of its aesthetics or its style, but rather because it was the expression of 'a dynamic artistic nature' (*dynamisch-künstlerische Natur*) (IX, 530). In Mann's first major work, *Buddenbrooks*, subtitled 'The Decline of a Family', the theme of decline reflected the contemporary interest in the notion of inherited degeneracy, definitively formulated in Max Nordau's *Degeneration* (1895). More generally, the doctrine of hereditary degeneracy had become a major motif in late nineteenth-century psychiatry. These themes had been anticipated in such Romantic works as *The Devil's Elixirs* (1815–16) by E. T. A. Hoffmann (one of Mann's favourite writers), and in his copy of Eckermann's *Conversations with Goethe*, Mann had noted Goethe's discussion on 12 March 1828 of Europe's apparently congenital decline. As ever, Mann's sources are numerous and, as so often, deliberately conflated. Moreover, in *Buddenbrooks* Mann drew extensively on his own experiences growing up in Lübeck, especially in the episode where Thomas Buddenbrook reads a work which, through its citation of a chapter title (I, 655), may be identified as Schopenhauer's *The World as Will and Representation*.

In 1895, Thomas Mann purchased the second volume of *The World as Will and Representation*, and in 'A Sketch of my Life' (1930) he recalls that reading it was one of his formative experiences (XI, 111). As he had already observed in *Reflections of an Unpolitical Man*, in his novel he transferred that reaction to Thomas Buddenbrook (XII, 72; cf. IX, 561). Or as he wrote in 1936, this part of *Buddenbrooks* was 'a monument' erected to the memory of that impression (IX, 483). In the novel, the senator Thomas Buddenbrook picks up a book he bought by chance years before at a reduced price, the second part of a 'famous metaphysical system' (I, 654; Part 10, Chapter 5). Reading it outside in his garden on a warm summer's day, Buddenbrook undergoes a kind of philosophical conversion (I, 654–9). The account lasts for several pages, but it has been frequently pointed out that the message Thomas Buddenbrook draws from the book he reads, if it is Schopenhauer, is wrong.[2] Although Mann's understanding in 1899 may have been equally flawed, by 1938, in his essay on Schopenhauer, he was able to offer a perfectly adequate account of the Kantian basis for Schopenhauer's philosophy, although he emphasises that he is not interested in the 'truth' of Schopenhauer's exposition, particularly in relation to Kant (IX, 571). And of Thomas Buddenbrook's interpretation of Schopenhauer, Mann said that it shows 'one can think in the sense of a philosopher without in the least thinking according to his sense' (IX, 561).

Nor is Mann's account of his own first contact with Schopenhauer entirely 'pure'. Another remark in his 1938 essay drops the following hint: 'Here, of course, we have the thoughts of someone who had, apart from Schopenhauer, also read Nietzsche, and transported the one experience into the other, creating with them the most extraordinary mixture' (IX, 561). Indeed, what Mann presents as an autobiographical account of his reading of Schopenhauer carries deep resonances of Nietzsche's recollections of buying *The World as Will and Representation* from a second-hand bookseller in Leipzig and being subsequently overwhelmed by it.[3] Thus the figure of Thomas Buddenbrook is not only triply related to its author as 'father, offspring and double', as Mann put it in *Reflections of an Unpolitical Man* (XII, 72), but is also a duplicate of Nietzsche.

As far as Thomas Mann is concerned, there can be no doubt about his credentials as a Nietzschean. In 'A Sketch of My Life', Mann wrote that he saw in Nietzsche, above all, 'the man who conquers himself': 'with him I took nothing literally, I believed almost nothing, but precisely this gave my love for him its multi-layered and passionate quality – gave it depth' (XI, 110). That depth was expressed in many ways, including two important lectures: 'Opening Words to a Musical Celebration of Nietzsche' (1924), delivered on the eightieth anniversary of Nietzsche's birth, and 'Nietzsche's Philosophy in the Light of our Experience' (1947), delivered to the PEN Club in Stockholm. Yet there is hardly an essay on another subject or writer that does not mention Nietzsche at least in passing, and Nietzschean motifs inform nearly all his short stories and novels.

A good example of Thomas Mann's complex interweaving of intellectual motifs is provided by a frequent remark he made about Nietzsche. In *Reflections*, Mann claimed that the Nietzsche who had made such an impact on him – 'the Nietzsche that really mattered to me and had the greatest pedagogical effect on me' – was 'the Nietzsche who had been, or remained, close to Wagner and Schopenhauer' (XII, 541). This Nietzsche was summed up for Mann by Dürer's famous picture *Knight, Death and Devil*.[4] In a later essay of 1928 Mann added that although Dürer had always reminded him of Nietzsche, it was Nietzsche who had provided him with the medium through which he had come to know the world of Dürer. Had Nietzsche, Mann wondered, ever mentioned Dürer? 'I could not tell' (X, 230). But he went on to quote Nietzsche's description of Schopenhauer as 'a man and a gallant knight, stern-eyed, with the courage of his own strength, who knows how to stand alone and not wait on the beck and nod of superior officers' (x, 230, from *GM*, III, §5). And in his speeches and articles written for Freud's seventy-fifth and eightieth birthdays, Mann took Nietzsche's encomium of Schopenhauer as 'a knight between Death and the Devil' (*BT* §20) and applied it to Freud (x, 465–6; IX, 480). In fact, that expression, referring to Dürer's picture, occurred in a passage intended to win support for Wagner. So not only had Nietzsche indeed mentioned Dürer, but Mann must have known this. More importantly, Mann used such intertextual references to create his own intellectual world, constructed from philosophy, biography and autobiography in equal proportion.

A further example of the extent to which Nietzsche's writings penetrated Mann's writing is provided by the following remark in his 1938 lectures on Goethe's *Faust*:

> What a poet can give himself and what he can make of himself, that is his own, that is what he is, and in the Homeric phrase 'The poets tell many lies', the word 'lie' has another and more powerful meaning than in ordinary life.
>
> (IX, 592)

Yet the source for this quotation is not Homer but Nietzsche, who attributes these words to Homer as the ironic conclusion to the section 'On the origin of poetry' in *The Gay Science* (§84).[5] Then again, when Mann asserts, as he does in his essay on Dürer, that the very name of Nietzsche summons at once 'the profoundest memories and the highest hopes ['höchstes Hoffen']' (x, 230), it is hard not to hear the echo of Zarathustra's promise of the Superman as the 'highest hope' ('höchste Hoffnung'), a phrase used at least nine times in *Thus Spoke Zarathustra*. Nietzsche's presence in Mann's writings can thus be allusive, but is no less significant for that.

Moreover, Nietzsche provided the basis for one of the most fundamental antitheses of Mann's early thinking: the dichotomy between culture (a positive notion, connoting a private, inward and self-centred, not necessarily rational ideal, closely allied to the German concept of *Bildung*) and civilisation (here a negative term, describing societies dominated by the political consciousness of democracy, such as England and France, where only rational values are recognised). Nietzsche's formulation can be found in his notes for the book posthumously published as *The Will to Power* (edited to the point of distortion by his sister, Elisabeth Förster-Nietzsche, whom Mann met in Weimar in 1921). In 'Culture contra Civilisation' Nietzsche wrote: 'The high points of culture and civilisation do not coincide: one should not be deceived about the abysmal antagonism of culture and civilisation' (*WP* §121). The extent to which Thomas Mann was impressed by this idea is made abundantly clear in one of his early, nationalistic essays, 'Thoughts in War' (XIII, 528).

Nietzsche was also to provide Mann with material for the novella *Tonio Kröger*, a work that pursued another central pair of Mannian categories, those of artist (*Künstler*) and bourgeois citizen (*Bürger*). In 1932, Mann claimed that the 'school' through which Nietzsche had passed was revealed in his linguistic style in general and his psychologically characteristic combinations of words. (That 'school', Mann believed, derived from Luther, via Goethe (IX, 353).) As Mann himself pointed out (IX, 481; XI, 110), *Tonio Kröger* contains the Nietzschean-sounding expression 'Erkenntnisekel' ('loathing of insight', VIII, 300). And section 4 of the novella is saturated with similar phrases and ideas taken from Nietzsche. As usual, the allusions are often indirect. For example, Tonio's remark to Lisaweta Iwanowna about the word 'Erkenntnis' (knowledge) – 'perhaps it is less a question of redemption than a freezing, a laying-on-ice, of feeling' (VIII, 301) – contains an oblique but unmistakable allusion to Nietzsche's famous comment in *Ecce Homo* about the conduct of his war against ideals, not by refuting them, but by laying them one after another on ice (*EH*, 'Human, All Too Human', §1).

So as well as using Nietzsche on the intellectual level, Mann was remarkably alert to the texture of Nietzsche's language, which he equated with music, praising it for its refinement of the inner ear, the masterly sense of cadence, tempo and rhythm, which in his view were without parallel in German and probably European prose (X, 181). Indeed, Mann attributed to Nietzsche a significance that was, to take his words literally, as global as it was epochal. In 1924, he hailed Nietzsche as 'seer and guide into a new future for humanity' (X, 182), 'the evangelist of a new alliance between earth and Man' (X, 184). In 1926 he wrote that the name of Nietzsche heralded 'dawn and epochal change' (IX, 189). And just before the outbreak of the Second World War, Mann provided his clearest explanation up to that date of why exactly he considered Nietzsche so important. Concomitant with his inversion of Schopenhauer, Mann argued, was Nietzsche's vision of life as an aesthetic spectacle:

> For when, in *The World as Will and Representation*, we read that 'the in-itself of life, the will, existence itself, is a constant suffering, partly pitiful, partly terrible; on the other hand, as mere representation, viewed purely or repeated through art, free from torment, it affords a *meaningful spectacle* ['*bedeutsames Schauspiel*']', then Nietzsche takes up entirely this justification of life, as an aesthetic spectacle ['ästhetischen Schauspiels'], a phenomenon of beauty, in no different a way than Schopenhauer takes up its 'disinterestedness'. He does so by giving Schopenhauer's thought a twist into an anti-moral and drunken affirmation, into a Dionysianism of justification of life, in which

Schopenhauer's moralistic, life-denying pessimism is admittedly hard to recognise, but in which it survives in another hue, with another label and an altered demeanour. (IX, 572; cf. *World as Will*, I, §52)

After two World Wars, Mann found it impossible to regard Nietzsche in quite the same way as at the beginning of the century. In his 1947 lecture, Mann offered a more critical appraisal of Nietzsche in the light of twentieth-century history. On this occasion, he charged Nietzsche with two major errors (IX, 695–6). First, he claimed that Nietzsche had misunderstood the power relationship between instinct and intelligence. There was certainly no danger of too much intellect on this earth, Mann maintained. And second, he rejected Nietzsche's opposition of morality and life. The real opposition, Mann contended, is between ethics and aesthetics. It would, however, be wrong to see this lecture simply as a reversal of his earlier views. As with all Mann's intellectual influences, it was a question of adapting or refining them.

Mann's most important attempt to come to terms with Nietzsche after 1945, however, is his late, great novel, *Doctor Faustus*. In that work, the life of the central character, Adrian Leverkühn, is closely modelled on that of Nietzsche: not only do both have a similar experience in a brothel, but they both collapse from madness at the same age (45) and die on the same day (25 August). In the novel, Mann explored the similarity between literature and music to its limits. Whereas in 1938 he had compared Schopenhauer's *The World as Will and Representation* to a symphony in four movements (IX, 556, 558), here music becomes representative of all art, including literature. In *The World as Will and Representation*, Schopenhauer singled out music as 'an immediate objectification and copy of the Will' (I, §52); in *The Birth of Tragedy*, Nietzsche claimed that it was only music that can give us an idea of what is meant by the justification of the world as an aesthetic phenomenon (§24). In Mann's novel, we ponder the possibility that the daemonic art of music, far from justifying life, may destroy it. Yet, as Mann knew, Nietzsche had once claimed that without music life would be a mistake (*TI*, 'Maxims and Arrows', §33), and elsewhere he quoted Nietzsche's confession that he did not know the difference between music and tears (X, 184; *EH*, 'Why I am so clever', §7). In *Faustus*, the music ends in tears. By the same token, the significance attached to music recalls its importance in the Pedagogic Province, that strange country conjured up in Goethe's late novel *Wilhelm Meisters Wanderjahre* [*Wilhelm Meister's Journeyman Years*]. As Mann had observed in 1922, music functions there as 'the most spiritual [*geistigste*] symbol of all the "regulated cooperation" of the manifold towards a cultural purpose and goal that is worthy of humanity' (IX, 160).[6] In *Faustus* that cultural goal has itself become inhuman. In a short essay on film (1928), Mann had spoken of art as being 'cold' ('die Kunst ist die kalte Sphäre'), quoting Goethe's view that art 'originates in reason' (x, 900; G xii, 467). But in *Faustus* Mann explores the view that if the real source of art is hell-fire, then it will generate a much higher temperature. Finally, by making the central figure of *Faustus* a musician, Mann was also able to pay appropriately ambiguous homage to another of his intellectual heroes, a figure whom Nietzsche had first regarded with well-known enthusiasm and later with no less notorious contempt. In 1904 Mann claimed: 'If I were asked whom I regarded as my master, I would name someone who would astonish my literary colleagues: Richard Wagner' (x, 837).

## Wagner

Thomas Mann first started listening to Wagner's operas when he was sixteen years old. Later, this enthusiasm may have helped him woo his wife, Katia, for her father was a devoted Wagner enthusiast. Mann's passion for Wagner remained with him throughout his life. Looking back in his sixties, Mann admitted in 1940 that his love of Wagner overcame his recognition, not simply of the pernicious use to which his music had been put, but of the genuinely dangerous elements in it: 'I find an element of Nazism not only in Wagner's questionable literature; I find it also in his "music", in his work, similarly questionable, though in a loftier sense – albeit I have so loved that work that even today I am deeply stirred whenever a few bars of music from this world impinge on my ear.'[7] Mann's attitude to Wagner, however, was always something of a love-hate relationship.

Wagner himself considered his own music to be (in the title words of one of his great essays, published in 1849) 'the art-work of the future'. And in *The Birth of Tragedy*, a work dedicated to Wagner (in both senses), Nietzsche suggested that in Wagner's art there lay the possibility of 'the rebirth of German myth' (*BT* §23), although he later polemicised in the strongest possible terms against this 'sick', 'decadent' 'Cagliostro of modernity' (*CW* §5). In 'On the Art of Richard Wagner' (1911), Mann hailed Wagner as 'the representative German artist' of the nineteenth century, but claimed that what he called 'a new classicism' would involve turning away from Wagner (x, 842). The emphasis in *Reflections of an Unpolitical Man* was, however, more personal. Here, Mann claimed that he owed much to Wagner in terms of actual artistic technique, including 'the epic mode, beginnings and endings, style as assimilation of the personal to the objective, the creation of symbols, the organic unity of the individual work and the biographical unity of the complete oeuvre' (xii, 80). In other words, his debt was almost incalculable.

Further on, Mann quoted Nietzsche's view of Wagner: 'I like in Wagner what I like in Schopenhauer: the moral fervour, the Faustian flavour, the Cross, Death and the Tomb' (XII, 541).[8] Mann quoted this phrase so often that it almost became his mantra. In the *Reflections*, Mann glossed Nietzsche's words as representing 'a symbol for a whole world, my world, a northern-moral-Protestant one, that is, a German one, that is strictly opposed to the world of ruthless aestheticism' (XII, 541).

In Mann's early writings, the presence of Wagner is, on the thematic level, unmistakable. In *Buddenbrooks*, Hanno's musical improvisations are distinctly Wagneresque in character. Quickly gaining insight into how tonality functions (I, 502), Hanno gives a performance of a piece that could easily have been written by Wagner (I, 506; Part 8, Chapter 6), as could one of his later compositions (I, 748; Part 11, Chapter 2). So perhaps Herr Pfühl, the organist, is right to reject *Tristan and Isolde* as violently as he does: 'This is not music... This is chaos! This is demagogy, blasphemy and madness! This is perfumed billows of smoke, suffused with flashes of lightning! This is the end of all morality in art!' (I, 498; Part 8, Chapter 6). Such sounds also constitute a foretaste of the music that will be heard in the compositions of Adrian Leverkühn. Later, Wagnerian music informs Mann's writing in terms of structure and compositional technique. In these terms, *The Magic Mountain* provides an excellent example of how the repetition of motifs can structure a complex prose work.

In the thirties Mann's attitude towards Wagner became more defensive, as can be seen in the essay 'The Suffering and Greatness of Richard Wagner' (IX, 363–426). At the same time, there was much about which to be defensive; and the political use to which Wagner's music was put by the National Socialists came as no surprise. Mann's cautious attitude is exemplified by the story *Mario and the Magician*, where the mischievous and menacing hypnotist, Cipolla, demonstrates not just his demagogic powers but the dangers of the uses to which the charismatic artist might put them. More generally, Wagner offered an example of the problem to which Mann returned, time and again, in his essays and novels. In 1924, Mann described 'the phenomenon of Richard Wagner, for whom Nietzsche's love knew no end, and which his commanding spirit had to overcome' in terms of 'the paradoxical and eternally interesting phenomenon of world-conquering intoxication with death' (X, 182). This perennial problem was called Romanticism.

## Romanticism

Mann did not hold a single view of Romanticism, although his attitude towards it forms a key part of his matrix of philosophical concerns. His approach to Romanticism is governed by his theory of its origin, which he arrived at through a conflation of two remarks made by Goethe, quoted in his 1921 essay on Goethe and Tolstoy (IX, 81). The background to these remarks is Schiller's treatise *On Naive and Sentimental Poetry* (1795–6), which had introduced the distinction between naive poetry (where the poet enjoys an immediate relationship with Nature) and the sentimental kind (where the poet is 'alienated' from Nature, and his relationship with it is mediated). First, in a conversation with Eckermann on 21 March 1830, Goethe said: 'The conception of classic and Romantic poetry that is going about everywhere today and has caused so much strife and schism came originally from Schiller and me.' And second, in his earlier conversation of 2 April 1829, Goethe remarked: 'I have recently thought of an expression which is not a bad way of describing the relationship [between classical and Romantic]. I call the classical what is healthy, and the Romantic what is sick.' Taken together, Mann argued, these statements identify, on the one hand, the naive with what is objective, healthy and classical; and, on the other, the sentimental with what is subjective, pathological and Romantic (IX, 81). Hence it is the sentimental – where we are separated from Nature, from the world, and from ourselves – which is equated with sickness and disease and, by implication, with the Romantic. On this account, Romanticism is the product of Man's separation from Nature by consciousness. In fact, we read that man is nothing less than 'the romantic being' (IX, 81). In other words, Thomas Mann saw Romanticism as a response to man's alienation, through consciousness, from both internal and external nature. But in his 'Opening Words to a Musical Celebration of Nietsche' he regarded it as an unhealthy response: as 'the song of homesickness for the past, the magic song of death' (X, 182). And in his view Nietzsche had been uniquely sensitive to the seduction of Romanticism: 'It was the fate, the mission of his heroism to prove himself against this musical power-complex, full of great magic, musical Romanticism and Romantic music – and thus almost what is German' (X, 182).[9] The master of Romanticism was, of course, Wagner.

According to Mann, Wagner glorified himself, but Nietzsche overcame himself.[10] Hence Mann praised Nietzsche as 'a friend of life, a seer of higher humanity, a leader into the future, a teacher who tells us to overcome everything in us that is opposed to life and the future, in other words, Romanticism' (X, 182). The reliance on Nietzsche for his critique of Romanticism is well displayed by Mann's examination of two aphorisms. In *Daybreak*, Nietzsche argued that 'the whole great tendency of the Germans was against the Enlightenment and against the revolution in society which was crudely misunderstood as its consequence' (*D* §197, quoted X, 256). And in *Human, All Too Human* (I, §26), he suggested under the heading 'Reaction as Progress' that the reactionary evocation of a past epoch can serve to draw attention to the weakness of progressive tendencies and, in so doing, in fact strengthen them. In particular, he pointed to Luther and Schopenhauer as apparently retarding (but, in the long run, enhancing) the growth of science. In this form, Nietzsche's aphorism is a version of the doctrine of indirection, expressed in the French phrase *reculer pour mieux sauter*, 'step back for a better leap' (x, 258). On the basis of these two aphorisms, Mann saw 'reaction as progress, progress as reaction' and believed that 'their embrace is a continually recurring historical phenomenon' (x, 259).

So in the 1920s Mann's strategy for dealing with Romanticism was a dual one. On the one hand he wanted to distance himself from the association of Romanticism with death (symbolised in *The Magic Mountain* by Schubert's setting of 'Der Lindenbaum' from *Eine Winterreise*), and even more from the dangerous irrationalism that sought its origins in Romanticism (exemplified by the archaeologist of matriarchy, Johann Jakob Bachofen (1815–1887); the 'biocentrist' metaphysician and, for a time, fellow Kilchberg dweller Ludwig Klages (1872–1956); and the right-wing Nietzschean Alfred Bäumler (1887–1968)). On the other hand, he tried to retain sympathy with Romanticism as an expression of the human condition, and with its forward-looking elements. For in the case of German Romanticism, Mann concluded, it would be wrong to think of it purely in terms of a reactionary and fundamentally anti-intellectual movement. Although in its interest in history it might seem reactionary, in the end, he asserted, it proved to be progressive: 'German Romanticism is essentially not historically determined but is oriented towards the future, to such an extent that one can call it the most revolutionary and the most radical movement of the German mind' (x, 266). In 'Culture and Socialism' (1928), Mann condemned 'the actual inadequacy of traditional intellectualism in Germany' for 'its powerlessness to aid the mind turned futurewards' (XIII, 648). Nowhere did Mann see a better expression of the forward-looking nature of Romanticism than in the idea of 'die eigentlich bessere Welt' (the really better world), an expression found in the Romantic poet Friedrich von Hardenberg, better known by his pseudonym Novalis (x, 266).[11] But, as Mann must have known, Novalis, who himself died young from tuberculosis, was also the poet *par excellence* of the desire for death, and of the cult of the *Liebestod* that reached its apogee in Act III of Wagner's *Tristan and Isolde*.

## Psychoanalysis

Mann offered his commentary on Nietzsche's two aphorisms in 'Freud's Position in the History of Modern Thought' (1929), the first of his two major lectures on Sigmund Freud (x, 256–80). The starting-point for Mann's view of psychoanalysis might be considered to be the following remark by Freud: 'As a psychoanalyst, I must of course be more interested in affective than in intellectual phenomena; more in the unconscious than in the conscious mental life' (SE, XIII, 241). As Mann recognised in 1929, however, Freud's investigation of the affective sphere by no means degenerated into the glorification of the object of his research at the expense of the intellectual sphere (x, 276). Acutely aware of the 'quite remarkable' relationship between Freud and German Romanticism (x, 277), particularly Novalis, Mann acknowledged the important affinities between the founder of psychoanalysis and the nineteenth century's opposition to rationalism, intellectualism, and classicism (x, 260). In fact, Mann wrote that, precisely because of 'its emphasis on the daemonic in nature, its investigative passion for the night side of the soul', psychoanalysis was 'as anti-rational as any expression of the new spirit that is locked in victorious battle with the mechanistic and materialistic elements of the nineteenth century'. 'In this sense', Mann concluded, psychoanalysis was 'completely revolutionary' (x, 275).

More important, however, is Mann's assimilation of psychoanalysis to his positive understanding of Romanticism by uncovering the striking similarities between Freud and Novalis. These led Mann to argue that both psychoanalysis and Romanticism believed in 'the transcendence of disorder, in ever higher stages, and in the future' (x, 280). From this perspective, Mann commended psychoanalysis to the young generation as 'one of the forms of modern research into life which, more effectively than any other, frustrates the attempt to misuse it for the purposes of obscuring the concept of revolution' (x, 274). This was the basis of Mann's enthusiastic attitude towards psychoanalysis, and his essay of 1929 concluded with the following words of praise: 'It is that manifestation of modern irrationalism which unequivocally resists all reactionary misuse. It is one of the most important foundation stones that have been laid at the foundations of the future, the dwelling-place of a liberated and conscious humanity' (x, 280). Freud, in his letter of 23 November 1929, expressed gratitude to Mann for this defence against 'the accusation of reactionary mysticism'.[12]

Yet Mann's praise was even more lavish – indeed, suspiciously so – in 1936, in a speech delivered in Vienna on the occasion of Freud's eightieth birthday (and later presented to Freud personally). Whereas in 1929 Mann had concentrated on the parallels between Freud and Novalis, here he drew attention to Freud's affinities with Nietzsche (IX, 480–1) and Schopenhauer (IX, 483–8). In particular, Mann suggested that the id corresponded to Schopenhauer's notion of the will, and the ego to Schopenhauer's view of the intellect (IX, 487; cf. 578). Furthermore, he argued, the chapter entitled

'Transcendent Speculations on Apparent Design in the Fate of the Individual' from the second volume of *The World as Will and Representation* pointed to 'the most profound and mysterious point of contact' between Freud's 'natural-scientific world' and Schopenhauer's 'philosophical' one. For Mann, that point of contact constituted the core of psychoanalysis: 'In the mystery of the unity of the ego and the world, of being and happening, in the perception of the apparently objective and accidental as something which is organised by the soul, I believe I recognise the innermost core of psychoanalytic theory' (IX, 488; cf. 479).

One might think that such a view has very little to do with Freud; and one would be right to do so. Indeed, Mann himself admits as much when he says he wants to use this 'festive occasion' to 'indulge in a little polemic' against Freud, primarily by citing with approval the words of C. G. Jung, 'a clever but ungrateful offspring of this [analytic] doctrine' (IX, 488). And he goes on to discuss Jung's introduction to the *Tibetan Book of the Dead*, in which, according to Mann, Jung 'uses analytical results to form a bridge of understanding between Western thought and Eastern esotericism' (IX, 489). Hence it is via Jung and another analyst, Ernst Kris, and not via Freud, that Mann comes to his discussion of the *Joseph* tetralogy in 'an hour of ceremonial encounter between poetic literature and the psychoanalytic sphere' (IX, 490). In return, Freud informed Mann that the biblical figure of Joseph had been a mythical model for Napoleon, the secret daemonic force behind Napoleon's complex career (letter from Freud, 29 November 1936; cf. diary, 13 May 1936).

Although there is no direct evidence that Mann ever encountered Jung personally, it is likely that the two men met in Munich in 1921. For a time, both lived in Küsnacht near Zurich: Mann lived at Schiedhaldenstrasse 33, up on the slope of the village, between 1933 and 1938, while Jung's home for most of his life was at Seestrasse 228, by the lake. In fact, Jung's influence on Mann was arguably much greater than Freud's, and Jungian ideas can be seen to inform Mann's work in various ways. In particular, his notion of the collective unconscious becomes, in Mann, a kind of cultural unconscious (a less metaphysical, and hence perhaps more defensible notion). For example, Mann writes that through Dürer we come to meditate on 'what is the most profound and the most super-personal, lying outside and below the corporeal limits of our ego but still determining and nourishing it' (X, 232). Then again, in his essay on Schopenhauer he suggests that 'our most intimate self . . . must have at its root a connection with the foundations of the world' (IX, 529). In the famous 'Snow' chapter of *The Magic Mountain*, Hans Castorp achieves the following quasi-Jungian insight: 'One does not just dream from one's own soul, but I should say we dream anonymously and communally, albeit each in his own way. The great soul, of which you are but a part, dreams through you, in your way, of things which, secretly, it always dreams' (III, 684; Chapter 6). In *Joseph* Mann explored the notion of a collective self, a realm where 'the borders between the ego and the cosmos are opened, and the ego loses itself and mixes itself up' (V, 1721–2; *Joseph the Provider*, Part 6: 'The Restored', 'I Will Go and See Him'). And in *Doctor Faustus* Mann's understanding of the rise of Nazi Germany and the causes of the Second World War is similar to that expressed in Jung's essays on the War in several respects, not least the tendency to view Germany through the prism of paganism, centring on the figure of the Greek god, Dionysus, or his Germanic 'cousin', Wotan.[13]

In *Reflections of an Unpolitical Man* Thomas Mann wrote that there was probably some truth in the charge that the Germans were heathens, secretly praying to Odin (XII, 46). In 'Thoughts in War' (1914) he spoke of 'the German soul' as being characterised by 'something very deep and irrational' (XIII, 545). In a letter to the Stockholm newspaper *Svenska Dagbladet* in 1915, he described Germany as 'above all a great psychic fact' (XIII, 553). And in 1922 Mann compared German fascism to a pagan folk religion and, more specifically, to the cult of Wotan (IX, 169). Not only did Mann and Jung find an explanation for fascism in terms of mythical rather than political phenomena, but both men regarded the Faust legend as offering insight into what Mann called the 'antiquated and neurotic underground' of the German soul (XI, 1130). In 'Germany and the Germans', a speech originally given in English on 29 May 1945 in Washington, Mann argued that there existed 'a secret connection between the German mind [*Gemüt*] and the daemonic', which was symbolised by the story of Faust (XI, 1131). Jung's rejection, in 1936, of the Faustian 'yearning, hungry unrest for the unattainable' was as vigorous as Mann's had been in 1932 in 'Goethe as Representative of the Bourgeois Age' (IX, 321).[14] Moreover, Mann and Jung saw a prefiguration of Germany's fate in the madness of Nietzsche. From his diary entries in 1933 and 1934 (XII, 684–6) to his 1947 lecture on 'Nietzsche's Philosophy in the Light of Our Experience', Mann tried to draw a link between aspects of Nietzschean thought and the Third Reich (IX, 707–8). Both men regarded Hitler as an hysteric; and both were aware, each in his own way, of an uncomfortable sense of affinity with what happened in Germany – so much so that, in 1939, Mann contentiously called Hitler his 'brother' (XII, 845–52). The culmination of Mann's novel on the war conflates the Dionysian and the daemonic, as the final paragraph of the novel depicts Germany trying to recover from its drunken and dangerous revelry (VI, 676).

This aspect of Mann's work and his relationship to Jung serve as a reminder of some of the murkier figures in which Thomas Mann displayed an interest, such as Klages and Bäumler. Equally, however, Mann entertained connections with contemporary intellectuals on the Left, including Max Weber (1864–1920), Georg Lukács (1885–1971), Ernst Bloch (1885–1977), and T. W. Adorno (1903–69). Mann's overall political attitude is perhaps best summarised in the words of his letter dated 13 March 1952 to Ferdinand Lion: 'My democratic attitude is not really genuine, it is merely an irritable reaction to German "irrationalism" and the swindle of its profundity... and to any form of fascism, which I really and honestly cannot endure.' In 'Goethe and Tolstoy' (IX, 170) and 'Culture and Socialism' (XII, 649), Mann expressed his views more positively when he said that Karl Marx should read Friedrich Hölderlin: scientific socialism needed to be supplemented by visionary Romanticism.

## Weimar classicism

Moving away from the figures just mentioned, who are relatively minor influences on Mann, let us examine a more important tradition of thought in which Mann consciously placed himself, namely Weimar classicism. In 'Freud and the Future' Mann claimed that the imitation of Goethe 'can still unconsciously lead and mythically determine the life of an artist' (IX, 499), and this was certainly true of Mann himself.

In *Reflections of an Unpolitical Man* Thomas Mann referred to the notion of *Bildung*, a German concept of long standing, describing it as 'an insufficiency and sense of discontent when faced with one-sidedness' (XII, 505). A prime example of such one-sidedness and its resultant discontent is provided by the figure of Gustav von Aschenbach, the (anti-)hero of *Death in Venice*, the first of many works which reflect Mann's interest in Goethe. For the infatuation of the middle-aged Aschenbach with the youthful Tadzio is, in part, based on Goethe's love, late in his life, for the seventeen-year-old Ulrike von Levetzow ('On Myself'; XIII, 148), and in his letter to Carl Maria Weber of 4 July 1920 Mann said that while writing this work he had read Goethe's novel *Die Wahlverwandtschaften* [*Elective Affinities*] five times. In 1922, Mann published a lengthy essay on Goethe and Tolstoy, and many of the passages in this piece are taken up and used in Mann's later essays and lectures on Goethe. Thus it is right to speak of a strong continuity in Mann's view of Goethe, in which, at most, the emphasis is modulated.

In his 1922 study Mann drew attention to the theme of anatomical study and surgical training in *Wilhelm Meisters Wanderjahre* to illustrate how the hero's interest in theatre and medicine were expressions of his 'sympathy with the organic and its highest revelation, the human form' – an interest and a sympathy Mann regarded as 'not far removed from Eros' (IX, 147; cf.

'On the German Republic', XI, 846). In the *Wanderjahre*, Wilhelm comes across in the dissecting-room 'the most beautiful female arm that ever twined itself around the neck of a boy', and hesitates to cut into it (Book III, Chapter 3). Mann refers specifically to this episode, which adumbrates some of the most startling passages in the Mannian oeuvre where characters expound on medicine and the body. For example, in *The Confessions of Felix Krull, Confidence Man* (published 1954, but begun in 1909 and worked on periodically in the 1920s), Professor Kuckuck undertakes a dissection of a woman's arm in evolutionary terms, reminding Krull that it is it is nothing other than what has become of the hooked wing of the primordial bird and the pectoral fin of the fish (Book III, Chapter 5; VII, 541). Then again, *The Magic Mountain* recalls Goethe's *Faust* in its very title: the section 'Walpurgisnacht' alludes to the annual orgy celebrated by witches on the Brocken mountain, and especially to *Faust*, line 3868, where the mountain is called 'zaubertoll' (mad with magic); and the novel is replete with meditations on the human body and on the relationship between sickness and health, life and death, and the physiological and the psychological. In his lectures, entitled 'Love as a pathogenic force' (Chapter 4, 'Hippe'; III, 164), Dr Krokowski declares that a symptom of disease is the disguised activity of love, and that all disease is transformed love (III, 181). According to his diary entry of 26 July 1921, rereading the *Wanderjahre* left Mann 'astonished at the truly Goethean aura of *The Magic Mountain*'. And in his letter to Arthur Schnitzler of 4 September 1922, Mann described *The Magic Mountain* as a kind of *Bildungsroman*, in which the hero is led by the experience of sickness and death to the ideas of man and the state.

In 1939, Thomas Mann entered as fully as was possible into the persona of Goethe by attempting, in *Lotte in Weimar* (known in English as *The Beloved Returns*), to recreate the thoughts of the great man of German letters. According to his letter to Anna Jacobson of 13 November 1936, composition of this novel allowed Mann 'the fantastic pleasure of putting Goethe personally back on his feet again'. The stream-of-consciousness passages interweave fresh Mannian material with extensive quotation and allusion, and Mann was so successful in recreating the cadences of Goethe and his circle in Weimar that the British prosecutor at the Nuremberg Trials, Sir Hartley Shawcross, mistakenly attributed a line written by Mann in the novel to Goethe.

The impulse behind the work which, with good reason, Mann referred to with the Goethean phrase 'my main business' ('mein Hauptgeschäft') – the *Joseph* tetralogy, the composition of which stretched across more than a decade – was also, at least in part, Goethean. For in his autobiography *Dichtung und Wahrheit* [*Poetry and Truth*], Goethe wrote that he had always wanted to write a version of the Biblical story of Joseph (Part 1, Book 4); Goethe's version has been lost, but Mann's prodigious four-part series was presumably intended to make up for this. Of the tetralogy, Mann wrote in 1940: 'This novel is a Joseph-game. The imitation of God in which Rachel's son indulges corresponds to my *imitatio* of Goethe: an identification and *unio mystica* [mystical union] with the *Father*' ('On Myself', XIII, 169).

Finally, just as *Doctor Faustus* investigated the mad artist-musician Adrian Leverkühn's pact with the devil to reach the sources of creativity, so Mann had earlier discerned, in no less a figure than Goethe himself, 'something elemental, dark, neutral, something maliciously confusing and devilishly negating' (IX, 119); or, as he also put it, 'a synthesis of the daemonic and the urbane' (IX, 352; cf. IX, 582). For genius, Mann observed, is closely allied to the psychopathic (IX, 322).

Concurrently with the Goethean overtones of his novels, Mann's essays continued to develop his thinking about Goethe. In 1922, Mann noted that the bourgeois, humanistic, liberal epoch was coming to an end: could classical humanism, he wondered, survive it (IX, 166)? In his epilogue to a 1925 edition of *Elective Affinities*, Mann expounded the notion of 'ethical culture' which he found in this text (IX, 183). In 'Goethe as Representative of the Bourgeois Age', a lecture delivered in March 1932 in Berlin to commemorate the centenary of Goethe's death, he explored what he regarded as the virtues of that epoch, praising the bourgeoisie in a manner almost reminiscent of Marx in the *Communist Manifesto*, albeit also lamenting its decline. Above all, Mann celebrated Goethe not simply as the master of the German cultural epoch of classicism, nor just as an almost god-like individual and one of the greatest human manifestations to have walked the earth, but rather as a representative of the epoch of the bourgeoisie (a period extending, for Mann, from the fifteenth to the nineteenth centuries). Next to Schiller's poem 'Das Lied von der Glocke' ['The Song of the Bell'], Mann wrote, Goethe's domestic epic *Hermann and Dorothea* was 'the purest and most conscious glorification and transfiguration of that human mean which we call the German bourgeois sphere' (IX, 301–2). Sensing an affinity, as Freud had done, between Goethe and Leonardo da Vinci (IX, 301; *SE* XI, 75), Mann described the chief characteristic of Goethe's work in terms of 'unforced, unambitious, quiet and natural, almost vegetative growth from unprepossessing beginnings to universal significance' (IX, 307).

In his second great commemorative lecture of 1932, delivered in Weimar, Mann considered Goethe's career in a more personal light, this time as a 'Schriftsteller', or man of letters. And in his lecture on *Faust*, delivered in April 1938 at Princeton University (where, a month later, he was awarded an honorary doctorate), he offered a detailed commentary on that work, drawing on Goethe's rejected drafts. In the same year, Mann claimed that Goethe had been able to unite in himself both the classical and the Romantic: 'That, indeed, is one of the formulas in which one may express his greatness' (IX, 576). Later essays examined Goethe's novel *Die Leiden des jungen Werther* [*The Sorrows of Young Werther*] (1941; IX, 640–55), conjured up an image of the man in 'Goethe: An Imaginative Portrait' (1948; IX, 713–54), and interrogated the significance of Goethe for democracy (1949; IX, 755–82).

For all his self-stylisation as the successor to Goethe, Mann's last major intellectual essay was on Schiller (1955). On the occasion of the 150th anniversary of his death, Mann said of Schiller: 'This spirit was and is the apotheosis of art' (IX, 873). His enthusiasm for Schiller went back to his school days, and is reflected in one of his early short stories, 'A Weary Hour' (1905). Here, Mann depicted Schiller struggling to complete his play *Wallenstein* – much as Mann himself had had difficulty writing *Fiorenza* – and trying, perhaps also like Mann, to overcome his ambivalence towards Goethe. And in *Tonio Kröger* (VIII, 276), the hero tries to persuade Hans Hansen to read Schiller's *Don Carlos*, particularly Act 4, Scene 23, where the courtiers report that the King has wept (an example of Mann's interest in passionate emotion, not just the solitary, friendless suffering he associated elsewhere with Schiller). In his essays, Mann frequently hailed the importance of Schiller's essay *On Naive and Sentimental Poetry*, describing it in 1922 as 'the classic and comprehensive essay of the Germans, which encompasses all the others and renders them superfluous' (IX, 61; cf. IX, 177; IX, 313; XII, 569–70). Moreover, he contrasted the different attitudes towards freedom held by Goethe and Schiller (IX, 95–100). And not only, according to Mann, was Schiller kinder to his visitors than Goethe was (IX, 77), but Schiller emerges, à la Tolstoy, as almost saintly (IX, 63). In 1955 Mann spoke of Schiller's persistence in writing despite his critical medical condition (IX, 925), and Mann's own health when he was composing his lecture was extremely poor. Yet Mann may have sensed an affinity with Schiller on a far more fundamental level. In the case of Goethe, Mann had emphasised the importance of the senses (IX, 135; cf. IX, 93). As one of Mann's biographers has pointed out, the observation by the contemporary writer and friend, Kurt Martens, that Thomas Mann was 'attached to nothing that did not emanate from himself' anticipates Mann's comment about 'a certain troubling affinity' with Schiller in his letter to Karl Kerényi of 5 December 1954: 'The world of the eyes is not actually my world either, and at heart I want to see nothing – just like him.'[15] Yet such remarks point to a central divergence in aesthetic principles between, on the one hand, Thomas Mann, and, on the other hand, Goethe and Schiller, the school of Weimar classicism.

Throughout his writings, Mann investigates the relationship between the aesthetic, the epistemological and the moral; between art, knowledge and action. In the case of Schillerian aesthetics, the relationship between the aesthetic and the moral was a complex one: the aesthetic was a precondition for the moral, yet it should also accompany its expression. Schiller argued in his *Letters on the Aesthetic Education of Mankind* that the 'sense-drive', by which we absorb sensory experience, and the 'form-drive', by which we shape our experience, jointly gave rise to a third, the ludic drive ('Spieltrieb'), and similarly he envisaged, in the midst of the destructive realm of natural forces and the sacred realm of moral laws, a third realm of play and semblance ('ein drittes, fröhliches Reich des Spiels und des Scheins').[16] Mann made frequent allusion to this 'drittes Reich' (e.g. XI, 564, 847, 867), although its connotations have, in the wake of National Socialism, frequently been misunderstood. When Mann remarks that, in ethical culture, 'social and religious contra-natural tendencies become good morals through good manners' (IX, 182), he is recalling one of the most practical aspects of the third realm, Schiller's notion of aesthetic social conduct.[17]

In Mann's works, it is the relationship between the aesthetic and the moral that, time and again, he investigates; indeed, that is their central theme. In *Death in Venice* and *Tonio Kröger*, the presence of this theme is almost palpable. In his essays, it can be found in his discussion of the Goethean notion of 'innate merit' ('angeborenes Verdienst') (IX, 101; IX, 549–50; G IX, 475). He reminds us that in Schopenhauer's system the aesthetic state is subordinate to asceticism (IX, 544–6; cf. 555, 570–1). In the final book of the *Joseph* tetralogy, Jacob warns Serach that 'poesy is always a dangerous, seductive and tempting thing', because 'the essence of song [*Liederwesen*] is unfortunately not far from dissoluteness [*Liederlichkeit*]', adding: 'The game is beautiful, but the spirit is holy' (*Joseph the Provider*, Part VI: 'The Holy Game', 'Annunciation'; V, 1712). And in *Doctor Faustus*, Serenus Zeitblom invokes the question of 'Schein' (semblance), asking whether 'beautiful semblance', that key term derived from Schillerian aesthetics, has become nothing more than a lie (Chapter 21; VI, 241). In the same year, the essay 'The Task of the Writer' ponders the possible limitations to aesthetic education (X, 781). Yet even here Mann goes on to argue that 'the work of the intellect' ('das geistige Werk') represents 'the apotheosis of life' (X, 782). Correspondingly, at the end of Adrian Leverkühn's mad, bad masterwork, the symphonic cantata *Dr. Fausti Weheklag*, the raucous dissonance fades away to leave a final note, played on the cello, like a light that shines on in the darkness, leaving neither 'silence' nor 'night' unchallenged (Chapter 46; VI, 651).

Despite his celebration of the bourgeoisie in *Reflections of an Unpolitical Man*, and his emphasis in 1932 on Goethe's bourgeois roots, Mann was prepared, as early as 1922, to wonder whether classical humanism, and the intellectual world it inhabits, would be able to survive the end of the bourgeois era (IX, 166). From this point of view, Mann's entire literary output represents an attempt to answer this question in the positive, or, as Nietzsche's Raphael did, to say 'yes' and do 'yes' (*TI*, 'Expeditions of an Untimely Man', §9). Hence Mann saw his task in terms of 'a conservatism of the future' (IX, 189), the preservation of a core of values around which, in beautiful forms, the new might crystallise (XI, 829). As he wrote in 1926, the function of the modern writer is to mediate between the greatness of the past and the new (IX, 361). Thus Mann's concern was to open up to the reader the riches of the intellectual world outlined above. And the hermeneutic imperative to understand that world becomes, as Thomas told his son Klaus in his letter of 22 July 1939, the means by which each generation inherits it: 'But in the end, to inherit something, one has to understand it; inheritance is, after all, culture.'

## NOTES

1 See Wagner's letter to Emilie Ritter, 29 December 1854, in Richard Wagner, *Sämtliche Briefe*, 11 vols. to date (Leipzig: Deutscher Verlag für Musik, 1967–), VI, 308–11.

2 See e.g. Hugh Ridley, *Thomas Mann: 'Buddenbrooks'* (Cambridge: Cambridge University Press, 1987), p. 64.

3 'Reminiscence of my Two Years in Leipzig' (Nietzsche, *Werke*, III, 133).

4 A chapter in Ernst Bertram's book on Nietzsche is entitled 'Knight, Death and Devil'; see Mann's diary, 12 September 1918.

5 See also Mann's letter to Arnold Schoenberg, 17 February 1948; and *Thus Spoke Zarathustra* (*Werke*, II, 345 and 382). The phrase attributed by Nietzsche to Homer is quoted by Aristotle in *Metaphysics*, 1:2:983a, where it is described as proverbial. According to other sources, however, it is assigned to Solon by the scholiast on Plato, although this attribution is uncertain: Ivan M. Linforth, *Solon the Athenian* (Berkeley, CA: University of California Press, 1919), pp. 171, 245.

6 For 'regulated cooperation' ('gesetzliches Zusammenwirken'), see *Wilhelm Meisters Wanderjahre*, Book II, ch. 8.

7 'To the Editor of *Common Sense*', in Mann, *Wagner und unsere Zeit* (Frankfurt am Main: Fischer, 1963), p. 158.

8 'Mir behagt an Wagner, was mir an Schopenhauer behagt, die ethische Luft, der faustische Duft, Kreuz, Tod und Gruft', from Nietzsche's letter to Erwin Rohde, 8 October 1868.

9 In his letter to Ernst Fischer of 25 May 1926, Mann spoke of 'Romanticism's self-transcendence in Nietzsche'.

10 'Wagner [war] ein mächtig-glücklicher Selbstverherrlicher und Selbstvollender, Nietzsche dagegen ein revolutionärer Selbstüberwinder' (X, 182).

11 Novalis, *Schriften*, ed. Paul Kluckhohn and Richard Samuel, 5 vols. (Stuttgart: Kohlhammer, 1960–88), III, 469.

12 But see also Freud's letter, 28 July 1929, in Sigmund Freud and Lou Andreas-Salomé, *Letters*, trans. William and Elaine Robson-Scott (London: Hogarth Press, 1972), pp. 181–2: 'Th[omas] Mann's essay is certainly an honour. It gives me the impression that he had an essay on Romanticism ready to hand, when he was requested to write something about me, and so he furnished the front and back of the essay with a veneer of psycho-analysis, as the cabinet makers say; the bulk is of a different material. However, when Mann says something, it has real substance.'

13 See C. G. Jung, *The Collected Works*, ed. Herbert Read, Michael Fordham and Gerhard Adler, trans. R. F. C. Hull, 2nd edn (London and Princeton, 1970): 'Wotan' (1936), x, 179–93; 'After the Catastrophe' (1945), x, 194–217.

14 See Jung, *Collected Works*, x, §423, and cf. Goethe, *Faust II*, line 8202.

15 Ronald Hayman, *Thomas Mann: A Biography* (London: Bloomsbury, 1996), pp. 143, 608; Klaus Schröter, *Thomas Mann im Urteil seiner Zeit: Dokumente 1891–1955* (Hamburg: Wegner, 1969), p. 15.

16 Friedrich Schiller, *Letters on the Aesthetic Education of Mankind*, ed. and trans. E. M. Wilkinson and L. A. Willoughby (Oxford: Clarendon Press, 1967), pp. 214, 215.

17 For Schiller's concept of 'schöner Umgang' see *Aesthetic Education*, Letter 27, and *Kallias oder Über die Schönheit*, in his *Sämtliche Werke*, ed. Gerhard Fricke and Herbert G. Göpfert, 5 vols. (Munich: Hanser, 1958), v, 408–26.

## FURTHER READING

Bishop, Paul, 'Thomas Mann and C. G. Jung', in Paul Bishop (ed.), *Jung in Contexts: A Reader* (London and New York: Routledge, 1999), pp. 154–89

Bridges, George, 'The Almost Irresistible Appeal of Fascism, or: Is it okay to like Richard Wagner?', *Germanic Review* 64 (1989), 42–8

Furness, Raymond, *Wagner and Literature* (Manchester: Manchester University Press, 1982)

Kelley, Alice van Buren, 'Von Aschenbach's *Phaedrus*: Platonic Allusion in *Der Tod in Venedig*', *Journal of English and Germanic Philology* 75 (1976), 228–40

Lyotard, Jean-François, 'Adorno as the Devil', trans. Robert Hurley, *Telos* 19 (spring 1974), 127–37

Pütz, Peter (ed.), *Thomas Mann und die Tradition* (Frankfurt am Main: Athenäum, 1971)

Reed, T. J., 'Thomas Mann und die literarische Tradition', in Helmut Koopmann (ed.), *Thomas-Mann-Handbuch* (Stuttgart: Kröner, 1995), pp. 95–136

Robertson, Ritchie, 'Primitivism and Psychology: Nietzsche, Freud, Thomas Mann', in Peter Collier and Judy Davies (eds.), *Modernism and the European Unconscious* (Cambridge: Polity, 1990), pp. 79–93

Tuska, Jon, 'Thomas Mann and Nietzsche: A Study in Ideas', *Germanic Review* 39 (1964), 281–99

Zeder, Franz, *Studienratsmusik. Eine Untersuchung zur skeptischen Reflexivität des 'Doktor Faustus' von Thomas Mann* (Frankfurt am Main: Lang, 1995)

# 3

MICHAEL MINDEN

# Mann's literary techniques

We no longer believe that truth remains
truth once its veil has been removed.
Nietzsche
(*GS*, preface, §4)

In olden days a glimpse of stocking
was looked on as something shocking,
now, heaven knows, anything goes.
Cole Porter

Thomas Mann is chiefly known as a novelist in the European tradition. The novel is an artistic hybrid of storytelling, immoral behaviour and moral consciousness. This holds true for Thomas Mann's fiction, although in his case it is complicated by specifically German factors.

The first is that the German novel tradition has characteristics of its own. Both Goethe and the Romantics made distinct contributions to the literary genre of the novel, usually in the form of attempts to modify its hybrid constitution in one way or another. The Goethean *Bildungsroman* concentrates on the moral development of one individual character, and the artistic aspect of the novel's composition is enhanced not only by this thematic focus, but also by the belief in the meaningful shape of the education process itself.[1] As the protagonist is formed, so is the novel. The Romantics promoted the hybrid heterogeneity of the novel, its mixture of narrative and essayism, to the status of a defining principle of all art. For them it was (at least theoretically) the only art form equal to the task of capturing the metaphysical interpenetration of subjective and objective realities. Thomas Mann was conscious of both these strains in the German literary inheritance, and we shall return to them.[2] But it is from Wagner's music drama, which was understood by Mann and others to be the last flowering of Romanticism, that Mann most clearly derived aspects of his literary technique, aspects that strained against the novel form's own pragmatic heterogeneity.

This heterogeneity goes back at least to the seminal eighteenth-century English novelist Samuel Richardson. The cunning mixture of immorality and morality can be seen as a form of historical self-consciousness, an effect of the novel's history as a medium in which the new reading public of the

European middle classes viewed its satisfactions and duties in literary form. If we allow that literary techniques are primarily a matter of engaging the reader's pleasure, then the sort of pleasure involved in the reading of the novel, from the eighteenth century until more or less the time of Mann's own beginnings as a novelist, is twofold. On the one hand the reader identifies with imperfect characters and their social circumstances, and on the other she is put in possession of the moral criteria necessary to be discriminating about them. Both sensations promote a feeling of belonging. The reader can enjoy the representation of immoral actions without herself feeling immoral; on the contrary, reading increases the sense of moral security.

With Wagner there is a completely different kind of pleasure, requiring different skills of the artist. Here, the deep literary and moral involvement with a given readership is replaced by the sovereign mastery required to forge all the artistic media together in the creation of a postulated world. Composition, form, becomes more important for its own sake, so that, as Kandinsky said, Wagner's art anticipated abstraction.[3]

Not only does this kind of art not recognise an existing social world with its own readership and repertoire of representations: it seeks to create a public for itself by developing a theory of its own reception and creating the environment (Wagner's theatre at Bayreuth, for example) to bring it about. It brings with it its own theory of collective identity based upon the power of the *Gesamtkunstwerk* (total work of art), especially the power of music to speak directly to the senses. The scandal of Wagner, as well as his overwhelming appeal to so many in the nineteenth century, were bound up with the sensual, even sexual appeal of the music, and the narcotic effect it brilliantly produced. The inner intensity created by music drama is held to transcend or at any rate transform the sphere of morality. As the scandalised music teacher famously exclaims in *Buddenbrooks* on first hearing *Tristan* played on the piano: 'This is the end of morality in art!' (1, 498; Part 8, Chapter 6), only to succumb himself to its seduction on the next page.

Wagner's notion of art (he despised the purely literary) and the pragmatic sociability of the novel could hardly be further apart.[4] To express the difference antithetically, the novel is consumed in private but addresses the public sphere, indeed confirms the reader's membership of it; the Wagnerian orgy of form is experienced in public, but addresses the most private areas of personal experience. From here, the will towards a new public sphere is projected. The two modes of artistic representation work in opposite directions.

In Mann, then, the Wagnerian seduction of form is superimposed upon the pragmatic heterogeneity of the novel. It is appropriate that his children called him 'the magician': it takes an unusually gifted illusionist to hold these two things together. Mann's illusionism too has a specifically German background.

Wagner was deeply influenced by Schopenhauer, and it is in relation to this thinker, precursor of Darwin and Freud, that we can sketch a philosophical context for Mann's literary illusionism. In Schopenhauer's model of the world as 'will and representation', the world of human experience, from sensation all the way through to philosophy, is a complicated system of illusion constructed upon a ground of mere blind striving. His pessimism derives from his belief that there is no escape from this state of affairs, since it is inseparable from the fundamental illusion that consists in our sense of being individuated persons. Our pleasures can never lead to satisfaction because they are the expression of the undifferentiated will: though given to our experience as particular, they are in fact the movements of a boundless flux which sets all against all.

Schopenhauer includes in his philosophy a special function for art. He adapts the notion from idealist aesthetics that aesthetic pleasure is categorically distinct from any pleasure associated with the appetites. The difference consists in the circumstance that, apart from a lifelong practice of asceticism, only possible for a few saintly individuals, it is only the contemplation of art that can afford liberation, albeit temporary, from our constitutional enslavement to the will. Schopenhauer's view of what one might call the novelistic world of human moral experience as fundamentally illusory (and his related belief in music as the ultimate art) inspired Wagner, but the philosopher's view of the enjoyment of art as a sub-category of self-denial did not. While classical aesthetics saw pleasure in art as transcending the appetites, Nietzsche quotes the definition of pleasure in art as '*une promesse de bonheur*', a promise of happiness, given by Stendhal (a novelist!) (*GM* III, §6); and this development from classical aesthetics to Nietzsche has the deepest implications for Mann.

While it is likely that Mann did, at bottom, see the world in a more or less Schopenhauerian way, it is clear enough that his view of the role of art and the artist came from Wagner and, especially, from the complex and contradictory role Wagner plays in Nietzsche's thought. What concerns us here is that the philosopher put a notion of art as 'the paradigm of human activity' at the very centre of his critical project.[5]

Nietzsche began as a great enthusiast for Wagner as an artist capable of galvanising contemporary Germany into the kind of collective implied by the passion of his operatic effects. Later Nietzsche turned away from the composer, his disillusion intensified by the very passion of the hope in which he felt disappointed. He felt that Wagner's art had 'fallen' into the vulgar reality of Wilhelmine Germany. Wagner now became the paradigm for the modern artist as reactive, weak, fragmented and resentful. Nietzsche continued to hold that art, properly practised, can be supremely important, not as the bodying forth of a higher kind of truth, but as a manifestation of the world's own investment in illusion. As Gilles Deleuze puts it, for Nietzsche, art is the 'highest power of falsehood'; 'the activity of life is like a power of falsehood, of duping, dissimulating, dazzling and seducing. But, in order to be brought into effect, this power of falsehood must be selected, redoubled or repeated and thus elevated to a higher power.'[6]

This powerful propagation of life-enabling errors thus adds an affirmative aspect to the significance of illusion in Mann's work. The extreme model for Mann's illusionism, in which for a brief moment Schopenhauer, Wagner and Nietzsche all converge in a founding mythical scene, is Nietzsche's brilliant analysis in *The Birth of Tragedy* of the effect of Act III of Wagner's *Tristan und Isolde*. In this view, the pleasure generated by art is so great that it threatens to exceed the ability of the recipient to enjoy it: 'how could anyone fail to be shattered immediately, having once put their ear to the heart of the universal will, so to speak, and felt the raging desire for existence pour forth into all the arteries of the world...?' (*BT* §21). What protects the hearer from this self-destruction is the interposition of the narrative of tragic myth and the figure of the tragic hero. They are the *forms* that screen the opera-goer from what threatens to be the collapse of all forms, even the individual human form, into an ecstatic reunion with the primal oneness behind appearances. Nietzsche calls this primal lure the Dionysiac. Tragic myth and tragic hero, narrative and impersonation, transform the kind of pleasure the hearer and observer experiences from that of overwhelming ecstatic self-abandon into that of illusion: 'this is where the power of the *Apolline*, bent on restoring the almost shattered individual, bursts forth, bringing the healing balm of a blissful deception' (*BT* §21). The embeddedness of an individual creative artist in his time and culture assumes, at this climax of Nietzsche's argument, a power almost as great as that of the Dionysiac that threatens to destroy the individual: 'with the enormous force of image, concept, ethical doctrine and sympathetic excitement, the Apolline wrenches man out of his orgiastic self-destruction' (*BT* §21).

It is notable that, in a culture of which Nietzsche approves like that of the Greeks of Sophocles' time or (as he thought then) of Wagner's Germany, the relation between art and morality is unproblematic since 'ethical doctrine' can be accommodated as part of the repertoire of the life-sustaining illusion of the Apolline. This holistic view was later available neither to Nietzsche himself nor to Thomas Mann. Mann inherited not only the doctrine of the vital existential power of illusion from Nietzsche, he also inherited his critical moralism. As a novelist Mann is thus doubly inspired by

Nietzsche. His narrative art, his storytelling, is compositional, illusionistic, forming and performative rather than mimetic, and as such engages a pleasure that exceeds familiar social experience and threatens it. The moral consciousness proper to the novel genre takes the form of Nietzsche's fierce critical moralism, which sees through all morality in Schopenhauerian *Erkenntnis* (knowledge, insight), but which is also fired by the almost unbearable disappointment at the absence of the redemptive art of which a real possibility has been glimpsed.

To take the matter once again from the point of view of pleasure: in Mann's fiction the balance of immorality and moral consciousness specific to the novel has been fundamentally disturbed. On the one hand the flirtation with immorality has grown monstrously into a Dionysian pleasure that threatens to burst the individual and society asunder. On the other there is a homeless critical consciousness that suffers from the knowledge that this redemptive satisfaction is impossible in the given historical world. The novel's historical compromise has become polarised into what Mann called 'art' and 'intellect'.

This configuration underlies the early stories in which Mann said he had made his first breakthrough to a public literary identity or mask (letter to Otto Grautoff, April 1897). In 'Little Herr Friedemann' and 'The Joker' (both 1897), a Nietzschean critical voice displays with cold impassivity the Wagnerian dream of redemptive passion in grotesque contrast to the mundane reality of Germany's Wilhelmine Empire. The idiom of the novel, with its precise social settings, its differentiated psychology and erotic relations, especially adultery, is ironically relativised by the eruption of a grotesquely incongruous passion. The stylistic point is not that these are erotic adventures of the sort that take place in any decent novel from *Tom Jones* to *Le Rouge et le Noir*, but that the passion conceived in the breast of the protagonist is ridiculous. Where Tristan's and Isolde's *Liebestod* (love-death) occurs on the symbolic threshold of land and sea, little Herr Friedemann declares his heartfelt but absurd love for Frau von Rinnlingen only to be predictably laughed at, and then, in a clear parody of the Dionysiac moment ('did it become an access of self-disgust, a craving to annihilate himself, to tear himself to pieces, to blot himself out...?', VIII, 105), drowns himself in a river at the edge of an ornamental garden, not deep enough to cover his own backside.

In the moral vacuum that opens up between the obviously redundant morality of the real world and the yet-to-be-imagined morality that would accord with our deepest subjective desires, narrative details become self-conscious and function as compositional markers. This patterning force of narrative detail remains constant throughout Mann's career.

In terms of pleasure, these early stories present a problem. The kind of pleasure literature can provide within the real world ('[little Herr Friedemann] was well versed in all the latest publications both in Germany and abroad, he knew how to savour the exquisite rhythms of a poem, he could appreciate the atmosphere of a finely written short story', VIII, 81) is shown to be obviously incommensurate with the only kind of pleasure that demands to be taken seriously, namely erotic desire. Herr Friedemann's precarious epicureanism, or the Joker's pleasure in anticipating the next edition of an entertaining periodical (VIII, 122), are simply elements of the cultural material they use to make their nests, which are then effortlessly swept away by the sexual storm. Sexual passion, on the other hand, does not promise satisfaction or even tragedy, but abject ridicule and the impossibility of self-respect.

The stand-off between these two kinds of pleasure needs to be subsumed in a third kind, namely the kind the implied reader is expected to gain from the formal achievement of the 'finely written short story'. One can accept Mann's claim that in finding this style, he felt he had found a social possibility for himself as an individual. However, Herr Friedemann's obvious unsuitability as a role model for a self-respecting reader implies that there is a gap where our pleasure as readers should be. To put this the other way round, Mann's early texts imply the need for a new kind of pleasure, and thus the need for a new kind of individual.

In a sense, Mann finds a voice by aligning himself with the *fin-de-siècle* fashion of aesthetic decadence, but the implications are deeper than mere fashion. The empty place where the reader's pleasure ought to be reflects the historical pressures bearing upon the modern individual. On one side, modern consciousness is denied an identity formed in relation to the pleasures and duties of a given social reality, by the modernising processes of rationalisation and untempered capitalist profit-seeking which galvanise social change. On the other side, it is tantalised by the redemptive promise of personal gratification, where once religious faith had provided the backdrop to aspirations beyond daily satisfactions and sacrifices. Thomas Mann's specific approach to decadence is, he says, at once to embrace it and to seek to overcome it (XII, 201), to adopt its world-weary detachment and counterbalance it with a will to form. More than is explicitly the case with Nietzsche, Thomas Mann relies upon the secularised 'Protestant ethic' to come to terms with the anomaly of unregulated pleasure.[7]

In his next two major works Mann went on to explore the contested boundary between private and public life in both the public and private directions. He found means of transcending what was on the face of it, artistically, a deeply unpromising historical moment, by contriving to address a readership at once familiar with and sceptical of existing forms of address. This was essentially an *ironic* solution. In finding it, Mann's natural talent as a creative novelist emerged.

*Buddenbrooks* clearly marks an advance over the sarcastic narration of sacred moments by finding more satisfactory form for the serious illusion of literature. In his first and best-known novel Mann succeeded in making an entire social-realist panorama transparent upon its own nullity. This is perhaps the most brilliant balancing act of his whole career. As a result of it we believe in the story and the characters as morally and artistically real, and Mann comes closest to the Nietzschean creative ideal of showing the vitality of a lived 'ethical doctrine'. Yet our very sympathy with the characters and their lived world leads us to see across into the world of myth, indeed beyond that, into the world of musical form where pleasure is imagined as unmediated by representation or individuation.

How is this astonishing feat achieved? Mann displays bewildering skill in entwining a naturalist narrative with aspects of abstract composition. One strand can be isolated as a demonstration. Mann establishes a pattern out of the successive eldest male members of the Buddenbrook family. He thematises representation by offering the reader four carefully contrasting death scenes for each of the four primary male Buddenbrooks: Johann, Jean, Thomas and Hanno. Each one dies younger than the last, each one dies in a more unaccommodated manner: Johann in bed in the bosom of the family at the end of a long and fulfilled life; Jean indoors, but at the desk of the family holiday house and in the afternoon, with a romantic storm raging outside; Thomas in the street in grim naturalist style; and finally, Hanno, not even in the text itself. Hanno's death escapes the idiom of the novel entirely. The poles of art and intellect both miss it. An impersonal scientific account of death by typhoid fever is necessary to avoid the account of the death itself, which, as a realistic event, could hardly have been free of the aesthetic 'mildew' of melodrama, the warm Dickensian gratification of kitsch.[8] There is no longer any place in realism for Hanno's death, nor therefore for Hanno, nor for the family or for the world it inhabited. By the time we reach the end of the novel, the world that seemed to make it possible simply no longer exists. This vanishing act points to another world, which it cannot, by definition, show.

*Tonio Kröger* is also a qualitative advance from the device of sarcastic form used as a mask to transform self-revelation into social identity. It does not travesty the personal experience of the author, as the early stories had done, but rather points to it as existing in that other world which can never be directly represented, but which is nevertheless the scene of a very real longing. The transition from the private to the public is at once recognised as impossible, and achieved by an ironic but serious representation of this impossibility. The story is about a character whose feelings are impracticably intense, but who grows up to be a Nietzschean critical moralist. The polarisation takes place *within* his character, and he moreover becomes conscious of this and wills to overcome it. This is expressed as a problem of the artist: 'There's no problem on earth so tantalising as the problem of what an artist is and what art does to human beings' (VIII, 299).[9] The absurdity of this assertion (barely ten years before the First World War!) vanishes if one accepts that Mann's art does in fact track and register disturbances in the history of consciousness. What Tonio Kröger is talking about is not 'the artist', but the historically specific predicament of modern consciousness. It is the European mind, excited but bewildered by the power of desire liberated from traditional restraints and coping anxiously with the countering force exerted by the secular and psychological legacy of religious asceticism.[10]

The defining difference between Mann and Nietzsche is that what in Nietzsche is a form of self-overcoming which makes it possible to dispense with the craven accommodations of what passes for morality in the given world, becomes in Mann a morality of self-discipline and service defined by his own background, and reinforced by the self-discipline required at that time of homosexuals to deny and sublimate their desires. This self-overcoming thus means the formation of character in a much less absolute way than Nietzsche finally intended, a way that is tied into existing social and psychological determinations, yet, through literature, negotiates them creatively. Where, for Nietzsche, art is 'the paradigm of human activity', for Mann it is 'the paradigm of *responsible* human activity'.[11]

At the time of *Tonio Kröger* one could define Mann's sense of the social meaning of artistic composition as the model for a system of patterns and repetitions that stitch our inchoate inner lives together with the agreed social world of conventional meanings. The culmination of this phase of his writing, *Death in Venice*, both perfects this kind of exquisite form and suggests that the social compromise implied is not going to work. The novella displays with unparalleled clarity that liminal quality that Mann derives from the metaphysics of Schopenhauer, Wagner and Nietzsche. Two opposing value-systems are left suspended in mutually exclusive equipoise. When Gustav von Aschenbach dies he is a pitiable figure, even though he dies at a more dignified water's edge than his unfortunate predecessor, little Herr Friedemann. However, the point of view from which he is pitiable is the very point of view that he has abandoned by falling in love. It is exposed as merely a point of view, an apparatus for seeing. This is perhaps the significance of the arresting image of the abandoned camera that stands on the beach as the great writer dies (VIII, 523).[12] Moral clarity, which in Aschenbach's past had been compatible with the artistic cultivation of beautiful form, is now swept away by passion which, as the story conveys clearly enough, is aroused by the contemplation of physical beauty. Form itself is thematised as fundamentally ambiguous: 'And is form not two-faced? Is it not at one and the same time moral and immoral?' (VIII, 455). Mann is offering prose fiction, a story (significantly, a story in the highly patterned genre of the German novella rather than the hybrid sprawl of the novel) as a means of reconciling this difference between the moral and the immoral. But in formulating so perfectly this genuinely profound rhetorical question, Mann has actually exhausted its rhetorical possibilities. Such an exquisite address cannot on its own call forth the new reader the need for whom it identifies, capable of existing between a tired old world and an unimagined new one. Only a change in objective circumstances could do this. Such a change was, indeed, not far away in 1912.

With *The Magic Mountain* and *Joseph and his Brothers*, Mann entered the twentieth century. These two vast encyclopaedic novels are literary experiments in a world where the search for new forms is not a question of an artist's choice but a political and historical necessity. Mann the successful and widely read novelist, who as a result of a combination of private and social circumstances had become the master of providing literary pleasure on the threshold between the public and private spaces, could hardly have been better suited to respond to this challenge. To his lasting credit, despite his innate conservatism, and despite his deep love for Nietzsche, who would have turned in his grave at the word democracy, Mann affirmed the democratic aspiration of the Weimar Republic and set his two faces of form against the many cultural forces that opposed it.

The implied reader of the exquisitely formed and metaphysically ironical *Death in Venice* is the somewhat utopian one of a Schopenhauerian with a patrician disdain for the quotidian but a real moral consciousness. The reader of these two great modern novels, on the other hand, is closer to the ordinary educated middle-class person who has traditionally been the reader of novels and has found the moral issues of his class and day reflected in them. Yet in the absence of the shared social and moral world of the earlier members of the Buddenbrooks family, without an implied mimetic contract (where author, character and readers all know and belong to recognisably the same world), these novels have to construct the form that will give pleasure inventively, from the cultural materials to hand. And the social meaning of this inventiveness is that the individual reader is also involved in the need for self-invention. Story-telling, immorality and moral consciousness are combined afresh to serve the purpose of educating democratically responsible individuals.

Therefore, with *The Magic Mountain* Mann turns, although he claims it was unconscious,[13] to that element in the specifically German novel tradition that programmatically aligns literary form with significant human form. The

*Bildungsroman* is based upon the premise that individuals are capable of being morally formed, of unfolding from within according to regularities proper to them, which will only fail to develop if the circumstances are adverse. Mann places this Enlightenment optimism wittily in the context of a Germany, and indeed a Europe, which needs to redefine itself in the aftermath of the First World War.

The *Bildungsroman* depends upon the reader identifying with, yet remaining morally critical of, the main character around whose development it is organised. It is like a healthy attitude to oneself. Mann adopts this structure of identification, and this is the most important change in his literary strategies after the First World War. It is a vital expression of solidarity between author and reader. The problem of the artist has at last explicitly become a question concerning how human inwardness generally (and this includes the basically narcissistic human disposition for pleasure) relates and should relate to the responsibility of belonging to a collective. The problem with the optimistic German *Bildungsroman* has traditionally been that no objective society existed capable of accommodating the rounded human personality the genre celebrated. In the circumstances in which Mann found himself returning to the genre this uncertainty was welcome. It made it possible to adumbrate a model of healthy personality as a hope rather than a certainty; as something for which each individual must himself in some measure take responsibility.

Hans Castorp's relationship with pleasure and responsibility is thus placed at the centre of the novel's development. Again a pattern, again four defining moments at which representation itself is thematised. Mann's basic ploy of transposing the protagonist from normal life into a TB sanatorium has the effect of removing him, and the reader, from a sense of familiarity and belonging. The loss of the familiar shared social background upon which the traditional novel was based is made explicit. The world Castorp leaves behind, which is described in retrospect in the second chapter, is recognisably the world of the Buddenbrooks. Instead, we are put into a less regulated relation with the Schopenhauerian material flux through the omnipresence in these surroundings of disease, desire and death.[14] The individual, as it were, has his outside stripped away and has to start from scratch with the creation of a new one.

The pattern Mann constructs begins with a charming vignette about the socialisation of desire within the old order. The Wilhelmine schoolboy Hans has an infatuation with a model pupil called Pribislav Hippe. Although Mann describes the sensations of infatuation with his habitual precision, Castorp's feeling is nameless until he finds a way to give it outward expression by way of a suitable performance. He finds his opportunity when the need arises to borrow a pencil for an art class. The loan of the pencil from a model pupil permits Hans to take part in his drawing class, an unexceptionable action, while secretly rejoicing inside that his feeling now has an outside to it, that it informs a public action. The responsibility that accompanies this pleasure is likewise perfectly discharged: the pencil is returned. There is no residue, no excess of unnameable, illegitimate, Dionysiac feeling. It has vanished into a social act. There can be no doubt that Mann knew the experience of sublimation very well indeed from the inside.[15]

The loan of the pencil is then consciously restaged by Hans Castorp to allow Mann with deft humour to sketch out a real sexual encounter. Now Hans Castorp's desire does not vanish into conventional forms: he dares to act on it with Clawdia Chauchat, that brilliant pastiche of a *femme fatale*. She has the same eyes as Hippe – it is, after all, the same desire, only the object is different – but is far from being a model pupil. It is carnival time, and everything is out of joint, albeit with institutional approval (III, 461). The pencil is borrowed for the disreputable purpose of drawing the tail on a pig when blindfolded, but it is never used, and its return is the excuse Clawdia gives to Hans to visit her room later that night.

This is an important advance on the sad accommodation of the earlier infatuation. In that case the exercise of responsibility consisted in the procrustean sacrifice of one's inchoate feelings to the existing order. Here Mann conveys, with the artistic skill that consists in telling the obvious and familiar with the force of a new insight, that the first responsibility of an autonomous subject lies in recognising that the other is in fact an autonomous subject too. The negotiation between Hans and Clawdia takes place between two independent and desiring people without relying on convention.

The third time the pencil is returned is during the novel's climactic scene, when Hans Castorp really does step outside what Rilke would call 'the interpreted world' to go for his famous walk in the 'Snow' chapter. While the situation in which Hans seduced Clawdia, or possibly the other way around, was out of joint, the disorientation of the storm far exceeds the staged disorder of carnival night. Now Mann makes his inevitable thematic connection between sexual desire and the infinite, formless universe with which we are familiar from Schopenhauer. It is now the effects of the elemental mountain landscape which remind Hans of the eyes of his beloveds. They had always been associated with the allure of distant mountains and now the protagonist and the reader are somehow *there*. The difference between Apolline and Dionysian pleasure is that the former is in looking and the latter is in *being*. Before, with Hippe, Hans was entirely passive, and with Clawdia it was hard to tell who was the passive and who the active partner. Now it is Hans who is active: this time it is he who lends the pencil, and enjoins the implied borrower to take care to return it, just as Hippe and Clawdia had done to him (III, 661). It is in this chapter, of course, that the commitment to the love of humanity, albeit in full knowledge of the dark underpinning of all life, is expressed in the form of Hans's hallucination, in which civilised people walk in serenity and light while nearby old hags dismember a baby. It leads to the formulation of a new humanist commandment: '*For the sake of goodness and love, man shall let death have no sovereignty over his thoughts*' (III, 686).

In this progression of moments linked by repetition of details, Hans Castorp's situation as a subject in relation to the meaning of his own desire is changed step by step. *Form* at this point in Mann's career is defined as love, as that which mediates between what Mann called two kinds of death: death as excessive form, as in an ossified social order, and death as formlessness, or self-abandonment (XI, 371). With the help of the structure of identification of the *Bildungsroman*, the familiar liminal moment has now been imbued with an explicit moral significance. Storytelling, immorality and moral consciousness have been brilliantly and creatively recombined.

When Clawdia Chauchat returns to the Magic Mountain with Mynheer Peeperkorn, the self-evidently phallic pencil is no longer required to slyly suggest a link between desire and representation, since Peeperkorn is himself a walking phallus, 'God's own wedding-organ' (III, 867).[16] In relation to Peeperkorn, and in co-operation now with the former object of his own sexual love, Hans Castorp forms an alliance to support the ailing patriarch. This is now the practical ethical application of the only superficially forgotten insight gained in the snowstorm. Hans's *Bildung* is complete.

Hans Castorp and the reader have gone from a morally threadbare society, through the Dionysian temptations of complete self-abandon, to the formulation of a new morality. Now it is up to them to bring into being the strong yet flexible model of a personality able to succeed to the authoritarian structure of responsibility abdicated by Peeperkorn.[17] By committing suicide Peeperkorn symbolises the self-destruction of European patriarchal authority in the First World War. But before Hans Castorp can succeed to anything he must survive the Dionysian carnage of the battlefield, and there is of course only a modest likelihood that he will.

The point to emphasise here is that this great work, for all its democratic commitment, is still essentially a performance on the threshold between worlds, the essence of which is captured by the Nietzschean interpretation of Act III of *Tristan and Isolde*. Hans Castorp's snow dream amounts to an affirmation of the beloved illusion as a survival strategy: one just has to try to believe that this beloved illusion and the reality of democratic politics can be compatible. The four moments of the pattern expounded above are essentially time-bound for at least two reasons: they point to stages in Hans's *Bildung*, and they address a historical need for democratic responsibility. Yet Mann takes care to brush each one with the colour of timelessness: there is that eye-colour, common to all three of the moments, or all four if we include Clawdia's involvement in the conspiracy to help the failing Peeperkorn. Moreover, as Hans goes round and round in the snow, linear time is suspended. The circle of timelessness is also implied by Peeperkorn's means of killing himself. He uses a contraption to administer snake poison: the phallus bites itself, thus performing the figure of the snake that bites its own tail – the figure of infinity. Thus the novel is still, at some level, an ironic composition on the edge of musical abstraction, the implication of which is the failure of 'meaning' and 'being' to map onto each other.[18] The traditionally problematic match in the *Bildungsroman* between the development of a healthy personality and a society unable to accommodate it was welcome to Mann not just because it supported the modality of hope: it also supported the modality of irony. The morally questionable pleasure in infinite prevarication enriches the encyclopaedic organisation of themes by implying the proximity of the negation of their humanistic message. The carnage of the Great War with which the novel closes thus has a double function: both as the reality that must be overcome, and as the timeless abyss that attends all precarious human accommodations.

The circumstances would never again be so propitious to Mann's peculiar genius. Never again could complete mastery of certain literary techniques combine moral profundity with ludic irony for a real historical constituency so well. By the end of the Weimar Republic, the enemies of the Republic identified *The Magic Mountain*, a novel that had made such a substantial contribution to the creation of democracy, with 'the talking shop' of an enfeebled liberalism.[19] Mann's other great experimental democratic novel, *Joseph and his Brothers*, is already largely the product of an exile, which took the integrated body of his readers and his moral purpose away from him.

Nevertheless, the *Joseph* novels recognisably grow from Mann's earlier literary development. The way that the biblical story is used raises the mysterious thresholds between different types of storytelling to the status of an explicit theme. The inevitable function of illusory appearances in the never-ending transactions between 'intellect' and 'art', the latter now rechristened 'soul', is placed at the heart of the composition. Jacob's wedding night, for instance, recounted in *The Tales of Jacob*, encapsulates the cruel necessity of illusion in the progress of human affairs. The coat of many colours deludes the patriarch-to-be that he is at last possessing his beloved Rachel, a gratification so long deferred, and so imbued with human and spiritual meaning. But Leah has been substituted for Rachel. The horrible, and irreversible, truth of this is only apparent in the morning. Significant human love and brute material possession are indistinguishable in the dark. Yet, so the novel persuades us, the progress of significant human life depends upon this particular combination of deceptive lure and unfolding fulfilment.

The identification of the reader with the protagonist, which marks the decisive shift in literary technique from the *Magic Mountain* onwards, is likewise maintained and taken further. While the narrative voice of that novel had had the monopoly on ironic 'intellect', now Joseph is both the 'blessed' protagonist and the bearer of an intelligence that learns to manipulate the world in his own interests and those of his fellow men. He is a self-lover who learns to love others as himself. The reader's pleasure in identification is conducive to his learning how to mediate between the narcissistic promptings of desire and the requirements of collective consciousness.

The *Joseph* tetralogy is the climax of Mann's ironical style. This style – Mann's signature from beginning to end – is encapsulated in the passage that follows the failure of Potiphar's wife to persuade her husband to remove the temptation of Joseph's beauty from her sight. Her response is veiled, although the reader is of course keen to know what it is:

> Yet much, indeed everything, supports the conjecture that this hidden countenance was radiant with joy, because she would continue to be permitted to be obliged to see the source of her agitation, and not therefore obliged to be permitted to forget him.     (*Joseph in Egypt*, Section 6, 'The First Year').[20]

The motif-based and patterned texture of Mann's writing is exemplified in the return of the modal verbs 'müssen' (be obliged) and 'dürfen' (be permitted) from Joseph's consolation of the dying Mont-Kaw (v, 998). The use of these verb-motifs is intensified to the point of over-fastidiousness in the double succession of three infinitives – grammatically correct to the point of ironising grammatical correctness itself. But not only does this virtuosity give delight to the reader, it is doing what Mann's virtuosity always does, namely playing a game of hide and seek with the reader's desire to see behind the veil: first 'much', then 'everything', yet just an 'assumption': it is a series of teases. And what does lie behind the veil is as obvious as it is unrepresentable: the euphoria of sexual longing, what Hans Castorp has filed under the heading of 'the advantages of shame'. And how perfectly does this desire – so manifestly beyond good and evil – contaminate and confuse those modal verbs of permission and obligation.

The essence of the trick is that the reader is permitted to *enjoy* being told of the illusoriness of all pleasure. The biblical plot allows this permitted pleasure to be amplified by the identification it offers with the character who defines his moral identity by resisting the very temptation so teasingly conveyed here. The democratic message is aligned with the fundamentally illusory nature of all representations and the amoral pervasiveness of all desire by a virtuoso display of storytelling, indeed, of the sustained manipulation of different types of storytelling.

Writing in a social vacuum, however, Mann tends to confuse literary technique with world-view. The brilliant literary device of building a whole mighty narrative project on the interconnections between the apparently incompatible narrative principles of causality and mythology is offered as a kind of humanist religion, according to which God needs to be invented, composed by men if he is to be God. The literary device of patterns and repetitions that characterises all Mann's writings becomes instead the living-out of this relationship as generation repeats and anticipates generation. Mann's inexhaustible Nietzschean irony, the pleasure of not knowing for sure, is promoted to a form of wisdom about this inscrutable interrelationship, the alternation of the 'sphere' of human meanings between moral dignity from above and Dionysiac subversion from beneath. The bitter post-Nietzschean antagonists 'art' (or 'soul') and 'intellect' are reconciled as characters in the significantly named 'Roman der Seele' (novel or romance of the soul) (IV, 42).[21] It seems that Mann might with some justice (despite extenuating circumstances) be accused of relapsing into the Romantic pseudo-religious exaggeration of the metaphysical and spiritual potential of the novel (the *Roman*) whence the term 'romantic' derives. There is an arbitrariness, albeit a hugely pleasurable one for those who have the time, about what is intended as authoritative wisdom.

In aesthetic terms, the mediation between 'high' and 'low' of the *Joseph* novels can be seen as an attempt on a Wagnerian scale to reconcile high art with popular culture.[22] This is reinforced by the protagonist's 'fall' into the secular world, a fall which nonetheless preserves the values of the spiritual one. In socio-economic terms, the novels' central strategy, which is to offer a more abstract reconciliation between collective responsibility and narcissism than *The Magic Mountain*, moves the entire project of Mann's work squarely into that contested space where democracy coexists with commodity capitalism. Before looking at the relation between the quintessential Mann and the capitalist commodity, a detour via another work is required.

Mann's own awareness of this relation can be examined clearly from the perspective of *The Confessions of Felix Krull, Confidence Man*. It was started in 1910, then set aside, and only taken up again and published in an extended form nearly forty years later, after Mann had completed his swansong, *Doctor Faustus*. The significance of this text for our argument can be divided into two parts: the socio-economic and the psychological.

The conflation of the artist and the trickster has a precedent in Nietzsche (*GS* §361), yet after the success of *Buddenbrooks*, Mann must also have taken a less theoretical interest in the public life of skilfully fabricated illusions. This is reflected in his finding inspiration for a new novel in the memoirs of the Romanian confidence trickster and society thief Georges Manolescu.[23] There are several aspects of this phenomenon which merit our attention. Not only had Manolescu got away with a series of glamorous scams, but he had repeated his success by writing about them, and in writing about them, embellishing and adding to them. The continuity between the illusions of the criminal with style and those of the extravagant inventor of fictions was palpable. Furthermore, Mann was interested by the fact that Manolescu's successes were based upon the increased mobility of society in the most concrete sense: his thefts often depended upon the carelessness, while staying in hotels, of those used to servants at home. Moreover, Manolescu establishes a link between his own determination to succeed by audacious trickery and the modern climate in politics, trade and industry, in which nothing is sacred any more. A series of connections is therefore set up between the practice of illusion, the climate of modern Europe, and the ability of the trickster, artist, confidence man or whoever is bold enough, to *sell* deception to a public avid to be deceived and pay for it. Manolescu certainly had Nietzschean traits – he insisted on absolute self-control in the creation of his personae – and Hans Wysling is also surely right to point out how easily the Manolescu problematic could be recoded into the metaphysical Schopenhauer-Nietzsche problematic. But the point can be made both ways: the other side of that grand illusion is the universal human desire to be deceived which breathes life into commodities and animates consumer capitalism.[24] Manolescu and Krull suggest that these two things are worryingly close.

The psychological issue is this. It will be clear that Mann's literary aesthetic is deeply determined by an ethic of discipline, a relative of Nietzsche's 'self-overcoming', but reflecting also Mann's Protestant work ethic, his inherited cultural elitism, and his repressed homosexual aesthetic (beauty is that which is sexually pleasing but forbidden). The achievement of formal composition is valuable to the extent that it reflects the terrifying yet real forces that threaten it and in the face of which it has been achieved. This applies as much, I think, to the democratic works as to the Wilhelmine ones; it is just that a transition is made from the artist to all human subjects, and from artistic form to the moral forms of collective life. Now, with *Felix Krull*, as Anthony Heilbut has persuasively argued, the identification is different.[25] In this case the writer gives up the disciplined control of his own identity implied in the commitment to form, throwing in his lot instead with the forces that threaten it. Felix Krull is an impersonator. His main trick is to assume the personality of the Marquis de Venosta. There is thus here a tentative imaginative acknowledgement of the fact that to surrender control of one's identity to the forces that threaten it need not result in Dionysiac dismemberment but can instead lead to the realisation – both disturbing and liberating – that identity is plural and fluid.

If we now put together the socio-economic and the psychological aspects we reach the capitalist-democratic constitution of the subject as defined by contemporary social theory. Where Herr Friedemann's and the Joker's precarious identities, fenced around by feeble social pleasures, were swept away by an incommensurably stronger pleasure, now we have the 'revisable narrative of self-identity', the condition of the modern subject whose burden, but also whose pleasure, consists in the composition of a self.[26] The *Joseph* tetralogy is completely at home in this culture of self-creation: '[In *Joseph and his Brothers*] Mann wishes us to see how much larger our individualities become when grounded in scores of mythical narratives and patterns, and how the corresponding multiple social roles and alliances of mass society can free us from stifling uniformities.'[27]

What this formulation does not stress is the extent to which this view of the constitution of the modern subject, and with it a view of the point of modern fiction, is bound up with commodification. The *Joseph* novels address the reader as if he were a consumer. Like the traditional novel, they contrive to reassure him that flawed individualism and moral responsibility are compatible. Unlike the traditional novel, however, they do not write of and for a shared moral community, since community is in flux. Instead, the tetralogy is a composition based on a shrewd but, in an important sense, arbitrary selection of materials. The very choice of the Joseph story – the same choice that thirty years on initiated the career of Tim Rice and Andrew Lloyd Webber – speaks to every individual's longing for recognition and distinction.

The influences of Freud and Jung on the tetralogy, extensively documented by scholarship, are also significant in this regard.[28] In composing a novel in which individual psychology and archetypal patterns intertwine, Mann naturally turned to psychoanalysis. This certainly reflects his desire to incorporate the irrational aspects of life in a humanistic world view, in opposition to the Nazis' attempt to co-opt them. Yet it also once again moves his production towards the status of a commodity: both modern fiction and psychoanalysis are complex purchasable apparatuses and models for the formation of one's own self. Whereas previous centuries had taken commodification only as far as sex, the twentieth extended it to friendship, love, and, turned inwards, the very construction of personality itself.

If the *Joseph* novels represent Mann's unintended arrival in the realm of the commodity after the great thematic and stylistic journey that had gone before, *Felix Krull* most clearly reveals the hesitant awareness throughout his creative career of the modern cultural-commercial world. Elsewhere, he held the temptations of immediate gratification at arm's length, thematising them as the forbidden banality of 'life'. In his own work, as we have seen, he fabricated a public identity for himself. Historical circumstances then unveiled that kaleidoscopic multiplication of his lonely effort which modern Western society in its non-totalitarian version requires of and permits each individual subject. Mann's arduously achieved formal compositions are available – much more readily than the productions of high modernism – for use in the self-creation of the modern consumer-subject. They offer narcissistic pleasure – the reader sees himself and his moral, philosophical and political concerns in them – and as best-selling quality fiction they bind readers into an implied moral community, quite regardless of the truth-value of their 'ideas'. Joseph and Felix Krull, both tricksters, both men who console the world with the deceptions it cannot do without, converge in the public identity of Thomas Mann the traditional novelist in the twentieth century, a world-class dissembler, who *plays consciously* with the most serious ideas.[29] From the start Mann's work had a trajectory towards the commodity and the consolations it offers for survival in a world that defies comprehension and does not promise redemption.

Consolation, noted Franz Kafka in his diary for January 1920, is no help precisely because it is only consolation.[30] Thomas Mann never accepted this stark assessment of the nature of consolation, not even during the Second World War, when he permitted *his* Doctor Faustus the glimmer of a hope of redemption. In this he remained to the end a disciple of Wagner – whom he called 'the great consoler' (XIII, 353) – against the advice of Adorno, who helped Mann with the musical themes of his great allegorical treatment of the fate of Germany under the Nazis.[31] This was the same Adorno whose abhorrence of popular culture and whose affirmation of the most difficult and user-unfriendly examples of modernism amount to an aesthetic of anti-consolation. Yet extreme modernists like Kafka and Adorno only deny consolation in the hope that this denial will bring redemption, which is the ultimate consolation and the only one worth having. Mann was indefatigable in his efforts to keep open the link between pleasure and redemption, to preserve the higher consolation of serious art amid the kaleidoscopic confusion of the modern capitalist world. For this he should be applauded, even if it means that his writing may well fade in the cultural memory of the twenty-first century, rather as the pleasure of having servants faded in the twentieth.

## NOTES

1 The term *Bildungsroman* has been translated in various ways, e.g. as apprentice-ship novel, novel of formation, novel of education or novel of self-cultivation.

2 See Diana Behler, 'Thomas Mann as Theoretician of the Novel: Romanticism and Realism', *Colloquia Germanica* 7 (1974), 52–88.

3 See Raymond Furness, *Wagner and Literature* (Manchester: Manchester University Press, 1982), p. 15.

4 For Wagner's views and Mann's objections to them, see *Quellenkritische Studien zum Werk Thomas Manns*, ed. Paul Scherrer and Hans Wysling (Berne and Munich: Francke, 1967), pp. 134–5.

5 Michael Tanner, *Nietzsche* (Oxford: Oxford University Press, 1994), p. 74.

6 Deleuze, *Nietzsche and Philosophy*, trans. Hugh Tomlinson (London: Athlone, 1983), pp. 102–3.

7 For analyses of the relation between Mann and the social theorist Max Weber, and especially Mann's address to a new type of reader, see Russell Berman, *The Rise of the Modern German Novel: Crisis and Charisma* (Cambridge, MA: Harvard University Press, 1986), pp. 261–86, and Harvey Goldman, *Max Weber and Thomas Mann: Calling and the Shaping of the Self* (Berkeley and London: University of California Press, 1988).

8 The term 'mildew' is borrowed from *Doctor Faustus*, where it denotes the debil-itating effects on art of the historical freedom of the individual.

9 David Luke's word 'tantalizing' is the right translation, but lacks some of the strength implied by the original (*Thomas Mann. Selected Stories*, trans. and with an introduction by David Luke (Harmondsworth: Penguin Books, 1993), p. 161). Tonio uses the word 'quälend' (literally 'tormenting'), so that the reader has more of a sense of what actually happened to Tantalus in the myth than is conveyed by the familiar word 'tantalising', which often means little more than mildly irritating. In our context, the sense that a satisfaction unbearably yearned for is denied is important. In the next sentence Tonio Kröger refers to *Tristan and Isolde*.

10 That this is what preoccupied Mann in the pre-war years is suggested, for in-stance, in the dream of a literature which will combine 'Askese und Schönheit', 'asceticism and beauty', where beauty bears the lure of Wagnerian seduction (*Quellenkritische Studien*, ed. Scherrer and Wysling, p. 149).

11 Tanner, *Nietzsche*, p. 74; T. J. Reed, *Thomas Mann: The Uses of Tradition* (Oxford: Clarendon Press, 1974), pp. 365–6, emphasis added.

12 'Abandoned' is the word used in Luke's translation; the original reads 'scheinbar herrenlos', connoting the absence of a master (*Herr*). Again, the translation is right, but inevitably loses nuance.

13 See 'Nachbemerkungen des Herausgebers', in Thomas Mann, *Der Zauberberg*, ed. Peter de Mendelssohn (Frankfurt am Main: Fischer, 1981), pp. 1053–4.

14 Mann took this triumvirate from Novalis (see XI, 849). It is just one of thousands of cultural appropriations that he wove into his text 'like an oriental carpet-maker' (de Mendelssohn, 'Nachbemerkungen', p. 1056).

15 On homosexuality in *The Magic Mountain*, see Karl Werner Böhm, 'Die homo-sexuellen Elemente in Thomas Manns *Der Zauberberg*', *Literatur für Leser* 3 (1984), 171–90; Gerhard Härle, *Die Gestalt des Schönen. Untersuchungen*

*zur Homosexualitätsthematik in Thomas Manns Roman 'Der Zauberberg'* (Königstein im Taunus: Athenäum, 1986).

16 On the pencil, see Härle, *Die Gestalt des Schönen*, p. 119, and for an elaboration of this construction, Jochen Hörisch, *Gott, Geld und Glück. Zur Logik der Liebe in den Bildungsromanen Goethes, Kellers und Thomas Manns* (Frankfurt am Main: Suhrkamp, 1983), pp. 206–39.

17 See Michael Minden, 'The Magic Mountain ("des Weiteren")', *Publications of the English Goethe Society* 64–5 (1993–5), 38–52.

18 These useful terms are taken from Charlotte Nolte, *Being and Meaning in Thomas Mann's Joseph Novels* (London: MHRA and The Institute of Germanic Studies, 1996). For a helpful account of Schopenhauer's continuing subterranean significance for Mann, see Nolte, pp. 13–15. The major Schopenhauerian reading of *The Magic Mountain* is Børge Kristiansen, *Thomas Manns 'Zauberberg' und Schopenhauers Metaphysik*, 2nd edn (Bonn: Bouvier, 1986).

19 See H. Stuart Hughes, *Consciousness and Society: The Reorientation of European Social Thought 1890–1930* (Brighton: Harvester Press, 1979), pp. 404–12.

20 'Aber viel, ja alles hat die Vermutung für sich, daß dieses Antlitz in der Verborgenheit strahlte, weil sie den Erwecker auch weiterhin würde dürfen sehen müssen und ihn nicht gerade würde müssen vergessen dürfen' (V, 1090).

21 On the link between the shape of a novel and that of a life, see Michael Minden, *The German Bildungsroman: Incest and Inheritance* (Cambridge: Cambridge University Press, 1997), p. 12.

22 Mann was attracted by Wagner's ability to produce great art at the same time as giving pleasure to a large number of real people: see *Quellenkritische Studien*, ed. Scherrer and Wysling, pp. 131–4.

23 On Mann and Manolescu, see Hans Wysling, *Narzißmus und illusionäre Existenzform. Zu den 'Bekenntnissen des Hochstaplers Felix Krull'* (Berne and Munich: Francke, 1982), pp. 153–70, from which most of the information used in this paragraph is derived. A man who denounced Manolescu for the theft of some pearls on a train journey to California bore the name Krull. See J. J. Lynx, *The Prince of Thieves: A Biography of Manolesco alias H. E. Prince Lahovary alias the Duke of Otranto* (London: Cassell, 1963), p. 86.

24 Wysling, *Narzißmus*, p. 165. Mark Seltzer notes that the widespread criticism of the culture of consumption as a culture of illusion may have less to do with a critique of illusion, which after all goes back to Plato, than with opposition to the democratisation of illusion as a social privilege: Seltzer, *Bodies and Machines* (New York and London: Routledge, 1992), p. 141.

25 Heilbut, *Thomas Mann: Eros and Literature* (London: Macmillan, 1996), pp. 245, 262.

26 See Anthony Giddens, *Modernity and Self-Identity: Self and Society in the Late Modern Age* (Cambridge and Oxford: Polity, 1991). The idea goes back to Georg Simmel's seminal essay 'Cities and Mental Life' (1910).

27 William E. McDonald, *Thomas Mann's 'Joseph and his Brothers': Writing, Performance, and the Politics of Loyalty* (Rochester, NY: Camden House, 1999), p. 183.

28 See McDonald, *Thomas Mann's 'Joseph and his Brothers'* (for Freud), and Nolte, *Being and Meaning* (for Jung).

29 Mann's own formulation, in the context of Schopenhauer's language scepticism. The emphasis is Mann's. See *Quellenkritische Studien*, ed. Scherrer and Wysling, p. 188.

30 Kafka, *Tagebücher*, ed. Hans-Gerd Koch, Michael Müller and Malcolm Pasley (Frankfurt am Main: Fischer, 1990), p. 851.

31 On the question of Leverkühn's possible redemption and Adorno's views, see Hans Rudolf Vaget, 'Mann, Joyce, Wagner: The Question of Modernism in *Doctor Faustus*', in Herbert Lehnert and Peter C. Pfeiffer (eds.), *Thomas Mann's 'Doctor Faustus': A Novel at the Margin of Modernism* (Columbia, SC: Camden House, 1991), pp. 167–91.

## FURTHER READING

Bahr, Ehrhard, 'Art Desires Non-Art: the Dialectics of Art in Thomas Mann's *Doctor Faustus* in the Light of Theodor W. Adorno's Aesthetic Theory', in Herbert Lehnert and Peter C. Pfeiffer (eds.), *Thomas Mann's 'Doctor Faustus': A Novel at the Margin of Modernism* (Columbia, SC: Camden House, 1991), pp. 145–66

Baumgart, Reinhard, *Das Ironische und die Ironie in den Werken Thomas Manns* (Munich: Hanser, 1964)

Behler, Diana, 'Thomas Mann as a Theoretician of the Novel: Romanticism and Realism', *Colloquia Germanica* 8 (1974), 52–88

Crick, Joyce, 'Thomas and Heinrich Mann: Some Early Attitudes to their Public', *Modern Language Review* 77 (1982), 646–54

Dedner, Burghard, 'Satire Prohibited: Laughter, Satire, and Irony in Thomas Mann's Oeuvre', in Reinhold Grimm and Jost Hermand (eds.), *Laughter Unlimited: Essays on Humor, Satire and the Comic* (Madison, WI: University of Wisconsin Press, 1991), pp. 27–40

Eichner, Hans, 'Aspects of Parody in the Works of Thomas Mann', in Inta M. Ezergailis (ed.), *Critical Essays on Thomas Mann* (Boston: Hall, 1988), pp. 93–115

Peacock, Ronald, 'Much is Comic in Thomas Mann', in Inta M. Ezergailis (ed.), *Critical Essays on Thomas Mann* (Boston: Hall, 1988), pp. 175–91

# 4

ANDREW J. WEBBER

# Mann's man's world: gender and sexuality

The punning title of this chapter has a particular rationale. It imitates a marked feature of Mann's own writing practice, where patterns of repetition are used to accentuate strategies of imitation. My argument here will be that this repetitive formulation of acts of imitation has a particular significance for the representation of gender and sexuality, and that these categories of identity, in their turn, have a special importance for Mann's project as a whole.

T. J. Reed has commented on how Mann's narrative voice in *Death in Venice* engages in mimicry of Aschenbach's own discourse.[1] He cites a narratorial judgement of the fallen artist, 'der in so vorbildlich reiner Form . . . das Verworfene verworfen hatte' ('who in such exemplarily pure form had . . . rejected the wayward as wayward') (VIII, 521) and points out that it sounds uncomfortably close to the uninflected vigour of Aschenbach's own earlier judgements. Specifically, it is an act of ironic citation, taking up the description of Aschenbach's moral pronouncements, the 'Wucht des Wortes, mit welcher hier das Verworfene verworfen wurde' ('the weight of words, with which the wayward was here rejected as wayward') (VIII, 455). The repetition works on several levels. It is inherent in the original collocation of 'Verworfene' and 'verworfen', which is in turn ironically framed by a grotesque sequence of repetitive sounds. The narrator is, in other words, performing Aschenbach's excessive speech act by larding it with further excess, with a too vocal 'weight of words'. The reiteration later in the text clearly replays this pronounced irony, and it does so all the more tellingly by juxtaposing it with notions of 'exemplarily pure form'. It is, in other words, a form which is designed to be copied, but not in the parodic style which the narrative voice vocalises. The savage irony of this distorted repetition of the exemplar from the master's copy-book is that the model form is designed not least as a lesson in the discourse of manhood. The 'Wucht des Wortes' is a discursive template of virile ethics for young men to adopt and it rebounds brutally on the master-turned-pederast. That is, an excessively masculine discourse marks the punishment of a man who fails to maintain the exemplary purity of his patriarchal function.

This is perhaps the most pronounced example of the economy of simulation which operates throughout the text and accounts for a large part of its irony. The title 'Mann's man's world' thus partakes of a logic of ironic mimicry which informs the narrative disposition of that world, not least in its relation to masculinity. A significant part of Mann's enterprise involves his own approximation to the idea of manhood, the mapping of Mann onto *Mann*. He is a writer who exhibits a special, acute, and ambivalent interest in manhood and rarely puts women and female experience centre stage. Many of his most significant works are driven by all-male configurations of interest, and when women are indeed focalised, there is often a suspicion that they are acting as foils or even as substitutes for men. Mann came into his chance patronymic at a time when the categories of gender and sex were beginning to be contested as never before. His own life's experience can also be understood as turning on a personal contestation of these categories. Mann, the father's name, was one that was therefore bound to become freighted with the issues of masculinity, of patriarchal conventions and their subversion, which were a key part of Mann's personal world and came to perform a no less key role in his fictional world. Mann is a writer who delights in punning play with the names of his protagonists. If he had not already registered of his own accord the persistent irony of fate produced by his own name, then Nazi propagandists, expert in the use of names, gender, and sexuality for crude ideological purposes, did it for him. They dubbed political opponents of the Mann sort 'Thomasmänner', thereby implying a sort of manhood which was not quite in order.

This essay focuses in particular on the sexually troubled character of masculinity and of male–male relationships for Mann. The partly open, partly concealed role of homosexuality in Mann's writing has received considerable attention from recent textual and biographical scholarship, most notably in Anthony Heilbut's recent literary biography, which sees homoerotic passion as the key engine of Mann's life and works from beginning to end.[2] Even critics of a more conservative bent have come to realise that homosexual interests in Mann's work have more than a purely symbolic value. It is certainly the case that for Mann homosexuality tends to be an object of sublimation, rarely rendered in straightforward representational ways, but, if nothing else, its sheer recursive persistence gives it the structure and the substance of real passion.

My argument here is that the direct or oblique representations of homosexuality have a paradigmatic function for Mann's depiction of identity at large and for his whole aesthetic enterprise. Homosexuality attains this function not least through being embedded in, and revealing the workings of, the moral and symbolic order of gender. Masculinity and homosexuality are seen to be constructed here in a dialectical relationship, one of mutual dependence and of often painful contradiction. The complex of gender and sexuality is a key territory for the working out of the sort of binary oppositions which are so fundamental to Mann's intellectual grasp of things (such binaries as spirit and nature, or culture and civilisation). The working out of the binarisms of male and female, heterosexual and homosexual, produces confusions both within and between the respective polarities. As such, this complex takes on a symptomatic character for the binary strategies of Mann's whole enterprise of cultural understanding.

In order to analyse the relationship between gender and sexuality, I will mobilise the categories developed over the last fifteen years by two influential theorists of gender and sexuality, Eve Kosofsky Sedgwick and Judith Butler. By extending feminist debates on gender construction to an understanding of the constitution and representation of homosexuality, Sedgwick and Butler provide a framework for working on the interaction of these concerns in Mann. Sedgwick's pioneering work in *Between Men* and *Epistemology of the Closet* has opened up a new understanding of how constitutive homosexuality, its anxieties and its closeting are for sustaining the whole order of culture in its historic development.[3] She has analysed a catalogue of literary texts and political scenarios to show how the scandal of homosexual desire functions as a foil to what she calls the homosocial, the pervasive networks of male–male desire, licensed by ostentatious homophobia. Like Sedgwick, Butler understands homosexuality as a function of social structures. In her ground-breaking *Gender Trouble* and subsequent works, she has developed a philosophy of gender and sexual identity which powerfully challenges any straightforward notion of these as natural or given, understanding them rather as made up and dressed up through acts of performance.[4] For Butler, our identity as gendered and sexualised subjects, and the trouble which can attach itself to these key types of subject status, rely on degrees of subjection to prescribed roles. The only type of relative autonomy open to the subject is the sort which is allowed by the parodic or other strategies of mock performance.

The theories of Sedgwick and Butler will allow us to see that the troubled status of gender and sexual roles in Mann is not merely a biographical effect, but fundamentally representative in both historical and transhistorical terms. On a historical level, Mann's depiction of homosexuality is part of the more general crisis in the hold of hegemonic heterosexual culture in the late nineteenth and early twentieth centuries which Sedgwick has scrutinised. In this sense, the breakdown in the sexual order of things is a culturally specific phenomenon, an indicator of systemic problems in the culture of realism. In the late nineteenth century the ideology of knowability which sustains realism can extend to giving a name to the hitherto nameless condition of homosexuality.[5] But the extension of knowledge of homosexuality on the level of sexological taxonomy is shadowed by obscurity, taboo and panic in the more general cultural field, where it becomes a ground for projection of broader social phobias. As Sedgwick has shown through detailed readings of the work of Mann's contemporaries, realism has a particularly fraught blind-spot or closet in the representation of homosexuality. Although the move into modernism appears to open such closures up, homophobia retains a powerful control over the representability of the homosexual subject in social and cultural contexts. The representation of homosexuality in modernism is thus only differently closeted, and homosexual desire is still constitutionally subject to the claustrophobic condition of hidden and confined spaces.

On a more general level, the work of Judith Butler can help to show that the specific structures of representation at work in Mann's man's world extend beyond the cultural models of late realism and modernism to allow an understanding of how gender and sexuality are constructed *per se*. Specifically, I would suggest that the dialectic of masculinity and homosexuality in Mann's writing is driven by structures characteristic of Butler's notion of the performative character of gender and sexuality. That is to say that both of these orders work through acts of performance in speech, behaviour and costume, acts which are citational, conforming to cultural scripting. Butler takes the founding constative sentence of identity, 'It's a girl' or 'It's a boy', assigning a sex based on genital difference, and argues that it in fact serves as the first act in the performative discourse of gender. A gender identity is pronounced for the new subject, one which has to be renegotiated and secured by the constant recital of versions of that sentence. And, as the child adopts the role of a sexualised subject, so those gender acts of speech and other social behaviour incorporate the normative sexuality which is identified with the respective gender status. The acts of the one order are implicated in those of the other: the performance of masculinity is always also a performance in relation to the oppositional structure of heterosexuality and homosexuality. In both orders, and between them, the regime of prescription is continually troubled by the mismatching of its subjects.

The representation of gender and sexuality will be shown here to operate through performativity. In as far as they work through patterns of imitation and repetition, it is argued that the orders of gender and sexuality can be understood as paradigmatic for Mann's whole aesthetic project, for his realism as for his modernism. If imitation and repetition are fundamental to any acts of representation, in the case of Thomas Mann they are self-consciously heightened and exposed to an unusual degree. The performance of gender and sexuality according to codes of representability thus comes to function as representative (that is, imitative and repetitive) of the whole business of representation. If we recall the phrase 'das Verworfene verworfen', we can see that it mimics an archetypal case of the performative, pronouncing certain forms of behaviour illicit in a judgemental gesture of casting away. The irony is that this performative condemnation is tautological, a reiteration of what should be constatively obvious. Its superfluity indicates an anxiety at the base of the representative speech act and of the order which authorises its performance.

The problem of representation, as focused on sexual identity, is a concern throughout Mann's writing career. The examples to be considered here will cover that span, though with special consideration of the text which has identified Mann, however ambivalently, as a pioneering modern gay writer, namely *Death in Venice*. Investigation of this theme across Mann's work as a whole will show it to function as a sort of intertextual leitmotif. It has become a commonplace of Mann criticism to see his individual texts as organised through leitmotif structures; and encounters with dissident sexual performances will be seen to undertake this role in some of the texts under review here. At the same time, the logic of emblematic repetition operates between texts and between life and text, or between the textualised life of the diary and the literary text. If individual acts in the performance of gender and sexuality are figured as repetitions or citations of culturally codified models, then their representations in Mann's writing can be understood as a series of citational repetitions of what has gone before in both his life and his work. As leitmotifs, they attain a certain cumulative pattern and meaning, but they also partake of the darker side of Mann's leitmotif structures, where repetition can be an empty masquerade or an uncanny compulsion.

The favoured scene for the leitmotif of illicit desire is the sea. It seems destined to act as backcloth, partly for reasons of biography and social history. Mann and his social like resort to the seaside in a regular, ritual fashion as a space which affords freedom from socialisation and workaday constraints. It provides a certain degree of openness and licence for the body, and makes a spectacle of the body's exposure for anybody willing to view. It is, in other words, a sort of carnival space, its irregular freedoms available only as a regulated counterpoint to social order. It is a space, furthermore, which is marked as liminal, a threshold between the social and the natural. As a scene of regular resort, it is tailor-made for the leitmotif function, marking returns through time in chapters of life and over life as a whole, in texts and over the whole textual corpus. In a personal sense, it is also the place to which Mann resorts in order to write more freely, and as such it links some of the most intense experiences of his life with the act of recording and representation. The extant diaries record examples of an archetypal scene which runs, with variations, throughout Mann's working life: the scene of the beach and the spectacle of naked or half-naked male forms. In its most telling form, its point of view is from a beach-hut, a structure at once open and enclosed, a sort of half-opened closet.

If the seaside performs such a fundamental role of structuring repetition for the meeting of life and work, it does so not least because of its peculiar material character. It juxtaposes the solid with the fluid, the apparently fixed with the recurrent. The sea becomes a particular object of fascination for Mann, above all because it is the most absolute instance of structural repetition. In the context of Mann's first major novel, *Buddenbrooks*, where the sea is a resort for the different generations, this structure is represented in the most radical fashion. The narrative flouts all conventions of mimetic representation by describing encounters with the sea, not through endless protean variety, but by brazenly copying itself. When the sea is first described during Tony's holiday it is in a classic act of realist imitation, as the order of mimesis seems able to incorporate even this liquid body. When Hanno goes down to the sea, however, the narrative resorts with him to acts of repetition; it simulates the work of mimesis, while actually reproducing verbatim the earlier reproductions of its own copy-book. If the sea is described as a shiny and metallic surface ('metallblank', I, 142, 635), then this prepares it for reflection and reproducibility; it is set to become a specular construct, 'mute and mirroring' (I, 635), as a screen for projections of word and image. The sequences mirror and parody the notion of mimetic reproduction as an act of origination, and so question at once the order of realism and the originality of the characters who move within its domain.

The leitmotif of the sea is thus established here as a framework for human scenarios of repetition and simulation. Specifically, it is prepared for recursive acts and encounters of desire which will work through the logic of the simulacrum. *Buddenbrooks* is a text which is profoundly troubled by that logic. It is famously introduced by a set-piece domestic comedy of imitation, as the young Tony is called upon to recite patriarchal articles of faith from the newly revised catechism of 1835. The comedy, cast in a bewilderment of competing languages and discursive levels, works as a crisis of linguistic performance. The text which is designed for parrot-like recital is a performative text, in the sense that speech-act theory would give to that category. That is, the act of speech performs its own meaning; the article of faith inscribes the subject as a believer. But it is only designed to be performed by a certain class of subject: adult, male, and land-owning, and while the young Tony can just about perform the performance, she can never properly qualify as such a subject. Her grandfather seems most amused by the idea of Tony owning land and livestock, but perhaps the more fundamental discrepancy is on the level of gender: a wife can never figure as part of Tony's property. This is what permanently excludes her from anything but a simulation of this performative act. She is destined to parrot speech acts without real agency.

Encoded in this opening performance, therefore, is a significant case of gender trouble.[6] The Buddenbrooks regime depends on an ethic of repetition or ritual imitation of what has gone before, as represented by the performative entries in the family copy-book. From the start it seems that this regime will be subject to disorder and decline, especially on the level of the performance of sexual identity. Christian's parasitic function as mimic is foreshadowed by his similarity to his father at the age of seven, where the appearance of patriarchal masculinity is 'almost ridiculous' (1, 17). When Thomas struggles to retain the appearance of patriarchal authority, he has recourse to the cosmetic methods which, by convention, should be used to heighten femininity. His masquerade exposes as much as it conceals gender trouble. This legacy of disorder is passed on to Hanno, when the masquerading father demands the postures of 'masculinity' (1, 485) from his son in the performance of a poem, and thereby transforms him into what he classifies as a as 'little girl' (1, 486), robbing him of any residue of masculine performance. The disorder will culminate in Hanno's dissident sexual identity, as he is courted by Kai Mölln. It is charted against the repetitive recourse to the sea, which thus becomes metonymically invested with symptoms of that disorder. It is the scene for Tony's illicit passion for a working-class man on the 'naked beach' (1, 131); for Thomas's fatalistic confrontation with the pathological failure of his patriarchal role; and for the completion of Hanno's erotic self-absorption and feminisation.

The vaudevillian talents of the sexually dysfunctional Christian, the elaborate 'theatre' of Thomas's public life, and the investment of Hanno's dissident sexual identity in his musical composition and performance establish a pattern which will recur throughout Mann's writing. These are all intimately related prototypes for the figure of the male artist who will occupy centre stage in so many of Mann's narratives. From the start, they represent a convergence of gender trouble with aesthetic production. When Thomas makes himself up for his social appearances, he engages in what the narrative calls the 'intoxication of self-production' (1, 615). Selfhood is a thing not given, but produced and reproduced through acts of performance. And identity as male and identity as artist seem destined to confuse and contradict one another. The male role in this bourgeois context is constructed according to the conventions of patriarchy, which are compulsorily heterosexual, but which also operate according to Sedgwick's notion of homosocial desire.

This is represented in *Buddenbrooks* through the grotesque male society of the school which parodies a neo-Platonic model of the education of boys by men in the ways of masculinity. For this homosocial order of aggressive male bonding, the bond between Hanno and Kai is deemed, in the characteristic language of homophobia, to be a thing of 'filth and opposition' (I, 720). While the homosocial institution of patriarchy holds them in the grip of its 'loving embrace' (I, 742) between men, the embraces between the two of them are seen as abject and oppositional by the institution. These tentative homoerotic embraces between an aspiring musician and an aspiring writer, both producing works which offend official sensibility, seal the relationship between sexual and artistic dissidence.

The embrace between schoolboy artists is one which, it seems, has to take place on a deathbed, under the sign of Hanno's mortal sickness. Its community of passion and art is a sort of fantasy counterpart to another sort of relationship which will act as a scene of perpetual recurrence for Mann. This is a scene where lover and beloved are profoundly different, and attraction can only work through estrangement. Both types of relationship are based on Mann's personal schoolboy experience, but it is this second scene which will become the more compelling template for configurations of desire in Mann's work. Desire is engaged by similarity (not least same-sex similarity), but always through the ambivalent mediation of difference. The scene is first recreated in Mann's early story *Tonio Kröger*. It is emblematically marked as a scene for repetition by the name given to the object of love. Hans Hansen carries the name of patriarchal self-replication and so of masculine continuity; it is a name which redoubles that of the archetypal Germanic boy. It approximates to Mann's man, a convergence of patronymic with gender identity. The subject of that first love, however, is given a name which famously fails to match itself, the exotic Tonio jarring against the claims of the patronymic. Thus the pattern is set: the subject as non-self-identical, out of kilter, and the object as confirmed in his German, bourgeois, and masculine identity. And if Hans Hansen seems like a fairy-tale Hans, a stylised figure of identity through syllabic repetition, then he is suitably prepared to repeat himself again and again. The recurrence of Hans Hansen in the circular structure of the story is also a sign of a more general, intertextual recurrence, most evidently in the admittedly more complicated person of his namesake Hans Castorp in *The Magic Mountain*.

Tonio Kröger is also set to return, in the ambiguous, irregular shape of the artist, whose self-identity is questioned not least on the level of gender. If the artist specialises in mimicry, the falsity of his performance extends to the reliability of his masculinity, as questioned by the protagonist: 'Is the artist in any sense a man?' (VIII, 296). Tonio's manhood is put in question from the very start by his passion for the man's man Hans Hansen. It is also parodied by his first encounter with artistic performance through the theatrical figure of the dance-master, whose name seems to connote an eccentric form of manhood: 'François Knaak war sein Name, und was für ein Mann war das!' ('François Knaak was his name, and what a man he was!') (VIII, 282). Just as Thomas Buddenbrook can only offer ambiguous tutelage to his son in male role-play, Knaak's strange name and correspondingly questionable manhood make him a dubious master for Tonio Kröger to follow. Thomas Buddenbrook produces himself as a man for the world, and similarly Knaak does not just present but re-presents himself: '"J'ai l'honneur de me vous représenter", sagte er' ('"I have the honour of re-presenting myself to you", he said') (VIII, 282). His identity is totally performative, constructed through repeated self-presentation. Hence his pedagogic transmission of gender roles through dance classes works through mimicry, through the representation of incorrect behaviour so as to elicit disgust. When Tonio symbolically gravitates to the side of the girls, he is thus ridiculed as 'Fräulein Kröger' by a man whose by turns graceful and shrill theatre is a sort of drag, a male representation of stylised femininity, designed to represent and disgust the transgressor. The foppish woman's man Knaak and the virile man's man Hans Hansen represent in their stylised forms, in negative and positive terms, the imperative of masculine behaviour. They also represent, respectively, the spectre and the allure of homoerotic possibilities.

On the model of Hans Hansen, the same-sex object returns for Mann through male images of similarity, of symmetry and repetition. Mann develops the figure of the *Doppelgänger* in this fashion, and in the time-honoured manner of that figure, the duplication of the erotic object at once redoubles the desire and corresponds to a splitting in the desiring subject.[7] As with Tonio Kröger, the passion for replication takes Mann back to the sea as an object at once of eternal specular similitude and of constant breaking, of utmost identity and of radical non-identity. Here the objects of his interest are always marked out by forms of specular similarity, like the Italian boys on a beach in 1934, who interest him through their graceful 'Gleichmäßigkeit' or symmetry (diary, 24 July 1934) and record their own reproducibility when one takes a photograph of the other. Similarly, after a visit to the beach in 1919, he records a recurrence of his first experience of love (for Armin Martens) and does so in a fashion which doubly recognises the repetitive character of this model passion: 'Tonio Kröger, Tonio Kröger. Each time it is the same and the emotion deep' (diary, 24 July 1919). In a reflexive sequence, art imitates life which in its turn imitates art. Tonio Kröger, the non-identical literary subject, is repeated in the writer's life, in his literary texts, and in the text which records his life, each time the same.

If the objects of Mann's homoerotic interest can encompass the Italian and the archetypally German, then it seems that the condition of being a Tonio Kröger is that of being different from both, and both are the same in as far as they are self-identical and self-reproducing. Thus the lure of that which is different, because the same as itself, can also take the form, first in biographical and then in literary terms, of a young Pole. Each time the same, but also different, the desiring subject goes down to the sea (the Baltic now become the Adriatic) and is captivated by a figure which is marked by its graceful symmetry ('Gleichmaß', VIII, 490), the Tadzio of *Death in Venice*.[8]

In *Tonio Kröger* the sea helped to transport the protagonist through its combination of dreams and intoxication. It is on board a ship, and under the influence of the sea, that he encounters the young man from Hamburg who feels encouraged to share with him a moment of poetic intimacy which, like his sea-sickness, fills the amateur poet with shame, and draws from him the masculine compensation of a soldierly greeting. Thus the pattern is set for deviations from the norm in the relations between men, sustained by sea-borne dreaming, intoxication and poetry. 'Dream' was to become for Mann a watchword for the realisation of homosexual desire, as recorded in a diary entry of 20 February 1942 (citing another entry, of 1927, from a diary which was subsequently destroyed) where an embrace with Klaus Heuser on the island of Sylt is described as a 'leap into the dreamlike' ('Sprung ins Traumhafte'). In *Death in Venice*, the leap into the dreamlike is effected, as elsewhere, under the influence of the sea. And the dream experience of the protagonist Aschenbach is represented in terms of the model of dream work developed by Freud in his *Interpretation of Dreams*: an encoded form which dissembles what it represents principally by the twin processes of condensation and displacement.[9] While the patterns of performativity which were noted in the earlier texts are maintained here, they are complicated by the intervention of the sort of strategies of representation which characterise the Freudian unconscious. Freud exposes another level of representability and one particularly attuned to Mann's (by convention) unrepresentable subject: a means of signification which works through strategic distortion in order to accommodate but also outflank the forces of censorship and repression. It represents, in other words, an arrogation of the 'productive drive' ('des produzierenden Triebwerkes', VIII, 444) of the Ciceronian writer, by 'Triebwerk' of another kind, the type of drives that are produced by unconscious desires.

The Freudian strategy is signalled by the sort of discrepancy between classical surface and inner confusion which characterises Freud's analysis of Jensen's *Gradiva*. Aschenbach is represented as a rearguard classicist who resists the 'indecent psychologism of the times' (VIII, 455) after the model of St Sebastian, one of surface elegance which hides to the last the 'inner undermining' (VIII, 453) of decay. While Sebastian is used here as a model of masculine self-control, Mann will not have been unaware of his history as an icon of homoerotic sensibility. The anti-analytic classical posture is, accordingly, itself ironically undermined from the start by a Freudian counter-figure. The lure of travel, which opens up initially into a lurid Freudian jungle of lascivious ferns and hairy palm-trees, is embodied by an anti-classical figure, a figure of 'distortion' ('Entstellung', VIII, 446). Applied thus, in isolation, to the wanderer figure, this term might innocently be read as representing only physical 'disfigurement'. When it is repeated, however, its context projects a Freudian logic back over the opening pages. The wanderer figure initiates a chain of falsified and disfigured agents, the theatrical hunchback who sells Aschenbach his ticket and the grotesquely made-up 'false youth' on the boat. And the spectacle of the second of these prompts an encoded realisation that Aschenbach's adventure, with its strange 'dream logic' (VIII, 521), is more specifically following a Freudian dream logic: 'Ihm war ... als beginne eine träumerische Entfremdung, eine Entstellung der Welt ins Sonderbare' ('He felt as if a dreamlike estrangement were beginning, a distortion of the world into the curious') (VIII, 460). Here, 'Entstellung' demands to be read as what is standardly translated as 'distortion', the fundamental principle of dream-work in Freud's account, a term, however, which resonates for Freud both with the meaning of physical 'disfigurement' and with the etymological root of 'displacement' or 'removal'. Thus it is that this dreamlike estrangement is accompanied by the displacement of the ship onto the familiar element of dreams, the sea, accompanied by Aschenbach's visions of the 'strange shapes' of his disfigured fellow travellers, their ambiguous gestures and 'confused dream-words' (VIII, 461). This then, a scene where the framework of representative reality is shot through with the slippery representations of the unconscious, is ready for a more explicit sort of seaborne encounter between men, one subject less to the social censorship through disavowal of *Tonio Kröger* than to the censorship through distortion of the psyche. 'Das Verworfene', the depraved behaviour which we saw that Aschenbach had rejected ('verworfen'), and which ironically rebounds upon him, might thus seem closer to 'das Verdrängte', Freud's notion of the repressed, which is always set to return in disguised forms. This return of the repressed is figured not least through the sequence of disfigured figures which attend Aschenbach's journey as projections of his own self-repressive desires.

In a way which is familiar from the earlier texts, the 'false youth' on the ship embodies an exposure of the performative, a gender masquerade, but one which is distorted here in the manner of a dream figure. By performing a made-up version of youthful masculinity, the old man only accentuates his dissidence as a male subject. The false performance of gender represents a sexuality which, for the narrative as focalised through Aschenbach, is as abhorrent as it is ambiguous. The playing of a young man in order to seduce young men represents an extension of the drag act performed by Knaak in *Tonio Kröger*. It accords with Butler's contention that the performance of a same-sex role can also be a kind of drag. Indeed Mann acknowledged this himself in his diary entry of 24 January 1934 after seeing the film *Viktoria*, where a girl performs as a female impersonator, and the confusing same-sex 'Geschlechtsverkleidung' ('disguise of sex') strikes him as being at once ridiculous and of significance for a philosophical understanding of the emotions.

A similar significance seems to be at work in the travestied gender performance here. While Aschenbach flees the attentions of the masquerader, he is unable to escape the symbolic logic of the dream. Under the influence of the disfigured, masquerading homosexual, the world tends to take on a grotesquely distorted physiognomy (again the keyword is 'entstellen' (VIII, 462)). Aschenbach's displacement into a Freudian dream world is accompanied by the sort of motions which classically characterise such worlds. As the ship sets off, the voyager has the sensation of swimming with the 'heavy and dark body' of the vessel as the engines 'work back and forth' producing a dirty slick on the water (VIII, 460). As Aschenbach beholds the drunken masquerader, he sees him 'pulled back and forth by the intoxication [*vom Rausche*]' (VIII, 462). This pulling back and forth, a rhythmic displacement over which the intoxicated subject has no control, becomes, in the language of dreams, a representation of the ambivalent lure of homosexual desire.

This sexual disfigurement is cemented by the keyword 'Rausch', which operates, as throughout Mann's writing, as a figure of Dionysiac intoxication in the Nietzschean style, but is mediated here by a Freudian logic. 'Rausch' is the intoxication which is engendered by the 'Rauschen', the rushing noise of the sea which recurrently intoxicates Mann's protagonists when they become subject to its ambiguous propulsion. The compounding of the ocean with intoxication as 'Meerrausch' (VIII, 491) completes a process which was introduced in the drunken descriptions of the sea's 'Rauschen' in the earlier texts, where it is figured in the ecstatic Dionysiac terms of Nietzsche's *Birth of Tragedy*. When Aschenbach is abducted by the rogue gondolier, the strategic contamination of 'Rauschen' by 'Rausch' is exposed. As the voyager is propelled further into his homoerotic adventure through a more intimate, manual continuation of the rhythmic push and pull, 'so gently rocked by the beating of the oar by the unauthorised gondolier at his back' (VIII, 466), he is lulled by a confusion of 'Reden und Rauschen',[10] of the intoxicating rush of the sea with the obscure dream-talk of the gondolier. In psychoanalytic style, the narrative thus ensures that, in accordance with Aschenbach's later realisation, Eros is an ever-active, if encoded, presence 'in the word' (VIII, 492), operating through strategic 'Entstellung' in the word of the text.

This 'Entstellung' is at once dreamlike and fundamentally poetic. In other words, it embodies the Nietzschean element of 'das trunkene Lied' (VIII, 1069), the drunken song to which Mann alludes when he discusses *Death in Venice* in his *Gesang vom Kindchen* [Song of the Baby]. While the narrative is objectified as what he calls there a 'moral fable', it retains the vestiges of poetic intoxication, or 'Rausch', in a sort of dialogical relationship with the more impersonal narrative structure. While the structures of control and containment represent the sort of masculine bearing which Aschenbach sees as continuing a patriarchal legacy, the vestiges of the 'drunken song' sustain a more uncontrolled sense of the seductive dangers of the homoerotic. The sea bears both the poetry and the desire in the overdetermined confusion of 'Rauschen' and 'Rausch', and, as in the earlier narratives, it does so through a compulsive rhythm of repetition. The push and pull of the sea voyage is extrapolated into the rhythmic draw of the sea for the protagonist, the underlying beat of the 'drunken song'. If the homoerotic hymn is subjected to the moral regulation of narrative form, then the sea, as 'unarticulated space' ('ungegliederter Raum', VIII, 461), represents both the morally unspeakable and a radical poetic resistance to articulate discourse.

This conflation of Nietzschean intoxication with Freudian dream logic is the poetic counterforce not only to the narrative regulation of the text, but also to another generic voice which stands in tension with both, that of burlesque theatre. While the intoxication of Nietzsche's Dionysus is designed to work dialectically with the Apollonian mask, here it is harnessed instead to the masquerade of aberrant sexuality. The burlesque theatre of sexual performance produces a series of repetitive acts which correspond to, but also parodically contaminate, the rhythm of 'Meerrausch'. The sexual 'acts' already witnessed on board ship deteriorate into a more general sort of burlesque sexuality which is correlated with the 'mask' of the plague. The lip-licking masquerader on the ship is repeated in the lip-licking ambiguities of the street singer, who also masquerades as the wanderer figure from the start of the narrative. The street singer's theatrical song is a grotesque anti-form to the 'drunken song' which Mann originally envisaged, one which collapses articulate verse into the contagious rhythm of laughter. The laughing song mimics the anti-social contagion of the plague as a form of performance which demands the performative mimicry of its audience. Aschenbach's own part in this contagious performance is to succumb to the repetitive travesty of gender and sexuality. His 'Rausch' adopts the mask not of tragedy but of the satyr play as he is made up for his homosexual adventure with the cosmetics and the costume (the red cravat and the coloured hat-band) of the masquerader on the ship. He becomes, in his turn, a false 'blossoming youth' (VIII, 519), a grotesquely made-up version of his object of desire.

As such, Aschenbach's final performance is a characteristically double one, at once a sort of hymnic repeat of classical models of homoerotic love, and a repeat of a more burlesque spectacle of abject and anomalous desire. When Aschenbach goes down to the seaside, in his act of repetition, for the final time, he shares the beach not only with Tadzio and his playmates, but also with an abandoned camera. The camera, on the one hand, stands as an apparatus of voyeurism, representing the narrative's attachment to the erotics of the gaze. It also seems to be an emblem of mechanical reproducibility, of the sort of repetition of scene which has structured the narrative and will, indeed, project beyond it into subsequent works. The abandonment of this apparatus of reproduction suggests an aporia of the work of representation, in a repetition of the scene earlier in the narrative where the Russian painter despairs of capturing the sea on canvas. Not only is a camera inherently incommensurate with the constant mobility of the sea, but it represents, by extension, the incommensurability of this archetypal object with any act of representation.

The abandonment of the apparatus of simulation also reflects the narrative's depiction of a breakdown in incommensurate relations between males. However, even as the symbolic object of the sea and its 'Rausch' elude representation, the narrative nonetheless returns to the project of representation of the artist's object of desire. The choreographic representation of Tadzio's movement seems to recuperate something of what was abandoned. It makes speakable an unspeakable desire and it symbolically articulates the disarticulated experience of 'Rausch'. While the sea as 'das Ungegliederte' ('the unarticulated') (VIII, 475) exceeds representation, its intoxicating disarticulation, the 'Gliederlösen' ('loosening of the limbs') which is the attribute of Dionysus,[11] is incorporated into the desired body. As they turn and then seem to loosen from each other – 'die Hand aus der Hüfte lösend' ('releasing his hand from his hip') (VIII, 525) – the body-parts gesture towards a vision of embodied disembodiment commensurate with 'Rausch'. Against the ironic emblem of the abandoned camera, Mann thus constructs a daring allegory of the representability of passion, one which has recognised the incommensurability of its constituent parts and yet constructs through the desired boy a bodily movement towards transcendence through 'Gleichmaß', which the desiring man moves to imitate. In spite of the ostentatiously ironic abandonment of his protagonist, Mann seems here to commit himself to the ultimate test of performing life through art. While *Death in Venice* exposes the apparatus of performativity through false performances of gender and sexual identities, it also, at its end, gestures towards a truer act of performance beyond irony.

As Mann recognises in his letter to Carl Maria Weber (4 July 1920) on *Death in Venice*, the text at once sublimates and pathologises 'forbidden love'. Whatever it may achieve in terms of the representation of homosexual passion, it seems that it must follow the model of the mortification of that passion which was demanded of Hanno in *Buddenbrooks*. It can only be immortalised under the sign of sickness unto death. The narrative thus imposes a sort of sacrifice upon itself as compensation for what it has released. In his diary for 4 February 1935, Mann records, with an exclamation mark, proposals for an early film version of the story with Tadzio transformed into a girl, indicating the powerful censorship that acts on homosexual desire in a culture of compulsory heterosexuality. This censorship is perhaps inevitably internalised to the extent that Mann restricts any substantial depiction of homosexuality to the passing phase of first love or the terminal 'amour fou'.

Homosexuality thus functions as an episode, or episodes, in the disparately projected lives of Mann's men. In the novella form, the episode can approach the status of the whole story. In the economy of a narrative like *The Magic Mountain*, a mock version of the *Bildungsroman* genre, it is formulated as an episode, but one which is formative for the life story, formative in the sense that it sets up a performative logic for what comes after. A significant part of Hans Castorp's formation is a sentimental education in gender and sexuality. The novel plays throughout with the possibility that intellectual and moral experience is ultimately reducible to the erotic, as informed by the (albeit ironically edged) presence of psychoanalysis. The explicitly sexual adventure with Clawdia Chauchat is part of a general network of more implicit passions which motivate the educational interests of Castorp's progress. Late in the novel, when Castorp comes to the realisation that his masculinity is not routine, not inspired by the rivalry with other men over female objects which the social definition of masculinity would expect, his mentor Settembrini finds himself on slippery ground, recognising that his own masculinity also inverts the social order by engaging in jealous rivalry over Castorp (III, 812).

In spite of the focal female figure of Clawdia Chauchat or the female anatomy given to the allegory of life, *The Magic Mountain* is essentially a narrative between men. While the enchanted world of the novel creates opportunities for heterosexual licence, it also charges the educational and therapeutic relations between men with a sense of seduction. The ostentatious heterosexuality of Settembrini's professions of interest in female patients or of Behrens's exposures in the X-ray cabinet are shadowed by the pursuit and exposure by men of the male body and mind.

Hermann Kurzke has noted that *The Magic Mountain* is a novel full of male societies of various kinds.[12] It seems that these conform to the model set out by Hans Blüher in his influential book *Die Rolle der Erotik in der männlichen Gesellschaft* [The Role of Eroticism in Male Society] (1917). Blüher's analysis of the erotic character of masculine social and political bodies, which Mann read and greatly admired, can be understood as an understanding *avant la lettre* of the homosocial. While this analysis is informed by an essentially conservative spirit, based on the male bonds of the patriarchal state, it does challenge predominant, essentialist views of sexual identity. The homosexual male is thus seen, not as a biological gender hybrid (as, for instance, in the theories of Weininger), but as an identity which can be fully masculine. Blüher thus prefers the term 'Sexualität' to 'Geschlechtlichkeit', as the former implies for him less the idea of subjective essence than that of object choice.[13] It is perhaps under the influence of this more constructionist view of the relationship between gender and sexuality that Mann is able here partially to disengage the homoerotic from the burlesque theatre of gender role-play. As the letter to Weber shows, however, Mann's view of homosexuality is also informed by the flip-side of Blüher's argument, by the figure of the *typus invertus neuroticus*, the repressed 'invert' whose gender and sexual identity merge in the sort of third sex 'mimicry'[14] which Blüher and Mann both abhor.

While the relationship between Hans Castorp and Clawdia Chauchat is, notwithstanding the narrative's decorous failure to show the scene where Hans returns the pencil to Clawdia, the most fully sexualised experience in Mann's writing up to that point, it is also a relationship which works through a logic of substitution. The lure of Clawdia Chauchat simulates not only the childhood passion for Pribislav Hippe, but also, intertextually, the concoction of orientalism and illness embodied by Tadzio (boy and plague both being identified as coming from the East). The relationship seems always to be marked with this homoerotic template. This works less through the strategy, employed elsewhere, of masculinising physical features of the female body (notably in *Felix Krull*), than through one at once more subtle and more crude: that of the fetish. In the encounter with Hippe, the extendable mechanism of the red propelling pencil is straight out of the Freudian dream-book. Indeed, the propelling pencil features as an especially appropriate phallic symbol in the dream section of Freud's *Introductory Lectures* (*SE* xv, 155). In the context of the dream where Castorp receives the pencil from Clawdia Chauchat, the heterosexual gift is transferred in classically, perhaps parodically, Freudian style into a more homosexual scenario, which ends in a clinch between the analyst Dr Krokowski and Hans Castorp's trouser-leg as the latter desperately seeks to climb a flag-pole (iii, 130). While

Mann has a very erotic woman present the phallic object to Castorp, it is a fragile version of the original (half-length in the dream and barely usable in reality). As with that other classically Freudian object, the cigar, here known as Maria Mancini, female characterisation would appear to be a device for the more homoerotic desire of the phallic fetish. The fetish, as a part-object which inspires compulsive attachment, thus serves as an index of how the episode of first love can function as formative and return in a sequence of performative acts. The novel is accordingly structured around the fetish of homosexual passion.

In its ending, *The Magic Mountain* appears to envisage the collapse of a benevolent homosocial order into the self-destruction of the man's world. Here the narrator enters into the male bonding of the text in order to confess his own pedagogical interest in Hans Castorp, as represented by an imitation of the tear in Settembrini's eye. The gesture is characteristically performative, an archly ironic expression of love, but it seems to help the final line to gesture in its turn towards the tentative possibility of love surmounting violence. The historical reality of the First World War, however, clearly deals a blow to the ideology of male eros, and in subsequent works history intervenes insistently to distort and pervert the performances of gender and sexuality.

Thus, in the satirical story *Disorder and Early Sorrow*, the narrative oscillates between bewildered excitement at new sexual manners and a sense of more general historical anxiety and melancholy. Gender roles, as a paradigm for social behaviour at large, are in a condition of performative upheaval, allowing men to use make-up and to dance with other men. But, in accordance with Butler's theories, the performative character of gender is not simply a theatre of free choice, it is more fundamentally a system of constraint and hence of duplicity. In the context of this narrative, gender performance becomes a measure of a crisis in history. The two young children are at once similar in appearance and differentiated by their gender. While the older children experiment with the boundaries of gender, the young Beisser suffers from a precocious case of gender trouble. While he performs masculinity with an excess of gesture and diction, the masquerade is not fixed in his nature; as a child of 'desolate disturbed times' (VIII, 625), his gender performance is haunted by neurotic instability.

In *Mario and the Magician*, too, the march of history is enacted in the theatre of sexual identity. The vision of Blüher's masculine eros takes on a grotesque form here in the figure of the fascist illusionist and his sexually charged games with the young men of Torre de Venere. The showman makes a show of masculinity; as one who has failed to match up to the nationalist standards of manliness by fighting in the war, he overcompensates in his taunting of the young men with their show of sexual prowess. The performativity of the earlier texts reaches a height of parodic intensity, as the histrionic magnetiser mimics the virile postures of his audience and has them expose the performative character of their own naturalised performances. The 'false youth' of *Death in Venice* is repeated here in the magician's grotesquely false performance of femininity, a performance which casts doubt on the most 'natural' of matters. Through his imposture as a woman, the illusionist lures Mario into a homosexual embrace, thereby showing the extent to which nature is susceptible to the powers of performance.

Cipolla, the master impersonator, figures at once as an allegorical embodiment of the spectacular lure of fascism and as its parodist. If this allegory has to work, for Mann, through a grotesque performance of homoerotic seduction, then he embraces a widespread model of mixing fascism with homosexuality, one which, at least in part, betrays homophobia.[15] His suggestion that *Death in Venice* reads, in retrospect, as a prophetic vision of fascism (diary, 26 January 1938) seems to suggest a similar confusion, a confusion which also plays into the demonised depiction of male–male attachments in *Doctor Faustus*. Relationships between men become infected with fantasies of power and of death, and the self-destructive excesses of the homosocial order are projected onto that which is partially assimilated with that order but is also anathema to it, the homosexual.

It is only in *Felix Krull* that Mann seems able to envisage a more benignly satirical picture of dissident forms of sexual identity. Krull embodies the ultimate instance of performativity. He is perpetually 'in disguise', so that any sense of unmasked identity is 'in fact absent' (VII, 498). What Mann calls his 'homosexual novel' (diary, 25 November 1950) reads as a celebration of the flexibility which the performative character of sexuality can allow. Here, the protagonist is a consummate embodiment of both homoerotic 'symmetry' ('Ebenmaß', VII, 284) and performative variety and interchangeability, without the pathological symptoms, moral and political, which attach to this elsewhere. He is able to perform heterosexually and homosexually by turns, never more impassioned than by the sexual double act of the brother and sister at the Frankfurter Hof hotel. Ironically enough, it takes a picaresque confidence trickster as narrator to achieve the sort of healthy candour about sexual identity which so painfully eludes the earlier texts. The perverted magnetism of Cipolla is replaced here by a magnetic allure which can break down the most entrenched of heterosexuals (the General Manager of the hotel) and which can expose the sorts of repressed desires which sustain the homosocial authority of an institution like the army. The figure of Krull seems to allow Thomas Mann a confessional mask for coming to more balanced terms both with the forms of masquerade which operate in the construction of gender and sexuality and with those which determine his project of aesthetic representation.

Given the trouble which has gone before in both aspects of Mann's world, it is hardly surprising that this valedictory vision should also have to incorporate, in the figure of Lord Kilmarnock, the melancholy of unfulfilled desire. The performance of sexual identity remains an ambiguous quantity, like the actor Herzl in *Disorder and Early Sorrow* a troubling hybrid of 'Schwermut' and 'Schminke' ('melancholy' and 'make-up', VIII, 637). This contradictory performance, at once essentially felt and ironically constructed, is of paradigmatic significance for Mann's man's world.

## NOTES

1 T. J. Reed, *Thomas Mann: The Uses of Tradition* (Oxford: Clarendon Press, 1974), p. 149.

2 Anthony Heilbut, *Thomas Mann: Eros and Literature* (London: Macmillan, 1996).

3 Eve Kosofsky Sedgwick, *Between Men: English Literature and Male Homosocial Desire* (New York: Columbia University Press, 1985); *Epistemology of the Closet* (New York and London: Harvester Wheatsheaf, 1991).

4 Judith Butler, *Gender Trouble: Feminism and the Subversion of Identity* (New York and London: Routledge, 1990).

5 The term first appeared in two pamphlets of 1869 attributed to Karl Maria Kertbeny.

6 For further discussion, see Elizabeth Boa, '*Buddenbrooks*: Bourgeois Patriarchy and *fin-de-siècle* Eros', in Michael Minden (ed.), *Thomas Mann* (London and New York: Longman, 1995), pp. 125–42.

7 Mann corresponds here to a set of writers effecting revivals of the Romantic fantasy figure in the age of modernism, as discussed in my book *The Doppelgänger: Double Visions in German Literature* (Oxford: Clarendon Press, 1996).

8 'Gleichmaß' or 'Ebenmaß' are recurrent markers of the even measurement of the homoerotic object in Mann's writing. They sustain a fantasy of similitude for the desiring subject who gauges their symmetry but can never measure up to it himself.

9 While most commentators are reluctant to date any serious engagement with Freud to before the early twenties, there have been tantalising suggestions that the influence dates back to the composition of *Death in Venice*. See Manfred Dierks, 'Der Wahn und die Träume in "Der Tod in Venedig": Thomas Manns folgenreiche Freud-Lektüre im Jahr 1911', *Psyche* 44 (1990), 240–68.

10 It is perhaps symptomatic of the discursive confusion at work in this passage that the *Gesammelte Werke* text has 'Reden und Raunen' ('speaking and whispering') (VIII, 466) rather than the 'Reden und Rauschen' in, for instance, T. J. Reed's 1983 Hanser edition of the text. 'Raunen' has occurred elsewhere in the passage, and its more ready collocation with 'Reden' would seem to account for its appearance at this point in the *Gesammelte Werke*.

11 As described, for instance, by Friedrich Nietzsche in 'Die Geburt des tragischen Gedankens', in *Sämtliche Werke: Kritische Studienausgabe*, ed. Giorgio Colli and Mazzino Montinari (Berlin: de Gruyter, 1988), I, 594.

12 Hermann Kurzke, *Thomas Mann: Epoche – Werk – Wirkung* (Munich: Beck, 1985), p. 178.

13 Hans Blüher, *Die Rolle der Erotik in der männlichen Gesellschaft: Eine Theorie der menschlichen Staatsbildung nach Wesen und Wert* (Stuttgart: Klett, 1962), p. 52.

14 Ibid., p. 137.

15 For a discussion of this phenomenon, see Andrew Hewitt, *Political Inversions: Homosexuality, Fascism, and the Modernist Imaginary* (Stanford: Stanford University Press, 1996).

## FURTHER READING

Böhm, Karl Werner, *Zwischen Selbstzucht und Verlangen: Thomas Mann und das Stigma Homosexualität* (Würzburg: Königshausen & Neumann, 1991)

Feuerlicht, Ignace, 'Thomas Mann and Homoeroticism', *Germanic Review* 57 (1982), 89–97

Heilbut, Anthony, *Thomas Mann: Eros and Literature* (London: Macmillan, 1996)

Woods, Gregory, *A History of Gay Literature: The Male Tradition* (New Haven and London: Yale University Press, 1998)

# 5

MARK M. ANDERSON

# Mann's early novellas

As T. J. Reed has remarked, Thomas Mann never seems to have experienced the language crisis characteristic of the early development of many German writers at the turn of the century.[1] Hofmannsthal's 'Chandos Letter', Rilke's *Notebooks of Malte Laurids Brigge*, and Kafka's *Description of a Struggle* are paradigmatic moments of a general malaise concerning the function and authenticity of poetic language at the turn of the century that seem to have passed over Mann completely. From his earliest novellas to his 'breakthrough' novel *Buddenbrooks*, from *Tonio Kröger* to the great novellas and novels that followed it for more than half a century, Mann seems always already himself, the sovereign master of a voice and narrative manner whose relation to the empirical world of facts, people and events is never seriously in question. Nevertheless, in one short, almost didactic story of 1896 entitled 'Disillusionment' (VIII, 62–8), Mann gestures towards a discrepancy between words and things that is indicative of a larger metaphysical concern. Set against the 'magnificently theatrical façade' of San Marco in Venice, the story consists of an older man's bitter monologue to an unnamed narrator about how 'life' has always disappointed him because it has never lived up to its linguistic description. Precisely because of his sensitivity to language, to the 'big words' of the poets, 'life' appears to him as a shadow that feebly limps behind his linguistically charged imagination. In earliest childhood he experienced a great fire that destroyed his house and almost killed his family; but while it was raging, a 'vague presentiment' of something much more terrible and terrifying made the actual fire appear to him 'dull', devoid of excitement, a pale simulacrum of the picture ('Vorstellung') in his mind. This has been true of everything in a long life of travel and experience: the real world of things and facts, of 'Tatsächlichkeiten', leaves him profoundly bored and unmoved. And so he bitterly concludes that even his approaching death, that ostensibly sublime, terrifying moment so celebrated in literature, will only occasion a final disappointment: 'So this is death? I will say to myself in the final instant: now I'm experiencing it! *Is that all it really is?*' (VIII, 68).

Like Hofmannsthal's Chandos, Mann's unnamed character is struck by the artificiality of 'big words'; but unlike Chandos he has no intense, epiphanic experience of the plenitude of life for which language is inadequate. Unlike Rilke's Malte, Mann's character is not beset by hallucinations of a grotesquely threatening, aggressively modern reality. And unlike the various narrators in Kafka's *Description*, he is not afflicted by the vertigo or 'seasickness on firm ground' generated by the arbitrary relation between signs and signified.[2] What seems to oppress him rather is the stultifyingly drab, uninteresting nature of reality itself when compared with the individual's yearning for unmediated emotional plenitude. As such the 'disillusionment' articulated in this early story seems not so much a modernist *Sprachkrise* as a belated response to the problem of individual imagination in a disenchanted, desacralised, bourgeois world: the problem of realist fiction since the late eighteenth century. It is perhaps for this reason that Mann's character quotes Goethe's Werther, who laments that 'man, the celebrated demigod', is repeatedly denied fulfilment of his yearning: 'And when he rises up in joy or sinks down suffering, isn't he always dragged back to that dull, cold state of consciousness at the very moment he thought he would lose himself in the plenitude of infinity?' (VIII, 67).

Though constituting only a slight tear in the narrative fabric of his writing, this spectre of a 'dull, cold' consciousness of quotidian experience marks a real anxiety in Mann's realist project. For if reality is not inherently interesting, if it is not charged with a higher, animating principle but is just a random collection of 'Tatsächlichkeiten' without greater meaning, what can justify the realist novelist's gargantuan effort to represent it? Or the reader's effort to understand it? In the following remarks I will attempt to trace his response to this anxiety in his early stories – not because it is confined to them, but because it is more openly articulated there in ways that will allow us to see it in the later, more complexly ironic and self-conscious writings. My argument will be that Mann's work defends itself against this spectre by turning reality into an elaborate stage performance of largely non-verbal exchanges, a performance of gesture, tableau and accentuated visuality that stems from the tradition of melodrama and anticipates to some extent the techniques of early silent cinema.[3] As we shall see, this understanding of Mann goes against the grain of most readings of the early stories, which have emphasised his ironic, decadent, ethically distanced or uncommitted posture. It reveals him rather as the passionate stage director of a single, unchanging human drama: the truth of desire and its struggle for liberation and expression within the confines of bourgeois life.

As Peter Brooks has shown in an influential study, melodrama is crucial to the historical development of realist fiction from Balzac to Henry James and

Proust.[4] 'Melo-drama', literally drama accompanied by music, sprang up as an extremely popular form of theatre during the French Revolution and the first decades of the nineteenth century. Historically, the genre evolved out of the 'low' forms of the puppet show, pantomime and farce which, because they did not have government patents for full verbal representation, developed an 'aesthetics of muteness' emphasising visual elements of gesture, tableau, simplified plot lines, gross characterisation through clothing, make-up and signifying names. 'Subjects are evidently conceived for their plastic figurability, the dramatic interplay of posture and gesture', Brooks notes. 'The spoken word is rarely used toward the formulation of significant messages; it is largely confined to emotional utterance, outburst, expressive cadenzas' (p. 63). In the very purity and crudity of melodrama, as Brooks argues, we find a polarisation of extremes and an aesthetics of 'excess' deriving from a basic understanding of human reality. Melodrama stages

> an intense emotional and ethical drama based on the manichaeistic struggle of good and evil, a world where what one lives for and by is seen in terms of, and as determined by, the most fundamental psychic relations and cosmic ethical forces … Man is seen to be, and must recognise himself to be, playing on a theatre that is the point of juncture, and of clash, of imperatives beyond himself that are non-mediated and irreducible. This is what is most real in the universe.
>
> (pp. 12–13)

Brooks's understanding of the term thus goes far beyond the historical development of a (now defunct) theatrical genre to encompass a broad aesthetic and metaphysical response to bourgeois society *per se*, and specifically to the French Revolution as the great epistemological cut in modern European consciousness, the event signalling the demise of the sacred as the governing principle of society, philosophy and art (p. 15). The more interesting, pervasive and influential role of melodrama concerns its afterlife outside its own genre in the infiltration of other discourses: popular forms such as Harlequin romance and television soap operas, but also such 'high' forms as grand opera and the novel. 'Melodramatic novelists' such as Balzac, Henry James and Proust (though not Flaubert or Kafka) conceived of reality as a coherent system of signs concealing beneath its surface the great 'drama' of modern life. The novelist's task, according to Brooks, was thus not at all to chronicle the world of facts and things, but to stage this ethical drama between the forces of good and evil, virtue and necessity. As a result, reality – even Werther's 'dull, cold' bourgeois reality – is reinvested with an essential aura, mystery and urgency, and the realist project is granted aesthetic legitimacy.

Critics have long noted the theatrical nature of Mann's prose writings, seen in devices such as the inclusion of a play or opera within a story; the use of dramatic dialogue and 'blocking'; or the scenic quality of narrative events.[5] Wherever this theatricality comes from, Mann himself was aware of it early on, as we can see from his emphatic response to a passage in Nietzsche's *Daybreak* describing the 'third eye' of a theatrical apprehension of reality. 'What! You still need the theatre!' Nietzsche exclaims:

> Learn sense and look for tragedy and comedy where they are better played! Where the play is more interesting and interested! No, it's not exactly easy to remain just a spectator, – but learn how! And in almost every difficult and painful situation you will have a little door opening onto a joyful refuge, even when your own passions assail you. Open up your theatre eye, the great third eye, which looks through the other two into the world! (D §509)[6]

Note here Nietzsche's comment that reality's 'theatrical' nature, properly intuited, is both more 'interesting' and more 'interested' than mere dramatic representations. The theatricality of a 'third eye' consists in splitting the subject into an experiencing self and a spectator self, with the latter providing a kind of refuge from and ironic distance towards the 'passions' of life – precisely the dilemma of the old man in 'Disillusionment' and of so many of Mann's worldly narrators. Mann's theatrical devices within his narratives would thus correspond to his generally ironic posture of distance and parody, which has received so much comment from his readers since his first stories were published in the 1890s.

To read Mann's theatricality in terms of melodrama, however, results in a subtly different picture: one in which irony is merely a surface ploy to conceal a passionate drama of human values and deep epistemological truths. Nietzsche's theatricality is not melodramatic; his deconstructionist relation to language and metaphysics, to the language of metaphysics, prevents the 'third eye' from becoming anything but a temporary heuristic tool. Mann, however, has an abiding faith in the ability of language, and specifically poetic language, to lay bare and give form to what he sees as the elementary moral, human drama behind the brute surface of things. Again and again in his stories, this 'deep truth' comes to the surface in highly staged, theatrical moments of passion, recognition and understanding, often manifesting itself in physical 'symptoms' or markings on the characters' bodies. Mann's 'third eye' of theatrical observation and presentation, of *Vorstellung*, is ultimately melodramatic, at once passionate and ethically committed, even when bourgeois morality itself seems to be under attack.

'Fallen' (1894), Mann's first story of any narrative consequence, already exhibits the constitutive tension in Mann's writing between melodrama and irony. The story itself is given a theatrical setting: the unnamed hero is an idealist – 'pure in body as in soul' (VIII, 14) – who falls in love with a beautiful young actress at the 'Goethe Theatre' in a provincial town. Naive and shy, he is encouraged to court her by a drinking companion, who slyly assures him that the actress, Irma Weltner, is of unimpeachable virtue and has rebuffed all previous suitors. The courtship runs its predictable course, the two become lovers, and the hero is appropriately ecstatic. But shortly thereafter he surprises her with an older man who turns out to be his rival and, in fact, a paying customer. Mann stages the encounter between the two suitors as farce, a comic and largely silent pantomime of exaggerated gestures and spluttering remarks. More interesting, pathos-laden and melodramatic is the recognition scene between hero and actress: also a virtually silent pantomime in which the hero suddenly discovers the terrible moral truth beneath the surface of things. 'Put those away', he says to her casually, referring to the banknotes lying on her dresser. But then he suddenly realises what these notes signify:

> Suddenly he became pale as wax, his eyes grew wide and his trembling lips parted.
>
> When he entered the room with the banknotes, she had raised her eyes up to him, and he had *seen* her eyes.
>
> Something disgusting ['Etwas Abscheuliches'] in him rose up with bony, grey fingers and held him fast by the neck.      (VIII, 39, Mann's emphasis)

Thus enlightened, the hero flees to his room in despair and wordlessly contemplates the image of his beloved, once 'so sweet and pure', while the 'lamenting' tones of a cello rise up from a neighbouring apartment.

To be sure, Mann has protected himself against the charge of 'mere' melodrama with a number of distancing devices, including a frame narration with four 'experienced' men debating modern questions such as the morality of 'woman' ('das Weib'); one of them, described as 'the ironist', is a doctor who narrates the above story of disillusioned love. Within the story itself, Mann also deploys the irony of both Goethe and Hoffmann in poking fun at his hopelessly lovesick, naive hero. The sly drinking companion is compared to Mephisto, so that Fräulein Weltner becomes an ironic Gretchen figure to the hero's unwitting Faust, more 'Frau Welt' than the personification of village innocence, whose lack of virtue is known to everyone in town. The melodramatic love affair thus becomes an elaborate joke at the hero's expense, who comes to resemble the truly deluded Nathanael in Hoffmann's *The Sandman*, the only one in town unaware that his beloved Olimpia is actually a mechanical doll.

Despite these devices, however, Mann's story turns on the young hero's extreme emotional trial, which the frame narration validates rather than suspends, as an essential truth below the layers of experience and cynicism. The three listeners are 'deeply moved' by the story, and finally the 'ironic' doctor reveals himself to have been the naive hero years earlier. For all his 'experience' and his medical, scientific detachment, he is still caught in the thrall of the deluded love of his youth. On one level Mann has thus clearly renounced the melodramatic device of a virtuous heroine who has 'fallen'; his modern novella, in naturalist fashion, has a doctor reject all idealistic blather about 'moral justification'. But in another sense he retains the melodramatic positioning of his characters around a key moment of revelation and insight (*Erkenntnis*) about a basic human drama of suffering and renunciation, here literalised in the highly visual, stagy figure of a 'disgusting' hand holding the hero by the throat. In a single charged moment of intense vision and insight, the protagonists *see* through the veil of surface phenomena into the ground of their moral existences. Schopenhauer may have provided the content for this drama, but the arrangement is anti-mimetic, contrived, operatic – and straight out of the popular tradition of melodrama.

Of the eleven stories Mann published before 1900, six use death – 'the most extreme and potentially melodramatic ending', according to Reed[7] – to resolve a plot conflict. The remark is intended as criticism, for it suggests an arbitrariness in Mann's handling of plot that patently strains the limits of realism and hence the reader's willingness to go along with the basic fiction. But if one understands melodrama in an extended, epistemological sense, the 'contrived' use of death becomes a logical necessity to his narrative. The subject of 'Luischen' (1900), we are told by the narrator at the outset, is a marriage whose bizarre nature can only be compared to the 'absurd conventions' of the theatre, in a farce or 'Posse'. The story consists of preparations for a skit at a party in which an exotic, empty-headed young woman publicly humiliates her obese, older and slavishly devoted husband so much that he drops dead on stage. Dressed up *en travesti* in a ridiculous pink tutu and tights, the husband sings the popular song 'Luischen' (we are not far from the actual origins of melodrama on the French stage) while being accompanied on the piano by his wife and the equally fatuous composer with whom she is having an affair. Only while performing does the husband realise the nature of his marriage. Again, the narrative climax is organised melodramatically, as a wordlessly enacted scene of gesture, seeing and being seen: 'While an awful silence reigned over the assembled guests, unbroken by a single sound, he let his ever widening eyes wander slowly and uncannily from the couple at the piano to the public and from the public to the couple . . . ' And again, the story culminates in a moment of *Erkenntnis* that is so profound, existence-shattering, and absolute that the only possible outcome (according to the logic of melodrama) is the husband's instantaneous death: 'A flash of insight suddenly seemed to cross his face, a rush of blood flooded his face . . . and the fat man came crashing down on the boards' (VIII, 186).

In traditional eighteenth-century melodrama, such extreme passions were usually grouped around familial relations, such as a mother's love for her long-lost but suddenly recovered child; or around a frustrated love relation between a young man and woman who yearn to establish a family. Mann modernises these passions by shifting them to illicit and uncanny forms of sexual dependence, domination and narcissism. We have left the realm of 'wholesome' bourgeois love for ostensibly decadent, criminal, perverse moral terrain, which for Mann always constitutes the hidden signified of human relations, or what Brooks terms the 'moral occult'. Consider for instance 'Little Herr Friedemann' (1897), the apparently Naturalist story of a baby dropped on its head by an alcoholic nurse, who grows up to be a physical misfit, renounces all claim to sexual love, and lives with his unmarried sisters. On the surface of things, Friedemann lives 'in peace' (Mann's 'speaking' names are themselves melodramatic). But this is only the façade of quotidian, bourgeois reality that in Mann's morally inflected universe is a great lie or, in Ibsen's phrase, a 'life-sustaining lie' ('Lebenslüge'). Exposure comes in the form of a melodramatic, 'fated' encounter with a woman named Gerda von Rinnlingen, whom he first sees driving a horse-drawn coach and brandishing a riding crop. They scrutinise each other in silence, without uttering a word, Gerda's features appearing in close-up detail, as if in a movie. The same wordless encounter repeats itself soon afterwards in the theatre, when the two 'accidentally' share a private box ('Box 13'). Friedemann is mesmerised by her physical appearance, cannot take his eyes off her and consumes her with fetishistic attention: 'Frau von Rinnlingen had removed the glove from her left arm, which lay on the red velvet balustrade – a round, pale white arm with pale blue veins running through it, like her unadorned hand. He kept looking at her arm; that couldn't be altered' (VIII, 88–9). 'Das war nicht zu ändern' ('that couldn't be altered'): the phrase is telling for what one might term Mann's melodramatic realism, for it suggests not only Friedemann's helplessness in gazing at the fate that will rip apart his bourgeois lie, but the 'fated' quality of realist detail itself. Seemingly insignificant scraps of the physical, bourgeois world are depicted as having such elementary force, mystery and truth that the characters are ineluctably caught in their spell. Nothing is accidental or contingent.

The rest of the story unfolds in an almost *pro forma* coda to this intensely visual scenario of metaphysical necessity. We watch Friedemann succumb to what is not really a woman at all, but a kind of supernatural goddess of cruelty, an 'ice princess' reminiscent of Andersen's tale or the Venus of

Sacher-Masoch's fantasy. His insight (*Erkenntnis*) into this truth comes again as a wordless moment of sudden, unexpected, life-altering insight, of seeing himself as he truly is through the eyes of this uncanny, pitiless judge: 'Suddenly the expression of her face changed. He saw how it contracted into a barely visible look of derision, how her eyes were levelled at him, again with that uncanny, trembling gaze that was yet icy and probing' (VIII, 96). The operatic finale takes place in her garden, by the lake, in which she confirms what he already knows about the false happiness of his previous life. This encounter with a divine order of reality sitting in judgement on his 'sins' ('My God' seems virtually his only form of address to her) cannot be sustained, and he drowns himself in grotesque fashion while the 'restrained' laughter of the distant party guests provides an appropriately ironic, unenlightened form of applause.

Music is of course an integral part of Mann's aesthetics and has often been understood, perhaps too quickly, in terms of Wagner's leitmotif technique for the opera. For music is also part of the larger issue of a melodramatic presentation of reality in realist fiction, just as Wagner's use of the leitmotif has its origins (through the grand operas of Halévy and Meyerbeer) in classical melodrama. As Brooks notes, the function of music in melodrama was part of its general concern with making its signs 'clear, unambiguous, and impressive'.[8] Music was used to mark a particular character's entrance on stage, to underscore the dramatic nature of a particular moment, or to signal to the audience a change or heightening of mood. Often dramatic action would come to a halt for a musical interlude, sometimes accompanied by a ballet. Because of the wholesale appropriation of these techniques by cinema, their origin in melodrama is often obscured or confused with the conventions of grand opera or cinema, its inheritors. But throughout the nineteenth century, including the period of Mann's early stories, this functionalisation of music within narrative derives from the stage; his use of the 'lamenting' sounds of the cello in the final tableau of 'Fallen', to cite only one example, is unmistakably melodramatic (and not at all Wagnerian).

This is true even of Mann's Wagnerian novellas, 'Tristan' (1903) and 'The Blood of the Volsungs' (1906), both of which depend on a narrative *mise en scène* of a Wagner opera for the resolution of plot. In the latter story, a deadly satire on assimilated Jews caught up in *fin-de-siècle* Wagner-mania, the drama begins at the dining-room table with two interrelated sources of dramatic tension: the generational conflict between parents and children, and the 'racial' conflict between the Jewish Aarenhold family and the German outsider, a government official named von Beckerath who is engaged to the beautiful daughter Sieglinde. Music defines the characters and the plot: first of all through their 'speaking' names (Sieglinde and her twin brother

Siegmund are named after the heroes of Wagner's *Valkyrie*); but also through their entrances into the text (one of the brothers taps out Hunding's motif when von Beckerath appears at lunch); through the musical interlude at the opera which substitutes for psychological development; and finally through the twins' re-enactment of the incest in Wagner's opera at the end of the story.

In addition to its musical organisation, however, the text also depends on the melodramatic acting-out and discovery of and the response to the hidden moral drama governing the characters' lives. The lunch scene provides von Beckerath (and the reader) with a number of visual clues about these conflicts, which are partially hidden by the family's veneer of German culture, liberalism and hypocritical politeness. But 'truth' in this story is constituted by 'blood' and the deep physiognomic marks of what Mann refers to as the Jewish (and possibly homosexual[9]) 'Art' – a difficult word to translate which can mean species, kind or type. The story unfolds as the progressive uncovering of this truth, first in the brother's dressing room as he contemplates his racial features in a mirror and then in the theatre as he contemplates them again, by their absence, in the Germanic hero Siegmund after whom he is named. What is enacted as high tragedy and noble suffering on stage is re-enacted as cheap melodrama and vulgar revenge in the Aarenhold bedroom. The story's conclusion, however, confirms Brooks's notion of 'epistemological melodrama' when the underlying truth and moral exigency of Jewish 'blood' are made visual as a physical mark on the body for a single expressive moment: 'and for a moment the distinguishing marks of his kind stood out clearly on his face' (VIII, 410).

Melodrama in the sense that I have tried to give it can be found in most of Mann's early novellas, since it is not merely one narrative device among others but an integral part of the author's very conception of writing; it informs his apprehension of, and interpretative response to, reality. It responds further to a central anxiety of realist fiction: the brute, unmotivated facticity of the real in a post-sacred, utilitarian era. And it does so not merely with a highly visual aesthetics of excessive (indeed, often fatal) emotion, but with a vision of the world that invests it with, if not sacred, at least metaphysical ethical content. Reality for Mann (as opposed to radically sceptical writers like Flaubert, Kafka, Musil, or Robbe-Grillet) is not inert matter, not a random collection of arbitrary surfaces covering over the void, but a system of signs animated by a deeply human, ethical drama. The kind of 'epistemological melodrama' I have attempted to describe here does not exclude the ironic, parodic, or distancing aspects of Mann's writing, indubitably present, but it does claim that they are subordinate to the demands of this elementary conflict of human passions.

The implications of this view for Mann's later novels are considerable, for it means understanding the patently excessive, contrived, theatrical novellas of his early years not as an immature stage to be overcome, but as the basis for the aesthetic, philosophical and ethical dimensions of his writing generally. One would need to look at his use of melodrama in works like *Buddenbrooks*, *The Magic Mountain*, the Joseph tetralogy and *Doctor Faustus*, as well as his essayistic work, to gauge its full range and significance, an analysis that goes beyond the scope of the present essay. But a brief look at the final scene in *Death in Venice*, indisputably one of Mann's finest and most characteristic stories, can gesture in this direction. The presence there of the 'unmanned' photographic 'apparatus' on the beach, shrouded by a black cloth, which silently records Aschenbach's demise, has often been taken as an emblem of Mann's own clinically cold, modernist mode of narration, perhaps even of a cinematic, mechanical apprehension of reality. An alternative reading of the scene would stress rather that Aschenbach's passion has been reduced to a mute tableau of gazes and gestures corresponding to the logic of melodramatic excess, which strips away superficial conventions, even language itself, to lay bare the elementary drama of the character's unanswered, unanswerable desire. The camera serves as an index of the scene's visuality. Highly stylised, operatic, almost contrapuntal in its deployment of Aschenbach's and Tadzio's signifying bodies, Mann's story culminates in this final mute vision, which coincides with a life-shattering, indeed fatal insight (*Erkenntnis*) into the nature of desire. Through this melodramatic orchestration of Aschenbach's death, which exposes and judges an entire life, Mann resacralises 'bourgeois' reality with a signifying, silent tableau that almost makes us forget the words through which we perceive it. As such, it might well be taken as his triumphant response to the doubts about the legitimacy of realist narration voiced fifteen years earlier in 'Disillusionment' (which was also, let us remember, set against the 'magnificently theatrical façade' of Venice): the great melodramatic illusion of words turning into expressive bodies.

## NOTES

1 T. J. Reed, *Thomas Mann: The Uses of Tradition* (Oxford: Clarendon Press, 1974), p. 29.
2 Franz Kafka, *'Description of a Struggle' and 'The Great Wall of China'*, trans. Willa and Edwin Muir, and Tania and James Stern (London: Secker & Warburg, 1960), p. 48.
3 Most of the work on melodrama in German literature is related to eighteenth-century drama; apart from a few scattered articles, little attempt has been made

to link melodrama with later prose texts, and none (to my knowledge) with Thomas Mann. Much interesting work has been done, however, on the relations between melodrama and early cinema by film critics such as Thomas Elsaesser, Laura Mulvey, Charles Musser and Stephen Heath; see especially Heide Schlüpmann, 'Melodrama and Social Drama in the Early German Cinema', *Camera obscura* 22 (1990), 73–87; and Miriam Hansen, *Babel and Babylon: Spectatorship in American Silent Film* (Cambridge, MA: Harvard University Press, 1991).

4 Peter Brooks, *The Melodramatic Imagination: Balzac, Henry James, Melodrama, and the Mode of Excess* (New Haven: Yale University Press, 1976; 2nd edn, 1995).

5 See Albert Ettinger, *Der Epiker als Theatraliker. Thomas Manns Beziehungen zum Theater in seinem Leben und Werk* (Frankfurt am Main and New York: Lang, 1988).

6 See the discussion in Reed, *Thomas Mann*, p. 21.

7 Ibid., p. 33.

8 Brooks, *Melodramatic Imagination* (2nd edn), p. 48.

9 Without entering into a biographical reading of the story, one can note the narrator's voyeuristic fascination with Siegmund's body as he dresses for the opera. Critical readings that stress the story's anti-Semitic animus often lose sight of this sexual identification with Siegmund, who is typed physiognomically as both Jewish and homosexual. See Anthony Heilbut's insightful biography *Thomas Mann: Eros and Literature* (New York: Knopf, 1995).

## FURTHER READING

Anderson, Mark, M., ' "Jewish" Mimesis? Imitation and Assimilation in Thomas Mann's "Wälsungenblut" and Ludwig Jacobowski's *Werther, der Jude*', *German Life and Letters* 49 (1996), 193–204

Reed, T. J., 'Text and History: *Tonio Kröger* and the Politics of Four Decades', *Publications of the English Goethe Society* 57 (1988), 39–54

Sheppard, Richard, '*Tonio Kröger* and *Der Tod in Venedig*: from Bourgeois Realism to Visionary Modernism', *Oxford German Studies* 18/19 (1989–90), 92–108

Turner, David, 'Some Rhetorical Functions of the Present Tense in the Shorter Prose Narratives of Thomas Mann', *Oxford German Studies* 29 (2000), 155–80

Vaget, Hans R., *Thomas Mann: Kommentar zu sämtlichen Erzählungen* (Munich: Winkler, 1984)

Ward, Mark G., 'More than "Stammesverwandtschaft"? On Tonio Kröger's Reading of *Immensee*', *German Life and Letters* 36 (1983), 301–16

White, John J., and Ann S. White (eds.), *Tonio Kröger*, Blackwell's German Texts (London: Duckworth; Bristol: Bristol Classical Press, 1996). German text with detailed introduction and notes in English.

Young, Frank W., *Montage and Motive in Thomas Mann's 'Tristan'* (Bonn: Bouvier, 1975)

# 6

RITCHIE ROBERTSON

# Classicism and its pitfalls:
## *Death in Venice*

While staying in Venice with his wife and brother between 26 May and 2 June 1911, Thomas Mann, like his fictional Aschenbach, was fascinated by a handsome Polish boy whom he watched playing on the beach. This 'personal and lyrical experience', as Mann later described it in a much-quoted confessional letter, prompted the story *Death in Venice*.[1] And just as Mann's protagonist Aschenbach is inspired by the sight of Tadzio to write 'a page and a half of exquisite prose' on an unspecified problem of taste and culture (VIII, 493), so Mann wrote a short essay on his changing attitude to Wagner. Having idolised Wagner for many years, he confessed, he was now turning away from the composer's steamy Romanticism and towards a new classicism:

> But if I consider the masterpiece of the twentieth century, I imagine something which differs from Wagner's profoundly and, I think, for the better – something decidedly logical, formal and clear, something at once severe and serene, evincing no less will-power than Wagner's, but intellectually cooler, more refined and even healthier, something that does not seek greatness in Baroque grandeur nor beauty in intoxication – a new classicism, I fancy, must come.     (X, 841–2)

His novella was itself intended to embody this ideal. Mann wished, for a time at least, to emulate certain contemporary writers who advocated 'neo-classicism' and who had the approval of Samuel Lublinski, a critic who had praised *Buddenbrooks* in a review that is quoted verbatim in *Death in Venice* (VIII, 453).[2] In retrospect, Mann's desire to climb on the bandwagon driven by such now-forgotten writers as Paul Ernst looks a very modest ambition. In his attempt to revive classicism, however, he also looked beyond his contemporaries and engaged with a long tradition in German literature, represented above all by the classical Goethe. We can also find in Mann's text traces of the new understanding of Greek sculpture pioneered by the eighteenth-century art historian Winckelmann, whose work formed an important basis for Goethe's classicism. In 1768 a shocked public learnt that Winckelmann had been murdered by a stranger at an inn in Trieste, and suspected (wrongly, it seems) a link with his known homosexuality. Winckelmann's death in Trieste may have helped to inspire Aschenbach's death in Venice.[3] Mann alludes unmistakably to one of his own favourite writers, August von Platen (1796–1835), 'the melancholy and enthusiastic poet' whose Venetian sonnets come to Aschenbach's mind as he approaches Venice from the sea (VIII, 461). Although the precision of Platen's odes and sonnets gave him a reputation as 'a man of severity, of cold symmetry, of classicist formalism' (IX, 268), Mann knew that Platen was essentially a Romantic poet in his urge to express his own personality, especially his distress over the repeated experience of unrequited homosexual love. And finally, since Mann was steeped in the thought of Nietzsche, the story also registers the radical shift in the understanding of Greek culture instigated by Nietzsche's *The Birth of Tragedy* (1872).

In paying homage to this tradition, Mann dramatises the strengths, the weaknesses and the pitfalls of classicism, in its different versions, through the career of a writer dedicated to a classical ideal. There was, above all, a contradiction between the public and private faces of classicism. Classical art is pre-eminently public. It is suited to public buildings, like Palladio's church of San Giorgio Maggiore which Aschenbach sees as he approaches Venice. In literature, it marks an exemplary public style which is to be shared and imitated, just as Aschenbach's formulaic style is held up as a model for schoolboys. But any real acquaintance with classical Greece soon reveals that it was a society markedly and disturbingly different from the modern cultures that claim it as an ancestor. In particular, homosexual relations between men and boys were an accepted part of Athenian life, whereas such a form of love has been officially frowned on since the rise of Christianity. Hence a preoccupation with classicism, especially with classical ideals of male beauty, has often enabled the homosexual imagination to find a satisfaction that was rare, dangerous or unattainable in reality, and in both life and literature visits to the Mediterranean have often brought about a sexual awakening. Oscar Wilde and E. M. Forster are two familiar examples among many.[4] *Death in Venice* assumes a prominent place among a series of texts in which travellers from Northern Europe have their sexual horizons enlarged by visiting the South.

More specifically, though, *Death in Venice* continues and comments on the long-standing German fascination with Greece and Greek sculpture. Sculpture is the pre-eminently classical art form. Free-standing, self-contained, detached from the spectator, the statue seems to be the 'art object' *par excellence*, best suited for the disinterested contemplation that Kant defined as the aesthetic attitude. Yet most of the statues surviving from the ancient world invite us to admire the naked human (often male) body, and such delighted contemplation is close to the sensuous desire for a living body. In particular, appreciation of sculpture can let men express covertly the homosexual desire that is officially prohibited. Does art sublimate desire, or release it? Nietzsche formulated this problem by juxtaposing Kant's definition of aesthetic experience with Stendhal's description of it as 'une promesse de bonheur', and asking: 'Who is right, Kant or Stendhal?' (*GM* III, §6) Mann explores the unstable relation of art and desire through his devotee of classicism, Gustav von Aschenbach.

When the story begins, Aschenbach is already a classic writer, in two of the senses which Goethe gave the term. First, he represents the type of 'classic national author' ('Literarischer Sansculottismus', G XII, 240) which could not exist in Goethe's fragmented Germany and did not yet exist in Mann's Wilhelmine Empire. Unlike most of Mann's early protagonists, Aschenbach does not come from Lübeck or Hamburg, but from the town of 'L.' (Liegnitz) in Silesia. His paternal ancestors were soldiers or administrators in the service of the Prussian state which formed the core of a united Germany. And in one of his major works, dealing with Frederick the Great, Aschenbach has evoked a national subject from Prussian history. Second, he is an exemplary writer. Extracts from his works are reproduced in school readers so that schoolboys may model their style on his. It represents the 'pure style appropriate to its subject' (G XII, 243) which Goethe considered classical. In addition, Aschenbach is a classical writer in the obvious sense of emulating the classics. He admires, and tries to imitate, the order, balance, harmony, and restraint deemed characteristic of classical literature.

Mann himself followed this precept to the extent of emulating the classic prose of Goethe. While working on the story, he steeped himself in Goethe's later works, especially *Elective Affinities*. Aschenbach's infatuation with Tadzio has much in common with Eduard's love for Ottilie in *Elective Affinities*. Mann also drew on 'The Man of Fifty' in *Wilhelm Meister's Journeyman Years*, where the elderly Major has himself made up to attract his niece Hilarie (G VIII, 178); and on Goethe's actual infatuation with Ulrike von Levetzow, to whom he proposed marriage in 1823 although she was fifty-five years his junior (letter to C. M. Weber, 4 July 1920). Moreover, many formal features of Goethe's classical narratives are present in *Death in Venice*.[5] The reader is distanced from the action, and allowed to form a considered judgement, by the narrator, who is not a distinct person but rather a distinct voice, sometimes close to Aschenbach, sometimes explicitly critical. The story begins *in medias res*, with the awakening of Aschenbach's restlessness one afternoon in Munich; only afterwards are we given an account of his previous life and career. Instead of pressing towards a climax, the narrative is retarded, as Goethe recommended, by Aschenbach's abortive attempt to leave Venice. The passage of time is blurred, making it hard to say how long Aschenbach spends under Tadzio's spell. And finally, the empirical world is not described in the fullness of detail we might expect of realism; instead, details are exploited for their symbolic value, as in the famous evocation of Venice, 'half fairy-tale, half tourist-trap', in Chapter 5 (VIII, 502–3).

In other respects, however, the classicism of Mann's style is qualified. He favours hyphenated adjectives, e.g. 'feurig-festlich' ('fiery and festive') (VIII, 496), hypotactic sentences, and such periphrases as 'betagtes Fahrzeug' ('aged vessel') for an old ship, 'Kollation' for a snack and 'Bäderinsel' for the Lido. However, neoclassicism is coupled with naturalistic detail. Mann evokes the jerky motion of the steamer taking Aschenbach to Venice, and the flakes of coal-dust falling on its damp deck (VIII, 461); later, in a dilapidated square, Aschenbach smells the stench of carbolic acid (VIII, 521).

Moreover, Aschenbach's deliberate classicism accompanies, and perhaps over-compensates for, his Romantic affinities. The text invites us to trace his creativity back to his mother, the daughter of an orchestral conductor from Bohemia. Music, for Mann the quintessential Romantic art, is also suggested by Aschenbach's visual resemblance to Gustav Mahler, news of whose death reached Mann just before his holiday, and by the fact that Wagner too died in Venice. Besides, Venice is a post-classical city. It originated in the fifth century AD when the inhabitants of towns along the Adriatic fled from Germanic invaders to the neighbouring islands, which they later extended and strengthened by driving wooden piles into the clay bed of the lagoon. Though happy to draw on his own stay in Venice, Mann could, had he thought it appropriate, have sent Aschenbach to Rome as well as making him a Prussian. His attraction to Venice underlines his Romantic leanings.

These two aspects of Aschenbach, the classical and the Romantic, are apparent in the biographical sketch provided by the narrator in Chapter 2. For Goethe, Schiller and their like-minded contemporaries, classicism included the physical health and harmony, the sense of being happily at home in the world, that they ascribed to the Greeks. Aschenbach is far removed from such an ideal. His health is poor. His substantial oeuvre is the product of determined self-discipline which enabled him to use all his available strength for literary work. Evidently Aschenbach's frail physical powers, including his creative energies, are controlled by an iron will. His feminine, intuitive abilities, his maternal inheritance, are under the firm guidance of his masculine, rational character: at least until the experience of homosexual love dissolves the rigid antitheses which frame his life.

Unattractive though Aschenbach's rigidity may sound, he is initially portrayed as an admirable character. In overcoming his physical weakness, he is a characteristically modern hero, with a special appeal for readers who themselves live likewise on the verge of exhaustion. We need not question the narrator's good faith at this point. After all, Mann ascribes similar qualities to the admired novelist Fontane. In his 1910 essay 'The Old Fontane' Mann portrays him as a nervous, irritable character who, by his own confession, wrote with difficulty, and interprets his achievement for that very reason as heroic: 'he must have been one of those whose achievements assume heroic proportions because they think they are making no progress' (IX, 12). The passive heroism celebrated by Aschenbach, and illustrated, in a self-referential allusion, by Thomas Buddenbrook as well as by St Sebastian, is also the quality praised by Winckelmann in the Laocoon statue, where the priest, entwined by huge snakes, is controlling his pain with dignity.

Doubts creep in, however, when we learn about Aschenbach's past. As a young man he was intent on *Erkenntnis*, on psychological analysis of a sceptical and cynical sort (VIII, 454). We may imagine that, like Thomas Mann, he had learnt from Nietzsche how to question conventional morality and to seek its unacknowledged motives. However, Aschenbach grew tired of constant negative questioning. He realised that too much analysis could paralyse the moral will. Instead of inviting his readers to question and learn, Aschenbach commanded them to resolve and take action. Misbehaviour like that of the protagonist of Aschenbach's story 'Ein Elender' ('A Miserable Specimen') should not be understood, still less forgiven; it should be roundly condemned. Mann's choice of words, particularly the inane repetition, suggests that Aschenbach's forceful moralism is both heavy-handed and banal: 'The weight of words ['Die Wucht des Wortes'] with which vileness was reviled proclaimed a rejection of all moral scepticism, of any sympathy with the abyss' (VIII, 454). As the moral content of Aschenbach's works became simpler, their form became more accomplished, with a purity, simplicity and symmetry that are recognisably classical. Their style became more refined. Subtlety and nuance were abandoned in favour of standard, polished formulae. Even in his speech, it seems, Aschenbach now follows the example of Louis XIV (no less) in avoiding all commonplace words. He is equally solemn in his devotion to writing: it is a quasi-religious act, full of fervour ('inbrünstig'), in which his energy is made a sacrifice ('Opfer') to his art; he works with two candles in silver candlesticks on his desk. His dedication to his duty becomes, in artistic terms, a crude overstatement, a rejection of ambiguity and irony. Formal perfection goes with diminution of content. Yet classical restraint is only a virtue if, as with Laocoon, there is something to restrain.

Though the classical Aschenbach may be an exemplary figure to his public, he is not so to the narrator, who, however discreetly, retains the commitment to understanding (*Erkenntnis*) that Aschenbach himself has discarded. In the essay 'Sweet Sleep' (1909), Mann defines the morality of the artist:

> The artist's morality is composure ['Sammlung'], it is the power of self-centred concentration, the commitment to form, shape, limitation, corporeality, the rejection of freedom, infinity, dozing and drifting in the limitless realm of feeling – in a word, it is the will to produce a work. But how ignoble and immoral, how bloodless and repulsive is the work that is born of cold, calculating, virtuous, self-contained artistry! The artist's morality is self-abandonment, straying and self-loss, it is struggle and hardship, experience, insight and passion ['Erlebnis, Erkenntnis und Leidenschaft']. (XI, 338)

In this declaration, and in his critical portrayal of Aschenbach, Mann is affirming the artist's duty to inquire, to probe, to reach what will often be uncomfortable insights into human character. He is siding with artists like Fontane, whom he described as being 'devoted not to intoxication but to insight' ('nicht auf den Rausch, sondern auf Erkenntnis gestellt', IX 20). Hence Aschenbach has aptly been called an 'anti-Fontane'.[6]

Aschenbach, however, places enthusiasm above reflection. His self-command has not extinguished his imagination. Rather, his intuitive powers have retreated from his control. He is in the situation of many people approaching middle age who, to attain success, have channelled their energy in a single direction, allowing other aspects of their personalities to wither or, more likely, to become repressed. Such a person is ripe for the 'mid-life' crisis, well described by Jung, in which buried aspects of their self make their presence felt through significant dreams, hallucinations and outbursts of emotion.[7] Aschenbach's crisis begins as he is waiting for a tram in Munich, facing a stonemason's yard full of funerary monuments and a mortuary chapel adorned with epitaphs. Amid these symbols of death, suggesting his inner desiccation, he is recalled to life by the sight of an unknown male traveller, which arouses not only a sudden urge to travel but also an intensely vivid hallucination. Aschenbach's inner vision shows him a tropical swamp with 'lascivious growth of ferns', the 'hairy stems of palm-trees' and the eyes of a crouching tiger peeping through a bamboo thicket. This 'primeval wilderness' ('Urweltwildnis') (VIII, 447) could not be more different from the apparently solid edifice of Aschenbach's professional life. It is sensuous, erotic and frightening, with a suggestion, in the tiger, of brutal appetite. Although this primeval, tropical scene is distant in time and space, it reminds us that Venice too was built on a swamp.

The traveller who unleashes such an inordinate response in Aschenbach is one of a series of wanderers who cross his path. The elderly fop on the boat to Venice, made up to seem youthful, the gondolier who insists on taking Aschenbach direct to his hotel and the malevolent street musician are all described emphatically, yet none is necessary to the narrative. Why introduce them? One, inadequate, answer is that Mann actually encountered such people in Venice:

> Nothing in *Death in Venice* is invented: the traveller by the Northern Cemetery in Munich, the gloomy boat from Pola, the aged fop, the dubious gondolier, Tadzio and his family, the departure prevented by a mix-up over luggage, the cholera, the honest clerk in the travel agency, the malevolent street singer, or whatever else you might care to mention – everything was given, and really only needed to be fitted in, proving in the most astonishing manner how it could be interpreted within my composition. (XI, 124)

How then are these figures to be interpreted? They have often been seen as mythic figures, variously identified with the Devil and the gods Hermes and Dionysus. However, one should be wary of projecting onto the early Mann the later fascination with comparative religion and myth that finds expression above all in the *Joseph* tetralogy and the correspondence with Karl Kerényi, in which Mann affirmed his liking for the combination of 'myth plus psychology' (letter, 18 February 1941). In *Death in Venice*, 'mythic' experience is shown by the sceptical narrator to be projected onto his actual experience by the increasingly enraptured Aschenbach. If a day on the beach is 'strangely exalted and mythically transformed' (VIII, 496), that is because his infatuation with Tadzio colours his view of the scene around him. The wanderers who cross Aschenbach's path likewise derive their disturbing aura from his emotional projections. Not only are these figures wanderers, like Aschenbach, but they also share some of his traits: the slight build, the loose mouth and the short nose. They represent the unacknowledged and unwelcome shadow-side of Aschenbach himself, the rootless, bohemian aspect which he has done his best to repress.[8] Jung has shown that the heightened sensibility accompanying a mid-life crisis can generate precisely such visionary embodiments of psychic forces.[9]

The story gradually reveals what Aschenbach is repressing – his power to love, his capacity for homosexual love, and the areas of experience it opens up. His repressed emotions appear just where he thought he was safest: amid his devotion to classicism.

Aschenbach first appreciates Tadzio aesthetically. On first sight, Tadzio's perfect beauty reminds him of 'Greek sculptures of the noblest period' (VIII, 469). Later he breaks into a classical hexameter – 'there, like a flower in bloom, his head was gracefully resting' (VIII, 474). A long, ecstatic appreciation culminates in calling Tadzio 'this divine sculpture' (VIII, 490). He is specifically compared to the Spinario (Boy Extracting a Thorn), a Greek statue formerly thought to date from the fifth century BC, but now considered Hellenistic; it shows a seated boy, one leg bent over the other, intent on extracting the thorn from his foot. The figure is notable for his thick, flowing hair, like Tadzio's 'honey-coloured hair' (VIII, 469) and for his complete absorption in his task. His self-sufficiency recalls the self-delight ascribed to Tadzio, whose smile is that of Narcissus contemplating his own reflection (VIII, 498).[10]

As Aschenbach becomes infatuated with Tadzio, he tries to preserve the aesthetic character of his feelings by interpreting them in accordance with Plato's doctrine of beauty. Mann compiles a montage of quotations from classical sources, especially Plato's dialogues *Phaedrus* and the *Symposium*, to present the claim that beauty, alone among Ideas, is palpable to sight. It gives people a visible reminder of ultimate reality. Thus it links us to the higher realm as other Ideas, lacking sensible embodiment, cannot. Hence a man 'is amazed when he sees anyone having a godlike face or form, which is the expression of divine beauty; and at first a shudder runs through him, and again the old awe steals over him'.[11] This experience, however, separates the wise from the merely sensual. The former practise self-control, 'enslaving the vicious and emancipating the virtuous passions of the soul',[12] while the latter rush straight to physical enjoyment and never attain spiritual happiness. For the Platonic ladder is like a real ladder: to reach the higher rungs, you must leave the lower ones behind.[13]

By this stringent standard, Aschenbach's Platonism is false. He thinks that in Tadzio he beholds 'beauty itself, form as a divine idea', 'a mirror of intellectual beauty' (VIII, 490); but his recollection of Plato's *Phaedrus* leads him, not to wisdom, but to intoxication, as the narrator makes clear by calling him 'the enthusiast' ('der Enthusiasmierte') (VIII, 51) and 'the bewildered one' ('der Verwirrte') (VIII, 503), and deploring 'the manner of thinking of one beguiled' ('des Betörten Denkweise') (VIII, 504). Love leads Aschenbach to such extravagances as stopping outside Tadzio's bedroom door and resting his forehead against the hinge 'in complete inebriation' (VIII, 503). Eventually it leads him into moral transgression, which we are to see, not in his homosexuality, but in his conscious decision to refrain from informing Tadzio's family that Venice is infested by cholera. In thus discovering the intricate relation between classicism in art and the experience of passion, Aschenbach is following in the footsteps of Winckelmann, Goethe and Platen, who explored the shifting boundary between aesthetic appreciation and sensual desire. Winckelmann takes male statues like the Laocoon, the Apollo Belvedere and the Antinous (representing the lover of the Emperor Hadrian) to illustrate the beautiful style, which, far from inviting cool observation, overwhelms the beholder and threatens to dissolve the firm borders of the self.[14] In his tribute to Winckelmann, Goethe said that in these descriptions a normally dry writer became a poet (G XII, 120). Platen praised Winckelmann for his lyrical descriptions of sculpture, 'breathing souls into blocks of marble'.[15] Platen too expressed his own emotions indirectly by describing male statues, and later by describing actual males in statuesque language.[16] Thus an ode to a beautiful male model he met in a friend's studio in Rome combines nature and art by praising the symmetry of his build with the spring-like fullness of his growing limbs; the young man's face, though, shows 'kaltblütige Gleichmut', the cold equanimity of an aesthetic object or, possibly, of a self-obsessed narcissist – anticipating the narcissism of Tadzio.[17]

Aschenbach's Venetian experience re-enacts, in different ways, Goethe's experiences in both Venice and Rome. Erotic attraction brings the classical world to life around him, as it did for the Goethe of the *Roman Elegies*, through his love affair (whether real or fictional does not matter here) with a young Roman woman. Similarly, as Aschenbach's infatuation mounts, classical reminiscences turn into lived experience. At first Aschenbach simply draws on his classical education for suitable quotations. Thus the spoiled Tadzio reminds him of Homer's hedonistic Phaeacians, and a line from Voss's translation of the Odyssey comes to his lips (VIII, 473). Once Aschenbach has yielded to his passion, however, the surrounding world is subjectively transfigured into mythic grandeur. Classical references are frequent and dense in section 4: the sun becomes 'the god with fiery cheeks' (VIII, 486), the waves are Poseidon's horses (VIII, 496), Aschenbach feels transported to the Elysian Fields (VIII, 488), and Tadzio, playing ball, is identified by Aschenbach with the boy Hyacinth, loved by both Apollo and the West Wind (VIII, 496). Goethe too, in a famous passage, finds his appreciation of sculpture heightened by intimacy with his beloved's body (G I, 160).

There is, however, a more specific association between Aschenbach and Goethe. Goethe's visit to Venice in spring 1790 gave rise to the *Venetian Epigrams*. Here Mann found the famous comparison of a black gondola to a coffin (VIII, 464; G I, 176). More centrally, several epigrams celebrate a group of street acrobats, including a preternaturally agile girl called Bettina. Watching them as a tourist, Goethe is in a position like that of Aschenbach watching Tadzio and his friends. Moreover, Bettina's appeal comes partly from her boyishness. She reminds him of the 'boys' in paintings by Bellini and Veronese; when she stands on her hands with her legs (and bottom) pointing skywards, Goethe pretends to fear that the sight will attract Jupiter away from his boy-lover Ganymede.[18] Goethe was tolerant towards male homosexuality. In a conversation recorded in 1830, he remarked that pederasty

(*Knabenliebe*), even if against Nature, was part of Nature.[19] It has been suggested that a homosexual encounter formed part of his sexual awakening on his Italian journey.[20]

For Aschenbach, the balance between art and desire soon tips towards physical passion. The prospect of Venice laid waste by cholera, with law and order collapsing, opens up dim, unformulated, but exciting possibilities. Rather than relinquish these, Aschenbach will take the risk that both he and his supposedly beloved Tadzio will die of cholera. This conscious decision releases violent unconscious forces in a horribly vivid dream, in which men and women, with sinister ululations, dance round a gigantic wooden phallus and copulate promiscuously.

In this orgy we see the unacknowledged underside of Aschenbach's classicism. For its participants are worshipping the god Dionysus, and such rites, in which intoxication (Aschenbach's 'Rausch') is taken to such extremes as incest and self-mutilation, are attested from classical sources. Mann took the details from a study of Greek religion, *Psyche*, by the classical scholar Erwin Rohde.[21] But he had already encountered this shadow-side of classicism in the work of Rohde's friend Nietzsche, *The Birth of Tragedy*, in which the sunlit world of Greek sculpture, called 'Apolline', is contrasted with the dark, violently sensual, 'Dionysiac' world that finds expression especially in music. A civilised Greek had to accept that 'his whole existence, with all its beauty and moderation, rested on a concealed underground of suffering and insight [*Erkenntnis*], which was disclosed by that Dionysiac element' (*BT* §4). It was only in the experience of tragedy, Nietzsche argued, that these two discordant truths, the truth of Apollo and the truth of Dionysus, could be held together in a single thought.

Thus *Death in Venice* examines the precarious balance between two forces. On the one hand, we have 'classical' clarity and control; on the other, the sensuous pleasure which forms part of the experience of art, which can grow into love, and which, sometimes in frightening and destructive forms, is also part of classicism. Too rigorous control can swerve into its opposite, self-abandonment. Mann's ideal of critical understanding (*Erkenntnis*) may offer a way of holding both together.

## NOTES

1 To Carl Maria Weber, 4 July 1920. On the background, see Anthony Heilbut, *Thomas Mann: Eros and Literature* (New York: Knopf, 1995), esp. p. 247.

2 See Hans Rudolf Vaget, 'Thomas Mann und die Neuklassik. *Der Tod in Venedig* und Samuel Lublinskis Literaturauffassung', *Jahrbuch der Deutschen Schiller-Gesellschaft* 17 (1973), 432–54.

3 Lionel Gossman, 'Death in Trieste', *Journal of European Studies* 22 (1992), 207–40 (p. 214).

4 See Robert Aldrich, *The Seduction of the Mediterranean: Writing, Art and Homosexual Fantasy* (London: Routledge, 1993).

5 Discussed (with reference to *Wilhelm Meister's Journeyman Years*) by Wolfdietrich Rasch, 'Die klassische Erzählkunst Goethes', in Hans Steffen (ed.), *Formkräfte der deutschen Dichtung vom Barock bis zur Gegenwart* (Göttingen: Vandenhoeck & Ruprecht, 1963), pp. 81–99.

6 Joyce Crick, 'Thomas Mann: How Late is Late?', *Publications of the English Goethe Society* 68 (1998), 29–44 (p. 33).

7 See Anthony Stevens, *On Jung* (London: Penguin, 1991), pp. 164–5.

8 See Heidi M. and Robert J. R. Rockwood, 'The Psychological Reality of Myth in *Der Tod in Venedig*', *Germanic Review* 59 (1984), 137–41.

9 Stevens, *On Jung*, p. 175.

10 For an illustrated account of this figure, see Francis Haskell and Nicholas Penny, *Taste and the Antique: The Lure of Classical Sculpture 1500–1900* (New Haven and London: Yale University Press, 1981), pp. 308–10.

11 *Phaedrus*, 251a, in *The Dialogues of Plato*, trans. B. Jowett, 4th edn (Oxford: Clarendon Press, 1953), III, 158.

12 *Phaedrus*, 256a–b, in *The Dialogues of Plato*, III, 163.

13 See T. J. Reed, *Thomas Mann: The Uses of Tradition* (Oxford: Clarendon Press, 1974), pp. 156–71; the doctrine ascribed to Socrates is summarised in the social context of Greek homosexual practice by K. J. Dover, *Greek Homosexuality* (London: Duckworth, 1978), pp. 160–5.

14 See Alex Potts, *Flesh and the Ideal: Winckelmann and the Origins of Art History* (New Haven and London: Yale University Press, 1994), esp. p. 128.

15 Sonnet 32, 'An Winckelmann', in Platen, *Lyrik* (Munich: Winkler, 1982), pp. 384–5.

16 See Wolfgang Adam, 'Sehnsuchts-Bilder: Antike Statuen und Monumente in Platens Lyrik', *Euphorion* 80 (1986), 363–89.

17 Platen, *Lyrik*, p. 463.

18 Goethe, *Sämtliche Werke: Briefe, Tagebücher und Gespräche* (Frankfurt: Deutsche Klassiker Verlag, 1986– ), I, 451.

19 Ibid., XXXVIII, 249.

20 Sander L. Gilman, 'Goethe's Touch', in his *Inscribing the Other* (Lincoln and London: University of Nebraska Press, 1991), pp. 29–49.

21 For Mann's excerpts from Rohde, see his work-notes in *Thomas Mann: 'Der Tod in Venedig'. Text, Materialien, Kommentar*, ed. T. J. Reed (Munich: Hanser, 1983), pp. 92–3.

## FURTHER READING

Berlin, Jeffrey B. (ed.), *Approaches to Teaching Mann's 'Death in Venice' and Other Short Fiction* (New York: Modern Languages Association of America, 1992)

Gronicka, André von, ' "Myth plus Psychology": a Style Analysis of *Death in Venice*', *Germanic Review* 31 (1956), 191–205

Reed, T. J., *Death in Venice: Making and Unmaking a Master*, Twayne's Masterwork Series no. 140 (New York: Twayne, 1994)

'The Frustrated Poet: Homosexuality and Taboo in *Der Tod in Venedig*', in David Jackson (ed.), *Taboos in German Literature* (Oxford and Providence, RI: Berghahn Books, 1996), pp. 119–34

Reed, T. J. (ed.), *Der Tod in Venedig*, Blackwell's German Texts (London: Duckworth; Bristol: Bristol Classical Press, 1996). German text with detailed introduction and notes in English.

Rockwood, Heidi M. and Robert J. R., 'The Psychological Reality of Myth in *Der Tod in Venedig*', *Germanic Review* 59 (1984), 137–41

Vaget, Hans R., 'Film and Literature. The Case of *Death in Venice*: Luchino Visconti and Thomas Mann', *German Quarterly* 53 (1980), 159–75

# 7

ALAN BANCE

# The political becomes personal: *Disorder and Early Sorrow* and *Mario and the Magician*

*Disorder and Early Sorrow* (1925) and *Mario and the Magician* (1930) have often been linked because they conveniently span the life of the Weimar Republic and its two major crises. The eponymous 'disorder' of the earlier story concerns the economic distress resulting from the disaster of a lost war, whereas *Mario and the Magician* presages the political crisis which will follow a new financial crash. How short the period between Weimar's first and second crises was in reality, and how brief it must have seemed to Thomas Mann, is underlined by the fact that only five years separate the publication of the two tales. Both stories have obvious autobiographical elements.

The use of the term 'disorder' is in one sense an understatement. It covers a recent German history of terrible experiences. But the upheavals in German society after the First World War were too well known to German readers in 1925 to need spelling out. And however dramatic the events, unless directly involved in them, individuals generally experience such crises in trivial terms of day-to-day survival and adjustment to changing moral and social conditions. This is how Thomas Mann chooses to present the period: through the situation of one family and the eyes of one individual in particular.

Since knowledge of the events leading up to *Disorder and Early Sorrow* can be taken for granted by the author in his German readership, there is no mention of the overwhelming fact of the recent defeat and the resulting insecurity. The modern reader must bear in mind too that the collapse of the old order in Germany in 1918 followed upon severe wartime suffering from food shortages and inflation. Of those who experienced the hardships of the post-war inflation up to 1923, most had already endured the starving 'turnip winter' of 1916–17. A black market flourished and substitute (*Ersatz*) foods were developed, prefiguring the makeshift menus and the ingenious expedients for acquiring food seen in the Cornelius household in Mann's story.[1] The living standards of many members of the middle class declined during the war, especially those on fixed incomes.

Germans had seen a succession of calamitous or unprecedented events, collectively known as 'the German Revolution': naval mutiny, the enforced abdication of Kaiser Wilhelm II, socialists in government for the first time. From the political shambles of 1919, two rival soviet governments of Bavaria emerged there. After a week of savage fighting in April and May 1919, the Munich soviets were destroyed amidst vicious right-wing reprisals. In Berlin, the local civil war of the Spartacist (proto-Communist) uprising early in 1919 and its violent suppression by the SPD (Social Democratic) government in collusion with the army culminated in the murder of the Spartacist leaders. The right-wing Kapp putsch of 1920 provoked strikes in central Germany and particularly in the Ruhr, and there were abortive KPD (Communist) risings in 1921 and again in 1923. Munich, the setting of Mann's story and his home at the time, was a city particularly hard hit by post-war political turbulence. Hitler's failed 'Beer Hall Putsch' in 1923 was an expression of his initial admiration for the Italian fascist leader Benito Mussolini, whose 1922 'march on Rome' he tried to emulate in this 'march on Munich'.

Mussolini, a charismatic renegade socialist who lends some of his rhetorical prowess and theatrical swagger to the figure of Cipolla in *Mario and the Magician*, had joined with the Italian nationalist movement supported by hordes of disappointed ex-soldiers (blackshirts). The nationalists broke up socialist meetings and linked with extreme right-wing groups to form the fascist movement, targeting their violence particularly upon the Italian Communist Party which was founded in 1920. Then, in November 1921, the Fascist Party was formed and a kind of respectability descended on the movement. The so-called 'march on Rome' was actually a summons by King Victor Emmanuel III to form a government.

Meanwhile, the effect on the post-war German economy of 'revolution', strikes, the loss of territory, the problems of demobilisation, and the unrealistically generous social welfare arrangements of the early Weimar governments was to bring about massive inflation, and additional mischief resulted from the way the country had financed the war by internal borrowing. The inflationary spiral was exacerbated by the Allied demand for reparations, which caused the crisis of 1923 that is the setting for *Disorder and Early Sorrow*. Those who experienced inflation told of rooms decorated with redundant banknotes in place of wallpaper, and workers being paid their wages and rushing with barrow-loads of notes to buy scarce provisions before their money ceased to have any value at all.

The degree of disorder recorded in *Disorder and Early Sorrow*, set in this inflationary period, seems tame by comparison. But disorder is a matter of scale, and Thomas Mann is rarely the writer to seek out sensational events. In both stories, the narrator or narrative focaliser experiences the eruption of new and unpleasant events into his private life, and is forced into confrontation with an outer world which he would rather keep at arm's length. This dichotomy of public and private is central to Thomas Mann's being as an artist, and not surprisingly rises to particular prominence in these stories set in times of public crisis.

The motif of a private world turned inside out is signified quaintly and harmlessly enough in *Disorder and Early Sorrow* through the invasion of Professor Cornelius's home. The household is normally a citadel of privacy organised around the professor's dignified academic routine. Today, however, his adolescent children are holding a jazzy 1920s-style party, which throws his home into sudden disorder – the more sudden for the professor because he has stereotypically forgotten the date of the event. A potentially more sinister, parallel invasion of his privacy is that of the great inflation, which, like all such vast monetary landslides, devalues and discredits more than just the currency. As we see them in the story, however, Cornelius and his upper-middle-class family are more or less holding their own against the chaos, and the sense of crisis is defused by a gentle humour epitomised in the professor's conscientious tolerance of his rumbustious young guests and his rueful rather than bitter attitude towards the genteel poverty of his family's reduced circumstances.

The real threat, by contrast, lies in the 'early sorrow' of the story's title, an incursion into the professor's most intimate family sphere which is not immediately related to the public disorder of Weimar society. Cornelius's youngest daughter Lorchen is heartbroken over her helpless love for the charming student Max Hergesell, who has turned her infant head by 'dancing' with her at the party. Worst of all for Cornelius, he must suppress his jealousy of this usurper of his daughter's affections, because he depends on the young man to quell her inconsolable sobbing. The pain of this invasion of his private emotional space is exacerbated by Max's jocular liberty-taking with the child's name. His use of the form 'Loreleyerl' is not, as it was once called, 'a totally irrelevant allusion', even though she is obviously unrelated to the Lorelei of German Romantic literature, 'the bewitching temptress who lures men to their death'.[2] The allusion forecasts the inevitable separation which will come about between father and daughter as she grows to sexual maturity, the first foreshadowing of which is painfully apparent in the child's discovery of the attraction of the opposite sex in the shape of Hergesell.

The pain belongs to father and daughter alike, but in the case of Cornelius it strikes to the root of his most intimate and private being, both as a man and as an academic historian. In an earlier passage close to third-person inner monologue, the Professor broods on his 'excessive' love for his favourite, and confesses to himself that it is in some way connected with his love of the past, which is timeless and eternal. And yet he loves the past also precisely because it is *not* the present. In the best possible sense, from his point of view, the past is dead. That Romantic 'empathy with death' ('Sympathie mit dem Tode') which is a theme of Mann's early works, and which the hero of *The Magic Mountain* strives to overcome, is here a refuge from the turmoil of a vexatious present.

Professor Cornelius, from whom the narrator is careful to distance himself,[3] exhibits the remnants of a decadent *fin-de-siècle* sensibility in his love for the melancholy past and his 'empathy with death', reminiscent of Mann's own love of Romantic decay expressed in *Buddenbrooks*. *Disorder and Early Sorrow* deploys a number of well-known Mann motifs along with the disturbing novelties of contemporary life that begin to complicate their significance. Political disorder is related in an oblique way to the 'sexual disorder' (early sorrow) with which it is associated in Cornelius's mind. The professor's reveries about the Spain of Philip II and the doomed Counter-Reformation evoke thoughts about the reality of his students' political 'disorder', which means that he has to be careful how he presents his reactionary ideas to them in his seminar the next day. Whereas old-fashioned decadence is a kind of permanent aesthetic fascination with states of decay, real-world decline precedes changes which are unpredictable and possibly revolutionary. The danger of associating his reveries with his love for his daughter is obvious. Fatherly love may be unchanging and eternal, but daughters must change, precisely through the workings of time seen in the moment of 'early sorrow' around which Mann builds the story.

Between the private and public worlds of Cornelius a subtle connection is established, which lies in the violation of privacy brought about by change. The preservation of privacy can often strike the reader as the essence of Thomas Mann's style. There is an inherent paradox, though, in his continuing to cultivate a fastidious, distancing, self-protective style while projecting a representative public persona with claims to pedagogical status that are characteristic of leading German writers. It is provocative to some that he takes upon himself the burden of representing European culture. On the one hand, to his credit his position is admirably non-nationalistic. On the other hand, his cosmopolitanism appears to be the view from above, and not in the least democratically minded.

It is within this context that we can view the democratising and the international influences reflected in *Disorder and Early Sorrow*. Inflation has had a great levelling effect in post-war German society, and it is the democratisation lived out by Cornelius's upper-middle-class household that provides much of the bitter-sweet humour of the story. The internationalism of the period is present not only in the impact of the American-inspired jazz age and the colourful repertoire of folksongs of all nations sung by the young people at the party. More seriously, this is a post-revolutionary age where Germany's fate is not in its own hands; where, in fact, the Weimar Republic is as much an international construct as a German state. (It is significant that *Mario and the Magician* also has an international setting.) The contrast with Mann's cultivation and cosmopolitanism (not at all diminished by his conversion to republicanism and increasing sympathy for the Left after the Great War), with its assumptions of social control by an educated European elite, could not be more painful. It is precisely that control which *Mario* shows finally and utterly to have broken down.

The story of *Mario* is told by an educated middle-class narrator, recalling events which took place during a family seaside holiday in Mussolini's Italy in the late 1920s. At the end of their month in an up-and-coming resort called Torre di Venere, the respectable German family, aware of certain unpleasant xenophobic and nationalist attitudes in the Italians, are looking forward to returning home. As a final treat, the parents reluctantly agree to take their two children to see a performer billed as a 'magician', who turns out to be a flamboyant, unscrupulous, and also physically deformed show-business hypnotist. During the evening the charlatan demonstrates his powers to dominate and then degrade his audience. Though clearly still fascinated by the experience, the narrator struggles to come to terms with the horror of the performance and its effect on his children, particularly in view of the macabre turn of events which concludes the evening and the Italian holiday. At the climax of his show, the magician, Cavaliere Cipolla, mesmerises a young waiter called Mario, well known and liked by the family. In his hypnotised state, Mario is induced to believe that Cipolla is the girl who is the object of his unrequited love, and the young waiter plants a kiss on the cheek of the old charlatan. Immediately afterwards, apparently coming to his senses, Mario draws a pistol and kills the magician.

Mann demonstrates in the story a seismographic ability to sense and express the movements of 1920s politics. For instance, although the self-appointed, charismatic leader-figures of inter-war Europe easily lend themselves to caricature (as in Chaplin's *The Great Dictator*), Mann succeeds in conveying through Cipolla in *Mario* the menace of charisma, despite his potentially comic, grotesque appearance. His perception of Hitler (once a would-be painter) as a fellow-artist, whose raw material is now humanity itself, in the essay of 1939 entitled 'Brother Hitler', acknowledges an affinity between himself and the Führer, based on a critical self-knowledge which endows him with special political insight. Cipolla's techniques result from Mann's acute observation of leadership methods; for example, the trick of persuading the public that he, Cipolla, bears the enormous burden of carrying out their will, rather than his own. Cipolla's effect on his audience may be compared with the analysis by a contemporary of the 'Psychopathology of Dictators': 'as more and more people join the leader, their merged inferiorities become a superiority...They partake of the flesh of his authority. They become part of his soul and substance, and he of theirs. They share in his Authority Complex. Germans, for instance, say that they don't fight for Hitler, but that Hitler fights for them.'[4]

Many attributes of Mussolini, the 'Duce' (Leader), are echoed in the figure of Cipolla. Both remind the onlooker of Cagliostro, the Italian arch-impostor of the eighteenth century.[5] The Duce exercised the privilege of keeping the audience waiting for his appearance, as does Cipolla. There are further parallels in the fact that the dictator was always as it were on stage, acting a part, and that he was solitary, isolated, misanthropic and aloof. Cipolla-like in hating to be laughed at, he similarly prided himself on his great intelligence, iron will and perfect sense of timing. Like Cipolla, Mussolini was initially not taken seriously, and resorted to sadistic measures to intimidate the opposition. Both dislike, and treat with disdain, persons of character and culture, but both play on cultural nationalism and the 'national awakening' for their demagogic effects. Both treat the masses of ordinary people like children. The puritanism imposed by the Italian fascist regime is present in the prudishness of the Roman holiday-makers in the scene on the beach in *Mario* where the narrator's young daughter's innocent nudity arouses their somewhat synthetic anger. The hypnotic power and the oratory of the dictator and the magician alike sap all resistance, to the point where 'the man in the street...find[s] an infectious joy in an uncritical obedience to his slightest whim', 'the joy of obedience to a single will' as irrational and involuntary beliefs spread like a contagion.[6]

The deeper psychic sources of inter-war political irrationalism are reflected in the central role of sexuality in the novella. Passionate sexual drives permeate the story: a 'Frau Angiolieri' is seduced on stage away from her husband; a virile and challenging young spectator, who arouses the magician's sexual jealousy, is forthwith humiliated; Mario's unrequited love for Silvestra is exploited to delude him into a 'perverted' public display of love for the magician; and Cipolla himself demonstrates a compulsive need to woo, seduce and dominate a whole audience.

For those desperate to oppose such a malicious assault on human dignity, the political climate of mass hypnosis and irrationality appears to urge the abandonment of reason in favour of passion and violence; the primary need is to resist the demagogue's will and save the mob from insanity, through just the kind of violent solution the narrator endorses in *Mario*. But Thomas Mann's position is that resistance needs to comprehend the power of unconscious drives and use them for positive ends, rather than merely be infected by the same irrationality. In a lecture to Viennese workers in 1932, taking up a position that opposes the abstract rationality of Marxist analysis, he pleads an equation between the artist's intuitive and unselfconscious creative process, and the similarly non-rational impulse that is the source of humane socialism: 'you falsify art, just as you falsify humanity, if you see it as simply the product of reason or simply the product of instincts' (XI, 898).

It should be borne in mind, however, that fundamental to Mann's creative observation is a distance from political commitment. Essentially, all social processes are grist to his artist's mill. He cares at least as much about giving a satisfying shape to his observations as he does about their implications in the real world of action, and delights in a plenitude of expression and description irrespective of the object observed. Cornelius is made in his mould when he works up his reflections about history and the doomed Spain of the Counter-Reformation into nicely turned sentences and, God-like, finds his creation good. At this moment he fits the template of the typical Thomas Mann artist-figure, for whom political concerns take second place to the achievement of aesthetic effect.

*Mario and the Magician* concerns the nightmare of a private persona inescapably caught up in a public crisis and forced out of the typical Thomas Mann position of detached, ironic observer. The narrator of the story is not just exposed to more contemporary history than he can stomach, he becomes morally implicated in it, just as no one who lived as an adult through the Hitler years in Europe could remain a private and disinterested party. The fascinating ambiguity of the novella lies in the narrator's attempt retrospectively to master the events he recalls.

In *Mario*, literature and political responsibility become the implicit crux of the tale, but in part by negation: the artist-narrator shapes his story as the magician on stage shapes the evening and the audience's responses. In telling the story of the show-business hypnotist who illicitly manipulates minds and commits the crime of stealing his audience's souls, Mann voices his familiar suspicions about the 'ulterior' motives of art through the very medium in which it asserts its magic. Not for nothing was he known to his family as 'der Zauberer', the magician. They knew his tricks only too well.

A creative imagination like Mann's claims, or cannot shake off, an 'irresponsibility' which he would like to see as a kind of higher responsibility. His desire to be true to his own insight is the key to an understanding of the charlatan on stage and therefore also, by extension, of the phenomenon of fascism, for which he acts as a cipher. Fascism is not alien to Mann, because it too uses aesthetic and mind-manipulating magic. The dubious nature of the artist is further underlined in *Mario* when the narrator (an artist by def-inition, since he is shaping his tale to achieve certain effects), who is also a parent with a duty to protect his children, is confronted with an evil from which he ought to be shielding them. He is left helpless on the sidelines as the evening progresses. As a parent, let alone as any kind of potential saviour of human dignity, he is a failure in this situation, but as a narrative voice he has the compensation of being able retrospectively to express that condition and explore the tricks of his fellow artist – with an admixture of respect for professional skill, and the appropriate horror.

Between *Disorder and Early Sorrow* and *Mario and the Magician* there is one clear shift of perception. In *Disorder*, change is shown as open to interpretation: it may be registered as no more than that, merely change, or it may be viewed as development. By metaphorical implication, the assimi-lation and subordination of post-war German disorder to the growing pains of young Lorchen leaves open a reading of the condition of Germany as a natural development leading to growth, rather than as an unmitigated dis-aster. Cornelius then appears as a character with whom we can sympathise, but ultimately as yesterday's man – or yesterday's Mann, for there is a sense in which Thomas Mann, the convert to republicanism (who would indeed want to see the convulsions of postwar Germany as birth-pangs) is saying farewell through the figure of Cornelius to his earlier, supposedly apolitical, metaphysical and conservative imagination. Modernity is entertainingly pre-sented through the older Cornelius children's breezy manner and their easy egalitarianism. The sense of loss inevitably felt by a member of Cornelius's social class after the First World War is diverted into the personal and away from the political, while the story culminates in a tragi-comic dénouement with sentimental overtones.

By the time of *Mario*, on the other hand, disorder can in no way be con-strued as containing the potential for development. The story fits into the cat-egory of the disaster tale particularly well represented in Weimar Germany by such mid-twenties works of fiction as Heinrich Mann's 'Kobes' and Leonhard Frank's 'Im letzten Wagen' ['In the Last Carriage']. The first is a story of the destruction experienced by the middle class of Weimar at the hands of big business during the economic turmoil up to 1925; the second deals with a railway carriage which has broken away from the body of the train and is careering downhill – an obvious allegory of contemporary Germany.

Development can be thought of in connection with *Mario* only in terms of the narrator's own gain in insight, which would again foreground the narcissism of the Mann-type artist. Otherwise, disorder is purely destructive. In a kind of negative inversion of the triadic Marxist structure of historical development (note that the route taken by the narrator and his family to the venue of the fatal show leads from the aristocratic area of Torre di Venere, with its imposing *palazzi*, via the bourgeois quarter to the working-class district), the story suggests that while the age of the masses has arrived, those masses are nothing more than raw material for a malevolent leader to work upon. Against the background of this unpromising predicament, Mann's choice of a working-class saviour offers a significant statement of faith, or at least of hope.

Yet there is something deeply problematic about the middle-class narrator's reaction to the liberating act of Mario in shooting the magician, which vicariously allows him to cut through the moral complications of the evening and his recounting of it. Mario's act is apparently instinctive and, in its Southern European context, at least warrantable, if not excusable, as a crime of passion. It is more problematic when the narrator embraces this outcome which – he 'cannot help feeling' – is 'a liberating ending all the same' (VIII, 711). This conclusion in itself produces a highly ambiguous ending, suggesting at least two levels of interpretation: the guilt of the liberal humanist at finding himself willing to sanction a murder, albeit the murder of somebody who does not respect human dignity or integrity; and the guilt of the intellectual (in the broad sense of educated or professional person) who has explored what his liberal politics tell him is forbidden territory, and who will never truly be 'liberated' from an experience which spoke to the dark places of his own mind.

Here Mann's narrator – and Mann himself? – betrays that he is already infected with a moral malaise that was to invade even the most right-thinking minds of the 1930s intelligentsia. 'Infection' could indeed be the key metaphor in relation to *Mario and the Magician*. The infection of nationalism or xenophobia in the air of Torre di Venere and of Mussolini's Italy attacks the liberal cosmopolitan narrator himself, so that he experiences a 'nordic' distaste for the superficiality of the Italian population and the brazenness of the southern climate, and develops a most illiberal impatience with Italian culture as a whole. A kind of infection is discernible in the way that the 'disease' of fascism spread to Germany from Italy. (Ironically, when in *Mario* the motif of infection becomes overt, this Italian-to-German contagion is reversed, according to the narrator's drily humorous remark about the irrational fear of the aristocratic Italian family at the Grand Hôtel that the whooping-cough of the narrator's youngest child may prove to be 'acoustically infectious'.)

The threatening political mood poses a danger that strikes at the very heart of the narrator's – and, by extension, Mann's – delusion of control, expressed in his *Meisterstil* ('style of a master'). Mann had already parodied his own distinctive style in *Death in Venice*.[7] In *Mario* the narrator's pretensions to linguistic mastery amount to a kind of hubris. He attempts in vain to place the barrier of his educated culture between himself and the world, in a manner both condescending and ironic. Since we have access to the events of the story only through his self-censored recall, which includes a large element of self-justification, Mann is clearly inviting us to be wary of the narrator's attempt to impose his command after the event by means of irony. Even the delight in description and the plenitude of language which the narrator shares with his creator Thomas Mann can no longer be regarded as neutral, in a time of increasing European crisis. For it implies an irresponsibility built into the ability of the 'chameleon Poet' (in Keats's phrase) to immerse himself in the immediate object of his contemplation irrespective of the circumstances.

There is no easy answer to the question of the relationship between literature and political responsibility, as we see when the question reaches a crux in the narrator's verdict on the death of Cipolla – 'a liberating ending'. Where the creative imagination emerges from its role of pure contemplation and the artist (in the shape of Mann's narrator) for once adopts a moral standpoint, there is a danger of infection by the worst contagion of all, one which was to haunt the literary culture of the 1930s: the disease of absolutism. It is summed up in the famous words of W. H. Auden's Spanish Civil War poem 'Spain': 'the conscious acceptance of guilt in the fact of murder'. Willing the end – resistance to fascism – also appears to mean willing the means, commensurate with the evil manifested. Many writers in the 1930s took upon themselves the task of shaking off the lethargy of the inter-war years (summarised in the wonderful title of the book about the period that Robert Graves co-authored, *The Long Weekend*) and reasserting the will-power of the civilised world; 'the will' is of course a theme of the 1930s which is prefigured in *Mario*. With the polarising of politics in that decade because of the rise of extreme right-wing mass movements, the most humane of writers drifted in desperation towards an absolutist stance. Auden himself, Koestler, Sartre, Brecht, all embrace extreme and violent left-wing politics in defence of the 'good'.

These attitudes are anathema to an artist like Thomas Mann and the kind of creative imagination which lives off ambiguities, not absolutes; which enjoys the complexities of Cipolla's performance, and loses itself in them. Mann may be immune to the dubious forces he describes, but he cannot expose them without revealing a good deal about himself, for they correspond to the darker side of his artistic nature.

The irony which places a distance between the author and his public has been read as a kind of inauthenticity, even hypocrisy. Such charges were given added credence with the publication of Mann's private diaries and their confirmation of his covert homosexuality. His self-imposed role as a representative of 'white European *bürgerlich* masculine culture'[8] nowadays provokes resistance not only on account of its narcissism, not to speak of its eurocentric and sexist cultural self-assurance, but also because of its clear contrast to revelations about the 'private', and therefore the 'real', Thomas Mann. The fashionable view need not be accepted uncritically. Certainly, from the time of his vast First World War essay, *Reflections of an Unpolitical Man* (1918), we have the spectacle of a very private ('unpolitical') person who chooses to go public. After the publication of the essay, Mann could never again revert to being merely a private citizen. But it is precisely the balance between private and public aspects of his writings that is so fascinating. *Mario* is a case in point.

There are public political morals to be drawn from *Mario and the Magician*, though they remain implicit. They are threefold, and the third is the most important and the least explicit: first, you cannot rely on rescue (hero-figures such as Mario will not always come forward); second, it is never too early to call a halt to the process of entanglement ('we should have left Torre after experiencing its xenophobic atmosphere, then we would never have been exposed to Cipolla'); and third, reason and passion ought to augment each other in resistance to political evil. The reader has to work to extrapolate these lessons from the novella. They are not spelt out, for the story of Mario contains more introspection on Mann's part than direct political analysis. But the interrogation of fascism may be all the better for being in part a self-analysis. Thomas Mann once again emerges as representative.

## NOTES

1 Henry Cowper *et al.*, *World War I and its Consequences* (Buckingham: Open University Press, 1990), p. 165.
2 *Thomas Mann: Two Stories* (Oxford: Blackwell, 1957), ed. W. Witte, p. 118, n. 43.
3 On narrative distance, see David Turner, 'Balancing the Account: Thomas Mann's *Unordnung und frühes Leid* ', *German Life and Letters* 52 (1999), 43–57.
4 John Gunther, *Inside Europe* (London: Hamilton, 1936), p. 35.
5 These observations about Mussolini are taken from Denis Mack Smith, *Mussolini* (London: Weidenfeld and Nicolson, 1981).
6 Ibid., pp. 151, 168, 127.
7 See A. F. Bance, '*Der Tod in Venedig* and the Triadic Structure', *Forum for Modern Language Studies* 8 (1972), 148–61 (p. 153).
8 Michael Minden (ed.), *Thomas Mann* (London and New York: Longman, 1995), p. 22. See Minden's nuanced reflections on this question, pp. 21–2.

## FURTHER READING

Bance, Alan, 'The Narrator in Thomas Mann's *Mario und der Zauberer*', *Modern Language Review* 82 (1987), 382–98
Bolkosky, Sidney, 'Thomas Mann's *Disorder and Early Sorrow*: The Writer as Social Critic', *Contemporary Literature* 22 (1981), 218–33

# 8

JUDITH RYAN

# *Buddenbrooks*: between realism and aestheticism

One of the most astute early reviews of *Buddenbrooks* was written by a young poet who was Thomas Mann's exact contemporary, Rainer Maria Rilke. What strikes today's reader is not so much Rilke's positive response to the novel as his perceptive grasp of the inner tensions that give *Buddenbrooks* its unique and innovative character. Rilke describes Mann as having reconceptualised the traditional role of chronicler in a modern way. At the same time as Mann builds up an increasing sense of material concreteness in what he depicts, he also works over the surface of his presentation with 'a hundred furrows', producing an unusual richness of detail. While avoiding authorial intrusions in which 'a supercilious writer bends down to the ear of a supercilious reader', Mann maintains a narrative objectivity that nonetheless gets us involved, just as if we were reading our own family documents, discovered 'in some secret drawer'.[1] Rilke's review, published in 1902, recognises fundamental aspects of the position of *Buddenbrooks* in the first year of the twentieth century. Rilke is fully aware of the novel's double character as a record of an actually experienced reality and a carefully constructed and intricately developed work of art. He assesses quite deftly what has since been called Mann's 'irony': his ability to hold sympathy and critical distance in balance.

From today's vantage point, we might say that Mann's *Buddenbrooks* occupies a crucial place in the transition from realism to aestheticism. To be sure, the two movements were less fundamentally opposed than the terms we use for them suggest. Realism, especially as practised by Flaubert and his German counterpart Fontane, was far from a straightforward representation of external reality. In all of its many forms, European realism, ostensibly an objective mode of presentation, was sensitive to the idea that reality can only be perceived from a particular point of view. Realism also depended heavily on the use of significant detail, chips of reality that serve in the first instance to build up the materiality of what is presented, but also, through repetition and variation in the course of the narrative, become invested with symbolic meaning. Descriptions of costume, interior decor, and outdoor settings, but also characteristic gestures and repeated turns of phrase, were particularly favoured by the realists as they worked to create a thick accretion of detail. The prominence of pictorial elements in realist works paved the way for aestheticism, with its love of decoration and ornament. Many descriptive passages in realist novels, notably those of Flaubert, can be read as early forms of aestheticism. By the same token, aestheticism itself was not a one-dimensional movement, despite its emphasis on intricately beautiful surfaces. From the beginning, the aestheticist movement contained within itself a strong self-critical streak, an awareness that the purely decorative could lead dangerously away from practical reality: Joris-Karl Huysmans's *A rebours* [*Against the Grain*] (1884) is a good example of this self-critique at work. The dialectical relationship between realism and aestheticism is brilliantly exploited by Thomas Mann in *Buddenbrooks*, with its accurate depiction of a North German Hansa town (Lübeck, though the name is never actually mentioned) in the course of the nineteenth century, and its close attention to the way in which aesthetic vogues infiltrate its citizens' otherwise largely mercantile lives.

The social, economic and historical reality that underlies *Buddenbrooks* is Germany from 1835 to 1877, the years in which the novel begins and ends. In addition to indicating these specific dates, *Buddenbrooks* allows glimpses of the German revolution of 1848 and the introduction of general male suffrage in Lübeck; the appointment of Otto von Bismarck as Prussian chancellor in 1862 and his promulgation of pragmatic politics known as *Realpolitik*; the ending of Danish sovereignty over Schleswig-Holstein in 1864 and the consequent greater participation of towns like Lübeck in German economic prosperity; the Austro-Prussian war of 1866 which caused soldiers to be billeted in places like Lübeck; the controversy about whether Lübeck should join the North German Customs Union; the early emergence of colonialist aspirations well before the founding of a German overseas empire in 1884; the rise of German industrialism including the expanding importance of railroad and postal systems; increasing modernisation charted by the shift from oil lamps to gas lighting and finally to electricity; and a shift in educational values from traditional humanistic disciplines to the more practically oriented *Realschule*. While *Buddenbrooks* can be read without special knowledge of these historical, economic and social developments – the more so because they are cunningly relegated to what at first glance appears to be the 'background' of the story – the symbolic network set up by the narrative comes into sharper relief when these events are brought into play.[2] In this respect, *Buddenbrooks* resembles Zola's *Nana* (1880), in which the French Second Empire and the preparations for the Franco-Prussian War form the backdrop for a fictive figure, Nana, who at first appears to be the object of socio-psychological study but ultimately becomes a kind of allegory for the period as a whole. 'Background' and 'foreground' relate similarly in *Buddenbrooks*. History is both the setting for the *Buddenbrooks* family and the larger complex for which the family stands (the novel's title, by the way, should properly be rendered in English as *The Buddenbrooks*).

Thomas Mann himself claimed that *Buddenbrooks* was 'the only naturalist novel in Germany' (XII, 89). What he meant was not the kind of naturalism that sought its interest in characters from the lower social classes, as in Gerhart Hauptmann's novella *Bahnwärter Thiel* (1888), but rather that naturalism which, in the wake of the French diarists and novelists Jules and Edmond de Goncourt, based its narratives upon actual observation. In the case of the Goncourt brothers, Edmond was the one who did the 'naturalising' (a word formed in parallel to 'botanising' – gathering botanical specimens on rambles through the countryside). It involved mingling with ordinary people, listening to their conversations and stories, observing their behaviour almost in the manner of an anthropologist, and keeping careful notes on everything seen, heard, encountered. The Goncourts were deeply interested in human psychology. They believed that this kind of observation could provide new and more accurate insight into the workings of characteristic personality types. They called the material they collected 'documents humains' ('human documents'). While working on the early versions of *Buddenbrooks*, Thomas Mann had been reading the Goncourts, in particular their novel *Renée Mauperin* (1864).[3] Though Mann did not actually do much 'naturalising' to accumulate the basic information for *Buddenbrooks*, he did collect a good deal of material in the form of family documents and letters, stories and anecdotes about relatives. These included a 28-page document written by his sister, Julia Mann, about one of their aunts, and some historical and economic information provided by his cousin Marty.[4] In this sense, Mann could claim, with good justification, that his novel was grounded in empirical reality, on 'human documents' just as firmly based in real life as those of the Goncourt brothers.

The most extensive documentary evidence Mann used, his sister's information about Elisabeth Haag-Mann, became the basis for one of the central figures in the novel, Antonie (Tony) Buddenbrook. While the narrative covers four generations of the Buddenbrook family, the main emphasis is placed on three siblings from the third generation – Thomas, Christian and Tony – and one child from the fourth – Thomas's son, Hanno. The story of Tony Buddenbrook forms in many ways the narrative backbone of the novel. *Buddenbrooks* begins when she is eight and ends when she is fifty; she is a key figure in both the opening and closing scenes of the book.

Although many readers find their sympathies most absorbingly engaged by Thomas and Hanno, and few will forget the appealingly comic figure of Christian, Tony is a crucial figure, no less important to *Buddenbrooks* than her two brothers.[5] The siblings form, as it were, a triple-souled complex at the very heart of the novel. Most readers grasp intuitively that Thomas, Christian and Hanno derive in part from Thomas Mann's ironic perception of his own psychology, but Tony, too, bears features of her creator. To put it in more literary terms, she is an heiress to Flaubert's claim, 'Madame Bovary, c'est moi.' Even though she does not give her name to the novel in which she appears, Tony belongs to a series of central women figures from the realist-naturalist tradition: Balzac's Eugénie Grandet, Flaubert's Emma Bovary, the Goncourts' Germinie Lacerteux, Zola's Nana, Fontane's Effi Briest. In part, the proliferation of female protagonists in nineteenth-century novels reflects a readership that consisted mainly of women; but it also reflects an increasing interest on the part of male novelists in the challenge of representing the psychology of the opposite sex. Tony's portrayal owes much to the Goncourts' Renée Mauperin, with her lively personality and intense devotion to her father. Tony is, in fact, a much more complex character than has previously been recognised. A good deal of this complexity is doubtless due to the Goncourts' theory that individual psychology was never either simple or consistent.

Like the Goncourts, Mann begins his novel in the middle of a conversation. This contributes to what the naturalists called the 'slice of life' effect, as if the events narrated are part of a larger continuum that exists before and after the reader is privileged to participate in it. As in the Goncourts' *Renée Mauperin*, which opens with a dialogue between a young man and woman who turn out to be swimming in a river, there is a touch of lightness and humour in the first scene of *Buddenbrooks*, where Tony's grandfather, old Johann Buddenbrook, teasingly quizzes the exuberant little girl on her knowledge of the catechism. Renée, the unconventional young woman of the Goncourts' river overture to *Renée Mauperin*, is more than superficially a model for the rambunctious Tony Buddenbrook. Though Hugh Ridley mentions 'obvious affinities' between the two characters, notably the 'pertness which always bounces back',[6] there is another crucial aspect of the two figures that critics seem to have overlooked: their psychological androgyny. Unlike her older sister, who fills the traditional female gender role to perfection, Renée regrets that young women cannot remain 'garçons' for life.[7] As a young girl, Tony alarms her family by her wild and uncontrollable behaviour, which includes the kind of practical jokes more traditionally played by schoolboys. Even the grown-up Tony Buddenbrook is given to cheeky remarks and prankish behaviour. While courting her, the fun-loving

Alois Permaneder affectionately refers to her as 'a liaber Kerl' ('a dear chap') (1, 333). As young women, both Renée Mauperin and Tony Buddenbrook behave outrageously – and distinctly childishly – in their attempts to discourage unwanted suitors. Impertinent and unladylike turns of phrase come readily to the lips of both young women. Even in her forties, Tony affectionately addresses her former nurse Ida Jungmann as an 'altes Möbel' ('old stick of furniture') (1, 460) and her cousin Klothilde as a 'camel' (1, 757), both terms the sort of slangy expressions one might expect from a schoolboy. Renée is described by an early critic as a 'girl Amazon',[8] and Tony, during the tirade in which she convinces her brother that she should get divorced from Permaneder, strikes 'a warrior-like pose' (1, 386), which, ridiculous though it is on one level, has a certain persuasive charm on another. Like the Goncourts before him, Thomas Mann succeeds brilliantly in representing the seductive effects of a female figure who is at once a tomboy and a virago.

Extending the Goncourts' theories about the fundamental instability of human character, Mann uses Tony Buddenbrook to explore problems of individual identity. Repeated references throughout the novel to Tony's childish and easily provoked tears suggest continuity of character; her changes of name and role during her two marriages and that of her daughter, Erika, which Thomas wittily terms Tony's 'third marriage' (1, 447), suggest discontinuity. When the narrator refers to her as 'Madame Grünlich' or 'Madame Permaneder', we can be sure that Tony has embarked on one of her role-playing episodes where she appears as a married woman of some importance and no little haughtiness. The name-plate Tony puts up outside the apartment she buys after her mother's death elides the fact of her two divorces by falsely identifying herself as a widow (1, 608). The narrative almost flaunts the interplay between the Tony who is always, in the last analysis, herself, and the Tony who likes to present herself in a sequence of different social roles.

The various aspects of Tony's personality find reflections in other figures in the novel. Although the members of the family are clearly distinct, individualised characters, they also have much in common. The clashes among the three siblings Thomas, Tony and Christian are due as much to their similarities as to their differences. Without hidden affinities, they would be less repelled by one another's weaknesses. With Thomas and her father, Tony shares pride in family tradition; with Christian, high-spirited mockery; with old Johann Buddenbrook, distrust of conventional religion; with her mother, a concern for outward self-presentation. The tomboyish girl who was the young Tony is reversed in the girlish boy who is Hanno. While in one sense the family is the concept that links all these figures, in another, Tony is frequently the glue that holds the action together.

Throughout the novel we can observe Mann working hard to develop Tony as a multifaceted figure driven by fundamentally conflicting motivations that she herself scarcely understands. At one point, the novel presents an extraordinary assessment of Tony's psychology. Adopting a position close to that of Thomas Buddenbrook, the narrator sees her talkativeness as the personality trait that has freed her from the nervous crises that plague her brothers. Far from silently accepting misfortunes and grievances, she has never hesitated to put her feelings into words: 'Nothing unspoken gnawed at her; no mute experience weighed on her' (1, 670–1). This is a remarkable diagnosis, especially as the three years of *Buddenbrooks*' gestation (1897–1900) precede Freud's first independent publication and the fuller development of his ideas about the talking cure. Through this analysis of the mainspring of Tony's psychological resilience, the psychologising gaze of the Goncourts finds its first truly modern successor.[9]

At the same time as he depended on close observation of real human beings, Mann continued in *Buddenbrooks*, as he had done in his early short stories, to draw heavily on other works of literature. Some of these are specifically mentioned in the novel, others remain more discreetly in the background. The aesthetic construct he creates is a highly self-conscious one. The clearest example of this effect is contained in the description of the stories invented by Hanno's friend Kai. Inspired by fairy tales read aloud by Hanno's nurse, Kai's stories 'gained interest by the fact that they were not entirely built in the air, but took their point of departure in reality and put this in a strange and mysterious light' (1, 520). In a similar manner, *Buddenbrooks* finds its starting-point in factual information about nineteenth-century Lübeck and in autobiographical experiences of Mann himself, yet fashions these into an entirely new, aesthetically transformed composite. The relation between 'reality' and 'fantasy' is a central theme of the novel, developed in such a way as to give neither side primacy over the other. Mann's dazzling ability to keep the two opposites in counterpoise lies at the very heart of his enterprise. It also accounts for a division of opinion among its critics, including not only its first readers (with the exception of Rilke, who recognised its delicate balance), but also more recent scholarship.[10] T. J. Reed is not wrong to say that Mann first began to find his feet as a writer when he decided to draw more openly upon autobiographical material;[11] but neither is Lilian R. Furst when she claims that the Lübeck of *Buddenbrooks* is less a specific historical and geographical location than 'the mind's own place'.[12] Furst calls the two poles of this opposition 'referentiality' and 'textuality'. Although the novel itself uses more everyday terms to identify this polarity, it continually draws attention to the reciprocal relationship between the world of the factual and the world of the text: to the way, in other words, in which creative imagination gives shape to individual perceptions and understandings of reality.

In depicting the Buddenbrooks' world, Mann is torn between two different nineteenth-century approaches to observing empirical reality: one which, in the tradition of the Goncourts' naturalising, might be called 'clinical', and another which, following the emerging psychological theories of the 1880s and 1890s, might be called 'introspective'.[13] The fulcrum shifts somewhat as the novel proceeds, first giving more weight to the clinical observation of psychological types such as the hypochondriac Christian Buddenbrook, then tipping the balance more towards the introspective in its analyses of Thomas and Hanno Buddenbrook towards the end. Throughout the novel, however, the narrative point of view is constantly sliding from inside to outside and back again. Sometimes we see the characters grouped as if they were figures on a stage, at other times we view events partially through the registering mind of one or another character. Frequently the perspective is that of an anonymous 'one' that mediates subtly between reader and characters.

Interior and sometimes exterior scenes are not only settings for the action, but also objective correlatives, symbolic near-equivalents to the psychological make-up of the predominating character in a given episode. The 'Säulenhalle' ('pillared room') in the old house, with its white figures of antique gods against sky-blue wallpaper, represents the survival of classical tradition into modern times and is thus not accidentally the locus of important family occasions, such as Tony's first marriage. The rocks by the sea in Travemünde, where Morten Schwarzkopf often sits alone but where he also tells Tony Buddenbrook about the revolution and his student fraternity's support of its ideals, become a shorthand reference for independence and freedom in Tony's mental vocabulary. The 'Penséezimmer' ('pansy room') in Grünlich's house, with its fashionable floral decoration, is the place where Tony first hears of Grünlich's bankruptcy ('pensée' means both pansy and thought). The source of the unfortunately named river Au (Thomas recalls that they had pinched each other as schoolboys in order to hint at the river's name, pronounced 'ow!', I, 348) forms a telling backdrop to the scene where Permaneder makes his awkward and ultimately disastrous proposal to Tony. The music room in Thomas Buddenbrook's house, with its music-making Cupid figures, suggests the power of the harmonious art in awakening sexual feelings: it is the place where Thomas's wife Gerda spends so much time playing duos with the rather suspect Lieutenant von Throta and where Hanno Buddenbrooks indulges in clearly erotic piano improvisations. And the chemistry classroom in Hanno's school, which looks more like a theatre auditorium and is used by the chemistry teacher 'to make a few explosions and coloured puffs of smoke' (I, 735), represents the uneasy mixture of intimidation and entertainment that characterises late nineteenth-century educational method. In these and many other instances, the boundary between historical or cultural observations, on the one hand, and symbolic representation, on the other, is dramatically broken down. Exterior and interior worlds, fact and fantasy, are so complexly interwoven that it is impossible to say where observation of the external world ends and introspective reflection begins.

This strategy of making the real symbolic and the symbolic real is supported by Thomas Mann's adaptation of the 'leitmotif' technique from Wagner's operas. In Wagner, specific musical phrases are consistently associated with particular characters, so that a certain melody can presage the appearance of the figure with whom it is linked. Furthermore, these phrases create a dual optic that allows the audience to glimpse the characters' hidden or subconscious motives and comments on the action as it takes place. Finally, the leitmotif technique, by creating complex links of sameness and difference between earlier and later parts of the text, enables time to be represented in a subtle and sophisticated way.[14] Thomas Mann was not the first novelist to adopt the technique for narrative purposes. In fact, his predecessor Fontane, who depicts contemporary debates about Wagner in several of his novels much as Thomas Mann does in the discussion between Gerda Buddenbrook and her piano accompanist Herr Pfühl (1, 498–9), makes extensive use of recurring details, gestures or phrases in his novels. In *Buddenbrooks*, the leitmotifs include the typical Buddenbrook hands with their long, fine fingers; the blue vein on Thomas's temple; the blue shadows around Gerda's eyes; the little trumpeting snorts Tony makes when she pronounces the names of her two despicable husbands; the nerve pains in Christian's left leg; Sesemi Weichbrodt's repeated injunction, 'Sei *glöcklich*, du *gutes* Kend' ('Be *happy*, you *dear* child'); Elisabeth Buddenbrook's reproving 'assez!' ('enough!') whenever conversation becomes too heated; and the way in which the condition of various characters' teeth is read as an indicator of their physical and mental health. The significant details of European realism, such as Emma's erotic licking of her pricked finger in *Madame Bovary*, become in Mann's *Buddenbrooks* an elaborate and carefully articulated system of shorthand signs that ingeniously bridge the gap between reality and fiction. In this way, the leitmotifs give the novel a symbolist aspect that goes beyond its realist or naturalist base.

Punctuated by leitmotifs, the novel also develops a more explicit and extensive probing of the problem of authenticity. Elisabeth Buddenbrook's reddish hair, first natural, then dyed with a subtle Parisian tincture, and finally (though no one can tell exactly when this occurs) replaced by an identical-looking wig, is just one of many motifs that examine the relation between the real and the fake. Grünlich's account books, good enough to be framed, as Tony's father thinks at first (1, 113), but ultimately exposed as fakes that 'mit der rauhen Wirklichkeit nicht völlig übereinstimmen' ('don't completely coincide with harsh reality') (1, 229), are another. Honey in the comb is 'a pure, natural product' (1, 123), Tony is told by the medical student Morten Schwarzkopf, and it follows that it must be good for your physical health. Yet Morten also recognises that the chemical formula for water would have to be considerably more complicated than $H_2O$ if it were to describe the natural, but not entirely pure water at the beach in Travemünde. Tony's mother's death cramps are mere reflexes, according to the family doctor, which make her appear to be in pain when she really isn't; yet the family members present note that she was clearly fully conscious (1, 566). How sincere is Morten Schwarzkopf when he kisses Tony's hands after she declares her love for him (1, 145)? Does his devotion equal that of Kai for Hanno, who kisses his friend's hands on the latter's deathbed (1, 758)? Why does Tony, who derives so much satisfaction from the entries she makes with her own hand in the family records, find Christian laughable when he says that 'one's hands feel content' after a satisfying day's work on correspondence and accounts in the offices of the family firm (1, 270)? The boundaries between authentic self-expression and theatrical exaggeration are very troubling.

Questions of honesty are bound up with the dilemma of authenticity, and they assume considerable importance within the business context of the family saga. The description of Hanno's schoolday makes abundantly clear that much success in the classroom is actually the result of cheating. When boys get good marks this way, everyone in the class feels that they have rightly deserved their success. When a pupil is caught out, the whole class feels that he is a blot on their escutcheon (1, 733). Christian Buddenbrook offends his brother by claiming that all businessmen cheat. Tony's first husband, Bendix Grünlich, not only faked his account books but also claimed to be hopelessly in love with Tony, when he was really enamoured of her money. Hugo Weinschenk, the man who marries Tony's daughter Erika, at first appears to be a model husband, but eventually has fits of temper during which he starts throwing crockery; ultimately, he goes to jail for embezzlement. Thomas, engaged in a questionable business deal involving some unharvested rye, feels that nature has played him a dirty trick when the grain is ruined by a hailstorm and he loses a substantial sum of money. Deceptive behaviour and cheating are interpreted positively or negatively according to the needs of the moment and the person who is doing the deceiving.

Tony Buddenbrook herself is an interesting case in this respect. Unlike her brother Christian, the consummate mimic, Tony has trouble disguising her emotions. When she thinks (mistakenly) that her father expects her to claim she loves Grünlich even in the face of his impending bankruptcy, her 'childishly dissimulating face' (I, 213) unwittingly gives her true feelings away. One of her letters home is so transparent that Thomas bursts out laughing as his mother reads it aloud; he claims that his sister is incapable of dissembling even when she wishes to do so (I, 310). Tony's parents reprimand her for displays of strong emotion; yet on at least one occasion – when she leaves her second husband, Permaneder – her brother Thomas regards her tempestuous departure as mere theatricality (I, 380). Indeed, a good deal of Tony's life is spent performing the role she believes her family and the bourgeois society of Lübeck expect of her.

Many critics have commented on the motifs of acting and the theatre that permeate the novel. Christian, with his gifts for comic mimicry and his love of theatre, is the main bearer of this theme. His grandfather calls him a monkey; later, Hanno and his classmates are required to memorise an English poem in which a monkey is addressed as a 'merry punchinello' (I, 739). In Christian's depiction of the horrible consequences that might result from swallowing a peach kernel, reality and performance intersect uneasily: acting out what *might* happen, he cuts such a true-to-life picture that his mother and the nursemaid jump up in fright: 'Heavens, Christian, you haven't swallowed it?!' (I, 70). And although Christian is just putting on an act, for a long time he actually doesn't eat peaches any more.

For Christian, the inauthentic and the theatrical are linked with the exotic. Yet however inflated his adventure yarns may be, the overseas world is very much part of Christian's real business experience. In this respect, he stands for German colonial aspirations in their early phase. When he returns from an eight-year period in South America, his suit has a tropical look to it and he brings with him the bony proboscis of a swordfish and a large piece of sugar cane (I, 258–9). Late in life, before he is finally committed to a mental hospital, he briefly tries to learn Chinese. This is presented as a foolish and unproductive whim, but we should not forget that trading with the Far East was very much a part of German business life at the time. When the Buddenbrooks' old house has to be sold, the real estate agent scornfully asks if they expect 'a nabob from India' to show up offering to pay their rather stiff asking price (I, 593); but in fact, the house is bought by Hermann Hagenström, a man who has gained his wealth by means of colonial trading (I, 597). The exotic overseas world, which staid bourgeois tradition regards as the product of an overheated imagination fed by too many adventure stories, is in fact an intimate part of nineteenth-century business and political life.

Thomas's own crisis of nerves is brought on by a feeling that his identity as a businessman is a fake and that his existence – not unlike Christian's – is 'no longer anything but an actor's' (1, 614). A joke begins to circulate that Thomas Buddenbrook's presence at the stock exchange is 'merely decorative' (1, 611). This linkage of his apparently solid bourgeois self with the theatrical and the aesthetic shatters Thomas's confidence. Is his position at work and in society merely a kind of sham? In this moment of profound doubt about the stability of individual identity falls his chance encounter with a book by Schopenhauer. Although this episode is based on Thomas Mann's own involvement with Schopenhauer's philosophy during the period when he was writing the later parts of the novel, it would not be accurate to turn Thomas's response to Schopenhauer into the master statement of *Buddenbrooks* itself. It matters little whether Thomas Buddenbrook understands the philosopher's writings correctly or incorrectly. Much more important is the fact that Thomas uses his reading of the speculative philosopher, rather than the more worldly, sceptical rationality of his grandfather Johann Buddenbrook, to counter his temptation to put an end to his own life. In this respect, Thomas exemplifies a central dilemma of nineteenth-century positivism. If we can no longer believe in traditional religion – as Johann Buddenbrook more than merely implies in his teasing of young Tony about the catechism – what reason can we give for deciding not to put an end to life when it becomes hard to bear? The question was one that Zola had already explored, in explicit reference to Schopenhauer, in his novel *La Joie de vivre* [*The Joy of Living*] (1884). *La Joie de vivre* depicts the relation between a melancholy young man devoted to Schopenhauer's philosophy and his optimistic, life-giving cousin. After struggling with Schopenhauer's philosophy himself, Zola had come to believe that his contemporaries, among whom Guy de Maupassant was particularly known as an ardent Schopenhauerian, needed to break their attachment to pessimistic beliefs. Thomas Buddenbrook derives hope from Schopenhauer's belief in an abstract 'life energy' that permeates all life forms and continues to exist beyond the limits of individual lives. Thomas's disappointment with his sensitive, sickly and timid son Hanno fades into irrelevance for him in the face of Schopenhauer's claim that each individual lives on in the life force itself:

> I don't need a son! . . . Where will I be when I am dead? But it is so brilliantly clear, so overwhelmingly simple! I will be in all those who have ever said 'I', in those who say it now and will say it in the future: *but especially in those who say it more fully, more strongly, more joyously.* (1, 657)

Thomas's ecstatic response to this conception is no less extravagant than Hanno's enthusiasm for Wagner; the description of Thomas's philosophical meditation is stylistically similar to that of Hanno's musical fantasies. Mann presents Thomas's thoughts about Schopenhauer in what is known as 'free indirect style' or 'narrated monologue',[15] which allows us to empathise with Thomas while not entirely losing our ability to take a step back from the overemotional perspective which even he himself recalls, the next morning, 'with a slight feeling of embarrassment about yesterday's mental extravagances' (I, 659).

Thomas Mann's original title for the novel was 'Abwärts' ('Downwards') – a title that, for his contemporaries, would clearly have alluded to aestheticist decadence, especially as depicted by Huysmans.[16] The opening scene of *Buddenbrooks*, in which Tony's recitation of the catechism is compared to a descent down the snow-covered Jerusalem Hill on a sled, functions as a narrative intimation of the downward movement of the family's history. The decline of the family is continually linked with motifs from 'decadent' literature of the late nineteenth century, such as the overpowering scent of flowers after Elisabeth Buddenbrook's death (I, 588).

The downward movement traced by *Buddenbrooks* is configured on one level as a decline in physical and mental health, on another as a complex shift in values. Conventional religion, family traditions, speculative philosophy, mythology, scepticism and economic pragmatism are the main components in the novel's portrayal of this shift. Mann is careful to avoid representing value systems in any simplistic way. It would be reductive to claim that religion is supplanted by scepticism or family traditions by economic pragmatism. Rather, these various value and belief systems are intricately interconnected. Sesemi Weichbrodt, firm believer in the Christian religion and life after death, is repeatedly attacked by rationalist thoughts against which she struggles valiantly (I, 87); and at the end of the novel she is depicted, not without irony, as a defiant prophetess (I, 759). As we have seen, the bourgeois family man, Thomas, ultimately succumbs to the temptations of speculative philosophy. When Grünlich comments on the religious associations of the first names of Tony's father, Johann, and her brother Christian, the reader is left to recall that her other brother, Thomas, bears the name of a doubter. Tony's own full name, Antonie, vacillates amusingly between pagan and Christian associations: we may think of the great lover Mark Antony, on the one hand, or of the resister of temptations, Saint Antony of Egypt. Either allusion seems ridiculous in connection with Tony Buddenbrook.

Tony despises conventional religion, mocking her mother's devotion to family prayers and the constant hovering of various ministers. One of the practical jokes she plays consists in serving a visiting pastor a North German vegetable and bacon soup palatable only to those who have been brought up on it. Tony is the one who expresses doubt, at the end of the novel, in an afterlife when we shall meet again. Yet Tony is far from being a rationalist. She believes, rather, in an ill-defined and unfathomable fate that descends without warning upon innocent victims. This mysterious force is represented by formulations such as 'something horrible, something terrifying' (I, 433);[17] she believes that dreadful events just descend upon her without clear reason (I, 369, 389). A humorous twist on Tony's self-conception as a victim of fate is given when she is shown in the pose of an 'ecstatic martyr' (I, 481) while trying to hold up the enormous memorial tablet at the firm's centenary celebrations. Tony's belief in inexplicable fate is accompanied by a carefully orchestrated complex of references to the fates of classical mythology. The three unmarried Buddenbrook ladies, Friederike, Henriette and Pfiffi, form a comic representation of the three fates,[18] and the hunchbacked Sesemi Weichbrodt, the similarly hunched real-estate agent Gosch and the nursery-rhyme figure of the hunchback mannekin who so upsets little Hanno are representations of the diabolical. So are the 'shortened nerves' in Christian's left leg (the devil is traditionally figured as limping). A light-hearted mingling of various forms of belief throughout the novel begins with the poem Hoffstede reads at the grandparents' dinner in honour of their move into their new house, a poem in which Johann Buddenbrook is referred to as Vulcan and Elisabeth as Venus Anadyomene. This theme emerges again when Thomas's bride Gerda is described as 'Hera and Aphrodite, Brünnhilde and Melusine in one' (I, 295). Yet, as even Thomas admits, the splendid Gerda is emotionally perhaps a little cold, and her breast shines through her lace bodice 'like marble' (I, 306), as if she were one of the white goddess figures in his grandparents' house or the white caryatids on the front of his own house. In elaborating this network of allusions to classical and Germanic mythology, Mann develops a central theme of his social criticism in *Buddenbrooks*.

The conflict between religion and mythology was a topic that had already been explored in Fontane's *Effi Briest* (1895), to which *Buddenbrooks* responds in multiple ways. Effi's preference for mythology over religion appears to her contemporaries and herself as an outward sign of her lack of a moral anchor. Hanno Buddenbrook's interest in mythology (he receives a book of Greek mythology as a Christmas present, I, 541) and his assimilation of it to the imaginative and aesthetic realms from which he draws what slight vitality he has, makes him a secret successor to Effi Briest.

When Richard Sheppard describes *Buddenbrooks* as a combination of 'realism plus mythology', he deftly locates the novel's curious position on the brink between the realist novel of the nineteenth century and the 'mythic novel' of twentieth-century modernism. Yet there is a crucial difference between *Buddenbrooks* and, for example, Joyce's *Ulysses*. By constructing the chapters of his novel so that they relate in certain ways to familiar episodes from Homer's *Odyssey*, Joyce encourages us to explore the distance separating the modern world from that of Homer; but his protagonist is not himself aware of the ironic connections the novel draws between his own wanderings and those of Ulysses. In *Buddenbrooks*, by contrast, mythologies classical and Germanic are often present in the minds of the characters, who use light-hearted, bantering allusions to this material as part of their communicative arsenal. At the same time, mythological allusions are also a central component of the narrator's collusion with his readers. In this layer of Mann's novel, the ironic relationship between characters and mythology takes on a darker aspect. As Sheppard has persuasively shown, Gerda appears as a cross between the Magna Mater or Great Mother and the Nordic earth-goddess, and the triads of women knitting or sewing suggest the Fates in classical mythology and the Norns in Scandinavian mythology.[19] *Buddenbrooks* is permeated by complex suggestions of secret powers, more of them malevolent than otherwise. In *Ulysses*, myth primarily underpins the macrostructure of the novel. In *Buddenbrooks*, it is in equal measure part of the macro- and the microstructure. Indeed, multiply conflated mythologies form an intricately interwoven pattern in the novel's very fabric. Mythological leitmotifs and allusions are particularly useful to Thomas Mann because of their ambivalent status: conjuring up classical tradition and the foundations of humanistic education, on the one hand, and appropriated by current fashion, on the other. Wagner's Germanic mythology functions as a switching point between the old and the new.

Gerda's debate with Herr Pfühl about Wagner articulates a fundamental issue in *Buddenbrooks*: the question of 'morality in art' (I, 499). By focusing the discussion on music, Mann is able to move immediately beyond simplistic views that locate the moral aspect of artworks in their thematic statements. Gerda and Pfühl differ in their judgements of Wagner, in large part because Gerda admires the emotional expressiveness and musical daring of *Tristan*, whereas Pfühl sees value only in certain parts of the *Meistersinger* (I, 499). Both believe, however, that ideology and form are closely connected, possibly even essentially identical. Pfühl sees Wagner's music as the end of morality in art because it is 'chaos! . . . demagogy, blasphemy, and insanity! . . . perfumed smoke with flashes of lightning in it!' (I, 498). Gerda argues that Beethoven, whose music Pfühl admires, had been seen as equally chaotic and unintelligible by his contemporaries; 'and even Bach, for heaven's sake, was reproached for lack of harmony and clarity!' (I, 499). Ironically, Pfühl is ultimately won over, not by the clear light of reason, but by his own unconscious emotional affinities with Wagner's music.

The puzzling relation between morals and aesthetics is explored from the very opening scene of the novel, in which Tony's recital of the catechism is counterpointed with descriptions of her grandmother's elegantly appointed sitting room and Tony's own delicate features and shot-silk dress (I, 9).

Numerous details throughout the novel support this interweaving of the moral and the aesthetic. The twin descendants of Paul Gerhardt, writer of a much anthologised poem of evening prayer, are sternly reproached by Elisabeth Buddenbrook for their unfortunate way of dressing: 'God sees into our hearts, but your clothes are not very neat... One must maintain self-respect' (1, 280). Given that the Buddenbrooks are Protestants, this emphasis on outward appearance is somewhat shocking, especially in the mouth of Tony's profoundly religious mother. A different kind of shock effect occurs when Hanno incorporates a childlike prayer motif and chords reminiscent of religious chorales into an aesthetic, erotic and even diabolical musical fantasy (1, 748–9). At its conclusion, Hanno's improvisation shifts from a minor to a major key, fading away wistfully (1, 750), indicating that formal resolution and moral temptation, optimism and melancholy can co-exist.

A long tradition in the novel consists of self-reflective moments in which readers' empathy with the protagonist is understood as a possible source of moral endangerment. Emma Bovary, in Flaubert's novel, brings about her own downfall in part by identifying too closely with the heroines of the Romantic novels she reads. Fontane's protagonist, Effi Briest, continues this tradition. Thomas Mann uses his famous narrative irony to address the problem of identification and its moral consequences for the reader. At times we laugh at Tony, at other times we empathise with her. One strategy by which the narrator achieves this double optic is his adaptation of a phrase from *Effi Briest*: 'arme Effi' ('poor Effi') (Chapter 36). Repeatedly, the narrative of *Buddenbrooks* is interrupted by the words, 'arme Tony!', an exclamation that calls upon our sympathy with the character while at the same time interrupting the flow of the story with what is clearly a rhetorical and (even in 1901) a rather old-fashioned device. To take a very different example, the chapter that describes typhus in the starkly objective tone of a medical textbook nonetheless calls forth tears from the reader, who knows very well that it is Hanno's death that is really being described. The subjective-objective or inside-outside narrative stance of *Buddenbrooks*, which Furst describes as 'dyadic' or 'two-pronged',[20] is the primary strategy Mann uses to guard the reader against simply being carried along with the story. In calling upon us to identify ourselves with but also distance ourselves from the fictional figures, Mann mediates between the seductive powers of the aesthetic and the need for moral reflection.

In its presentation of this dilemma, *Buddenbrooks* not only engages with one of the most urgent problems for writers at the turn into the twentieth century, but also recapitulates the complex ethical debacles of the later nineteenth century. The divide between religion and scepticism, metaphysics and positivism, humanistic values and economic pragmatism was by no means easy to negotiate for thinkers and writers of the period. In *Buddenbrooks*, Mann shows not only the struggle between individual positions, but also that within single individuals as they try to hold firm on the shifting moral terrain beneath their feet. The novel's easy narrative flow is deceptive; as Sheppard aptly puts it, there is 'a very different novel...behind *Buddenbrooks*' beguilingly realistic surface'.[21] After many decades in which critical attention has been drawn more frequently to the more reflective and abstract *The Magic Mountain* and *Doctor Faustus*, Thomas Mann's first novel is beginning to be rediscovered as a rich literary text that will repay further study. Behind the novel's detailed and precise representational mode, it already anticipates the more overtly mythic dimensions of Mann's later works. But neither element outweighs the other. *Buddenbrooks* holds the concrete and the abstract in brilliant equipoise. For this reason, it has much to offer our new sensitivity to how cultural realities intersect with aesthetic constructs. More than many of its contemporaries, *Buddenbrooks* is alert to the discursive and imaginative construction of culture. It does not simply transpose historical reality into narrative form; it shows this reality being created in human minds as they interact with others, driven at once by actual cultural history and by ambiguous, never fully articulable forces. Even its realist surface is far from straightforwardly referential in its conception. A theoretically sophisticated 'cultural studies' perspective may be the most productive way to view *Buddenbrooks* today. Such a perspective could comprehend how the novel registers nineteenth-century cultural realities while at the same time understanding them as imagined and constructed.

## NOTES

1 Rilke, 'Thomas Mann's "Buddenbrooks"', in *Sämtliche Werke*, ed. Ernst Zinn, 6 vols. (Frankfurt am Main: Insel, 1966), IV, 577–81.
2 For a helpful account, see Hugh Ridley, *Thomas Mann: 'Buddenbrooks'* (Cambridge; Cambridge University Press, 1987), pp. 10–19.
3 See T. J. Reed, *Thomas Mann: The Uses of Tradition* (Oxford: Clarendon Press, 1974), p. 72. See also Klaus Matthias, '*Renée Mauperin* and *Buddenbrooks*. Über eine literarische Beziehung im Bereich der Rezeption französischer Literatur durch die Brüder Mann', *Modern Language Notes* 90 (1975), 371–417.
4 See Ridley, *Mann: 'Buddenbrooks'*, p. 23.
5 My reading differs from that of Martin Travers, who claims that she 'plays a secondary role' (*Thomas Mann* (Basingstoke: Macmillan, 1992), p. 21). Ridley, while recognising her function as a 'measuring rod' (*Mann: 'Buddenbrooks'*, p. 10), nonetheless believes that 'Mann's major interest [among Thomas, Christian and Tony] clearly lies with Thomas' (p. 56). A stronger case for Tony's centrality is made by Eberhard Lämmert, 'Thomas Mann: *Buddenbrooks*', in Benno von Wiese (ed.), *Der deutsche Roman*, 2 vols. (Düsseldorf: Bagel, 1963), II, 190–233.

6 Ridley, *Mann: 'Buddenbrooks'*, p. 36. He also points out two important structural debts Mann owes to *Renée Mauperin*: the use of short chapters with witty breaks between them, and the technique of associating family history with national history (p. 25).

7 Edmond and Jules de Goncourt, *Renée Mauperin*, ed. Nadine Satiat (Paris: Flammarion, 1990), p. 54.

8 Jules Barbey d'Aurevilly, quoted in *Renée Mauperin*, p. 286.

9 Well known to Thomas Mann was another interface between literature and psychology, Paul Bourget's studies of literary works entitled *Essais de psychologie contemporaine* [*Essays in Contemporary Psychology*] (1883). Mann's predecessor in the German tradition of novel-writing, Theodor Fontane, also saw himself as a writer of 'psychograms'.

10 For an account of early responses to *Buddenbrooks*, see Ridley, *Mann: 'Buddenbrooks'*, pp. 94–103.

11 Reed, *Thomas Mann*, pp. 37–8.

12 'Re-reading *Buddenbrooks*', *German Life and Letters* 44 (1991), 317–29 (p. 323).

13 For more on the latter approach, see Judith Ryan, *The Vanishing Subject* (Chicago: University of Chicago Press, 1991), pp. 6–22.

14 See Hans Rudolf Vaget, 'Thomas Mann und Wagner. Zur Funktion des Leitmotivs in *Der Ring des Nibelungen* und *Buddenbrooks*', in Steven Paul Scher (ed.), *Literatur und Musik. Ein Handbuch zur Theorie und Praxis eines komparatistischen Grenzgebietes* (Berlin: Schmidt, 1984), pp. 326–48 (esp. pp. 330–2).

15 The latter term is Dorrit Cohn's. See her *Transparent Minds: Narrative Modes for Presenting Consciousness in Fiction* (Princeton: Princeton University Press, 1978), pp. 99–140.

16 Compare the title of the novel *A vau-l'eau* [*Downstream*] (1882). Elements of Huysmans' well-known aestheticist novel *A rebours* are present in the descriptions of interior decor, as well as in the intense way in which sensory impressions of all kinds are registered in *Buddenbrooks*. The dreadful experiences of Thomas and Hanno Buddenbrook at the dentist's office clearly owe much to the horrifying dental extraction scene in *A rebours*.

17 See Richard Sheppard's excellent analysis of this phenomenon in 'Realism plus Mythology: A Reconsideration of the Problem of "Verfall" in Thomas Mann's *Buddenbrooks*', *Modern Language Review* 89 (1994), 916–41.

18 See Sheppard, 'Realism plus Mythology', p. 921; Ridley describes them as "harpy-like" (*Mann: 'Buddenbrooks'*, p. 32).

19 Sheppard, 'Realism plus Mythology', pp. 920–3.

20 Furst, 'Re-reading *Buddenbrooks*', p. 327. Furst uses these terms in her discussion of the peculiar position of the novel's narrative mode between referentiality and textuality, but they are equally applicable to the issue of empathy and distance.

21 Sheppard, 'Realism plus Mythology', p. 918.

## FURTHER READING

Boa, Elizabeth, '*Buddenbrooks*: Bourgeois Patriarchy and *fin-de-siècle* Eros', in Michael Minden (ed.), *Thomas Mann*, Modern Literatures in Perspective (London and New York: Longman, 1995), pp. 125–42

Furst, Lilian R., 'Re-reading *Buddenbrooks*', *German Life and Letters* 44 (1991), 317–29

Moulden, Ken, and Gero von Wilpert (eds.), *Buddenbrooks-Handbuch* (Stuttgart: Kröner, 1988)

Nachman, Larry D., and Albert S. Braverman, 'Thomas Mann's *Buddenbrooks*: Bourgeois Society and the Inner Life', *Germanic Review* 45 (1970), 201–25

Ridley, Hugh, 'Nature and Society in *Buddenbrooks*', *Orbis Litterarum* 28 (1973), 138–47

*Thomas Mann: 'Buddenbrooks'* (Cambridge: Cambridge University Press, 1987)

*The Problematic Bourgeois: Twentieth-Century Criticism on Thomas Mann's 'Buddenbrooks' and 'The Magic Mountain'* (Columbia, SC: Camden House, 1994)

Sheppard, Richard, 'Realism plus Mythology: A Reconsideration of the Problem of "Verfall" in Thomas Mann's *Buddenbrooks*', *Modern Language Review* 89 (1994), 916–41

Swales, Martin, 'Symbolic Patterns or Realistic Plenty? Thomas Mann's *Buddenbrooks* and the European Novel', *Publications of the English Goethe Society* 60 (1989–90), 80–95

*Buddenbrooks: Family Life as the Mirror of Social Change* (New York: Twayne, 1991)

# 9

MICHAEL BEDDOW

## *The Magic Mountain*

In his impetuous youth, Gustav Aschenbach 'sent seed corn to the mill' (VIII, 454), but such rashness pales in comparison to how Thomas Mann, writing his Venetian novella, cast most of his own store of seed corn to the winds. The enumeration of Aschenbach's achievements (VIII, 450) assigns nearly all the projects in Mann's own notebooks and unfinished manuscripts to the accomplished oeuvre on which Aschenbach's fame rests. After that, visibly the same works could hardly appear in the bookstores under another author's name. The novella that depicts an aging writer's failing creativity dealt with its real author's mid-life creative crisis by forcing a clean sweep of plans which had long been engaging, but perhaps also blocking, his imaginative energies. That is the first thing that has to be recognised about the place of *The Magic Mountain* in Mann's literary biography: its themes and techniques emerged to fill the gap he had bravely, perhaps even desperately, created by letting Aschenbach complete his own previous plans. We, of course, now know that *Buddenbrooks* was not to be Mann's only work on the grand scale, but in July 1912, when *Death in Venice* appeared, he himself knew no such thing. What he did know was that the kind of fame he had tasted and longed to extend required more 'big' novels, and highly acclaimed ones at that, for its sustenance. He seems at first not to have anticipated that the 'novella' or 'story' which he first mentions in correspondence in the second half of 1913 as a 'humorous companion-piece' to *Death in Venice* would grow into one of the classic long novels of the twentieth century and would give a completely new dimension to his reputation, founding that view of him as an artist of encyclopaedic range which for the rest of his life he generally relished, though occasionally lamented.[1]

What turned the *The Magic Mountain* from a minor diversion into a major project was undoubtedly the outbreak of the Great War in August 1914, the controversies into which Mann was drawn by the hostilities, and his complex response to the defeat and the new republic which came in its wake. In a letter of May 1915, he refers to it for the first time as a 'novel'

(*DD* II, 455), and writing to the Swiss scholar Paul Amann he reveals that the work, though now termed just 'a longish story', is already something more ambitious than a comic 'chaser' to the serious fare of *Death in Venice*:

> Before the war I had begun a fairly long story, set in the Alps, in a TB sanatorium – a story whose basic intentions are pedagogical-political, where a young man is forced to come to grips with that most seductive of powers, death, and is conducted in a part comic, part gruesome way through the intellectual opposites of humanity and romanticism, progress and reaction, health and sickness, though more for the sake of exploring the ground and acquiring knowledge for knowledge's sake than with a view to taking a stand. The overall spirit is one of humorous nihilism, and if anything the balance is tipped to the side of sympathy with death.
>
> (to Amann, August 1915)

These remarks show that, even at this stage, the work had much of the ambivalence that has made it a source of unending contention among interpreters. There is an apparently clear declaration of a basic intention to educate and make political points, yet such an intention sits uneasily with the disavowal of taking a stand, which in its turn is hard to reconcile with the remark that the balance is tipped in a particular direction, even if that direction is characterised by a phrase that probably meant very little to the recipient of the letter, and which even the sender would only clarify to himself and, he hoped, to his readers, through many thousands of words still to be written in the decade to come.

By autumn 1915, the 'Hippe' section of Chapter 4 had been written and given public readings, but that, of course, did not take Mann very far into the work on its emerging new scale: in the current edition that section ends on page 175, with some 820 pages more to go. In October that year, he decided to lay *The Magic Mountain* aside in favour of the *Reflections of an Unpolitical Man*, the tortuous meditations on Germany and modernity which were to occupy him for most of the rest of the war. When he took up the manuscript again in April 1919, Mann still adhered to the 'anti-Western' and consequently anti-republican stance of the *Reflections*, and in diary entries of this period, occasional mentions of his problems with the advancing novel stand alongside remarks, like those recorded late in 1921, that he is reading the proofs for a second edition of the *Reflections* and reacting 'without anguish, indeed often with approval' to what he had written there (1 December 1921). Yet the following year, he wrote (in August) and delivered (in October) his speech 'On the German Republic', in which he astonished supporters and opponents alike by espousing democratic republicanism and warning sternly against reactionary irrationalism. This decisive, extremely public turn onto a political trajectory that was later to make Mann one of the most prominent and vehement opponents of National Socialism came during intensive work on what was originally to be published as the second volume of the novel (comprising Chapters 6 and 7), and we can get some measure of the way the work's compass was still expanding as he wrote from the fact that in May 1921, Mann had been reasonably confident that the manuscript would be finished by the same autumn (letter to Philipp Witkop, 21 May 1921, *DD* II, 464): in the event his estimate was some three years out, and it was September 1924 before the last words were written. The novel went on sale eight weeks later, since production of the earlier parts of the manuscript had been underway since mid-1923.

The chronology of its genesis indicates a second essential point about the place of *The Magic Mountain* in Mann's life-story. Irrespective of its literary quality, it is inestimably important as a cultural document, being one of the desperately few sources of insight we have into why Mann changed his political stance so dramatically. Anyone with the ambition to understand Germany in the twentieth century must be keen to have such insight, because of the historical significance of Mann's early and unexpected, but unfailingly sustained, commitment to the Weimar Republican cause and his implacable opposition from the very start to National Socialism and its precursors. Until he made his commitment to the new order, Mann had had impeccable patriotic and conservative credentials, having argued tirelessly and vehemently for the German war effort against both pacifists and supporters of the Entente. He viewed the Versailles settlement as a wanton humiliation far beyond what even a defeated nation had a right to expect and, being neither Jewish nor a communist, he had no particular vested interest in setting his face against the emergent radical right and urging others to do likewise. Hence the scandal that his biography represents to those who subscribe to the view that Hitler gained power by ingeniously exploiting the blinkered outlook of essentially well-meaning but politically naive elites. When all the respectable civil servants, academics and lawyers who had ignored, tolerated or even fostered Hitler's rise to power claimed they had been cruelly deceived, allegedly unable to perceive the Führer's true character and intentions until it was too late, Mann's biography testified that, deliberately or not, most of them were being less than truthful. If by 1923 someone so passionately and publicly committed to nationalist ideology could see the vast gulf between traditional German conservatism and the emergent far right and draw appropriate consequences, then countless others of similar background and outlook, including the former associates with whom Mann parted company, should have been able to do likewise, long before Hitler was allowed absolute power. That was the main source of the hostility with which Mann was treated by so many Germans after 1945, and a reason why Thomas

Mann studies took so long to establish themselves in the post-war Federal Republic. It may also be one explanation (alongside a *déformation professionelle* which places absolute value on pervasive ambivalence) why so many interpreters of the *The Magic Mountain* are determined either to deny that it offers any political message at all, or to argue that if political injunctions are indeed occasionally to be glimpsed, they are ironised to such an extent that only a hopelessly naive reader, whether in 1924 or our own day, could take them seriously.

When we first meet Hans Castorp, an 'ordinary young man' (III, 11) who is taking a short break between finishing his engineering examinations and starting his first job, it is August 1907. He will be kept at the forefront of our attention by an amiably garrulous narrator for close on a thousand pages and a narrated time-span of seven years, until he finally passes from view on a Flanders battlefield in 1914. Though his parents are long since dead, he stems from a well-connected family in an expanding city with a venerable past, a prosperous present and a promising future, as the weight of German trade and foreign policy shifts from the Baltic to the Atlantic seaboard, and he seems 'obviously on the way to important positions in life' (III, 54). By making him a citizen of Hamburg, a port that had expanded dramatically since 1871, largely at the expense of Lübeck, Mann associates Castorp with the relentlessly technocratic empire whose ascent had been portrayed in *Buddenbrooks* as poisoning the old ethos of Mann's home town. Castorp's choice of vocation aligns him, despite his personal distaste for excessive exertion, with the brash and pushful new order that let the Hagenströms' business put Hanno's family firm in the shade. It is not for nothing that the object of Castorp's great, if 'phlegmatic', passion (III, 824), Clawdia Chauchat, predicts (wrongly enough, as it turns out) that before long he will go back home 'pour aider à rendre son pays grand et puissant' ('to help make his country great and powerful') (III, 475): that is, after all, why the new Germany needs naval engineers, to construct a merchant and military marine that can wrest sea power from the British and rival them in imperial expansion. Tadzio had romped on the Venetian Lido wearing a sailor suit, like countless other children of the aristocracy and upper bourgeoisie in *fin-de-siècle* Central Europe, following a fashion quite deliberately set by Emperor Wilhelm II, who dressed his children to assert Germany's naval ambitions and geopolitical aims. Hans Castorp's reading material on the train to Davos, the subsequently much neglected *Ocean Steamships*, emphasises the dependence, for the time being, on English know-how; but he finds his military cousin occupying himself with Russian grammar, anticipating co-operation with a nation that might usefully keep the British occupied in the Pacific and on the Indian North-West Frontier while the German navy stretched its sinews in the Western seas.

Yet Castorp's life is on this track because it has been the line of least resistance. Early acquaintance with death, as first his mother, then his father and his grandfather died within little over a year, has lent him a measure of detachment from the work ethic, as well as bequeathing him a private income which means that he has no real need to earn his living, provided he is content with the modest degree of luxury he can afford in Switzerland as the Reichsmark appreciates against the franc. With hardly any recollection of his parents, his most influential memory from early childhood is the figure of his grandfather, who had to the last used his considerable political influence to fight the 'spirit of the new age' (III, 38). If he himself feels no particular inclination for such a fight, despite abiding and consciously cherished memories of his arch-conservative ancestor that were 'resistant to analysis' and 'purely and simply affirmative' (III, 39), it is because, as the narrator claims in a passage that Mann interpolated in 1919 when revising the sketch of Castorp's childhood first written some seven years earlier, people live not only their own personal lives as individuals, but also that of their 'epoch and contemporaries'. And if the general ethos of their age 'secretly reveals itself as devoid of hope, prospects or purpose' and offers 'no satisfactory answer to the question of what it is all for', the result will be 'a certain disabling effect' on all but the most robustly vital of individuals (III, 50). The addition of this passage is a marker of the process by which Hans Castorp's initial 'ordinariness' was made into something rather more complex than the original scheme of a comic counterpart to *Death in Venice* had envisaged. His self-satisfied social conformity and minimalist attitude to work are now attributed less to temperamental lassitude than to an obscure sense that what the world of his youth had to offer did not merit the full engagement of his qualities and talents. What was probably first conceived as amiable idleness was translated into a symptom of special, if as yet only subliminal, perceptiveness, so that by the time Mann realised he was indeed working on a novel, he had already given his harmlessly 'normal' engineer hero some of the essential traits of his artist-outsider figures, and allowed him the potential for spiritual explorations and adventures of a range and import that that would in the end rival, and even surpass, those of Aschenbach.

Shortly after adding this passage to the account of Castorp's childhood, Mann made a further change to the original stratum of his manuscript by shifting the childhood narrative from the first to the second chapter. This allowed him to begin the novel with Castorp's journey from Hamburg to Davos, and to present it in a way that anticipates Castorp's extraordinary 'development' in the 'new conditions' into which he is initiated. The account of the journey is rich in mythological and other symbolic connotations, intimating that it is not so much a trip from one point on the map to another as a passage into a dangerous and extraordinary other realm. A planned three-week visit to his cousin Joachim, who has been prevented by tuberculosis from realising his burning ambition to join the army, turns into a stay of vastly longer duration. Though it begins as a mere 'holiday escapade' (III, 203), his attraction to Clawdia Chauchat, a Russian patient who seems to embody the antithesis of all that he has previously lived by, develops into an all-absorbing obsession that binds him to the Mountain, though months go by before he even speaks to her. His preoccupation with Clawdia, and his all-embracing reflections on the significance of the intoxication she inspires in him, fuel new interests in biology, psychology, and even physics and astronomy, while the attentions of Settembrini, his would-be but none too successful mentor and advocate of progressive rationality, give him, and the reader, an extensive exposure to the philosphical and political programmes of liberal modernity. Seemingly deaf to all Settembrini's eloquent pleas to be reasonable, he becomes 'lost to the world' (III, 823), progressively abandons contact with what he and most of the other patients contemptuously call the 'Flatland' (III, 198 *et passim*), and makes the Mountain his new home. Clawdia leaves immediately after their one and only, much deferred, night of love, but Castorp stays on in anticipation of her return at some indeterminate time, even after Joachim, the occasion for his being there in the first place, tires of awaiting his endlessly-postponed discharge and leaves to join his regiment, against stern medical advice. Settembrini has little chance to take advantage of Clawdia's absence to work on Castorp unchallenged, for he soon acquires a more articulate and sinister rival for the biddable young man's intellectual and philosophical allegiance in the form of the 'conservative revolutionary' (III, 636) Leo Naphta, a Jewish Jesuit with Communist sympathies and an even greater addiction to interminable polemic than his Italian adversary. Later still, Mynheer Peeperkorn, the new lover with whom Clawdia returns, stands, with his 'powerful, if slightly blurred' (III, 765) personality, his expressive gestures belying his verbal inarticulateness, and his all-too-precarious vitalism, for yet another set of possibilities for Castorp to assess and mull over.

On various occasions Castorp is prompted to return to the workaday world, enriched by his 'adventures in the flesh and the spirit' (III, 994), but to no avail. In the first months, he has mild symptoms of a possible infection to furnish a pretext for devoting himself to the sanatorium routine and endless thoughts of Clawdia; but on the first anniversary of his arrival, he is emphatically declared fit to leave (III, 580). He insists the clean bill of health is not meant seriously, despite every indication to the contrary. Eventually, after Clawdia has returned and left again, this time with what is plainly a final farewell, and after Joachim, too, has come back to die while his cousin looks helplessly on, Castorp, unkempt and unshaven, accepts that he is there for good, no longer capable of even conceiving the thought of returning to the Flatland (III, 982). What prevents him from wasting the rest of his life in this wretched state is a purely external event, the outbreak of the First World War, which 'bursts the Magic Mountain asunder' (III, 984). But the release is very far from a return to the kind of life he had planned to resume seven years earlier, for it takes him onto the battlefield where, the narrator intimates at the close of the novel, he is probably to meet his death.

This overview, like most others in the literature on *The Magic Mountain*, including many much fuller ones, regrettably gives no hint that this is a characteristically funny book by one of Germany's most entertaining twentieth-century authors. The humour is nearly all comedy of character, arising from close observation of how a wide variety of personalities interact in the hermetic world of the sanatorium. At its best, the comedy is strongly entwined with the most serious themes of the work, and to appreciate it is simultaneously to discover threads of thematic coherence. Even apparently discrete laughter-provoking moments like Frau Stöhr's declaration (inspired by her doubtless strongly felt emotions at the sight of his corpse) that Joachim's 'heroic' death calls for a performance of Beethoven's *Erotica* (III, 745) increase her tally of cultural clangers while furnishing one more pointer to the secret roots of his mortal disease. More extensively, set pieces like the section 'An Attack Repulsed' (III, 588–608) in which Castorp's great-uncle ventures up from the 'Flatland' to reclaim the errant adventurer for the world of work, only to take to his heels in panic when the erotic spell of the Mountain makes itself hilariously felt in his 'ordinary' existence also, are at once masterpieces of comic construction in their own right and bearers of a dense network of references to other episodes in the fiction, as Castorp roguishly exploits his own memories of his 'initiation' into the Mountain's world to maximise his visitor's discomfiture and expedite his flight.

Such closely observed psychological interactions, which expect (while amply assisting) readers to hear and see the scene as though it were taking place on stage, are not used solely to comic effect. There is, for instance, the equally masterly dramatic narration in the immediately preceding episode, 'Fury' (III, 571–88). Behrens, the sanatorium's chief physician, explodes violently when Castorp says he 'can't be serious' (III, 580) when he declares him fully fit to leave the Mountain along with his cousin. The outburst, a riddle to Castorp and Joachim, is understandable enough to anyone attentive to the signs Mann has placed throughout the passage. Behrens has just decided, against his best medical judgement, to let Joachim leave to join his regiment, realising his patient knows full well that he is risking his life for the sake of his long-postponed vocation, and silently admiring the undemonstrative courage with which that risk is being borne. His reflections on Joachim's bluff bravery, and the powerlessness of medicine to avert its probably fatal outcome, are rudely interrupted by Castorp, the arch-civilian malingerer, questioning his medical judgement that he, unlike his cousin, is really and truly well enough to go. Thereupon, all the emotion Behrens cannot show towards Joachim is redirected into rage at Castorp's suggestion that he makes clinical decisions frivolously. What the young men put down to a fit of professional vanity actually stems from frustration at the impotence of his art and science to help a man he, like everyone else who gets to know him, cannot help fondly admiring. Our perception of all that, over the characters' heads but without any explicit prompting from the narrator, lends our reading experience a density characteristic of Mann's best fictional writing.

Again contrary to the impression produced by many critical accounts, some of the novel's more perilously discursive passages are embedded in contexts of psychological interaction and thematic reference that temper their wordiness. Few commentators can resist referring to Settembrini's collaboration on an encyclopaedic *Sociology of Suffering*, a project by the global League for the Organisation of Progress of which he is proud to be a corresponding member. Less attention is given to the dynamics and the implications of the actual episode – 'Encyclopaedia' (III, 330–50) – in which that collaboration is first revealed. At this point most of Castorp's day, when he is not dreaming of Clawdia on his balcony deckchair, or watching her across the dining room, is occupied with inventing pretexts for 'accidentally' encountering her, and his infatuated antics have made him an object of general amusement, with people actually gathering to watch him. One of the high points of his week is Sunday afternoon, when patients have to fetch their mail in person from the concierge's lodge, giving Castorp somewhere to linger with a strong chance of getting lucky, though he has patently no good reason for being there, since there is seldom any post for him. Settembrini, by contrast, is in constant correspondence with the world of campaigns and congresses from which his illness keeps him physically remote, so he frequently sees Castorp lurking while other patients have fun at his expense. In such circumstances, the narrator remarks, it was 'actually kind of Settembrini' to go out of his way to draw Castorp into a conversation, though the kindness is hardly appreciated by its recipient as Settembrini 'gets in the way' by asking if Castorp 'too' is expecting important post (III, 334). Settembrini knows what the answer will be, but the essence of his conversational gambit is in the 'too', and it falls predictably flat, for Castorp has no curiosity about the envelope his would-be conversation partner has just collected. 'You were asking about my mail', fibs Settembrini determinedly, and forcibly drags

Castorp away from the general gaze into a side room where the fabricated question can be answered without distractions (III, 339). The answer comes in several parts, linked together, in the absence of any response, interested or otherwise, by Settembrini's confident assertions that Castorp wants to know more, though in fact all he really wants to do is get back to his look-out position in the hallway. Its content is an account of the technocratic project so often cited as evidence of Settembrini's grandiose and self-important 'resolute philanthropy', to borrow a term Mann had mockingly harped upon in the *Reflections* as characteristic of his brother's rhetorically progressive stance (XII, 27 *et passim*). But its meaning within the texture of the novel merits more respect than it generally receives. Beyond the fact that this monologue determinedly posing as a conversation really is an act of kindness, an attempt to rescue Castorp from a situation where he is making a fool of himself, the obsessiveness which Settembrini displays (the conviction that others passionately share one's own special interests is after all a hallmark of an obsessive personality) is just his particular manifestation of something that afflicts all the inmates as they try to fill out the spiritual vacuum with which their timeless isolation surrounds them. Most of the patients cultivate both an obsession and a passion. Sometimes, as with Joachim, the obsession – joining his regiment – fights against the allurements of passion which draw him towards the ample bosom and irrepressible laughter of his fellow patient Marusja, eventually even gaining a Pyrrhic victory. With Castorp, passion and obsession are currently both directed at Clawdia Chauchat, and they are dragging him away from everything that once bound him to life. Settembrini's passion and obsession also seemingly have a single focus, his engagement via the pen with political schemes to change that world which his disease will not let him re-enter in the flesh, an engagement which is keeping him mentally, and possibly also physically, alive in this realm of the dead. But as we watch Settembrini's response to Castorp, we begin to realise that he, too, is under the sway of an erotic allurement which is not just the blandishments of a grand cause. Although he ostentatiously ogles passing village girls (III, 90), his heart plainly lies elsewhere; true to his classical allegiance, his desires for young men are sublimated into pedagogy, and this, we may surmise, is what allows those desires to fight against, instead of for, the disease within him. Settembrini's feelings towards Castorp are as clear as they are discreet and controlled. In devoting himself to 'life's problem child' (III, 429 *et passim*), he is living out his own desires in his chosen way, and it is the measure of his secret self-discipline that he is the one who, as early as Castorp's first evening, and then repeatedly afterwards, indeed in the aftermath of just this 'conversation', urges him to leave before it is too late. In other words, Settembrini actually does, again and again, what another pedagogic figure who identified with Socrates realised, once only, he ought to do: warn Tadzio's family to leave Venice before the city is closed off. Aschenbach's conviction that this is his moral duty, and his sense of delight in grasping that by not doing it he is knowingly locking himself and his beloved in a circle of death, usher in the first of his orgiastic dreams and take him irrevocably across the threshold of destruction (VIII, 514). Settembrini, determinedly channelling his desires into the hope that his 'problem child' can be won back to the cause of 'European civilisation', willing him to go for good where he, his mentor, cannot follow, is paying a price for his commitment to the 'organisation of progress' that lends it a dignity beyond its ideological deserts.

Life in the sanatorium benumbs any sense of leaving behind an irretrievable past and moving into a different future. At first, Castorp views the Mountain from the perspective of the Flatland: everything that happens is novel and unexpected, so his sense of advancing though time is 'refreshed' (III, 148). All too soon, though, he has experienced all the facets of the sanatorium routine, its daily, weekly and eventually even annual rhythms and rituals, so that he lives in a perpetual present, lacking even seasonal clues, since all kinds of weather appear haphazardly throughout the year. The loss of a sense of time leads him to start questioning other categories he has previously taken for granted, even on his first day, when, to his own surprise, he fastens on to Joachim's harmless enough remark that he likes taking his own temperature 'because it makes you notice what a minute really ['eigentlich'] is'. Castorp seizes on the word 'eigentlich', which, he insists, has no application to time, where only subjective measures really count. Joachim will have none of it: there are clocks and calendars, he says, and when the end of the month arrives, it arrives for everyone, no matter what they feel like. Yes, Castorp counters, but only because 'for the sake of order' people have agreed on measures that are 'in the end mere conventions' (III, 96). Most of Castorp's many and varied investigations in the pages that follow show this same pattern. Enquiring about things to which he has previously not given a second thought, he pursues what is 'really' the case, only to find that the sort of answer he has always presumed must be available evades him.[2] Here, his questionings take him into a fairly benign circle, in other instances they will lead him into infinite regressions or, most ominously of all, into regions where such truths as may be glimpsed are profoundly subversive of the things he had hoped to ground more firmly through his intellectual quest. He has to settle for the acceptance of conventions, fictions of practical value but problematic validity. What is time, what is life, what is love, and – the field where above all Settembrini and Naphta so insistently claim to offer their impassioned answers, sometimes contradicting themselves as much as they contradict one another (III, 644) – how should human beings organise and govern their collective and personal existence? All these questions are raised in and through Hans Castorp's story; and such answers as are intimated all entail a decision to impose articulation and structure on what remains in essence an elusive flux.

Castorp believes that although Settembrini is a 'windbag' he always means well, whereas Naphta is anything but well-meaning, even if he is 'nearly always right' when he disagrees with his enlightened opponent (III, 660). There is one occasion, however, where Settembrini is allowed to be 'right' as well as benign, expressing a viewpoint that matches very closely the conclusions Castorp himself reaches. Not for the first time, Castorp has been remarking that the 'boundaries' between reality and illusion are 'fluid'. Settembrini responds that, in that case, it is up to human beings to shown 'the moral courage to take decisions and make distinctions', to fix boundaries and limits according to values they have chosen:

> Man was the measure of all things, he added. His right to decide upon good and evil, truth and delusion in the light of his powers of knowledge was inalienable, and woe unto him who dared try to shake his belief in this creative right! It were better for him that a millstone were hanged around his neck and he were drowned in the deepest well.     (Chapter 6, 'Highly Questionable', III, 926)

This passage illustrates how Mann, in league with his 'discursive' characters, combines ideas from very disparate sources (III, 564, 586, 618, 643). The insistence that human beings have the 'creative' capacity to decide what is good and evil by the measure of their own interests is (almost) pure Nietzsche. That the exercise of this capacity is an 'inalienable right', namely one which no one may either suppress or renounce without violating Natural Law, is a Lockean notion very far from Nietzsche's thinking. The castigation of the offender who undermines 'belief' in this tenet is, of course, drawn from the words of Jesus about the lot of anyone who 'shall offend one of these little ones that believe in me',[3] and it anticipates the accusation Settembrini finally makes against Naphta of 'importuning defenceless youth' (III, 966), leading to their duel and his opponent's suicide.

The alternative to making decisions and setting limits is exposure to 'limitless' chaos, initially intoxicating maybe, but in the end the road to dissolution, as Castorp's apparently 'unlimited' stay on the Mountain seems set to show, until outside powers intervene. Settembrini is made to extend the application of this need to exercise the 'creative right' to set boundaries and make decisions to the realm of European politics, with Castorp, sympathetic to the pull of both 'Western' and 'Eastern' influences, as representative of Germany, the nation that must make crucial choices on which the whole of

Europe's future will depend (III, 714). The attempt make some kind of political statement, or at least to engage with political issues, is plain enough, though just what 'decisions' are being advocated is left vaguer than many readers have wished. The novel comes nowhere near to offering or advocating a political programme, but it does plead for, and try to ground in the represented experiences, a particular shift in attitudes to political matters, the same one that Mann had undergone during the work's protracted genesis.

In his second winter on the Mountain, Castorp, lost in a blizzard during a solitary skiing expedition, recognises in his own behaviour the classic preliminaries to death by exposure (III, 669). Resting in the meagre shelter afforded by the side of a locked hut, he succumbs to his drowsiness, yet he is in the event pulled back from the brink of death. The snowstorm is short-lived, though that is not what saves him. He is brought back to the living through a vision which passes over into a half-wakeful state and a train of thought that finally engages his will-power and gets him to his feet, and so back to life and safety. The vision's salutary effect is clear enough, but its broader meaning is harder to pin down, as the unending disputes among the commentators testify.[4] Castorp sees a community of people treating one another with a relaxed dignity which seems to stem from a bond joining all their minds and hearts ('Sinnesbindung') (III, 680). But there is more to the scene: in an ancient temple behind him, he finds two half-naked hags dismembering and devouring a living child. His struggles to escape this sight dislodge him from his position against the side of the hut, he slides to the ground and, jolted back to partial consciousness, he carries on dreaming 'no longer in images, but in thoughts' (III, 683). The dream-thoughts centre on the relationship between the scene on the shore and the horrors within the temple. What Castorp saw in the sanctuary is something the 'sun-people' know to be there; and, he surmises, their 'Sinnesbindung' which so enchanted him is a response to their knowledge. They live in a spirit directly contrary to what the temple holds: not out of ignorance or self-delusion, but as the result of deliberate collective choice to assert and so create what they value in defiance of what is the case.

The dream-thoughts build up to a formulation which Castorp calls his 'dream-saying' ('Traumwort'): *For the sake of goodness and love, man should not allow death any dominion over his thoughts* (III, 686). Despite or perhaps because of the over-demonstrative italics, interpreters have not always paid enough attention to why and with what implications human 'thoughts' are here singled out for defence against the dominion of death. This is in no sense a vote for Enlightenment rationalism against reverence for tradition. A moment earlier, Castorp described the raging controversies between his mentors as a 'confused din of battle, that is in no danger of deafening someone who keeps a little bit of a free head and a pious heart' (III, 685). The pious heart – a reverence for the past, and a recognition that in the present and likely future, there is much in human existence that the amenities of technocratic civilisation can neither remedy nor assuage – is not only not dismissed, it is emphatically honoured as the guardian of all worth. Such a heart is enshrined in the records with which Castorp 'falls in love' (III, 893, 896) after he commandeers the sanatorium's new gramophone, especially in the 'quintessentially German' piece, Schubert's *Am Brunnen vor dem Tore* ['At the well before the gate'], with which he is actually said to be 'besotted' ('vernarrt') (III, 905). Yet Castorp, in thoughts that the narrator concedes 'rise high above' (III, 907) the hero's 'simple' capacities, will reflect that his 'intellectual sympathy' ('geistige Sympathie') for this song, and the way of relating to the world that it encapsulates, need somehow to be 'overcome' if it is not to become a poison fruit to all who taste it (III, 906). This song and the 'world' of which it is a 'likeness' (III, 905) will always hold sway in Castorp's heart, and he will go to his death in battle singing it under his breath (III, 993), but he senses that it ought not to hold his thoughts in bondage.

There is a crucial parallel here to the phrase which Mann used in the preface he wrote for the printed version of the 1922 speech 'On the German Republic'. Denying accusations of desertion and betrayal from former comrades who had also served the German war effort with the pen, he was quite specific about what, from his perspective, had changed, and, more importantly, about what had remained the same: 'I may well have changed my thoughts, but not my mind' ('ich habe vielleicht meine Gedanken geändert, – nicht meinen Sinn') (XI, 809); and a little further on he spoke of the need to 'assert an abiding mind amid changed times' ('einen bleibenden Sinn behaupten in veränderter Zeit'). The claim may be elusive in some of its implications, but it is clear enough in itself: he is saying that it is for the sake of ensuring continuity of allegiance that he has made the choice to adopt a different line of thought about what his values require, if they are to be carried over into a new historical epoch. And he wants his hearers and readers to reflect that the converse applies: unless his contemporaries in general, and in particular those who were until now his ideological soul mates, realise that their abiding allegiances demand a different set of political commitments, their pursuit of the right values by what have become the wrong means will lead to a destruction of all that they cherish, infinitely worse than anything the democratic republicans whom they still consider their mortal foes are likely to bring to pass. As far as that goes, there is little that the wisdom of hindsight, schooled by the tragedy of German self-deception in the later twenties and thirties, could usefully add to what Thomas Mann tried to say to the contemporaries who were the first readers of *The Magic Mountain*.

MICHAEL BEDDOW

## NOTES

1 On the work's growth, see letters to Ernst Bertram, 24 July 1913; to Hans von Hülsen, 9 September 1913, *DD* II, 451; to Ida Boy-Ed, 4 November 1913; and Heinz Saueressig, 'Die Entstehung des Romans *Der Zauberberg*', in Saueressig (ed.), *Besichtigung des Zauberbergs* (Biberach an der Riss: Beck, 1974), pp. 5–53.

2 For the broader cultural and scientific background of this pattern, see Michael Beddow, 'The Climate of *The Magic Mountain*', in Michael Minden (ed.), *Thomas Mann* (London and New York: Longman, 1995), pp. 148–59.

3 Matthew 18:6, Mark 9:42, Luke 17:2. It is not clear why Mann (or his character) substitutes a 'well' for the sea in this quotation.

4 See Hans Wysling, '*Der Zauberberg*', in Helmut Koopmann (ed.), *Thomas-Mann-Handbuch* (Stuttgart: Kröner, 1995), pp. 397–422, and Wysling, 'Probleme der *Zauberberg*-Interpretation', *Thomas Mann Jahrbuch* 1 (1988), 12–26.

## FURTHER READING

Beddow, Michael, *The Fiction of Humanity* (Cambridge: Cambridge University Press, 1982), ch. 4: 'Reconstructions: *Der Zauberberg*'

Grenville, Anthony, ' "Linke Leute von rechts": Thomas Mann's Naphta and the Ideological Confluence of Radical Right and Radical Left in the Early Years of the Weimar Republic', *Deutsche Vierteljahrsschrift* 37 (1985), 651–75

Kowalik, Jill Anne, ' "Sympathy with Death": Hans Castorp's Nietzschean Resentment', *German Quarterly* 58 (1985), 27–48

Minden, Michael, *The German Bildungsroman: Incest and Inheritance* (Cambridge: Cambridge University Press, 1997), ch. 5: '*Der Zauberberg*'

Pascal, Roy, '*The Magic Mountain* and Adorno's Critique of the Traditional Novel', in Keith Bullivant (ed.), *Culture and Society in the Weimar Republic* (Manchester: Manchester University Press, 1977), pp. 1–23

Passage, Charles E., 'Hans Castorp's Musical Incantation', *Germanic Review* 38 (1963), 238–56

Swales, Martin, *Mann: 'Der Zauberberg'* (London: Grant & Cutler, 2000)

Weigand, Hermann J., *Thomas Mann's Novel 'Der Zauberberg'* (New York: Appleton-Century, 1933)

# 10

WOLF-DANIEL HARTWICH
TRANSLATED BY RITCHIE ROBERTSON

# Religion and culture:
## *Joseph and his Brothers*

Mann's work on the four novels *The Tales of Jacob*, *The Young Joseph*, *Joseph in Egypt* and *Joseph the Provider* spans a phase in his creative career in which the pressure of historical events obliged him to redefine his political attitude, his cultural identity, and his position as a literary author. While this monumental work was emerging, the Weimar Republic collapsed, the Nazis came to power, and Mann went into exile and emigrated to the USA, where he struggled to find a political attitude towards Germany and finally adopted a firm public stance opposed to Hitler. This anti-Nazi stance assumed increasing urgency for the writer with the outbreak of the Second World War. The remarkable persistence with which Mann pursued the *Joseph* project, however, also shows that he saw it as the great work of his later years.

At first sight, Mann's choice of biblical material, which as a *poeta doctus* he links with the mythologies of the ancient world, must seem surprising. The author himself comments to his publisher, Bermann Fischer, on the 'almost insane discrepancy between the work and our time'.[1] Hence the *Joseph* tetralogy has been interpreted as an escape from the historical present.[2] Only very recently have scholars sought to treat Mann's Egypt as a reflection of his own historical experiences.[3] The themes drawn from the history of religion now appear as a response to the political and intellectual situation that was defined by the growth of German fascism. Myth had been a political issue at least since the publication in 1930 of *The Myth of the Twentieth Century* by the Nazi ideologue Alfred Rosenberg. This programmatic text belonged to a tradition of nationalist and conservative writing in which a civilisation based on technology and rationality was contrasted with an archaic and mystical world order. Modern myth-makers transformed significant historical figures, from the medieval Emperor Friedrich Barbarossa to the philosopher Friedrich Nietzsche, into icons of anti-modernism.[4] The conception of the poet as spiritual leader, developed by the circle around Stefan George, acquired a political colouring. Thomas Mann was in close contact with two of the most prominent among these authors, Alfred Bäumler and Ernst Bertram. Responding to the 1930s' obsession with mythology, the theologian Rudolf Bultmann proposed to 'demythologise' biblical religion by adapting its ethical content to modern consciousness. Mann's *Joseph* tetralogy, however, opposes not only reactionary attempts to restore myth but also modernist attempts to eliminate it. Biblical Judaism appears as a transformation of mythical thought that overcomes such inhuman aspects of primitive cults as animal-worship or human sacrifice.

Beyond this contemporary polemical context, however, the *Joseph* novels represent the high point of Mann's lifelong literary involvement with religion as an aspect of modern society. In *Buddenbrooks*, Mann was one of the first writers to portray the significance of Protestantism for the secularisation of Christianity and the development of capitalism; yet elsewhere, notably in *Death in Venice* and *The Magic Mountain*, Mann considers attempts to restore myth and enchantment to the modern world. As early as *Fiorenza* and 'At the Prophet's', he depicts how religious charisma and its modern substitutes can be used to manipulate groups. Mann's works can be read as documenting and analysing the social transformation of religious belief in the nineteenth and twentieth centuries. In examining the religious history of bourgeois society, however, Mann differs from current trends in the sociology of religion. Instead of taking enlightened secularism as his sole standard, he develops a specific sensitivity towards religious outlooks. In *Joseph and his Brothers*, *Doctor Faustus* and *The Holy Sinner*, the late Mann goes beyond the description and analysis of religious matters and makes literature the vehicle for theological speculation. Neither theologians nor literary scholars have yet done justice to the religious aspects of these works, for they have reduced Mann's poetic and theological reflections to dogmatic concepts. The evaluation of Mann's theology within Protestantism depends on how authors see the relation between religion and culture. Those who consider religion an integral part of culture welcome Mann's enlightened view of the Bible.[5] Those who see the two as sharply opposed criticise Mann for reducing the divine to worldly terms.[6] Catholic theology, on the other hand, has succeeded in relating the novel to its more markedly ethical and mystical tradition.[7]

## Israel in Egypt: cultural memory and its media

Mann's portrayal of biblical Judaism in the *Joseph* tetralogy combines a revolutionary element with a conservative one. While the patriarchs' 'care for God' looks forward to the messianic liberation of the world, they shape their lives by forms which, having been handed down from primeval times, recall the beginnings of the divine promise and thus offer a landmark within the cultural diversity of the ancient Orient. Hebrew antiquity thus forms the historical paradigm of the combination of tradition with 'left-wing' humanism which the author constructs as an alternative to the anti-bourgeois, reactionary mass ideology of National Socialism and its nineteenth-century predecessors. The figure of Jacob is portrayed as the narrative incarnation of a spirituality that integrates cultural memory with intellectual innovation. His description speaks metaphorically of 'the old man's eyes, penetrating and exploring the depths of memory and thought, whose gaze came from below, almost getting tangled in his overhanging eyebrows' (IV, 92). Here the biblical patriarch appears in a mythical perspective which in the *Joseph* novels is always associated with 'depths', the 'well of the past' (IV, 9). The monotheistic idea of God is understood as part of a profound mythic dimension of the human personality, which is generated by a culture's collective memory and preserves its intellectual advances.

Jacob and his son Joseph mark closely adjacent stages in this process of religious and intellectual development. Jacob's predominantly ethical stance retains the normative aspect of religion which provides the criterion for faith, whereas Joseph transfers to the religious domain the model of aesthetic autonomy which frees art from the danger of instrumentalisation by stressing its fictionality. Both father and son are necessary for Mann's literary engagement with myth and religion. The author presents the sacred as ethically normative and, at the same time, as aesthetically autonomous.

Taking the life of Joseph as his example, Mann develops this ethical and aesthetic access to religion and myth. The *Joseph* novels reshape biblical history into a *Bildungsroman*. The protagonist's development stands for the growth of the early civilisations whose achievements have left a lasting mark on human history. Mann sees cultural evolution as determined by the discovery not only of God, but also of human individuality, which extends to the religious as well as the artistic domain. Cultural norms are grounded on collective memory until a personal ethics can develop. The *Joseph* novels anticipate the history of cultural memory that Jan Assmann, with frequent reference to Mann, has recently elaborated for Egypt.[8] The medium of this transformation, leading from cult to culture, is the development from orality to writing. Before poetic creativity became its dominant principle, literature was shaped by the narrative repetition of mythic patterns. Judaism exemplifies the transition from speech to writing by using both forms of communication to hand on its cultural memory, translating each into the other. While its veneration of the Torah makes Judaism the written religion *par excellence*, it also accords a central role to oral tradition and the art of remembering sacred events. Hence the communicative situation of parents and children, or of teachers and pupils, is particularly important in Jewish religion. Even in the 'Prelude' to *Joseph and his Brothers*, however, this technique of memory is universalised. Joseph's interest is not confined to his own Jewish tradition, but extends to foreign mythologies, which in his eyes have no religious authority but do have canonical status as literature. 'We have mentioned, for example, that Joseph knew by heart beautiful Babylonian verses which come from a great body of deceitful wisdom that exists in writing' (IV, 19).

In the chapter of *The Young Joseph* entitled 'Of the Oldest Servant', the figure of Eliezer, Joseph's teacher, serves to show the genesis of individuality from mythic consciousness. The 'oldest bondsman', an illegitimate son of his master who is later freed from slavery, appears as an institutional personality and a mythic authority:

> In short, he was an institution ... and when young Joseph contemplated him during their lessons, and the boy ... listening, looked into the face of the old teacher, who 'looked like Abraham' and could say 'I' with such splendid freedom, strange feelings crept over him. His handsome and well-favoured eyes still rested on the form of the storyteller, yet looked through him into an endless perspective of Eliezer figures who were all saying 'I' through the lips of the present manifestation, and as they were sitting in the twilight cast by the great shady tree, but the sunny breezes were shimmering in the heat behind Eliezer, this perspective of identities faded not into darkness but into light.  (IV, 422)

When Eliezer tells stories about his primeval namesake not in the third person, with its historical distance, but with the identification implied by 'I', such expressions are understood in *The Tales of Jacob* as part of a 'lunar syntax' that eludes rational definition. As a participant in the mythic language-game, Joseph has to accept 'that the old man's self (*Ich*) lacked firm boundaries, but was, as it were, open at the back' (IV, 122). Similarly, the narrator of the novel expects his readership to enter into a past mode of thought which 'for the idea of "personality" and "individuality" knew only such external terms as "religion" and "confession"' (IV, 123). Joseph's aesthetic outlook, however, overcomes the mythic and religious identification with the past by perceiving 'Eliezer's' various incarnations as facets of a poetic self-fictionalisation. Instead of becoming absolute, one particular cultural and historical definition of the self is relativised by the multiple identity of biblical humanity. Mythic obscurity is lightened, but it is a different light from that of modernity: it is illuminated as a forgotten possibility of human existence, involving a kind of self-awareness which is in no way inferior to modern individualism.

Mann masters the difficulty of 'talking about people who don't quite know who they are' (IV, 128) by making his protagonist's fate into a screen onto which mythological reminiscences are deliberately projected. This literary method attains its greatest intensity in the episode where Joseph's brothers throw him into a pit. The author makes a clear departure from his biblical text in ascribing to this action a religious significance, supported by a panoply of quotations from Egyptian, Babylonian, Jewish and Christian sources. When Joseph goes to see his brothers, who are working in the fields, their envy of Jacob's favourite is discharged in an outburst of brutal violence. Admittedly, this aggression also owes something to the frivolous conceit shown by Joseph in recounting two dreams in which God raised him above his family. The attack on Joseph is also linked with the central myths of Egyptian and Jewish religion. When Joseph's brothers seem about to 'tear him into at least fourteen pieces' (IV, 555), the allusion is to the mythic death of Osiris. In *The Tales of Jacob* Mann underlines the supreme importance of this cult for Egyptian civilisation: 'The reddish-skinned people of Mizraim saw the martyr Usiri as the benefactor who had originally taught them agriculture and given them laws, and been interrupted only by Seth's malicious onslaught' (IV, 26). After being slain and dismembered by his antagonist, Osiris is made Lord of the Underworld. Another tradition tells how Isis gathered up the members of her fraternal husband in order to give birth to Horus and thus to found the genealogy of the Pharaohs. Osiris' rebirth in seed and corn is celebrated in annual rites.[9] And when Reuben, seeking to protect Joseph by channelling their brothers' fury, calls 'Bind him!', this alludes to the sacrifice of Isaac, which is known in Jewish writings as *Aqedat Yitskhak*, the binding of Isaac.[10] Just as the resurrection of Osiris founds the fertility of Egypt, Isaac, once saved, becomes the ancestor of the Jewish people.

The chapter 'In the Pit' shows Joseph as 'the true son of Jacob, of the worthy thinker, the man learned in myth' and as 'pupil of old Eliezer' (IV, 581) when he attaches a mythic sense to his impending death. His intellectual play with the resources of memory now has nothing arbitrary about it, but becomes an existential necessity. His mythic outlook reveals its aesthetic character by enabling him to detach himself from his present situation and to order his emotions. In upholding the possibility of human existence even in the face of death, his mythic self-staging represents the opposite of a fatalistic belief in mythic destiny. Thus Joseph observes that

> the well . . . resembled the entry to the underworld, and symbolised death even through the round stone that normally covered it; for the stone covered its round opening as shadow covers the dark moon. What Joseph's attentive intellect could discern through events was the archetype of the dying heavenly body: the dead moon, which is not seen for three whole days before its tender reappearance; and the death of the light-gods, who must descend to the Underworld for a spell. (IV, 583)

Joseph undertakes to imitate the Sumerian god Dumuzi, whose mythic fate, according to the religious scholarship of Mann's day, 'embodies the withering and new growth of vegetation' and plays 'a prominent role in the

Babylonian mystery of death and resurrection'.[11] Since the beginning of the century, biblical scholars of the 'History of Religion School' had considered the resurrection narratives of the New Testament to be dependent on the ancient Oriental myths of Osiris, Dumuzi and Adonis.[12] The chapter in *The Tales of Jacob* entitled 'The Grove of Adonis' presents the festival of the Palestinian Tammuz, who belongs to the type of the dying and reborn god. The text here projects the religious formulae of the Christian Easter festival onto the pagan cult: 'Tammuz lives! The Lord is risen!...He is no longer there. The grave could hold him no more than three days. He is risen' (IV, 452).

The captive Joseph interprets his situation in terms of the sacrifice of Isaac, placing it in the context of the pagan idea of regeneration. Joseph's martyrdom thus fulfils the superhuman demands of a spiritual religion, while sublating them within the cosmic laws of a religion of nature.

> It was the abyss into which the true son descends...It was the underground sheepfold, Etura, the realm of the dead, in which the son becomes Lord, the shepherd, the martyr, the sacrificial victim, the dismembered god.    (IV, 583)

In the long reflective passage from which this quotation is taken, Mann is using the spiritualised interpretation of sacrifice that is found in Jewish martyr narratives of the Hellenistic period. In this sense the Fourth Book of Maccabees, for example, makes the sacrifice of Isaac the prototype of Jewish martyrdom. The bloody reality of martyrdom is compensated by the expectation of a heavenly reward, elevation to divine glory. Mann introduces into the story of Joseph the belief in eternal life which is unknown to the Pentateuch and represents a later development within Judaism.

The antithesis between Jewish and Pharaonic civilisation, and between their respective forms of cultural memory, is fundamental to the novel *Joseph in Egypt*. While the biblical Patriarchs are marked by 'divine concern for what is to come', the traditionalism of Egyptian religion is sharply criticised: 'Often venerable age can be a snare and a delusion, that is, when it has merely outlived its time and fallen into decay – then it only seems venerable, but in truth it is a stench and an abomination before God' (IV, 688–9). Admittedly, the text avoids the cultural stereotypes of Orientalism which deny Eastern civilisations the West's capacity for historical progress.[13] Egypt, in particular, became the paradigm of timeless stasis in which the humanists revered a source of ancient wisdom, Romantics found their inward experience reflected, and colonialists from Napoleon onwards found their activity justified. Mann's Egypt, however, is characterised by the coexistence of civilised progress and reactionary ideology. The juxtaposition of technical, bureaucratic rationality and cultic, mystical regression is made into a parallel to Western modernity.

In the chapter 'Conversation at Night', when the Midianite trader to whom Joseph has been sold explains to his slaves the peculiar nature of Egyptian civilisation, he concentrates on its culture of memory, which is clearly contrasted with the earlier presentation of Judaism. The collective memory of the Jewish religious community rests on personal identification with mythical prototypes; the cultic re-enactment of primeval stories stresses their symbolic and spiritual character. Rather than disclosing a sacred and profound dimension of human existence, on the other hand, Egypt's written culture organises a secular world in which the linguistic signs, far from evoking a presence, transpose reality into abstraction. 'The goods are greasy and sticky with gum: the merchant does not soil his hands with them, but deals with their written equivalent... Such a written list is like the *Ka*, the spiritual body of things, which is alongside the body' (IV, 680). The Egyptian cult, however, is characterised by the materialistic reification of the sacred, as seen in the primitive and inhuman rituals of animal-worship. 'Behold, in the beast god and man find themselves, and the animal is the sacred point where both touch and are united, sacred and honourable by its nature, and among the festivals that festival is held in highest honour where the goat cohabits with the pure virgin in the city of Djedet' (IV, 694).

While 'Conversation at Night' deals with the economic and cultic functions of writing, the chapter 'Joseph is Reader and Body-Servant' focuses on Egyptian literature. Joseph's master, Peteprê, owns 'a beautiful library of many pages, kept in the cases of both halls, and consisting partly of entertaining fancies and mirthful fables... partly of stimulating dialectic... religious and magical texts and treatises of wisdom... lists of kings... and annals of remarkable historical events' (V, 918–19). Egyptian literate culture appears in an advanced stage of artificial refinement, so that 'in most of these written works the substance and the story scarcely mattered, but all attention was given to the charms of style, the rarity and elegance of rhetorical forms' (V, 919). When Peteprê induces Joseph to pass judgement on his favourite books, the latter calls them 'very nice' but too 'simple' (V, 922). Joseph criticises the secularisation of Egyptian literature from the standpoint of the literary anthropology of Judaism, which is shaped by the religious idea of God's transcendence and His covenant with Israel. He contrasts the playful emotions of Egyptian love poetry with the absolute obligation seen in the sacrifice of Isaac. 'Our God is betrothed to us and is our eager blood-bridegroom, for He is solitary and burning for faithfulness. We are like a bride to his faithfulness, consecrated and set apart' (V, 922–3). While Jacob expressed moral reservations about secular literature, Joseph sketches a theological critique that questions the antithesis of good and evil. The mythic sacrifice of the Son symbolises a dialectic of sacred and profane that in turn mirrors the complex relationship of God to the world, of transcendence to immanence: 'For as it is forbidden, it is also denied and marked as a sin' (v, 923). In regarding the invention of sin as the main feature of the Jewish religion, Mann's Joseph could invoke Nietzsche's *Genealogy of Morals*. However, while Nietzsche charges the theology of sin with betraying life, Mann recognises in it an essential deepening of the cultural definition of man that draws his attention to his natural imperfection and his transcendental potential: 'God suffers too for our sins, and we suffer with Him' (v, 923). This conception implies a fundamental difference between the mythic self-definition of Judaism and the cultural memory of other cultures of antiquity. While the pagan world, in worshipping gods and heroes, celebrates its own collective virtues, the traditions of Judaism centre on its own shortcomings. Although the cults of Egypt are still on a pre-civilised level, Egyptian high culture has already forgotten the normative claims of its mythic texts. Yet when the Jewish Scriptures speak of the profane and contaminate cultic purity with ritual taboo, their awareness of sin actually sharpens the sense of ethical obligation. In transforming the Scriptures of the Old Testament into the modern form of the novel, Mann is simultaneously insisting that his *Joseph* retains a specifically religious meaning.

## Myth as psychology: the *Joseph* novels as a critique of psychoanalysis

Given that cultural memory forms a constant theme of the *Joseph* tetralogy, the text needs to be read in the context of Mann's involvement with psychoanalysis. Freud made the physical and psychic forms of remembrance and repression central to his psychology of the individual, from which he derived a theory of culture. During his preliminary reading for *Joseph and his Brothers*, Mann made a thorough study of Freud's works. His knowledge of psychoanalysis is already demonstrated by the figure of Dr Krokowski in *The Magic Mountain*. He first summarised his interest in this theory in his 1929 speech 'Freud's Position in the History of Modern Thought'. Mann's declared intention here was to defend 'the psychoanalytical movement as the only form of modern anti-rationalism which does not invite reactionary abuse'.[14] The *Joseph* novels were also inspired by the treatment of biblical material in the late Freud, especially in *Moses and Monotheism*, which also had an impact on Mann's story about Moses, 'The Tables of the Law' (1943).[15] Here Freud applies his theories of the Oedipus complex and parricide to Jewish history. Even earlier, Mann interprets the stories of biblical fathers that feature in the *Joseph* novels in the light of Freud's psychology of culture. In the following pages, the image of the father in *Joseph* will be compared with Freud's conception, and Mann's theory of myth, developed with reference to Joseph in his lecture 'Freud and the Future', will be assessed as an original alternative to the image of humanity in psychoanalysis.

The father–son constellation first attains significance when we are told about Isaac's death and the dispute between Jacob and Esau over their ancestral blessing. Here Mann draws on Freud's speculations in *Totem and Taboo* about the origin of culture and religion. Freud reads his own theory of Oedipal competition between son and father for the mother's favour into the ethnographic accounts by James Frazer and William Robertson Smith. According to Freud, human beings initially lived together in a primal horde ruled by the primal father. The chief of the horde, who claimed all the women for himself and thus castrated the younger men, was finally murdered and devoured by his sons. The memory of this event left its mark on early tribal societies. The primal father was worshipped in the shape of the totem from which the community traced its ancestry. The mythic parricide was re-enacted in the regular sacrifice of the divine animal and in the totem meal, which express both the triumph and the guilt of the murderers. For Freud, religious rites, like the compulsive behaviour-patterns of neurotics, are to be interpreted as the expression of a repressed trauma. Christian theology responds to this guilt complex when Jesus Christ sacrifices himself to atone for mankind's guilt towards God the Father. Henceforth Christianity need have no scruples about elevating the Son into God, with whom the faithful communicate by symbolically devouring His body in the Mass. The chapter 'Primordial Bleating' from *The Tales of Jacob* interprets the sacrifice of Isaac in the light of totemism. When the dying Isaac speaks 'of the blood of the he-goat which should be seen as his blood, the blood of the true son, shed for the atonement of all' (IV, 185), the text alludes to the interpretation of the Last Supper in Matthew 26:28. 'Indeed, shortly before his end he tried with remarkable success to bleat like a ram, and his bloodless face took on an astonishing resemblance to this animal's physiognomy' (IV, 185–6). In this metamorphosis Jacob sees the return of something repressed by cultural consciousness, and again we have an allusion to Freud's totem meal:

> an obscene apparition of the animal that was God, the ram, the divine ancestor of the tribe that was descended from it and had once shed and consumed its divine tribal blood, in order to renew its tribal affinity with the beast-god – before he came, the God from afar, Elohim, the God from outside and beyond . . . who had chosen them and severed the link with their primal nature.
>
> (IV, 186–7)

In the following chapter, 'The Red One', Freud's argument that biblical religion grew out of totemism is discussed at some length. While Freud sees human civilisation as shaped by the unconscious compulsion to repeat the primeval crimes, Mann stresses the ambivalence of the myth, which cannot be read as the expression of a specific psychological disposition. With the model of the 'swinging sphere', the novel anticipates the structural study of myth later undertaken by Claude Lévi-Strauss. Mann interprets myths of diverse provenance as variations on a single narrative pattern, within which roles can be exchanged. Hence there exists a 'reciprocal relationship between father and son, so that it is not always the son who slaughters the father, but the role of the victim can at any moment be transferred to the son' (IV, 192). Thus the sacrifice of the son and the murder of the father appear equally as fictional constructions of a mythological world-picture.

Once Jacob has cheated Esau out of their father's blessing, there follows a scene which has no counterpart in the Bible. In the chapter 'Jacob has to Travel', Esau, meditating revenge, encounters his uncle Ishmael, who was banished by Abraham for making homosexual advances to his half-brother Isaac. Mann makes this sinister, 'underworldly' figure (IV, 192) a spokesman for Freudian theories. Ishmael advises Esau, 'after slaying his father, to eat plentifully of his flesh, in order to incorporate his wisdom and power, the blessing of Abraham borne by the other' (IV, 215). Parricide appears here, not (as in Freud) as a primal fact of human culture, but as a revolutionary idea put forward by an individual who subversively questions traditional norms. 'He had thought of something new, while Esau had in mind only something traditional – fratricide', as prefigured in the myths of Seth and Osiris, Cain and Abel. 'Parricide was not among the possibilities in his mind; it had never happened.' Even on the primitive cultural level represented by the shepherd Esau, parricide forms an unimaginable sacrilege, so that it appears a fantastic suggestion stemming from a decadent phase of civilisation.

In exploring the totemistic background to Hebrew religion, Mann emphasises not the perpetration of parricide but the prevention of the sacrifice of the son. While Freud regards Judaeo-Christian religion as falling heir to primitive sacrificial cults, the patriarchs in the *Joseph* novels overcome totemism. Their blood relationship with their ancestor is replaced by their spiritual election by Yahweh. In his understanding of the biblical image of God, Mann employs an image of the father diametrically opposed to Freud's, and embodied especially in the figure of Jacob. While Freud understands the father–son relationship in biological terms, Mann sees it primarily as the channel by which cultural tradition is handed down. Hence the figure of the father in the novel is not tyrannical, but sympathetic and caring, compassionate and self-sacrificing. This image finds its principal literary expression in the description of Jacob's mourning for Joseph, whom he thinks dead. Thus Mann reverses the significance which psychoanalysis gave the father-figure for the psychic life of the individual as well as the community. While Freud traces the modern 'discontent with civilisation' back to the internalisation of the norm represented by the father, which restricts the individual's natural instinctual urges, Mann here recognises a positive force that contributes to civilisation. Rather than being a traumatic, punitive authority, the effect of the psychic father-figure on Joseph is salutary.

This revaluation is particularly apparent in the chapter from *Joseph in Egypt* entitled 'The Father's Face', with the culmination of the fateful love story between the protagonist and his master's wife Mut-em-enet. In the erotic sphere, just as in his relationship with his brothers, Joseph's narcissistic attitude brings about his downfall but also leads him to a higher level of individual and social development. Thus he flirts with the head of the Order of Hathor, who is vowed to chastity, while simultaneously eluding her attempts at making closer contact. However, when Mut-em-enet's passionate desire bursts all social bounds and rises to a pitch of madness, it becomes a threat to her beloved. The triangle formed by the young man, the father-figure Peteprê and the mature woman, who appears equally as an unapproachable icon and an incarnation of repressed instinctual urges, reflects the Oedipal constellation described by Freud. As in ancient Jewish literature, however, sexual seduction also appears as an alien threat to one's own religious and moral identity.[16] The novel provides a literary expression of Freud's analytic theory in the visionary description of Joseph's confrontation with the authority of the super-ego based in the father-imago:

> What enabled him to tear himself free and flee from her at the very last moment was this: Joseph saw his father's face...But it was not a picture with closed, personal features, that he might have seen here or there in space...It was a mental image, a warning sign, the image of the father in a wider, more universal sense...It gazed anxiously at Joseph with fatherly eyes. That saved him.
>
> (v, 1256)

The father does not appear (as in Freud) as the son's all-powerful judge, but as the merciful redeemer of his identity.

When Mann, in his lecture 'Freud and the Future', sets the *Joseph* novels in the intellectual context of psychoanalysis, he interprets the latter in a manner contrary to the intentions of its founder. Thus he treats psychoanalysis as a successor to the literary and philosophical psychology of Kierkegaard, Schopenhauer and Nietzsche, although Freud clearly distanced himself from these influences. On the other hand, Mann establishes a link between his poetic interest in the mythic world of ancient history and Freud's passion for archaeology:

> Freud has himself admitted that science, medicine and psychotherapy were for him a lifelong detour leading back to his youthful fascination with the history

of mankind, with the origins of religion and morality – the interest that, in his prime, finds such magnificent expression in *Totem and Taboo*. In the compound term 'depth psychology', 'depth' also has a temporal sense: the deepest layers of the human soul are also the depths of the past, the deep well of time, the home of myth, where it establishes the primal norms and forms of life.     (IX, 493)

In seeing the intellectual roots of Freud's teaching in a Romantic view of history, Mann ignores Freud's debt to the Enlightenment. While Herder and his successors sought the metaphysical bases of culture in the early history of national groups, Freud thinks that the mythic world-picture has been decisively vanquished by modern science. Thus the survival of archaic behaviour-patterns seems to him an atavistic regression and a pathological deviation from the norm of human values. Freud's theory of culture explains religion as a kind of collective compulsive neurosis which can be cured by insight into its historical and psychological causes. Hence, to justify his positive evaluation of myth and religion in the *Joseph* novels, Mann has to adopt two complementary psychological approaches which cross the boundary laid down by Freud between psychology and the holy. On the one hand, Mann appeals in a highly provocative fashion to Freud's renegade pupil C. G. Jung, who, by introducing mystical speculation about the unity of God and the human soul into psychoanalysis, influenced the psychology of the Israelite covenant with God as set out in the *Joseph* novels. On the other hand, Mann was guided (though without ever naming him) by the art historian and psychoanalyst Ernst Kris, who showed how biographies of artists in the Renaissance were modelled on typical patterns and thus changed 'psychological interest into mythical interest' (IX, 492). 'Life as quotation, life in myth' (IX, 497) is for Mann a ceremonial repetition of archetypal situations which places the individual life in a larger context and may still be relevant for modern man. If myth points towards the future, then, for Mann, it does not herald a cult-based collective but rather an individual form of life which adopts the principal of aesthetic autonomy and is prefigured in Joseph. 'The Joseph of the novel is an artist, inasmuch as he plays: with his *imitatio* of God he plays on the unconscious' (IX, 499).

In such works as 'Why War?' and *The Future of an Illusion* the late Freud offers a pessimistic prognosis for the future of civilisation, seeing the progress of rationality as constantly under threat from the power of man's instinctual urges and its mythological projections. Mann, by contrast, recognises in art the creative power of a humanism 'which will have a bolder and freer, more serene and more artistic relation to the powers of the underworld, the unconscious, the Id, than is possible for present-day humanity, toiling under the burden of neurotic anxiety and accompanying hatred' (IX, 500). The psychological treatment of myth in the *Joseph* novels is intended to explore the capacity of myth, even in its secularised forms, to unite the community. Mann retells the Scriptures, not (like Freud) as the records of mankind's illness, but as tales of the artist that also exemplify humanism.

## Metaphysics and politics: Mann's *Joseph* in its time

In Mann's work as a whole, the trio of mythology, psychology and aesthetics that is particularly accentuated in *Joseph* forms the central section of a long sequence that begins with metaphysics and ends in politics. In moving from metaphysics to politics, Mann gives a series of sensuous embodiments to the world of ideas. If in the metaphysical phase ideas appear as pure philosophical abstractions, they pass through mythic imagery, psychic representation and artistic portrayal, finally assuming practical form in political action. As early as in *Reflections of an Unpolitical Man* (1918) the political situation gave Mann the pretext for metaphysical reflection on the relation between life and intellect (*Geist*). There, in defining himself as conservative, in contrast to the left-wing progressivism of the *Zivilisationsliteraten* ('civilised men of letters'), Mann also distinguishes his stance sharply from a reactionary ideology of stasis. While political radicalism wishes to reshape life forcibly in accordance with intellectual principles, Mann's kind of conservative places life in an ironic relation to the intellect, thus relativising the claims to absolute validity put forward by political doctrines. Although, after the First World War, Mann became a *Vernunftrepublikaner* ('republican on rational grounds') and showed sympathy with socialism, he retained his metaphysical and political way of thinking until the period of exile. Resisting National Socialism, Mann became a popular spokesman for American democracy, without concealing his sympathy for Soviet Communism. Socialist revolution seemed to him an alternative to the bourgeois republic which had fallen prey to fascist populism. The changed political situation shows its effect in a new accent on the division between life and intellect. For the political threat no longer came from left-wing intellectual radicalism, but from a right-wing ideology of life that hypostatised 'blood and soil'.

The metaphysical model that contrasts life with the intellect is already expounded in 'Descent into Hell', the prelude to the *Joseph* novels. Taking the Gnostic myth that occurs in the various religions of salvation, Mann interprets it psychologically and poetologically as a 'romance of the soul'. The myth recounts the fall of the soul of the primal man, who is seduced by the sensual charm of matter. The union between the ideal form of the soul and the shapeless mass of matter gives rise to the cosmos. The intellect or the spirit, by contrast, appears as an envoy from the divine sphere who reminds the soul of its true origin and commands it to return. Radical intellectual reflection leads to a denial of the world of the senses. Mann reinterprets the mythic dualism of the spirit (or intellect) and the world as a sympathetic relationship mediated by irony. The novel's narrative principle thus receives a transcendental foundation. Since the spirit is 'unlawfully enamoured' of the soul, 'his words are changed in his mouth, so that, with a kind of affectionate wit, they speak against his own aims and in favour of life and forms' (IV, 44). The spirit's wilful deviation from the divine plan proves, however, to be a *felix culpa* or fortunate fall that makes possible their future reconciliation. 'God's mystery may lie ... in the mutual interpenetration of both principles and in the sanctification of each by the other, until mankind is blessed with a blessing from heaven above and a blessing from the depths below' (IV, 48–9). When Joseph, at the end of the tetralogy, is blessed by Jacob in the same words, he appears as a prototype of humanity's redemption into wholeness.

Although Mann transfers the metaphysical foundations of his fictive world to the universality of primeval myth, he does draw a historically detailed picture of political conditions in Egypt between 1352 and 1338 BC. Drawing mainly on the history of Egypt by J. H. Breasted, Mann chooses an epoch that was marked by violent political and theological conflicts. The Pharaoh Amenhotep IV introduced the monotheistic religion of the sun god Aton-Re and called himself Akhenaten, Son of Aton. This religious innovation met with fierce resistance from the priests of Amun, who had become the god of the state under Akhenaten's father, Amenhotep III. The religion and culture of the Akhenaten period perished with the death of their founder and were erased from Egypt's historical memory. It was only in the twentieth century that the monuments of the Amarna period (so called after Akhenaten's new capital) were discovered, with their fascinating air of modernity. Hence Freud, in his book on Moses, derived Jewish monotheism from the religion of Aton.[17] Similarly Mann identifies Amenhotep IV with the anonymous Pharaoh whose dream of seven fat kine and seven lean kine was interpreted by the biblical Joseph as prophesying a sequence of seven years of prosperity and seven years of famine.

In the Egyptian New Kingdom Mann was able to find counterparts to the modern phenomenon of political religions, that is, social movements that demand absolute faith and develop forms of cultic worship. Mann sketches a political typology that is shaped by the metaphysical principles of life and intellect. In *Joseph in Egypt* we meet a representative of a reactionary politics of life in the person of the priest Beknechons, whose disciples include Mut-em-enet. The latter uses fascistic phrases when she talks about the god Amun to her husband Peteprê, who inclines towards Amenhotep's reform party: 'he wishes the fibre of moral discipline to be strong in the land, as it always has been in Keme, and to have its children walk in the path of patriotic tradition'

(V, 1041). Beknechons's teaching represents not a conservative awareness of tradition but a forcible restoration of the past, reacting against 'laxity through foreign influence' (V, 1041). Recent research has stressed how much Beknechons corresponds to 'the reaction against the Weimar Republic that led to Fascism. He is nationalistic, xenophobic, conservative, and basically drawn to a barbaric and primitive past.'[18]

The Pharaoh Amenhotep stands for the contrasting principle of a politics of pure spirit which is opposed to 'the material, earthly and natural wellbeing of the world' and thus makes his successor incapable of acting as regent. 'The idea of his kingship was linked in his mind with the image of the black Egyptian soil . . . But he was an enthusiast for pure light . . . and his conscience was ill at ease' (V, 1384). While the Sun King proclaims a radical breach with tradition and denounces the elemental, earthy dimension of life, Joseph presents himself in the image of the moon as 'mediator' between heaven and earth, life and intellect, myth and rationality. Amenhotep succeeds in escaping from the division between his religious mission and his political obligations by appointing Joseph his 'Minister of Food and Agriculture' (V, 1499), while Joseph finds his way from an aesthetic existence, shown in his narcissistic construction of myths about himself, to social responsibility.

Joseph's worldly pragmatism translates Akhenaten's intellectual revolution into political terms without doing violence to the natural needs of the population. When Joseph's 'law of ground rent' introduces a fair method of taxing the rich and makes it possible for the state to look after the people, Mann is taking as his model the economic administration of the US President Franklin D. Roosevelt.[19] He considered the New Deal a successful synthesis of bourgeois democracy and socialist dictatorship. The similarities to the American model, however, go beyond the reference to current events and include the metaphysical dimension of politics. While Beknechons's theocratic regime rests on the identity of the sacral and the political, Joseph separates the state and religion, just as the US constitution prescribes in the spirit of the Enlightenment. This secularisation of religion appears as part of divine providence: 'however prudently he served the public, his inmost eye was always turned to private spiritual matters, to domestic matters of world significance' (V, 1499).

While the first three parts of the tetralogy assume a sharp division between Jewish and Egyptian cultures, Joseph has by now arrived at 'the time of enfranchisement', as the fourth section of the last novel is entitled. By distinguishing between outer and inner, Joseph manages to assimilate himself to Egyptian civilisation while maintaining his religious identity. Thus he marries an Egyptian and even becomes a priest of the new god of the state, Aton. He justifies crossing cultural and religious boundaries by the theological reflection 'that it would be an error and a folly, that is, a sin, to grant the God of his fathers a narrower horizon than Aton-Re' (v, 1520). The universal aspect of Jewish monotheism is here emphasised at the expense of the exclusive concept of election. 'The indulgence' granted Joseph by the biblical God 'took account of a worldly outlook which in turn ensured that there would never be a "Tribe of Joseph"'. Although the dying Jacob confirms the rediscovered Joseph as his 'favourite', it is Judah whom he makes his heir. While Judah's life has been shaped by the conflict with his sensual nature and his tormenting sense of guilt towards his brother, Joseph has always succeeded in 'finding favour before God and man'. According to Jacob, however, this blessing is 'not the highest nor the hardest' (v, 1804). The ancestor of Israel here reinforces the aesthetic character of Joseph's mission: 'It was play and play-acting... but not summoned and admitted in all seriousness.'

Mann's tetralogy gives Joseph and Judah equal status as representatives of Judaism. The author regards spiritual and worldly election, the individual sense of sin and the universal ethos, as aspects of biblical humanity that are important for the literature of the world. Thus the poet Mann, no less than the Jewish patriarch, declares Joseph his favourite, since for him it is only in the medium of art that modern religion can be revealed and accepted as the basis of culture.

## NOTES

1 Mann, *Briefwechsel mit seinem Verleger Gottfried Bermann Fischer, 1932–1955*, ed. Peter de Mendelssohn (Frankfurt am Main: Fischer, 1975), p. 130.
2 E.g. by Børge Kristiansen, 'Ägypten als symbolischer Raum der geistigen Problematik Thomas Manns. Überlegungen zur Dimension der Selbstkritik in *Joseph und seine Brüder*', *Thomas Mann Jahrbuch* 6 (1993), 9–36.
3 See Manfred Dierks, 'Kultursymbolik und Seelenlandschaft: "Ägypten" als Projektion', *Thomas Mann Jahrbuch* 6 (1993), 113–31; Dierk Wolters, *Zwischen Metaphysik und Politik. Thomas Manns Roman 'Joseph und seine Brüder' in seiner Zeit* (Tübingen: Niemeyer, 1998).
4 See Ernst Kantorowicz, *Kaiser Friedrich der Zweite* (Berlin: Bondi, 1927); Ernst Bertram, *Nietzsche. Versuch einer Mythologie* (Berlin: Bondi, 1918).
5 See Martin Doerne, 'Thomas Mann und das protestantische Christentum', *Die Sammlung* 11 (1956), 407–25; Friedrich-Wilhelm Kantzenbach, 'Theologische Denkstrukturen bei Thomas Mann', *Neue Zeitschrift für systematische Theologie* 9 (1967), 201–17.
6 Hans Egon Holthusen, *Die Welt ohne Transzendenz. Eine Studie zu Thomas Manns 'Doktor Faustus'* (Hamburg: Ellermann, 1954); Herbert Lehnert, *Thomas Mann – Fiktion, Mythos, Religion* (Stuttgart: Kohlhammer, 1965).
7 Diethmar Mieth, *Epik und Ethik. Eine theologisch-ethische Interpretation der Josephsromane Thomas Manns* (Tübingen: Niemeyer, 1976).
8 Jan Assmann, *Das kulturelle Gedächtnis. Schrift, Erinnerung und politische Identität in frühen Hochkulturen* (Munich: Beck, 1992); 'Zitathaftes Leben. Thomas Mann und die Phänomenologie der kulturellen Erinnerung', *Thomas Mann*

*Jahrbuch* 6 (1993), 133–58. See also Y. H. Yerushalmi, *Zakhor: Jewish History and Jewish Memory* (Seattle: University of Washington Press, 1982); Wolf-Daniel Hartwich, 'Prediger und Erzähler. Die Rhetorik des Heiligen im Werk Thomas Manns', *Thomas Mann Jahrbuch* 11 (1998), 31–50.

9 See Alfred Jeremias, *Die außerbiblische Erlösererwartung* (Sannerz and Leipzig: Eberhard Arnold, 1927), pp. 92–105.

10 Aharon Agus, *The Binding of Isaak and Messiah. Law, Martyrdom and Deliverance in Early Rabbinic Religiosity* (Albany, NY: State University of New York Press, 1988).

11 Dietrich Opitz, 'Tam(m)uz', in Hermann Gunkel and Leopold Zschernak (eds.), *Die Religion in Geschichte und Gegenwart* (Tübingen: Mohr, 1931), v, cols. 981–2.

12 See Jeremias, *Die außerbiblische Erlösererwartung*, pp. 27–9.

13 See Edward Said, *Orientalism* (London: Routledge & Kegan Paul, 1978). On Thomas Mann, see Andrea Fuchs-Sumiyoshi, *Orientalismus in der deutschen Literatur* (Hildesheim: Olms, 1984), pp. 136–55.

14 Letter to Charles du Bos, 3 May 1929, quoted from Mann, *Briefwechsel mit Autoren*, ed. Hans Wysling (Frankfurt am Main: Fischer, 1988), p. 179.

15 See Wolf-Daniel Hartwich, *Die Sendung Moses. Von der Aufklärung bis Thomas Mann* (Munich: Fink, 1997), pp. 188–200, 215–26.

16 See Maren Niehoff, *The Figure of Joseph in Post-Biblical Jewish Literature* (Leiden: Brill, 1992), pp. 78–80. Philo of Alexandria 'turns this confrontation into an encounter of Hebrew and Egyptian culture' (p. 79).

17 On the reception of Akhenaten in European history, see Jan Assmann, *Moses the Egyptian: The Memory of Egypt in Western Monotheism* (Cambridge, MA: Harvard University Press, 1997).

18 Dierks, 'Kultursymbolik und Seelenlandschaft', p. 124. Cf. Wolters, *Zwischen Metaphysik und Politik*, pp. 249–50.

19 See Wolters, *Zwischen Metaphysik und Politik*, pp. 302–9.

## FURTHER READING

Bishop, Paul, '*Jung-Joseph*: Thomas Mann's reception of Jungian thought in the *Joseph* tetralogy', *Modern Language Review* 91 (1996), 138–58

Borchmeyer, Dieter, '"Zurück zum Anfang aller Dinge". Mythos und Religion in Thomas Manns *Joseph*romanen', *Thomas Mann Jahrbuch* 11 (1998), 9–29

Kurzke, Hermann, *Mondwanderung: Wegweiser durch Thomas Manns Joseph-Roman* (Frankfurt am Main: Fischer, 1993)

Levenson, Alan, 'Christian Author, Jewish Book? Methods and Sources in Thomas Mann's *Joseph*', *German Quarterly* 71 (1998), 166–78

McDonald, William E., *Thomas Mann's 'Joseph and his Brothers': Writing, Performance, and the Politics of Loyalty* (Rochester, NY: Camden House, 1999)

Nolte, Charlotte, *Being and Meaning in Thomas Mann's 'Joseph und seine Brüder'* (London: MHRA, 1996)

Scaff, Susan von Rohr, 'The Dialectic of Myth and History: Revision of Archetype in Thomas Mann's Joseph Novels', *Monatshefte* 82 (1990), 177–93

Scheiffele, Eberhard, 'Die Joseph-Romane im Lichte heutiger Mythos-Diskussion', *Thomas Mann Jahrbuch* 4 (1991), 161–83

Wolters, Dierk, *Zwischen Metaphysik und Politik. Thomas Manns Roman 'Joseph und seine Brüder' in seiner Zeit* (Tübingen: Niemeyer, 1998)

# 11

SUSAN VON ROHR SCAFF

## Doctor Faustus

Thomas Mann began work on *Doctor Faustus* in May 1943, having just completed *Joseph and his Brothers*. A year earlier, as he was putting the finishing touches to the biblical tetralogy, he found his thoughts already turning towards this next novel, a daring new artist's tale that might, he believed, be the most bizarre and outlandish he had ever produced. A month before beginning the book Mann disclosed what he had in mind: to take up a project he had conceived as early as 1904, the story of an artist in league with the devil for the sake of creativity, a modern-day Faust who would sell his soul to make wondrous works of art (letters to Agnes E. Meyer, 21 February 1942, and to Klaus Mann, 27 April 1943). Art and artistry were of course familiar concerns for Mann, but why, we might ask, would he choose just now in the middle of the Second World War to devote an ambitious new novel to the tribulations of the artist? Living in exile along with other refugees in the United States, Mann was following the progress of Hitler's war with the distress of a German worried about the guilt and fate of his people. With the popularity of his translated works in America, moreover, he was becoming a prominent spokesperson on the German issue. Surely this was not the moment for him to rework the predicament of Tonio Kröger, Gustav Aschenbach, and the other frustrated artists who populate his tales, a strangely intellectual topic given the atrocities taking place in Europe. The author would have to make himself clear.

Mann did set out his purpose, and the answer to his choice of subject-matter lies in the connection that he draws between Adrian Leverkühn, the protagonist of *Doctor Faustus*, and the moral dilemma and culpability of the German nation. As Mann saw it, Leverkühn's stimulation by the devil illuminated the fascist frenzy and took on a political colouring (letters to Klaus Mann, 17 April 1943, and to Fredric Warburg, 27 September 1944). With this association between art and life *Doctor Faustus* extends a correlation present in all of Mann's work, for Mann believed that the artist represents the human spirit in its essence and that the pattern of life is contained in the work of art (XII, 799–800). The crisis for the human being as artist is sterility, an incapacity to realise one's creativity that Mann portrays as a terrifying paralysis. If we find ourselves unable to draw on our inner resources, we begin to feel as though we are dying inside, and when the artist fails in Mann's stories, we are threatened by the spectre of destitution. Artists inspire and bring out the best in us, but the foiled and maddened artist produces work that is repugnant and degrading, even criminal. It is this penchant for extremity that makes the artist a suitable figure for Mann's story of the troubled times. As the modern Faust Leverkühn stands at once for humanity's greatest potential and its most devastating frailties. With his brilliance and talent he shows just how high we might reach, but having made his deal with the devil, he is the very image of fallen humanity.

Leverkühn is also a musician, and his musical compositions stand at the heart of the novel. Music, in Mann's view, is a peculiarly powerful art-form, and it is morally charged. In hard times composers may draw upon deep inner reserves to write music that uplifts the audience, and whenever human beings fall victim to their worst instincts, music may replenish their faith and resilience (XIII, 862). But music may also be harmful. Settembrini, the Italian rationalist who advises Hans Castorp in *The Magic Mountain*, expresses Mann's grave reservations about music. Music can actually be hazardous to our mental and moral health, a gift of the devil, as he puts it, that corrupts the soul (III, 160–2). Writing pieces that drag down both composer and listener, Leverkühn has succumbed to the evil in his environment, and his work signals both the composer's inner corruption and the deterioration of the world around him.

*Doctor Faustus*, then, is a dialogical novel presenting an interplay between horrific public events and the tragic personal ones of a bedevilled musician. The book is structured to emphasise this reciprocity between the inner and outer worlds. It is told by Serenus Zeitblom, a retired grammar-school teacher living reluctantly in Nazi Germany who is writing the life-story of his childhood friend, and the story unfolds on two time planes, that of the narrator and that of Leverkühn himself. Zeitblom begins this writing when Mann began his, in 1943, and draws the tale to a close just as the war is coming to an end in 1945. As he relives his memories of Leverkühn, he intersperses news of the war with reflections on the culture and climate that enabled fascism to take hold in Germany. Alongside this commentary on historical circumstances and events, he characterises the inward life of his companion by reporting their conversations and correspondence, and, most importantly, by describing Leverkühn's works. The tie is made by juxtaposition and analogy between the state of the world and the spiritual condition of the artist. Zeitblom weaves back and forth, and the major themes and issues in Mann's novel could be said to lie in the link that he makes between the crisis of history and the artist's inner life, traced in the composer's music.

## The crisis of the times

In the course of his tale Zeitblom takes in virtually every aspect of German life from the public to the most private between 1885, the year of Leverkühn's birth, and 1945: the pre-fascist and fascist eras. The evocation of nationalist feeling, the perversion of theology, the failure of family love, the introduction of Leverkühn's shocking new music into the world of art – all are developed in gruesome detail. The effect is a doomsday atmosphere that intensifies as the Second World War and the memoir draw simultaneously to their ends. Relating the deaths by disease, murder, suicide and insanity that mark the end of Leverkühn's life-story, Zeitblom also relays news from the front portending the German defeat. At times he breaks into a biblical cadence, as in this passage prophesying the German demise, which recalls the Book of Ezekiel: 'the end is coming, the end is come, the dawn breaks over thee, O thou who dwell in the land' (VI, 576; Chapter 41). Mann himself saw *Doctor Faustus* as a book about endings and the final end (letter to Claude Hill, 18 November 1948). In his imaginary reworking of twentieth-century history the author creates a vision of the end that engulfs the present with apocalyptic rhetoric and creates a tone of unremitting fear.

Mann develops his revelation not only through the turmoil and terror characteristic of the biblical apocalypses, but also through a more local typology that he calls 'musicality'. In a talk entitled 'Germany and the Germans' given in 1945, he analyses the pact that he believes Germany has signed with its own devil, Hitler. Musicality is an introspective tendency epitomised in Faust, and to clarify it Mann turns to the dual nature of music itself. Music is a systematic structuring of sound, the product of mathematical calculation, yet it is also a spontaneous outpouring of feeling, inspired not by thought but by deep emotion (XI, 1131–2). Music thus promotes contrary extremes: excessive application of the intellect and indulgence of irrational feeling. Mann saw the work of the devil in this Faustian pattern, and he makes the Germans' vulnerability to musicality the model for their moral degeneration, an urge for purity that capitulates to hysteria.

Both tendencies are evident in the national feeling that Zeitblom has ample opportunity to observe. Around 1919 he and Leverkühn begin attending a salon in the home of one Sixtus Kridwiss, an art collector in Munich. Although he does not use the term 'musicality', Zeitblom describes the sentiments of these characters as an instance of it. Humane bourgeois values have been destroyed in the war just ended, and this is considered a good thing. What will replace them? Myths, lies, chimeras – all in the cause of in-stituting a tyrannical hold over the masses. The rationale for this autocracy is the purification of German society and the race. The weak, handicapped and diseased must be eliminated so that Germany can fortify itself for harsh and sinister times. Zeitblom says nothing of the counter-movement ready to establish a democratic society in the Weimar Republic at this time. In-stead, the people he meets in the company of Leverkühn declare their intent to achieve a perverted ideological goal. Its accomplishment would take the world back to the Dark Ages, a welcome return in their eyes to that epoch of war and persecution (VI, 492). As Zeitblom discerns, civilisation, in its desire for purity, is now set on a regressive course towards barbarism.

One might expect the Church to play a countervailing part to this com-pulsion for evil, but instead the opposite proves true. A Lutheran by birth, Leverkühn decides as a young man to study theology and enrolls at the Uni-versity of Halle. What he encounters there suits not only his well-developed proclivity for abstract thinking but also his fascination with the demonic. Covering such philosophical topics as ethics, and apologetics, and such practical disciplines as homiletics and church governance, the curriculum is strictly intellectual and ignores the New Testament gospel of love. This distortion of the Christian heritage finds loud spokesmen among the profes-sors, two of whom, Kumpf and Schleppfuss, show themselves to be obsessed with the devil. Kumpf evinces a hearty personality in the spirit of Martin Luther and does robust battle with the fiend. But Schleppfuss develops a learned rationalisation for his enthralment, arguing that evil contributes to the wholeness of the universe and that God, who is consummate, sanctions the evil abroad (VI, 139). In its grim combination of the cognitive and the diabolical, this education is distinctively Faustian. Taking place at the turn of the century within the very institution that might provide moral leadership, Leverkühn's course in theology presages the fascist way of thinking that will make its appearance among people like Sixtus Kridwiss two decades later.

In this deteriorating environment it is no surprise that family life is also affected, and Zeitblom's cultural biography is notable for its dearth of ful-filling love-relationships. Those marriages that do thrive, notably in the Schweigestill and Schneidewein families, subsist on the margin of society in isolated rural settings. Prominent in Zeitblom's tale is the story that he presents as emblematic of the age, the marriage of Inez Rodde and Helmut Institoris. Occupying lengthy sections of Zeitblom's narrative, the chronicle of this union follows the model of Faustian duality. Inez picks Helmut for his respectability and the security of a bourgeois life, and from the start her ideal of a proper home dominates their matrimony. Under what Zeitblom calls her compulsion for perfection, the accoutrements of family life are realised to the full: a grand house, daughters trained in every propriety, the decorous attendance of husband and wife in cultured circles. The other side of Inez shows itself in her passion for the violinist Rudi Schwerdtfeger and her erotic affair with him. In both components of her personality Inez is crazed: on the one hand, to keep up social appearances; on the other, to possess her lover body and soul. This saga of conflicting obsessions could only come to a tragic end. Rejected by Rudi and addicted to morphine, Inez shoots him in jealous fury. Inez has fallen victim to the twin traps of perfectionism and madness that form the dominant pattern in Zeitblom's depiction of a nation's woe.

Since Faustian evil has spread into every corner of civilised life, we must wonder about the role that Zeitblom plays in the story. In his persona as a good man Zeitblom agonises over the foibles and tragedies that he recounts while at the same time confronting them with brutal honesty. Perhaps this narrator who offers such a penetrating and sensitive analysis of what goes on around him stands beyond the influence of Faust. His responses are commendably humane. He reports feeling sick on hearing the talk of purification at the Kridwiss salon, and he bemoans the downward course of Inez Institoris, who has made him her confidant. Though his account of Leverkühn's student days at Halle is evidently factual, he colours it with ominous details – Kumpf's medieval oaths, Schleppfuss's dragging foot – that warn of demons on the loose. He evokes Leverkühn's talent with the highest esteem, sympathises through his friend's bouts of illness, and remains loyal even after learning about the composer's conversation and contract with the devil, reported to him in a letter. Zeitblom goes out of his way to set himself apart from his milieu as an observer and to express his sorrow for its casualties. If anyone has escaped the plight of the times it is this benign humanist in his shock at these abominations and the concern that he shows for his friends.

But the crisis is too big for one man to withstand, for understanding and compassion can only be compromised in surroundings that have gone so far wrong. Zeitblom shares the role of sympathetic bystander with another character, Frau Else Schweigestill. Proprietress of the farm outside Munich where the musician retires after finalising the pact, Frau Schweigestill provides a refuge for him in his work and warm care through his infirmities. It is she who rushes to Leverkühn's side when he collapses after the confession and farewell to his friends that so shocks the company, admonishing them to show some human kindness. Zeitblom and Else play complementary parts in the drama of succouring Leverkühn. As her name, Schweigestill, suggests, Else will 'keep quiet' about his life, not because she deliberately conceals evil but because in her simplicity she fails to recognise it. Zeitblom is the opposite, an artful narrator who does his best to persuade us that the musician is a genius who deserves compassion. Neither one nor the other can cover

Leverkühn's degeneracy from public view, however, and both sacrifice their own integrity in shielding him. Their implied complicity completes Mann's depiction of the corrupted times.

What of Leverkühn himself, this musician at the centre of it all whose life and work have so deeply affected his lifelong companion? What exactly does he *do* that deserves recrimination? Most obviously, of course, he makes a deal with the devil, and the meaning of this pact does much to explain his demise. In his letter to Zeitblom Leverkühn presents the scene in vivid detail, recounting his lengthy dialogue with Sammael, the angel of death. The meeting occurs just as Leverkühn is reading Kierkegaard's essay on *Don Giovanni*, and perhaps his imagination has been stimulated by the entrance of the ghostly *Commendatore* to claim Don Giovanni at the end of Mozart's opera, though Leverkühn emphatically denies that he has been hallucinating (VI, 294–6). The question is immaterial, however, for Mann's point is not to invite or deny a literal reading of the episode but to communicate the enormity of Leverkühn's sin. Taking as its source the original Faust legend from the time of the Reformation that ends in the damnation of Dr Faustus, Leverkühn's story draws its power from the tradition of the devil's contract immortalised by Goethe in *Faust* and by many others, including Carl Maria von Weber through Kaspar's deal with Samiel in the opera *Der Freischütz* (letter to Ernst Schertel, 29 September 1953). Leverkühn is a knowing and willing participant in the agreement. He has long awaited the encounter and admits that he welcomes it. In fact, the pact merely confirms the league that has implicitly been in effect for many years (VI, 296–9). Whether he signs the contract in the flesh or in the depths of his soul, Leverkühn is depicted in the devil's dialogue as a man who has sunk into depravity.

It might seem, nonetheless, that Leverkühn does not exactly commit immoral acts as a consequence of the pact. He is a composer, after all, and he simply writes his music. But music stimulated by the devil bears the mark of its origin, and in Mann's symbolic story Leverkühn's misdeeds are aesthetic. From the beginning of his career Leverkühn is heralded as an extraordinary musician. His works are stunning, arousing admiration, yet audiences also find them repellent. His first composition, *Meeresleuchten* (*Ocean Lights*), an orchestral work written in the Impressionist style, astonishes the critics with its brilliance but also appals them with its chilling mockery of Ravel and Debussy. Even after Leverkühn develops his own modern technique and wins widespread acclaim, the public reaction to his work swings between awe and repugnance. His opera, based on Shakespeare's *Love's Labour's Lost*, is esoteric and intellectual, beautiful in its own way perhaps, as Zeitblom muses, but more aptly termed heroic. In Zeitblom's summation, it is a 'breakneck game of art played on the edge of impossibility' (VI, 290; Chapter 34).

Here and elsewhere Zeitblom is forced to emphasise the daringness of Leverkühn's skill. This is music made to excite and agitate, not to edify or heal. The signature of the fiend is written everywhere in these productions, and Leverkühn's reputation as their maker never escapes the taint of notoriety.

Nevertheless, it is not so much what he does but who he is that defines Leverkühn's sinfulness. Leverkühn is fundamentally an abstract thinker, a lifeless and even dangerous character type, in Mann's view, like that of Nietzsche's Socratic man. In Nietzsche's *Birth of Tragedy*, Socrates stands for the supreme application of the intellect. Through the centuries Socrates' successors have overdeveloped the art of rational thinking, and the result is the lonely scholar and cogitator, Faust (*BT* §18). Exclusion of the life instincts requires their revival, however, and the artist is energised by a vital feeling that Nietzsche calls the 'Dionysian' in recollection of the orgiastic rites performed for the god Dionysus (*BT* §1). Leverkühn's intellectuality inhibits his creative power as long as he fulfils the Socratic tendency, and in order to generate his music, he infuses himself with the Dionysian life force. As a young man he intentionally contracts syphilis from the prostitute Esmeralda in a brothel scene that replicates an episode from Nietzsche's own life. Sickening and maddening the composer, the disease also stimulates his work. Nietzsche calls for a creative resolution of these polarities, but Leverkühn, under the influence of the devil, carries both to their outer limits and writes music that is at once too painstakingly designed and too raw in its projection of elemental feeling. It is this conjunction and clash between the mental and the vital that Mann has in mind when he speaks of Faustian musicality.

The salient feature of this conflicted personality is an inability to make contact with others, and Leverkühn subsists from childhood shut off in an inner world. Absorbed by the intellect, he lacks the human quality of care. His enchantment with music derives not from a pleasure in melody and song that could be shared but from a private fascination with the arithmetical and geometric structures of scales, chords and musical scores. His association with Zeitblom is intimate in the exchange of predilections and ideas, but never warm. Indeed, human warmth is exactly what Leverkühn never experiences. That he knows this about himself is revealed in a youthful admission to his music teacher, Wendell Kretschmar: 'I am a rotten fellow, for I have no warmth... I am decidedly cold' (VI, 174; Chapter 15). Sammael renders this curse conclusive when he forbids the warmth of love as a stipulation of the pact: the composer will be tossed between heat and cold, alternately inflamed by passion to write and compelled to retreat into the bitter coldness of his private life. Leverkühn rightly observes that by being forbidden attachment and affection he has been sentenced to a hell on earth (VI, 332–3). His fate is the misery of exile punctuated by frenzied bouts of productivity. Thus encumbered, he removes himself from the community to write his music. His sin is that he lives and works in this way; his damnation, the sorry condition of his soul.

Mann's protagonist contains the afflictions of the age within his very make-up. It is a loveless state, split between conflicting impulses, withdrawn and isolated. Though it is not typical of every figure in the story, for Zeitblom and Schweigestill are exceptions, it is conspicuous in most of the characters and carried to an extreme in Leverkühn himself. It reveals a moral dysfunction that extends from art into personal relationships and through all the principal institutions of society. The consequences of this collective pathology are harrowing. Zeitblom describes a corruption of civilisation so encompassing that no one, including himself, has a clear understanding of right and wrong. The confusion of standards and values has led an entire nation to misjudge its leader and the exalted promises made to them for a rebirth. Zeitblom speaks with compelling regret about the almost religious intoxication with which the Germans were animated to join the cause for their own betterment in 1933. Now with the war drawing to its end he dwells on the crimes committed and the inevitability of punishment: the deeds must be paid for (VI, 233). Within this apocalypse Leverkühn is accorded mythical proportions and made to stand for all that has gone wrong in the aesthetic, personal, religious and political spheres of life.

## The crisis in music

The story of Leverkühn's life is filled out and completed in the elaborate accounts that Zeitblom gives of the composer's music. In counterpoint to the main narrative, these descriptions relate the development of Leverkühn's musical style and profession. Complementing the musician's outer life, his music establishes an undercurrent of deeper meaning that speaks to the crisis in art as Mann saw it unfolding in the twentieth century, as well as to Leverkühn's personal plight. Leverkühn's career begins with his Impressionist parody in *Ocean Lights* and culminates in a cantata in the twelve-tone style titled *Dr. Fausti Weheklag* (*The Lamentation of Doctor Faustus*), which has particular significance for the reader's understanding of the musician's work and life. Between these pieces stretches a long line of songs, orchestral works, Leverkühn's opera, a violin concerto written for Rudi Schwerdtfeger, several pieces of chamber music, and a massive oratorio that Leverkühn calls *Apocalypsis cum figuris*, a revelation of the end of time. It would not be too much to say that the progress of Leverkühn's technique and themes forms a sub-plot with its own important story to tell. In other words, how we read Leverkühn's music contributes to how we comprehend the novel as a whole.

The issues surrounding his music are manifold, but they hinge on Leverkühn's 'breakthrough', promised to him by the devil and achieved, apparently, in *The Lamentation*. Sammael says that the composer will lead music into new times and enjoy the recognition of all who follow. To attain this fame the composer will have to break with the refinement of outworn conventions. He must dare to be barbaric (VI, 324). What the devil means by these enigmatic words and whether Leverkühn achieves a breakthrough worthy of congratulation are problems raised by the pledge. The matter goes beyond questions of style, taking on a broader cultural significance that extends from the aesthetic to the religious. If Leverkühn does break through to a new level of barbarism, this may bring his criminal activity to a climax and signal his downfall. On the other hand, if his breakthrough shatters the conventions that have trapped him and his contemporaries in a web of moral illusion, then he has confounded the devil and perhaps escaped the curse. Such a reading would set Leverkühn's story within the larger tradition of sin and redemption that Mann evokes in the story of the human fall. Mann frames the exploration of these life-and-death questions within a discourse on modern music that runs through Leverkühn's disquisitions on the theory and practice of the art and Zeitblom's analysis of the Leverkühn opus.

While any number of composers are mentioned or alluded to in the novel, the story of modern music begins in Mann's mind with Richard Wagner and ends with Arnold Schönberg. Leverkühn's musical development starts, accordingly, with his repudiation of late-Romantic Wagnerian grandeur and proceeds to his invention of Schönberg's cerebral twelve-tone method. Before he ever writes a piece of music Leverkühn makes clear his embarrassment about Wagner. In a letter to Kretschmar he gives a verbal description of the prelude to the third act of *The Meistersinger* that derides Wagner's sonority and heroic pretensions, a style, he says, that can only make him laugh (VI, 178–9). But mockery does not sum up Mann's own reservations about Wagner that stand behind Leverkühn's rebuff. Though he had a personal passion for Wagner's music, Mann believed that the Wagnerian style posed a moral threat. By the time he wrote *Doctor Faustus*, Wagnerian music was tainted by Hitler's enthusiasm for its blatant nationalism, but long before the rise of National Socialism Mann worried about the effect of Wagner's sweeping cadences. Wagner is cunning. His music seduces the listener with its sense of desire and can become all-consuming. With its insidious effect on the emotions it undermines resolve and strength of character. It is pernicious and dangerous (XII, 74–5).

Just how this harm is effected and why it is so important becomes clear in Mann's critique of decadence. Like Nietzsche in his earlier rejection of Wagner, Mann took the emotion induced by Wagner's lush melodies as an enticement to self-indulgence and lethargy. Nietzsche protested in *The Case of Wagner* that luxuriating in this music infuses us with a weary sense of floating and swimming. What is worse, letting ourselves go in this way weakens us and makes us sick, physically as well as emotionally (*CW* §5). Though he is not referring directly to Wagner, it is this kind of debilitating influence that Settembrini has in mind when he complains about the listlessness caused by music (III, 162). It is also the phenomenon that Mann describes through Hanno in *Buddenbrooks*. Along with his mother, a violinist, Hanno adores the Wagnerian style and seeks to imitate it in his own compositions. Improvising at the piano, he writes drawn-out cadences like Wagner's, expressive of his romantic adolescent yearnings. But this music consumes Hanno and eventually makes him sick, and his death indicates the danger to body and soul in giving oneself over to Wagner. More than thirty years after *Buddenbrooks*, in the speech that precipitated his exile from Germany, Mann commented again on the dangerously intoxicating sensuality of Wagnerian music, observing its power to allure the masses (IX, 414). Both for Hanno, the individual composer, and for the large audiences applauding Wagner in Germany, this music creates a beguiling world of illusion that undermines principle and integrity.

One might expect the rejection of Wagner to work a healing effect on the arts, but when Wagner is discredited as a reputable influence for the composer, a great deal is lost that is valuable, and Mann knows this. Wagner possessed the quality of expressiveness that Leverkühn misses in his creation. Despite all of his reservations about Wagner, Mann never gave up the personal pleasure that he took in Wagner's music, and in one of his many tributes to him speaks glowingly of Wagner's 'furchtbare Audsdruckskunst' ('formidable art of expression') (letter to Walter Opitz, 26 August 1909). The forfeiture of the Romantic art of self-expression in the twentieth century is accompanied, in Mann's fictional representation of it, by a shift in the artist's attitude toward the audience. A composer such as Leverkühn, who is by his nature cold and impersonal, does not make emotional contact. His music impresses listeners, but it does not move them, and even Leverkühn occasionally regrets this. In an uncharacteristic confession he admits that he would prefer a close relationship with his audience. Music must be released from its haughty isolation or it will wither and die, he tells Zeitblom, and his own aim is to create 'an art on intimate terms with humanity' (VI, 430; Chapter 31). With this incongruous acknowledgement of his own inadequacy, Leverkühn points to the transformation that might save modern music, the rediscovery and expression of feeling.

The bind of twentieth-century music depicted in *Doctor Faustus* is precisely Leverkühn's trap of cognition. Early in the century Mann had hoped that the Wagnerian extravaganza of the nineteenth century would be followed by a classical revolution in the twentieth. He looked forward to the introduction of an austere musical style, logical and clear in its form, confident and cheerful in its tone (x, 842). This was just a few years before Schönberg inaugurated the twelve-tone technique in 1915, and dodecaphony, with its formal precision, meets some of Mann's requirements for renewal. But when Mann heard Schönberg's new music, he found its dissonance jarring, and he was so disturbed by its abrasive tone that he came to look upon it as a harbinger of music's ruin. Schönberg, of course, who was Mann's fellow émigré in Los Angeles, objected to the author's use and characterisation of his work in the novel.[1] But, audacious as it was, Mann's point was to articulate as graphically as possible the straits of modern music and of the times. The switch from the mode of Wagner to that of Schönberg marked a reversal from emotion that was too heavily laden, to intellect that was overdeveloped in minds like Leverkühn's. Wagner operated seditiously on the souls of those unprepared to resist his seduction, but with the advent of dodecaphony in the avant-garde Mann saw a fall of a more heinous kind. The mental effort that the artist expended to produce each note displayed a deadening of feeling, the affliction of Faust, and the musician's need for a Dionysian awakening supplied by the devil signalled perdition.

Mann transposed his doubts about the new music into the apocalyptic outlook of his novel by linking dodecaphony to the approaching end of time. In its structure, the twelve-tone piece, instead of lengthening out in time, paradoxically seems to cancel time. This occurs as notes and phrases are doubled back in multiple patterns of repetition. The composition is built on a row or series of twelve notes based on the half-steps of the chromatic scale. In the course of the work this tone-row may be reversed or the intervals inverted, or both, but the series configured for the piece may not be altered. When Leverkühn explains this technique to Zeitblom, he emphasises its strictness. Every note has a predetermined place; no note is free (VI, 255–6). Preset in their design of interlocking and matching parts, the variations of the tone-row mirror one another, and the result is a tight construction featuring a few repeated musical ideas. Theodor Adorno, the author's consultant for music in *Doctor Faustus*, first drew Mann's attention to the temporal compression in dodecaphony.[2] In the novel, however, it is Sammael who elaborates the consequences of this restrictive method of composition, ironically quoting from Adorno's still unpublished *Philosophy of Modern Music*.

Because its parts are so tightly connected, he says, the piece eschews extra notes and phrases and provides little opportunity for thematic development, thus shrinking in time (VI, 320). Simply by giving these words to the devil Mann suggests the sinister effect of dodecaphony. Suppressing progression, the twelve-tone piece gives the audience the impression that time is coming to an end.

The structural repression of time parallels an impasse in the historical development of music that points towards another end. The problem is not so much stalled production, for music is still being written, but rather a standstill in significant new ideas. As Sammael explains and Leverkühn agrees, the composer's dilemma is the diminishing supply of musical material (VI, 318). By this late point in history virtually all musical ideas have been used and incorporated in the tradition, and the musician, like Leverkühn in *Ocean Lights*, is confronted with a superabundance of clichés. It is mortifying to repeat the old styles but nearly impossible to discover new ones, and an artist's only recourse is to recombine the stock of old inspirations in the hope that he may still squeeze some life out of them. In order to invent anything new, as Leverkühn does with the twelve-tone style, the musician must apply his mental powers to the utmost, but to write music by manipulating ideas is to turn it into a game. As modern composers concoct and elaborate their new styles, their field of opportunity diminishes, and if they continue much longer in this way, there will soon be no more new combinations to try. Without a breakthrough to a new way of composing reconnected with experience, the history of music will soon come to its end.

Leverkühn's *Apocalypsis cum figuris* brings the novel's theme of end-time to its most gruelling point of development in music. Compactly assembled in the circular twelve-tone pattern, it captures the end of time in its structure. Intended as a revelation, the oratorio also combines form with theme to give a hellish vision of the end. A peculiarity of this piece is its matching of contradictory elements. Though the pitch, orchestration and rhythms are changed, the music of the children's chorus reappears in a round of hellish laughter. Chorus and orchestra are confused in their musical function, and dissonance is associated with the solemn and pious while harmony is invoked to designate hell. The connection of the human voice with glissando, a primitive inhuman sound, shocks Zeitblom so much that he concludes that for cultural reasons it should be used with the utmost restraint (VI, 496–8, 502). In the way that it identifies opposites, the *Apocalypsis* reveals the final disintegration of things, disclosing the chaos and destruction foretold by Daniel and by St John the Divine in the Book of Revelation.

The crisis of modern music, illuminated in the *Apocalypsis*, shows Leverkühn at his lowest point, and as a commentary on the times it is a vision of depravity. Zeitblom describes the work at length in two chapters surrounding his account of the Kridwiss circle. Noting the parallels between the oratorio and the conversations of the company, he shows how this piece, produced in the same era as the Kridwiss gatherings, replicates their dogmatism. In its coercive formalism this music sums up the compulsion to perfect and control that distinguishes the fascist world-view. Outside the novel Mann also comments on the cultural implications of the *Apocalypsis*, saying that the tyrannical objectivity of the oratorio sets the audience back into a darkly primitive mythical time (XI, 174, 246). As an insight into the artist, finally, the *Apocalypsis* imparts the privation of the man who made it. For Leverkühn's labours have yielded no more than an iteration of hopelessness. He who produces such a masterpiece has, ironically, reached his nadir. In all these ways the oratorio tells of the failure of inspiration and the collapse into despair that Mann depicts as the terror of the artist and the nemesis of human life.

## The enigma of the endings

In a book that creates such anticipation and fear of the approaching end, the ending of the story takes on special significance. *Doctor Faustus* features several endings that coincide and conflict, and the way that we read the connections between them determines how we understand the end of the book. Zeitblom brings his tale to a close with his own apocalypse, Germany gripped by demons, staring into the abyss; and with this prospect he relives Leverkühn's crisis of faith in the *Apocalypsis*. Both the composer after the First World War and his friend at the end of the Second find themselves mesmerised by fear, their thoughts trained on a future that they envision as hell. Leverkühn's revelation is religious, replicating the tenor of the biblical apocalypses, and Zeitblom brings Leverkühn's vision to bear on the present catastrophe. In his ending Zeitblom apprehends the final retribution, the deserved conclusion to private and collective iniquities that the musician foresaw a quarter of a century earlier.

The novel also brings the life story of Leverkühn to an end with his death in 1940, ten years after his last piece of music, and this ending reinforces the fear of a calamitous end. Leverkühn's last act and fatal decline bring back two infamous precedents. In his farewell gathering and confession to his friends he re-enacts the prototype for this scene in the sixteenth-century chapbook version of the damned Faust. Though the musician is not fetched by the devil at midnight like the original Doctor Faustus, he falls into insanity, an earthly version of damnation that is the outcome of his syphilis. This second ending repeats Nietzsche's ten-year terminal decline from the same disease. Despite his lifelong admiration for Nietzsche, while he was writing *Doctor Faustus* Mann began to express doubts about Nietzsche's call for reinvigoration. This cry, he came to believe, had been misappropriated by the fascists, who were provoking the public into Dionysian madness in the spirit of Nietzsche's 'glorification of barbarism' (IX, 707–8). By condemning Leverkühn to Nietzsche's fate Mann endows the composer's punishment with a mythical force. In their eerie quality of repetition both Leverkühn's farewell and his Nietzschean demise operate like myths of the end, confirming Leverkühn's and Zeitblom's fears of judgement.

The story of Leverkühn's music also comes to a dramatic end with his composition of *The Lamentation of Doctor Faustus*. The cantata marks the end of Leverkühn's productive life by taking on a different tone from his previous work. For, unlike prior pieces, this work is invested with feeling. This at least is Zeitblom's perception, and the story behind the lament explains the transformation. Late in life Leverkühn is restored to feeling by his nephew, Nepomuk Schneidewein, called Echo, an angelic child come to visit, whose fondness for his uncle softens the musician's heart. But love has been forbidden Leverkühn, and when Echo is fatally stricken with meningitis, the devil, as Leverkühn sees it, takes revenge by slaying the child. Leverkühn's anguish turns him into a different kind of man, no longer deadened inside but full of torment. An outpouring of outrage and grief, the lament releases Leverkühn from the prison of inwardness and liberates him to a new power of expression. Reading through the work, for it is never performed, Zeitblom is moved: the music touches his feelings. This surely, he reflects, is the breakthrough that he and his friend have discussed so often, the resurgence of emotion that will revive and ensure the meaningfulness of music (VI, 643–4). As Zeitblom sees it, the *Lamentation* countermands the end-myths with a new revelation, the musician's reconnection with life.

Yet Zeitblom could be deluding himself here, and another way to take the lament is not as Leverkühn's salvation, but as the devil's accomplishment and victory. Propelling Leverkühn and enforcing fulfilment of their contract, it is Sammael who 'inspires' the piece that is simultaneously Leverkühn's triumph and defeat. What Sammael promised the musician was a revolutionary new style at the price of barbarism, and in the *Lamentation* Leverkühn has achieved that diabolic end. Having spent his career refining the twelvetone technique, the composer now perfects the method. The cantata is constructed in a pattern of expanding concentric circles that shocks and appals the listener in its monumental design. Zeitblom believes that by denying the composer choice in the arrangement of notes this mathematical style has freed Leverkühn to self-expression. But this paradox is difficult to grasp, and the consummate structure of the cantata suggests, on the contrary, that the twelve-tone method has bound him to a rigid circular path. On this reading, Zeitblom's belief that his friend has escaped to new life is only a wish, and this last piece of music functions, despite Leverkühn's apparent rebirth, to sustain the musician's isolation and all the myths that forebode the end of life and time.

Neither perspective offers the last word on the cantata, however, for the *Lamentation* also comes to its own unique end. In his fury Leverkühn has vowed to retract the Ninth Symphony of Beethoven. His lament will take back the affirmation of life at the end of Beethoven's symphony, the 'Ode to Joy'. With this aim he puts the Faust story, his own story, to music. Full of allusions to the chapbook Faust, the cantata sets the composer and his musical double on a headlong path toward damnation. But the piece does not hold to this course, carrying the listener instead through a series of reversals and breaking through in the end to a higher vision that Zeitblom describes as a religious miracle. The final note, a sustained high G for cello, glows in the night, reminiscent of the light that 'shines in the darkness' in St John's Gospel (VI, 651; John 1:5). Zeitblom is so moved by this conversion that he invokes it in his own ending. His very last words, surpassing his vision of horror, recall the 'light of hope' that he has perceived at the end of Leverkühn's music (VI, 676; Epilogue). In both endings, then, that of the lament and that of the novel, the terror of the end is superseded by the prospect, however dim, of a new life and time.

How we take this mixture of endings depends upon how we cast them within the novel as a whole. *Doctor Faustus* draws our attention again and again to the depravity of the times. Read with this emphasis, the book, like the cantata, operates as a dramatisation of sin, and the valid endings are those that justify its painful realism. Zeitblom's hopes are delusions, and Mann's novel unmasks the hollowness not only of Beethoven's symphony but also of Goethe's *Faust* with its redemptive ending and, by extension, the entire biblical tradition of grace.[3] The indictment of an age, *Doctor Faustus* expands like the *Lamentation* in widening circles to encompass the range of human sinfulness and repudiate shallow hope. The message is that of the chapbook, an *exemplum* of sin and retribution that warns of the price to be paid for wrongdoing, and the reduplicating myths of doom overwhelm Zeitblom's pathetic gestures toward salvation.

But the novel also invites another, more open reading that appreciates the possibility of recovery. Such an interpretation sets the tale within the biblical narrative of redemption that the author develops principally in humanistic terms. According to this view, God's grace is significant for Mann not as a doctrine to debate or as a test of belief or apostasy but as the defining myth of restoration. Just as he envisions the fall as a loss of morale, he imagines salvation as the repossession of inner strength. For the artist this means the ability to express in his art what he values most, and for Leverkühn, as for any human being, inspiration finds its source in his connection to life. The final concern of *Doctor Faustus* is not whether Leverkühn's sins merit forgiveness, but whether the sinner has reclaimed the feeling that Zeitblom believes he discerns in the Faust cantata. Mann's novel, like Leverkühn's lament, begins as an *exemplum* of sin and punishment, but towards the end it begins to break through to its own inspired vision. On this, I believe, more compelling reading, *Doctor Faustus* retells the myth of the fall but does not quite conclude with human damnation. A grievous tale of corruption, the novel opens out to a time beyond devastation, caught in the chance that the musician has recovered his humanity.

## NOTES

1 For the complexities of Mann's relationship with Schönberg and their disagreement over Mann's use of the twelve-tone method in the novel, see Jan Maegaard, 'Zu Th. W. Adornos Rolle im Mann/Schönberg-Streit', in Rolf Wiecker (ed.), *Gedenkschrift für Thomas Mann, 1875–1975* (Copenhagen: Verlag Text & Context, 1975), pp. 215–22. For a more recent review of the subject, see Bernhold Schmid, 'Neues zum "Doktor Faustus-Streit" zwischen Arnold Schönberg und Thomas Mann', *Augsburger Jahrbuch für Musikwissenschaft* (1989), 149–79, and (1990), 177–92. For an explanation of how Mann's fictionalised depiction of it departs from Schoenberg's dodecaphonic music, see Carl Dahlhaus, 'Fiktive Zwölftonmusik: Thomas Mann und Theodor W. Adorno', *Jahrbuch der Deutschen Akademie für Sprache und Dichtung* (1982), no. 1, 33–49 (especially pp. 40–1, 44).
2 See Adorno, *Gesammelte Schriften*, 20 vols., ed. Rolf Tiedemann (Frankfurt am Main: Suhrkamp, 1970–86), XII, 62, 74.
3 For this line of interpretation, see particularly Helmut Koopmann, '*Doktor Faustus* als Widerlegung der Weimarer Klassik', *Thomas-Mann-Studien* 6 (1987), 92–109; '"Mit Goethes *Faust* hat mein Roman nichts gemein": Thomas Mann und sein *Doktor Faustus*', in Peter Boerner and Sidney Johnson (eds.), *Faust through Four Centuries: Retrospect and Analysis* (Tübingen: Niemeyer, 1989), pp. 213–28.

## FURTHER READING

Beddow, Michael, *Thomas Mann: 'Doctor Faustus'* (Cambridge: Cambridge University Press, 1994)
Bergsten, Gunilla, *Thomas Mann's 'Doctor Faustus': The Sources and Structure of the Novel*, trans. Krishna Winston (Chicago: University of Chicago Press, 1969)
Carnegy, Patrick, *Faust as Musician: A Study of Thomas Mann's Novel 'Doctor Faustus'* (London: Chatto & Windus, 1973)
Durrani, Osman, *Fictions of Germany: Images of the German Nation in the Modern Novel* (Edinburgh: Edinburgh University Press, 1994)

Fetzer, John F., *Music, Love, Death and Mann's 'Doctor Faustus'* (Columbia, SC: Camden House, 1990)

Lehnert, Herbert, and Peter C. Pfeiffer (eds.), *Thomas Mann's 'Doctor Faustus': A Novel at the Margin of Modernism* (Columbia, SC: Camden House, 1991)

Robertson, Ritchie, 'Accounting for History: Thomas Mann, *Doktor Faustus*', in David Midgley (ed.), *The German Novel in the Twentieth Century* (Edinburgh: Edinburgh University Press, 1993), pp. 128–48

Ryan, Judith, *The Uncompleted Past: Postwar German Novels and the Third Reich* (Detroit: Wayne State University Press, 1983)

Scaff, Susan von Rohr, 'Unending Apocalypse: The Crisis of Musical Narrative in Mann's *Doctor Faustus*', *Germanic Review* 65 (1990), 30–9

'The Religious Base of Thomas Mann's World View: Mythic Theology and the Problem of the Demonic', *Christianity and Literature* 43 (1993), 75–94

'The Duplicity of the Devil's Pact: Intimations of Redemption in Mann's *Doktor Faustus*', *Monatshefte* 87 (1995), 151–69

Stein, Jack M., 'Adrian Leverkühn as a Composer', *Germanic Review* 25 (1950), 257–74

Stern, J. P., *History and Allegory in Thomas Mann's 'Doktor Faustus'* (London: H. K. Lewis, 1975)

Travers, Martin, 'Thomas Mann, *Doktor Faustus* and the historians: the function of "anachronistic symbolism"', in David Roberts and Philip Thomson (eds.), *The Modern German Historical Novel* (New York and Oxford: Berg, 1991), pp. 145–59

Vaget, Hans Rudolf, 'Amazing Grace: Thomas Mann, Adorno, and the Faust Myth', in Reinhold Grimm and Jost Hermand (eds.), *Our Faust? Roots and Ramifications of a Modern German Myth* (Madison, WI: University of Wisconsin Press, 1987), pp. 168–89

'tale' or 'novella' and, after growing to the size of a 'small novel', became a fully-fledged 'novel' only in 1939. These quantitatively motivated shifts in generic denomination were preceded, however, by fairly lengthy deliberations about generic quality. According to that first diary entry, as well as to many epistolary accounts of his fascination with the subject, Mann 'felt' for a long time 'the urge to write a play' about it,[5] an alternative still palpable in the final version of the novel put on stage with his approval and assistance in 1950, on screen in 1974, and on radio in 1996. The published text consists far more of dialogue and monologue than of authorial narration, and the author himself continued to call it an 'intellectual comedy' or 'dialogised monograph' rather than a genuine 'novel'.[6]

Another strikingly dramatic feature is that the actual 'meeting' is deferred until the eighth of the novel's nine chapters. Chapters 1 to 6 are devoted to the arrival of Charlotte, her daughter and their maid at the 'Elephant' hotel – which is seen 'as in a comedy' (XIII, 167)[7] from the humble perspective of an affected waiter called 'Mager' ('meagre') – and to a series of visitors whom Charlotte, who is besieged by a crowd of curious townspeople attracted by Mager's gossip, has no choice but to receive: Rose Cuzzle, an 'English' or rather 'actually' Irish autograph hunter and sketcher of celebrities (II, 395, 398); Friedrich Wilhelm Riemer, Goethe's assistant; Adele Schopenhauer, sister of the philosopher and a close friend of Ottilie von Pogwisch, Goethe's prospective daughter-in-law; and finally Ottilie's fiancé, Goethe's son August.

The time covered by the first six chapters overlaps and nearly coincides with the period encompassed by the next one, which starts an hour before Charlotte's arrival at the 'Elephant' and ends with August's departure for that hotel. The most modernist and 'audacious'[8] of all (given that Mann was not familiar with the Joycean 'stream of consciousness' with which the chapter has often been compared[9]), and emphasised by its definite article, '*The* Seventh Chapter' presents Goethe, 'though not from outside, but from within', offering 'associatively the thoughts which cross his mind on that morning when Lotte's note from the "Elephant" is going to surprise him'.[10] 'The murmur', as Mann privately referred to Goethe's 'interior monologue',[11] is interspersed with some dialogues with the people Goethe has to deal with that morning: his servant Schreiber, of whom he honestly approves; his secretary John, whom he profoundly dislikes; and his son August, who delivers Charlotte's note and is sent to the 'Elephant' with an answer at the very end of the chapter, so that the father's dialogue with his son cannot be read against what Goethe sincerely thinks either of August or of Charlotte's note. From the 'outside', at least, he does not seem 'surprise[d]' at all, and it takes more than ten pages for Goethe to react properly to the note by inviting Charlotte and her daughter to lunch along with a dozen local notabilities;

in the interim, his words wander from crystals to horticulture to tax and citizenship matters to Weimar court gossip to poetic fantasies, then suggest an answer in verse which, taken out of the context of the *West-Eastern Divan*, would make an extremely impolite impression: 'That geese possess a stupid mind / Is just an empty catch-word; / For now and then one looks behind / To tell me to go backward' (G II, 39).[12]

During the lunch, in line with its deliberately formal character, Goethe appears – and throughout Chapter 8 remains – cheerful, but courteously 'stiff' (II, 717, 758),[13] annoyingly detached and self-centred. Charlotte's deep disappointment with his strict avoidance of all intimate talk is eventually balanced in the last chapter. On her way back from a play which Goethe (in historically authentic wording) invited her to see using his coach and his box in the theatre, Charlotte has a strange encounter with him, the reality of which remains ambiguous throughout, although it seems far more likely to be a purely 'imaginary'[14] apparition which she, still thinking of the play and inspired by its rhythmic language, 'produces' in order to fulfil her need for 'a conversation' that 'sets things possibly to rights again'[15] and 'give[s] this story a tolerably redeeming close' (II, 756).

In accordance with its ambiguous reality, the conversation first revolves around the relationship between the 'eternal youth' of what is preserved in a literary work and the mortality of 'real' people, repeatedly indicated by the leitmotif of Charlotte's trembling head (II, 759). It finally culminates in Charlotte's open criticism of 'human sacrifice', a concept she uses – invoking Goethe's famous poem 'Selige Sehnsucht' ('Blessed Yearning') from the *West-Eastern Divan* – to characterise the subservient behaviour of Goethe's associates. Without responding to the criticism as such, Goethe inverts the roles of the 'sacrifice' and the beneficiary of the sacrifice through the same 'parable of the moth and the fatal, alluring flame': the burning candle too sacrifices its 'body'; 'and in the end the sacrifice was God' (II, 763).

As this and countless other allusions demonstrate, especially to the *West-Eastern Divan, Elective Affinities, Wilhelm Meister's Journeyman Years*, the poetic trilogy *Pariah* and of course *The Sorrows of Werther*, Mann drew in *Lotte in Weimar* on a profound knowledge of Goethe, not only of such canonical texts, but also of more obscure works and projects (for example, a version of *Cupid and Psyche* (II, 618)[16]), Goethe's scientific writings, diaries, letters and especially his conversations, as well as the documents produced by people around Goethe and the biographical and academic literature about him, including the most recent and most advanced. Thus, for example, an ethno-biological reflection by Mann's fictional Goethe about his genealogy is based on Joseph von Bradish's book *Goethe as the Heir of His Ancestors* (1933) – though incidentally, Mann, who himself had a Creole mother, emphasised the exotic Latin element in Goethe more strongly than von Bradish did. However, in enumerating his sources Mann omitted von Bradish, just as he omitted the book which had the most decisive influence on the picture of Goethe developed in *Lotte in Weimar*: Felix A. Theilhaber's *Goethe: Sexus and Eros* (1929), the first ever psychoanalytical study of Goethe.

The most sobering feature of this picture, which emerges more and more distinctly in Charlotte's conversations with Riemer, Adele Schopenhauer and Goethe's son, is explained ironically by Goethe himself in the 'Chinese... saying' that he offers his luncheon guests in the eighth chapter, and at which they laugh with such suspicious heartiness: 'the great man is a national misfortune' (II, 734). The great man in *Lotte in Weimar* is, and Goethe in reality was (though perhaps not to the same extent), an obstacle to the life's happiness of those around him: to the university career of Riemer (who was not working for Goethe at all at the time covered in the text); to Ottilie von Pogwisch's passion for the patriotic volunteer Ferdinand Heinke (which is historically authentic); to his son's friendship with the Romantic Achim von Arnim (which is greatly exaggerated); and more generally to August's desire to be a part of his own 'Romantic' and patriotically oriented generation, to whose hatred and contempt his father exposed him by forbidding him to participate in the 'Wars of Liberation' against the Napoleonic occupying forces in 1813–14.

The impression of Goethe's indifference to his fellow humans, of his inhuman 'coldness' (II, 446) and of his detachment from life which is built up by the 'slanders'[17] in the first two-thirds of the novel is confirmed and deepened in the following two chapters, in which he appears in person, symptomatically interested in the lifeless and the long dead. Thus Goethe's initial reaction to Charlotte's note is to give the messenger a lecture, occupying some two pages, about a 'crystal' (II, 685–7); and even after this he doesn't come to the point, but asks about the 'haymaking in the big garden' (II, 687). During the 'Table-Talk' (II, 726),[18] which he will end in order to keep the geologist Abraham Gottlob Werner alone with him and show him 'fossil fresh-water snails' (II, 747), Goethe tells the story of a 'feldspar twin crystal' which he interrupted a carriage journey to examine and which – this quotation is also authenticated – he addressed just like a human being: 'how did *you* get here?' (II, 725).[19]

In another anecdote, again addressed to Werner, the theme of coldness, alienation and mortification – as represented in the continuing motif of the silhouettes – is centred on art. This anecdote of the 'well-formed impression of a pair of pretty lips' which a 'young man' secretly left 'upon the cold glass' over a 'copy of Leonardo da Vinci's head of Charitas' in an exhibition features appropriately during the 'raspberry crème' course (II, 739–41, 760). In the seventh chapter, the smell of raspberries had already prompted Goethe's meditation about the kiss being 'of love the best', something which Goethe equates with the 'higher sphere' of 'poetry', and contrasts with the earthy act and consequences of 'procreation' (II, 467).[20] Against the background of this opposition 'between art and life', of this understanding of poetry as a 'spirit-kiss on the world's raspberry lips' (II, 467), the anecdote contains – as Charlotte's irrepressible physical reaction to it betrays (she 'got very red', II, 741) – the answer to the 'tormenting riddle' (II, 456) that ultimately drove Charlotte to Weimar: that is, why Goethe had originally fallen in love with her, another man's fiancée, without a hope of fulfilment, only to contaminate her with other female figures when he made use of this love in literature.

Goethe's joy in the anecdote casts an unforgiving light on Charlotte's 'mistake of confusing life with art',[21] on her folly in trying to evoke the long-past *Werther* epoch by her aged appearance, on the complete awkwardness of her still-white dress and of the ribbon missing from it, which recalls both the token that Lotte gives Werther for his birthday and the ribbon that Charlotte once really did send Goethe. Now, when the couple meet as widow and widower and there would no longer be any real obstacle to the eternal union that he supposedly swore to her as Werther did to Lotte, Goethe has absolutely no idea how to deal with Charlotte.[22]

The compulsive regularity with which Goethe, like that 'man' who tried to kiss the copy of a copy, seemed deliberately to seek unviable relationships of which he subsequently could make literary use, thereby betraying 'love and life and human beings to his art' (II, 647–8), reflects the problematical symbiosis which, according to psychoanalytical theories, art and sexuality must constitute in the 'genius', of whom Goethe serves as the prototype in German culture. Even for so early a commentator as Theilhaber, Goethe's genius was no longer simply a superhuman culmination of vitality and inspiration, but, on the contrary, an expression of deep-seated psychic problems. According to Theilhaber, Goethe had a profoundly troubled relationship to the purely physical aspect of sexuality ('sexus'), which his artistic productivity enabled him to sublimate all too comprehensively in 'eros'. Thus the erection with which the 67-year-old wakes at the beginning of the seventh chapter is definitely not a reflex of mechanistic drives; it is explicitly motivated by a dream which is not quite sexual, but involves a complex artistic sublimation of sexuality. Goethe dreamed of a couple in a painting, and moreover in a painting based on a literary motif: 'the l'Orbetto, the Turchi, from the Dresden Gallery, Venus and Adonis'. Goethe then associates 'Venus and Adonis' with 'Cupid and Psyche' (II, 617–18), and this tale again, according to his well-documented reception of it, meant for Mann a key mythical paradigm of the sublimation of sexuality.[23]

Mann's particular interest in the collusion between problematical sexuality and literary productivity, and especially in the 'androgynous' (II, 664)²⁴ and possibly homoerotic characteristics of Goethe – for example in connection with Goethe's admiration for a 'comely blond waiter' (II, 681)²⁵ – reveals something of the personal motives which made him imagine his way so deeply into Goethe's being. It was not simply that, like Goethe, Mann had not been educated systematically (II, 423), or that he too was a patrician of a 'Free City', or that his family too had to suffer under his great celebrity; for, as has only become known since the granting of access to Mann's diaries, he defined his own existence in terms of the two factors colluding in Goethe's genius: his literary vocation and what he regarded as his problematical sexuality, the homosexual half of which caused him suffering all his life (particularly because of his fondness for waiters such as Franz Westermeier in Zurich, whose erotic appeal inspired Mann to resume work on the *Felix Krull* fragment).

The philosophical basis of Mann's 'unio mystica' with Goethe (XI, 147), which in a sense allowed him to ennoble his own existential difficulties, was a concept of myth which was influenced by psychoanalytical theories of archetypes, and extensively tested in the *Joseph* novels, with which *Lotte in Weimar* is chronologically so closely associated. He considered his own idea of myth as 'return, timelessness, present-always' (IX, 229) to be identical with Goethe's understanding of myth,²⁶ and he could easily find his idea partially anticipated in the Goethe of the period covered in *Lotte in Weimar*, for in the *West-Eastern Divan* Goethe does indeed identify himself with the Persian poet Hatem (and Marianne von Willemer, in whom Mann saw a 'repetition' of the 'Lotte-experience',²⁷ with Hatem's Zuleika).

The concept of myth as dissolving boundaries between individual identities and, particularly, between generations is apparent throughout. Charlotte believes that she sees the young Goethe himself in Goethe's son (II, 564). Her own child, who accompanies her, is called 'Charlotte' like her, although the historical Charlotte Kestner was accompanied to Weimar by her daughter Klara.²⁸ In the novel Goethe calls his current servant Ferdinand by the first name of his predecessor, 'Carl'; and by a fortunate chance the secretary whom Mann has appear anachronistically, Ernst Carl John, had the same family name as his successor, Johann August Friedrich John.

As a means of representation, the concept of the mythical offered a possibility of overcoming the central problem, that of coming to grips with the essentially indefinable in Goethe's individuality. Thus the fundamental mythical paradigm of elusive identity, Proteus, is invoked (II, 445), and above all several fluctuating mythical and religious paradigms are superimposed on the single Protean person of Goethe: Goethe as the blessed son Joseph (II, 440) and as Joseph's typological equivalent, the Son sacrificed by God (II, 453, 467, 474),[29] but also, in accordance with the reversibility of the idea of sacrifice, Goethe as God the Father (II, 439, 490), His opposite, the Devil (II, 439–40), and His heathen equivalents Jupiter (II, 439, 466, 400, 731, 756) and Wotan 'the cloaked' (II, 763).[30]

There is no doubt that Mann's 'mythical' fusion of identity with Goethe achieved its most direct expression in *Lotte in Weimar*, in a manner of writing which imitated the vocabulary, idiom and spelling of Goethe's style, and of course most particularly in the 'murmur' of the seventh chapter – in Mann's claim that he could put himself into Goethe's skin. But his 'succession to Goethe' (diary, 29 September 1936) extended beyond this performance within the work: shortly before beginning the manuscript of the *Lotte* novel, in which Goethe suffers with historical authenticity from 'rheumatism in his left arm' (II, 625, 713), Mann was troubled by 'rheumatic pains...in the arm' (diary, 15 September 1936). In an autobiographical sketch written in 1936 he modelled his birth, even at the cost of patent untruth, on the opening of Goethe's autobiography *Poetry and Truth* (XI, 450). And it is said that the almost 80-year-old Mann walked up and down in a pose typical of Goethe, wearing the emblem of the Legion of Honour, of which Goethe was also a member.[31]

Although the argument that Mann organised the overall chronological sequence of his novels in conformity with Goethe's complete works may prove somewhat strained,[32] it nevertheless seems more than a matter of chance that he chose as his next novel project none other than the Faust legend, the material that forms the basis of Goethe's central canonical work. It is no accident that this material, which was in Mann's mind for almost half a century, appears together with the *Lotte in Weimar* project in that first diary entry of 1933. But on the other hand it seems equally significant that Mann had to procrastinate for so long about his considerably older *Lotte* project, and his project directly challenging Goethe's *Faust*, until they at last evolved into works which he could complete. Evidently he had been incapable of coming to terms with Goethe in literature before, and this incapacity had already become clearly apparent in at least one case, as *Death in Venice* had originally been planned as a novella about Goethe's final love, namely the embarrassing proposal of marriage which the 74-year-old had made to a woman 55 years younger.

The act of identification which succeeds only in the late works is the result of a development whose fixed points are discernible in two anniversaries in German cultural history, both of which Mann helped celebrate: the centenaries of Schiller's and Goethe's deaths. In 'A Weary Hour', which he published for the Schiller centenary in 1905, Mann made his first literary approach to

Goethe, but, most significantly, from the perspective of Schiller, a perspective which the narrator can already think himself into in very much the same way as only decades later he can think himself into Goethe's skin. In the logic of the narrative, which is also constituted by physical distance from Weimar, Schiller's perspective on Goethe appears as 'a mixture of hostility and yearning' (VIII, 372). This distance between Goethe and Schiller is maintained in *Lotte in Weimar*, but is now measured from the other side, that is from Goethe's perspective, which the narrator now adopts completely as his own, expressing Goethe's 'ambivalence' towards Schiller: 'Did I ever like him? Never' (II, 621).[33]

This identification with the person of Goethe, which is so clearly articulated in the narrative perspective of the seventh chapter, matches the tenor of the essays and speeches which Mann had written for the Goethe Year in 1932, such as 'Goethe's Career as a Writer'. The affinity which Mann had now achieved with Goethe as with a successful man who knew how to accommodate himself with the ruling powers, and whose accommodations with those powers did not baulk at repression and censorship, reflects Mann's own 'career as a writer', which he himself stylised as a fairy-tale progression from late-born member of a family in 'decline' to wealthy father of six, from high-school failure to Doctor *honoris causa*, honorary Professor and Nobel laureate (XI, 329–33).

Despite Mann's high degree of identification with Goethe in the 1930s, *Lotte in Weimar* retains the aggressive impulses towards Goethe which had already been revealed by 'A Weary Hour', and above all by Mann's literary interest in the biographical episode which would have permitted him to ridicule Goethe in the same way as he had humiliated the no less canonised and officially honoured Gustav *von* Aschenbach in *Death in Venice*. In *Lotte in Weimar* Mann at last 'realised' the 'old dream'[34] of performing a literary 'execution' on Goethe.[35] This is indicated even by the language he has Goethe speak in the novel. From his position as a northern German, whose dialect is much closer than Goethe's to the literary language, Mann mocks Goethe's dialectal deviations from the norms of the standard language, although these norms were far less clearly established in Goethe's time than in the twentieth century. Mann repeatedly puts peculiar Hessian forms into Goethe's direct utterances and explicitly points out that Goethe is 'yielding to the local practice of his home and leaving off the end-consonants' (II, 723).

Of all Goethe's deviations from the norms of speech, the most revealing is a 'slip' (II, 739, 741) with which he introduces that frivolous anecdote about the tension between art and sexuality: 'ich muß *Sie* was erzählen!' (II, 739; emphasis added). The erroneous substitution of the accusative pronoun for the dative is indeed authenticated in Goethe's *Conversations*, though only once in the whole ten volumes: 'Ich will *Sie* ... was zeigen!'[36] Significantly, Mann has removed the grammatical error from the context of 'zeigen' ('showing') and transferred it to the context of 'erzählen' ('telling'); that is, to a verb which is closely associated with a literary genre ('Erzählung', tale), and moreover with the only genre in which he could ever be considered a rival to Goethe.

In this rivalry, Mann's relationship to Goethe resembles that of a son to his father, and thus seems a model proof of Harold Bloom's theory that literary influence is an 'Oedipal' syndrome of simultaneous identification and aggression. The younger author, whose next literary project will enter into direct competition with Goethe's *Faust*, tries to take over the position of his at once admired and envied role model. Admittedly, the apparent value of *Lotte in Weimar* in confirming Bloom's literary theory is relativised by the fact that the author, though of course unfamiliar with the theory itself, was well versed in the theory's psychoanalytical preconditions, and that he himself had theorised his relationship to his literary 'precursor' in terms very similar to Bloom's. Mann conceptualised *Lotte in Weimar* as his 'unio mystica with the *father*' (XIII, 169), and in doing so he conceived of Goethe quite deliberately in psychological terms as his 'father-imago'.[37]

The fact that the idea of taking over the position of the 'father' first developed into a completed work in *Lotte in Weimar* highlights the close connections between this novel and the historical events of the time in which it was written. After the collapse of the Weimar Republic and under the circumstances of exile, Mann emerged as an author with a serious political commitment. Against the backdrop of this collapse, the place-name in the novel's title assumes a particular emphasis: 'Weimar' as the symbol of the failed republic, of Germany's political catastrophe; and 'Weimar' as the epitome of its cultural greatness. In the manner almost of an exorcism, *Lotte in Weimar* confronts National Socialist Germany with the greatness of German intellectual culture, epitomised by Goethe as its chief representative, a position to which Mann aspired and which in exile he even attained.

The confrontation of the historical reality with that ideal of a 'cultural nation' which has helped repeatedly to consolidate the German identity, from the dissolution of the Holy Roman Empire of the German Nation in 1806 by Napoleon (whom Goethe admired) to the unification of 1990, also influences the meaning of the final words of the novel's epigraph from the *West-Eastern Divan*: 'Dein Reich beständig!' ('Your realm enduring!').[38] Strictly speaking, the reference here is to a poem of homage by Goethe to Duke Karl August (who is not addressed by name). Removed from its original context of political and military power and placed at the beginning of the novel, the poem naturally takes on a completely different meaning. Only Goethe himself can be the addressee, and the 'realm' cannot be any territorially concrete one.

On the basis of a concept of 'Germany' divorced from territorial and institutional power – a concept which decisively influenced Mann's self-perception as an émigré ('Where I am, there is Germany'[39]) – exile seems paradoxically to be the form of existence inherently most appropriate to the Germans. In Mann's novel, Goethe, who himself is more or less exiled into an 'isolated' life in Weimar (II, 657), and who is about to renounce the citizenship of his home town of Frankfurt, prophesies that exile will be the Germans' punishment for their 'national narcissism' (II, 664). Using the ideal of his own personality, which he sees as fundamentally 'conceiving' and receptive (II, 664) – though from another viewpoint it seems also 'parasitic' (II, 466) – and contrasting this ideal with the Germans' pretensions to originality, he predicts for his compatriots that 'in exile only . . . will they develop all the good there is in them for the healing of the nations' (II, 665).[40]

This definition of the Germans as a people condemned to, but by the same token eschatologically chosen for, exile – a mission repeatedly invoked by the biblical quotation about 'the salt of the earth' (II, 665, 733) – constitutes the *tertium* of the comparison between Germans and Jews. Although, like the description of the Eger pogrom in the eighth chapter,[41] it is documented in Goethe's *Conversations*, this comparison inevitably had a far more provocative effect than Goethe could ever have intended when it was used in the late 1930s (and particularly in the mid-1940s, when Saul Fitelberg repeated it in *Doctor Faustus*). That Mann intended to preach a sermon to the Germans of his own day through Goethe's voice is shown very directly by the passage in the internal monologue in which Goethe explains his 'antipathy' for the 'vulgar strain' in his compatriots by referring to his own infusions of foreign 'blood'; that is, he explains his antipathy ultimately as an ethno-biological 'aloofness from the Germans' (II, 657):

> they abandon themselves credulously to every fanatic scoundrel who speaks to their baser qualities, confirms them in their vices, teaches them nationality means barbarism and isolation. To themselves they seem great and glorious only when they have gambled away all that they had worth having. Then they look with jaundiced eyes on those whom foreigners love and respect, seeing in them the true Germany . . . They think they are Germany – but I am.
>
> (II, 657–8)

As he himself admitted, Mann achieved the over-obvious link to his own predicament which is apparent here at the cost of abandoning the fidelity to his sources and making Goethe say something that cannot be authenticated in this or in any other recognisably similar form. This tendency to make links with the conditions in Germany at the time the novel was written also seems to have produced the deliberate confusion between the two real-life secretaries called John. Ernst Carl John, whose appearance in the seventh chapter significantly interrupts the 'murmur' about the Germans, although he had actually left Goethe's service before the period covered in the novel, embodies everything that Goethe has just been reprehending in his compatriots. Thus John unites several characteristics which excite Goethe's disgust, not all of which are historically accurate, particularly John's 'revolutionary errors' (II, 668), whereas the section of *Poetry and Truth* which Goethe is about to dictate to John begins with the contrasting statement that Goethe's 'position vis-à-vis the upper classes was most favourable' (II, 675). John's 'unnatural' desire 'to reform the world' (II, 668–9) derives from a misconception already present in Mann's sources. Although John was rightly credited with the authorship of a liberal tract, he had actually written as an *agent provocateur* attempting to entrap disloyal public officials. Hence John's alleged 'spirit of opposition' (II, 668) is diametrically opposed to his historically authenticated wish (which Goethe in fact fulfilled) to be recommended to a censorship office. This means that John no longer appears simply as the willing executor of official repression which probably he really was; rather, he gains an especial contemporary significance from the historical misconception, the supposed betrayal of the revolutionary ideas of his youth. John appears here as an opportunist of the type fostered by the political situation in Germany at the time the novel was written.

Despite the uncanny topicality with which the theme of Germans' ideological adaptability can be imbued since 1989, *Lotte in Weimar* is today sometimes considered Mann's least attractive novel.[42] Only five copies of the English translation reissued in 1990 have been sold in ten years in Great Britain. The lack of interest in the novel outside academic German Studies probably also reflects the lasting changes in the general understanding of Goethe, which have significantly detracted from the bold and spectacular quality of Mann's disrespectful portrait from the 1930s.

But the primary reason for the novel's decreasing attractiveness seems simply to be the increasing distance from the era which it criticised, as is suggested *ex negativo* by the acclaim and circulation which *Lotte in Weimar* enjoyed before that distance developed. The first English edition could be announced as 'the outstanding literary event of 1940', and *Lotte in Weimar* was the first of Mann's books issued in Germany after the war. Extracts from it had even been distributed clandestinely in Nazi Germany, under the title 'From Goethe's Conversations with Riemer', and including the historically inauthentic comments about the 'fanatic scoundrel'. After the war the British prosecutor at the Nuremberg Trials came across these comments, and quoted them in good faith as Goethe's own words, so that here at least Mann once really did take the place of his 'father-imago'.

## NOTES

1 Hayden White, 'Introduction', in Thomas Mann, *Lotte in Weimar: The Beloved Returns*, trans. H. T. Lowe-Porter (Berkeley and Los Angeles: University of California Press, 1990), p. xi. The translation was first published in 1940.
2 Letter of 29 November 1940 to Mrs George T. Paterson, in *Thomas Mann, Selbstkommentare: 'Lotte in Weimar'*, ed. Hans Wysling and Marianne Eich-Fischer (Frankfurt am Main: Fischer, 1996), p. 65; English original. References are to this volume in the 'Selbstkommentare' series, since it not only assembles as many as possible of Mann's references to this novel, but includes some letters that are not available elsewhere.
3 Mann, *'On Myself' and other Princeton Lectures*, ed. James N. Bade, 2nd edn (Frankfurt am Main, Berlin, Berne: Lang, 1997), p. 135; English original.
4 Mann, *Tagebücher 1933–1934*, ed. Peter de Mendelssohn (Frankfurt am Main: Fischer, 1977), p. 251.
5 *Selbstkommentare*, p. 65: letter of 11 December 1940 to Gertrude Howard; English original.
6 *Selbstkommentare*, pp. 45, 47, 50: letters of 19 January 1940 to Julius Schülein; 21 January 1940 to Hermann Kesten; 2 February 1940 to Ernst Benedict; 3 March 1940 to Heinrich Mann.
7 See also *Selbstkommentare*, pp. 45, 119: letters of 21 January 1940 to Hermann Kesten; 1 January 1954 to Hans Franck.
8 *Selbstkommentare*, p. 32: letter of 24 July 1939 to Menno ter Braak.
9 See *Selbstkommentare*, pp. 101, 105: letters of 11 January 1950 to Alfred A. Knopf; 1950 to Henry Hatfield (English original).
10 *Selbstkommentare*, p. 29: letter of 15 December 1938 to Ferdinand Lion.
11 *Selbstkommentare*, p. 47: letter of 29 January 1940 to Jonas Lesser; ibid., and *Selbstkommentare*, p. 105: letter of 1950 to Henry Hatfield (English original).
12 Goethe, *Poems of the West and East: West-Eastern Divan – West-Östlicher Divan*, trans. John Whaley (Berne, Berlin, Frankfurt am Main: Lang, 1998), p. 141.
13 Cf. *Goethes Gespräche*, ed. Woldemar v. Biedermann (Leipzig: Biedermann, 1889–96), V, 312–13.
14 *Selbstkommentare*, p. 67: letter of 7 August 1941 to Else Midas.
15 *Selbstkommentare*, p. 86: letter of 20 February 1947 to Fritz Grünbaum.
16 Cf. Friedrich Wilhelm Riemer, *Mitteilungen über Goethe*, ed. Arthur Pollmer (Leipzig: Insel, 1921), p. 218.
17 *Selbstkommentare*, p. 105: letter of 4 February 1951 to Eva Zimmermann.
18 Cf. Riemer, *Mitteilungen*, p. 243.
19 Cf. *Goethes Gespräche*, IV, 102.
20 Cf. *Goethes Gespräche*, III, 195.
21 White, 'Introduction', p. vi.
22 See Albert Bielschowsky, *Goethe: Sein Leben und seine Werke*, 8th edn (Munich: Beck, 1905), I, 167.
23 See Johann Jakob Bachofen, 'Die Lampe und ihr Öl im Mythus von Amor und Psyche', in *Urreligion und antike Symbole: Systematisch angeordnete Auswahl*

*aus seinen Werken*, ed. Carl Albrecht Bernoulli (Leipzig: Reclam, 1926), I, 312–21. Mann's two copies show signs of intensive use.

24 Cf. Joseph A. v. Bradish, *Goethe als Erbe seiner Ahnen* (Berlin and New York: Westermann, 1933), pp. 32–3.

25 Cf. *Goethes Gespräche*, III, 197–8, 205.

26 *Selbstkommentare*, p. 22: letter of 21 December 1937 to Kuno Fiedler.

27 *Selbstkommentare*, p. 31: letter of 16 February 1939 to Karl Kerényi.

28 *Selbstkommentare*, pp. 85, 113, 119: letters of 4 January 1947 to Lavinia Mazzucchetti; 18 June 1951 to Charlotte Kestner; 2 May 1953 to Hans-Heinrich Reuter.

29 The fictional Goethe himself reveals a particular affinity with Christ in his paraphrase of a 'Reformation Cantata' which the historical Goethe indeed planned to write (II, 618–19). Mann annotated a passage in Theilhaber's Goethe monograph with 'Jesus', and he had already equated Goethe's 'myth-making miracle personality' with Jesus Christ in an essay addressed (no doubt cautiously) to a Japanese readership (IX, 286).

30 Cf. *Selbstkommentare*, p. 86: letter of 20 February 1947 to Fritz Grünbaum.

31 Hans Wysling, 'Thomas Manns Goethe-Nachfolge', *Jahrbuch des Freien Deutschen Hochstifts* (1978), 498–551 (p. 533); cf. *Goethes Gespräche*, IV, 70, footnote.

32 Hans Eichner, *Thomas Mann: Eine Einführung in sein Werk*, 2nd edn (Berne and Munich: Francke, 1961), pp. 72–3.

33 *Selbstkommentare*, pp. 117–18: letter of 23 September 1952 to Beate Buchwald; 5 January 1953 to Lotte Schultheis.

34 *Selbstkommentare*, p. 22: letter of 28 December 1937 to Alfred Neumann; cf. p. 16: letter of 25 August 1937 to Lavinia Mazzucchetti.

35 Peter von Matt, 'Zur Psychologie des deutschen Nationalschriftstellers: Die paradigmatische Bedeutung der Hinrichtung und Verklärung Goethes durch Thomas Mann', in Sebastian Goeppert (ed.), *Perspektiven psychoanalytischer Literaturkritik* (Freiburg im Breisgau: Rombach, 1978), pp. 82–100.

36 *Goethes Gespräche*, V, 251; emphasis added.

37 *Selbstkommentare*, pp. 70, 72: letters of 27 April 1942 and 12 January 1943 to Agnes E. Meyer.

38 G II, 40; *Poems of the West and East*, trans. Whaley, p. 151.

39 See Helmut Koopmann, 'Lotte in Amerika, Thomas Mann in Weimar: Erläuterungen zum Satz: "Wo ich bin, ist die deutsche Kultur"', in Heinz Gockel, Michael Neumann and Ruprecht Wimmer (eds.), *Wagner – Nietzsche – Thomas Mann: Festschrift für Eckhard Heftrich* (Frankfurt am Main: Klostermann, 1993), pp. 324–42 (p. 326).

40 Cf. *Goethes Gespräche*, II, 232.

41 II, 727–8; cf. *Goethes Gespräche*, IV, 106–7.

42 Hermann Kurzke, *Thomas Mann: Epoche – Werk – Wirkung*, 2nd edn (Munich: Beck, 1991), p. 261.

## FURTHER READING

Asher, J. A., 'Thomas Mann's "Unio Mystica" with Goethe', *Publications of the English Goethe Society*, NS 25 (1956), 1–20

Dickson, Keith, 'The Technique of a "musikalisch-ideeller Beziehungskomplex" in *Lotte in Weimar*', *Modern Language Review* 59 (1964), 413–24

Siefken, Hinrich, '*Lotte in Weimar* – "Contactnahme" and Thomas Mann's Novel about Goethe', *Trivium* 13 (1978), 38–51

    *Thomas Mann: Goethe – 'Ideal der Deutschheit': Wiederholte Spiegelungen 1893–1949* (Munich: Fink, 1981)

    'Thomas Mann Edits Goethe: "The Permanent Goethe"', *Modern Language Review* 77 (1982), 876–85

Zweig, Stefan, '*The Beloved Returns*', in Charles Neider (ed.), *The Stature of Thomas Mann* (New York: New Directions, 1947), pp. 188–90

# 13

FREDERICK A. LUBICH

# The Confessions of Felix Krull, Confidence Man

The genesis of this work spans much of Thomas Mann's creative career. His collection of material dates back to 1910. In 1922 the first part of the book appeared under the title *Bekenntnisse des Hochstaplers Felix Krull. Buch der Kindheit* [Confessions of Felix Krull, Confidence Man: The Early Years]. In 1951, after his work on *Doctor Faustus* had once more delayed the continuation of the *Confessions*, Mann returned to this novel and to his former thematic trajectory. Hans Wysling, in his authoritative study, unfolds the multitude of literary influences and delineates the essential concepts and traditions which informed the *Confessions*.[1] According to Wysling, the two creative phases are marked by distinctive shifts of models. The early phase is inspired by three major models: Georges Manolescu's memoirs *A Prince of Thieves* (1905), Goethe's autobiography *Dichtung und Wahrheit* [*Poetry and Truth*], which is part of the great eighteenth-century tradition of autobiographical and confessional writing, and the fairy-tale motif of the *Glückskind*, the fortunate child. All three models are more or less refracted and modified by other concepts. For example, Manolescu's literary memoirs of a self-proclaimed confidence man are problematised by the Protestant ethic of self-examination and the psychoanalytical school of self-interrogation. Whereas Felix Krull's imitation of Goethe's *Poetry and Truth* lacks the aspects of societal integration and self-realisation so essential to the eighteenth-century ethos of *Bildung* or self-cultivation, the deployment of the fairy-tale plot of the *Glückskind* is enriched both by the psychoanalytical complex of primary narcissism, which is symptomatic for the early stage of childhood development, and by the mythological features of collective archetypes. The protagonist's name Felix, signifying the happy one, is onomastic testimony to the felicitous nature and fate of his composite psychomythic character.

The late creative phase of the *Confessions* is substantially influenced by three great German and European literary and cultural traditions. First, the genre of the picaresque novel from *Lazarillo de Tormes* to Grimmelshausen; second, the artist novel, infused with the increasingly decadent conception of the artist as an actor and dilettante, as developed by Schopenhauer, Lombroso and Nietzsche; and third, the Goethean concept of humanist *Bildung,* as exemplified in his *Bildungsroman, Wilhelm Meister,* and his *Bildungsepos, Faust.* Together, these influential traditions coalesce into a richly textured parodic portrait of the young hero as a comic criminal striving for culture and cosmic knowledge, which he ultimately attains in the sublimely ironic identification with the divine double of Eros/Hermes. Within this conceptual context the narrative unfolds, describing in autobiographical detail Felix Krull's early formative years in the Rhineland, his subsequent adventures and experiences as a young man, and his successful career as a winsome waiter in the dazzling hotel world of the Parisian *haute volée.* There he also encounters the young Marquis de Venosta, under whose assumed identity he travels on to Portugal, where he rises by his charm and chutzpah into the highest circles of Europe's late *belle époque* aristocracy.

In tracing genre models and literary antecedents, Wysling quotes several examples of textual similarities between the amorous exploits of Grimmelshausen's *Simplicissimus* and Thomas Mann's own protagonist, and he lists the various literary sources of artistic predecessors in nineteenth-century literature and cultural philosophy. As a confidence man, Felix Krull is bound to disappoint the high ethical standards of the *Bildungsroman* and to reflect the profound cultural parables and problematics of the *Faust* epic. In comparison to Mann's *Doctor Faustus* and its multi-coded cultural montage, the *Confessions* of Felix Krull are *Bildung* made easy. The *Glückskind* embraces the world of culture and knowledge not in order to understand it, but rather to enjoy it to its fullest: hermeneutic illumination gives way to hedonistic indulgence.

Intricately related to Felix Krull's personal and cultural confidence games and his trickster travesties of traditions is Schopenhauer's philosophy in *The World as Will and Representation,* with its central trope of reality as a great illusion, the veil of Maya. This Schopenhauerian trope permeates Mann's literary creativity from *Buddenbrooks* on and comes to full fruition in Felix Krull's many playful charades and masquerades. Even as a child he creates an elaborate fantasy-world which is further nurtured by his godfather Schimmelpreester, who drapes and disguises him in various roles, using him as a model for costume paintings. Young Felix thus becomes the ever-changing 'costume head' (VII, 284 *et passim*) which in his later years will so enchant and seduce the world. This make-believe life of an illusionary personality, which metamorphoses even further through the re-creative imagination of its autobiographer, provides the perfect stage to deploy and display the protagonist's narcissistic needs with theatrical ingenuity. Freudian

psychoanalysis has theorised narcissism as a form of psychological infan-
tilism with an attendant mother-fixation, whose psychodynamics trigger
powerful mood-swings ranging from feelings of utter inferiority to soaring
grandiosity. Throughout the yearning years of his adolescence, the fortunate
Felix Krull makes the very best out of this dysfunctional bipolarity. Given the
various cultural traditions and psychological preconditions of the narrative,
along with its fusion of the early and late conceptual stages, the *Confessions*
of Felix Krull provide a natural frame for an illustration of the aesthetic and
intellectual growth of Mann's creativity and the increasing complexity of
his psychomythic imagination. In the following pages the interplay of these
different elements will be traced and illuminated in exemplary scenes and
episodes.

In the *Confessions*, Thomas Mann's proverbial stylistic brilliance reaches
both its high point of cultivation and its parodic disintegration. No other
Mannian protagonist revels in such an 'exalted manner of speaking' (VII,
395) as Felix. Throughout his escapades in various countries and cultures he
parades his 'gift in general for all kinds of national tongues' (VII, 413) in such
a histrionic fashion that it becomes, as he has to admit himself, 'practically a
farce' (VII, 41). With all his poetic panache, he fails miserably in his attempt
to extol the beauty and romance of love and in its rhetorical wake to sweep
Zouzou, the demure object of his desire, off her feet. His linguistic *libertinage*
only provokes her comic counter-argument that the attractions of the human
body are a deplorable delusion, covering up the grotesque reality of its inner
truth: 'Der Mensch, wie schön er sei, wie schmuck und blank, ist innen doch
Gekrös' nur und Gestank' ('however beautiful, smart and smooth man may
be, inside he is but guts and stench') (VII, 633). This unadulterated Baroque
vision is a harshly ironic response to Felix Krull, the quintessential bourgeois
proponent of a thoroughly bohemian concept of love. Such are the deceptive
dynamics of the *Confessions* and their masquerades of make-believe. The
young inamorato should have known that in Thomas Mann's literary imagination, the magic moment of love is always shrouded in mystical silence
which his lovers – be they mythic or modern – can only break in stammering
if not multilingual confusion. Felix comes to the sobering realisation that
there are no 'new and noble words' (VII, 642) for the 'wordless primordial
state' (VII, 349). Echoing the much-discussed 'linguistic crisis' of his cultural
fellow-travellers through the *fin de siècle*, Felix concludes that in amorous
matters human language is condemned to fail. And to drive home his point
he even calls upon the ladies of the night advising them not to speak: 'for
the word is the enemy of mystery and a cruel betrayer of the quotidian'
(VII, 377).

Felix Krull's growing scepticism towards the word in all its verbosity and triviality is complemented by an equally deepening scepticism towards love in its pure carnality:

> Isn't the animal act of sex only the crudest form of enjoying what I once, in anticipation, called 'the great joy'? . . . Only when yearning, not when satiated, is one worthy of love. I for my part know much more refined, delectable and subtle forms of gratifications than the crude act . . . and in my opinion anyone who strives only straight for his aim understands little about happiness. My goal was always the realm of the great, the whole, and the infinite. (VII, 315)

Despite such erotic expostulations, Felix welcomes sexual adventures with open arms, and he is especially fond of imagining his objects of desire as doubles. His fascination with the two young elegant male and female siblings on the balcony of a Frankfurt hotel and his passionate involvement with the mother-daughter couple of the Kuckuck family are also sublimated *ménage à trois* fantasies. Not to mention the Scottish love-triangle of Lord Kilmarnock, his wife and daughter, who – at least at one point in the conception of the novel – were all poised to fall for Felix. Ingeniously, Mann caricatures himself in Lord Kilmarnock by endowing him with his own prominent nose, which has always been the favourite target of his caricaturists. (After learning that there was a real-life Lord Kilmarnock, Mann authorised for the English translation a name-change to Lord Strathbogie.) In order to live up to his admirers' and his own high and complicated expectations of love, Felix submits, as we will see, to a demanding – and rewarding – regimen of training his sexual faculties and erotic sensibilities.

The synthesis of Felix Krull's enjoyment of love and language is the 'delight of the eyes' ('Augenlust') (VII, 342): 'the gift of seeing was given to me, and it was my one and all' (VII, 344). In the visual realm, the verbal and sexual modes of communication form a higher synaesthetic union, and thus the eye becomes Felix Krull's most important sensory organ, 'the jewel of all organic formation [*Bildung*]' (VII, 348). In punning on *Bildung*, whose associative meanings range from formation and imagination to education and culture, Felix celebrates the eye as the central mediator between world and world-view, that is of sensory perception and its transformation into intellectual cognition and aesthetic appreciation. In addition, Felix's fusion of seeing and understanding is charged with a libidinal energy which clearly derives from both male and female sexual sources. Even as a youngster he developed a practice of contracting and expanding his pupils at will, thus exercising them in a fashion reminiscent of the physiology of male and female arousal. Its effects fill him with a sensation of 'satisfaction' which was 'almost terrifying and accompanied by a shudder at the mysteries of human nature' (VII, 274). The adolescent's joyful panic clearly anticipates already the panerotic rushes and epiphanies of his mature years. As an adult, the memoirist transforms his youthful, masturbation-like exercises into an aesthetic project which focuses explicitly on those 'extreme, silent regions of human relations [where] looks become wedlocked in a state of irresponsible, dreamlike unchastity' (VII, 349). This cross-fertilisation of the visual and the sexual was already the creative crucible for Aschenbach in *Death in Venice*. There, the protagonist's awakening to his erotic adventure is accomplished by a dramatic transformation of the suppressed sexual drive into an openly visual drive: 'Seine Begierde ward sehend' ('his desire became visual') (VIII, 447). This process reaches its powerful climax in the scene where Aschenbach begins to write while watching Tadzio on the beach. In a visual vertigo of erotic ecstasy, Aschenbach forges pure thought and pure emotion, Logos and Eros, into the perfect masterpiece, 'a page and a half of exquisite prose' (VII, 493). However, the psychological toll he has to pay for this aesthetic adventure is a subsequent torture of guilt, moral dissolution and ultimate death. Aschenbach's human demise is, conversely, Felix Krull's artistic rise. Where Aschenbach focused exclusively on his human object of desire, Felix embraces all the 'scenes of the beautiful world' (VII, 344). Intuitively following the Horatian adage *ut pictura poesis*, he strives to capture the essence of the 'Sinnenweide der Oberfläche' ('the sensuous pasture of the surface') (VII, 633) with an exuberant eloquence which is several times characterised as an endeavour to reproduce the recurring 'colourful panorama' in 'picturesque splendour' (VII, 647).

True to his picaresque roots in the Baroque age, Felix Krull envisions the beauty of the world as the multi-textured veil of *Frau Welt* (Lady World), who is the ultimate allegory of the Baroque world-view. Into her metaphoric fabric, the memoirist has woven a variety of Baroque themes and tropes. First, the motif of the fool: Madame Houpflé's affectionate appellations for her young lover include 'precious ignoramus' ('holder Dümmling') (VII, 443) and 'little fool' ('Närrchen') (VII, 450). Second, the trope of deception, to which Zouzou resorts when rejecting Felix Krull's amorous advances and which unfolds most explicitly in the performance art of Müller-Rosé, who is described both as 'unsavoury earthworm' (VII, 294) and 'blissful butterfly' (VII, 294). Third, the motif of transience which is most programmatically evoked by the aging Madame Houpflé, paramour-cum-poetess *par excellence*, and thus Felix Krull's congenial counterpart in all matters of love and poetry. Comically ignoring Felix's own erotic lesson that lovers should not be talkers, she obsessively intertwines her lusty caresses with learned laments about the transience of life (VII, 547), ultimately waxing rhapsodic in two languages: 'Nach Jahr und Jahren, wenn – le temps t'a détruit...Ja wenn das Grab uns deckt' ('after many years, when time has destroyed you – and when the grave covers us') (VII, 450). And last but not least, the Baroque motif of *carpe diem* ('seize the day'), which is the natural complement to the trope of transience, appears in the popular ditty: 'Enjoy life, as long as the lantern shines' (VII, 538); this song was already the motto in Felix's childhood home, and in its quaint folk wisdom it remains his guiding light through all his wanderings and adventures.

Given the Baroque baggage of a deep awareness of life's perennial deceptiveness and its inexorable limitations, Felix Krull embraces it with a vengeance, endlessly luxuriating in all its enticing manifestations, its 'desire-evoking images' (VII, 344). Throughout his memoirs he re-envisions lush sceneries and opulent *tableaux vivants*, which range from delicatessen shops and display windows full of jewellery to mass entertainment spectacles and the 'tumultuous celebration' (VII, 543) of life in the universe, in whose visionary evocation microcosm and macrocosm merge. He is introduced to the macrocosm by the paleontologist Professor Kuckuck who becomes his erudite cicerone through Lisbon's Natural History Museum. This guided tour is a veritable Faustian Walpurgis Night which turns the myriad manifestations of the organic and inorganic world into an awe-inspiring spectacle of wonders. Above it all presides Professor Kuckuck as a benevolent, all-knowing mock-mythic reincarnation of Wotan/Zeus.[2] This kaleidoscopic crescendo of the exploration of life writ large reflects Felix Krull's own deep desire for self-intensification and self-transcendence through and into the 'realm of the great, the whole, and the infinite' (VII, 315). Given its emotional and intellectual intensity, it triggers in Felix Krull the erotic-epiphanic moments of 'the great joy' (VII, 547) and the 'wordless primordial state', raising them to the cosmic level of 'universal sympathy' (VII, 548 *et passim*). The mystical qualities of these panerotic emotions have been compared to the 'oceanic feeling' which psychoanalysis associates with the infant's blissful memories of intra- and extra-uterine union with the maternal body. Felix Krull, the *Glückskind*, repeatedly recaptures this pre-oedipal *unio mystica* with the maternal body in his exuberant embrace of *Frau Welt*, cradling himself in her lap of sensuous mysteries and material luxuries.

The *Confessions* describe three major events whose spectacular nature not only exemplifies this intensive merging of the subject and object of vision, but also illustrates additional aspects of Felix Krull's increasingly complex view of life and art. The first is his theatrical experience with the actor Müller-Rosé, whose *outré* operetta performance makes a lasting impression on the fourteen-year-old. The incarnation of beauty, happiness and success on stage, Müller-Rosé represents the 'vain glory' (VII, 287) of a made-up histrionic – if not hysteric – who reveals himself backstage as the ugly and repulsive opposite of his theatrical self. His duplicitous identity, emblematised in the Baroque metaphor of worm and butterfly, is a modern *mise en scène* of the beguiling nature of *Frau Welt*. However, whereas the Baroque allegory preached ultimate disengagement and sober renunciation of the world, Felix Krull's modern morality play suggests just the opposite, that is, the passionate engagement between actor and audience: 'a mutual gratification, a nuptial encounter of his and their desires' (VII, 295). And contrary to the Christian warning that *Frau Welt* would ultimately trap her victims in the sensuous realm of sin and shame, Felix elevates Müller-Rosé's utterly secular spectacle into a 'church of enjoyment' (VII, 295). To top it off, he blends his reconstructed *Frau Welt* view with various Christian allusions to the 'Immaculate Conception' (VII, 295). This contravention draws the nuptial gaze of the viewer to the ultimate object of Catholic adoration, the divine image of the Virgin Mary. This thoroughly iconoclastic reconfiguration of Our Lady and *Frau Welt*, the two most emblematic models of Christian and pagan idolatry, is an exemplary illustration of Thomas Mann's complex parodic strategies.

The novel's second example from the realm of the spectacle is the world of the circus, in whose arena the acrobat Andromache performs her daring *salto mortale*. The erotic aura of the Müller-Rosé performance tightens into an erotic tension which is created by the colourful parade of wild animals and skimpily dressed acrobats on the one hand and the potential disaster of the beautiful high-wire equilibrist Andromache on the other. Together, this highly charged circus atmosphere amounts to a veritable 'assault on the senses, the nerves, wanton lust' (VII, 445). However, watching the aerialist's breathtaking stunts, the crowd's raw 'desire for her' (VII, 460) soon turns into a religious 'devotion' (VII, 460), and the enticing entertainment permutates into a scenery of sublime adoration, echoing the Madonna moments in Müller-Rosé's church of enjoyment. If Andromache's eyes and hands miss her acrobatic partner by just one split second, their aerial union will turn into a fatal crash. Thus, her perfect body-control transforms the erotic interplay between longing gaze and fleeting embrace into a complex symbolic work of art, wedlocking it, as it were, into elegant sublation: 'This was her way of intercourse with man, no other was conceivable, for one could easily see that this austere body invested and spent all that others give to love in its adventurous artistic performance' (VII, 460). In addition, as an 'Amazon of the air' (VII, 460), she is associated with making war rather than love, just like Aschenbach, whom Thomas Mann characterised after the outbreak of the First World War as a warrior of the mind. Given the intertextual web of associations referring to the cultural complex of psychosexual displacement and sublimation, Andromache's acrobatic act comes to represent the paradigm of civilisation proposed by Freud in *Civilisation and its Discontents*, according to which the dynamics of drives are transformed into sublime works of art. Closer to home, she also illuminates Thomas Mann's daily challenge of transforming his lifelong suppressed homosexual fantasies into increasingly hyperbolic parables. Andromache's graphically profiled androgynous features ('she was not a woman, but neither was she a man, and therefore not human', VII, 460) triangulate a cluster of meanings. First, she delineates Mann's own complicated bisexuality; second, she illustrates the hermetic nature of androgynous art; and third, as an angelic hermaphrodite she personifies the sublime union of both sexes in her body, i.e. the erotic ideal of permanent self-fulfilment and self-transcendence. Andromache's performance also anticipates and illustrates salient features of the *écriture féminine* in French post-structuralist theory. For example, Cixous' and Clément's influential manifesto *La Jeune Née* (1975) focuses on the spectacular world of circus and cinema. In those realms they find the 'mystical mythology' and the modern models for their much-touted theatre of the body: 'Women ... who are amazons, androgynous heroines, beyond bisexuality, and acrobats ... With the circus and cinema, we have moved into the institutionalisation of hysteria [... into the...] space ... for cathartic identification.'[3]

The third example of a mass spectacle with complex symbolic implications is the bullfight in Lisbon, attended by Felix Krull and the whole Kuckuck family. Again, the festive focus of this 'ethnic masquerade' (VII, 648), which is formed by the bull and the torero, is invested with a rich sexual imagery which reaches profound mythological proportions. To begin with, the bull exudes an 'irresistible concentration of procreative and murderous power', in which, the author surmises, ancient people would have seen 'a god-animal, an animal god' (VII, 651). Several times during the fighting ritual, the bloody confrontation between the bull and the torero is adumbrated as a momentary merging, as 'graphic visual unions of the powerful and the elegant' (VII, 654). When the bull finally lies dead in the sand, Felix perceives a mysterious 'equality and unity' between 'killer and killed' (VII, 652). With these allusions, this folkloric festivity of 'fun, blood and devotion' (VII, 652) turns into a veritable psychomythic spectacle. Psychologically speaking, it is a last echo of the sexual pathology of sadomasochism which is an aberrant undercurrent in the psychodynamics of Thomas Mann's literary universe. It surfaces most prominently in *The Magic Mountain* with Naphta's perverse fantasies about a magical union between the murderer and his victim in the act of killing. Mythologically speaking, the 'primeval folk features' (VII, 652) of the corrida evoke, as Professor Kuckuck's knowledgeable comments suggest, the ancient pagan connection between 'sacrificial blood' and 'divine blood' (VII, 657), a primordial connection which still reverberates in the mysteries of the Christian Eucharist. Contemplating this Christian blood mystery,

Donna Maria Pia perceives the final agony of the bull as that of a 'terrible martyr' (VII, 654). This double vision of the tortured creature as quasi-divine victim evokes in her deep and contradictory emotions, causing her to vacillate between 'clapping her hands and hastily crossing herself' (VII, 653). The torero's appearance in turn is reminiscent of Felix Krull himself – at least that is how the memoirist recreates it – since he wears a costume which is remarkably similar to that in which Felix's godfather Schimmelpreester once dressed him up as a youthful model. As these various momentous meanings feed on each other, Donna Maria Pia is being increasingly awed and aroused by the spectacle. It finally unleashes in her a 'whirlwind of archaic forces' (VII, 661) with which she embraces Felix Krull in intense passion: 'more tempestuously than in the Iberian blood game, I saw the royal bosom sway beneath my ardent caresses' (VII, 661). With this sentence, celebrating the *Glückskind*'s victorious return into a maternal ocean of love and desire, the memoirs of Felix Krull come to their climactic conclusion. The post-Freudian breakthrough into a pre-oedipal imaginary is a sublime moment of textual truth.

Pleasure and death, Eros and Thanatos, are the two borderline experiences in which humans perceive life most ecstatically, that is, beside themselves, and these two experiences are also at the core of the Eleusinian mysteries in which ancient devotees worshipped the Magna Mater or Great Mother. The psychosexual yearning for the maternal body, which breeds so many of the regressive phantasies of Thomas Mann's protagonists, is a longing for the uterine paradise, in whose mythical utopia love and death form a sacred whole. That utopian no-man's-land is matriarchy's lost horizon of which Faust's 'Realm of the Mothers' and his 'Eternal Feminine' are the last great poetic recollections in Christian culture. It was the Swiss school of Johann Jakob Bachofen, Carl Gustav Jung, Heinrich Zimmer, Karl Kérenyi and others whose research into matriarchal cultures increasingly engaged Thomas Mann's attention and inspired his later mythopoetic works. Whereas his early protagonists were haunted and attracted by a deeply rooted 'empathy with death', his later heroes were drawn to life at its fullest. In the bullfight's 'death-festivity brought up from the depths' (VII, 652), which turns into a tempestuous sexual experience, these two lifelong conflicting drives of Mann's protagonists become one through the Great Mother, who is the mythic womb and tomb of all life.

In the ancient mysteries of Eleusis, the matriarchal deities Demeter and Persephone, associated with the god Hermes, form the holy trinity of man's initiation into the sacred secrets of birth and death, creation and destruction. In Felix Krull's memoirs, the matriarchal mother–daughter dyad of Demeter and Persephone is clearly adumbrated in the strong mother–daughter relationship of Maria Pia da Cruz and her daughter Zouzou. The mother's name already encodes a highly mythical configuration, namely the Christian Mother of God and her close association with the ritual crucifixion of her son, the atavistic sacrificial Lamb of God. However, behind the Christian mother–son relationship stands the matriarchal myth of the mother goddess, who not only gives birth to her son, but also embraces him as her divine lover, only to devour him again in the end. This powerful mythic double bind of love and death still reverberates in the Christian iconography of the Pietà. Thus, the Kuckuck family becomes a sublime pastiche of the holy family, blending Christian dogma (Maria Pia), with Nordic mythologies (Wotan) and ancient matriarchal mysteries (Demeter/Persephone). Glimpses of the matriarchal archetype, which made a strong comeback in the European literature and cultural philosophy of the turn of the century, can be traced throughout Thomas Mann's work, especially in his multi-layered master narrative, *The Magic Mountain*. Since the *Venus Barbata*, the 'bearded Venus', is the androgynous archetype of the Magna Mater, she serves as the perfect sexual persona through which Thomas Mann can both articulate and personify his own polymorphous desires. From a French feminist perspective, Andromache and Donna Maria Pia create the spectacular aura and arena in which the Magna Mater can celebrate her comeback as the Newly Born Woman (pulling all the sparkling registers from cosmic to camp).

Since the matriarchal mother–daughter archetype is intricately linked with the figure of Hermes, it comes as no surprise that Thomas Mann's male protagonists throughout his narratives should reflect increasingly complex Hermetic features. The figure of Hermes itself underwent various metamorphoses during the course of its mythological genealogy. Originally a divine messenger moving between the upper world and the underworld, his initiatory character soon assumed additional features such as the god of love and seduction and the god of knowledge and textual interpretation (hermeneutics), thereby merging with the Egyptian deity and acquiring the sobriquet Thot Trismegistos. In Thomas Mann's work, Hermes makes his first appearance when the dying Aschenbach's original perception of Tadzio as an incarnation of Eros blends into a final vision of him as Hermes Psychopompos, the 'Psychagog' or guide of souls into the underworld (VIII, 525). The growing complexity of the Hermes figure in ancient myth is further explored in the lengthy disputation between Naphta and Settembrini in *The Magic Mountain*, which itself is a hermetically encoded narrative of elaborate initiations into the realms of sexual and spiritual knowledge. Finally, in the *Confessions of Felix Krull*, Hermes takes centre stage. As a Hermetic manifestation of Eros, Felix Krull preaches, practises and personifies, far more than any other Mannian hero, all the virtues of the god of love. Even as an infant at his nurse's breasts he awakes to the sensual pleasures of what he soon will call 'the great joy'. Growing up into a young man of exceptional physical beauty, he develops such androgynous features that both sexes end up falling for him wherever he goes. Fully aware 'that in me the enjoyment of love possessed twice as much sharpness and sweetness as in others' (VII, 314), Felix seeks and finds in Rosza a modern *hetaira*, who teaches him the age-old knowledge of physical love and erotic pleasures. Contrary to the late-Victorian misgivings about sexuality as 'enervating concupiscence' (VII, 384), Felix extols the 'virtue of love' (VII, 383) and 'strengthening of the nerves' ('Benervung') (VII, 384) which Rosza's *éducation sensuelle* has taught him. His initiation into the realm of the senses also doubles as a parody of the traditional *Bildungsroman*. Unlike Hans Castorp, who graduates to increasingly higher and older levels of knowledge and cultural understanding, Felix Krull's *Bildungsideal* is an ever-increasing 'refinement through love' (VII, 384). With his physical beauty, his penchant for colourful disguise and dissimulation, his visual and verbal luxuriance in the riches of the *belle époque*, and in his longing to embrace and transcend it all, he becomes a most natural and multi-talented son of *Frau Welt*. As a picaresque lover of women and the world, he sets out to disprove Freud's modern notion of civilisation as the source of increasing discontent. As a felicitous child he enjoys any civilisation with all his heightened senses as well as his copious capacity for intellectual enjoyment and amazement.

Complementing the erotic side of his personality, the Hermetic qualities of Felix Krull likewise inform all stages of his composite career as *picaro*, artist, lover and confidence man, but do not become fully evident until his amorous encounter with the much older Madame Houpflé. She invites his advances by encouraging him to steal her jewellery, thereby skilfully alluding to Hermes' original qualities as thief and seducer. As a sentimental poetess with a very strong weakness for younger men, who could all be her sons (hence a *magna mater rediviva*), she finally reveals Felix as the true embodiment of Hermes. In his naked beauty he appears to her as the 'statue of beauty', the 'god with the legs of Hermes' (VII, 444). Diane Houpflé's declaration of love for Felix is also Thomas Mann's own last and most explicit acknowledgement of his homoerotic feelings. In 1950 he met Franz Westermeier, a young waiter in the Grand Hotel Dolder in Zurich. Just watching him rekindled all the erotic, melancholy longing Mann had always felt for attractive young men. To his diary he confided on 6 March 1951: 'In half-sleep I dreamt that with a kiss I took leave of Franzl, the last loved one, as representative of the whole adored species.' Thus, in the eclipse of Thomas Mann's long life and career, the figure of Felix, the perennial fixed star on the horizon of his literary universe, merged with the figure of Franzl and became once more flesh and blood before vanishing into timeless myth. In the disguise of an overwrought Madame Houpflé, Thomas Mann embraces Felix-Franzl and – under the cover of caricature and sexual cross-dressing – articulates in simple words the 'great – forbidden – joy' of his life:

> Would you believe, beloved, that I have loved only you, no one but you since I was able to feel? . . . I live in my so-called perversion – in the love of my life that lies at the bottom of everything I am, in the joy and misery of this enthusiasm with its precious oath that nothing, nothing in the whole visible world equals the enchantment of youthful manhood. (VII, 445–6)

Since Felix Krull, like all Mann's leading protagonists, is also a projection of his own identity, Diane Houpflé's confession doubles as the author's own narcissistic declaration of love to the elusive image of his ideal self. In his diary entry of 18 July 1953, Mann wrote that he wept while working on the enchanted musings in the *Confessions* about the power of love.

As the divine lover in the mythic mask of Hermes/Eros, Felix Krull gains representative significance for Thomas Mann's late philosophy of art and life. The symbolic essence of his poetic persona becomes most obvious in the episode in which the military commission examines him in his immaculate nakedness. Under the probing eyes of the examiners, Felix Krull feels 'nameless, ageless, free and pure, floating in empty space' (VII, 357). As the statuesque embodiment of perfect physical beauty, and also as a skilful wordsmith who transforms the wonders of the world into perfect prose, Felix Krull stands for the harmonious union of life and art. In his bisexual faculty of conceiving and creating, he represents that androgynous genius of art which Mann's senescent Goethe in his novel *Lotte in Weimar* (or *The Beloved Returns*) has expressed thus: 'I am the brown woman from Lindheim in a man's body, I am womb and semen, the androgynous art, shaped by everything; but, shaped by me, what I receive enriches the world' (II, 664). Felix Krull's androgynous ideal of art is complemented by his androgynous ideal of life. In his bisexuality, 'not woman . . . not man either, but something wonderful in between' (VII, 374), he reflects that physical essence which was already characteristic of Tadzio and of which Norman O. Brown has written: 'The "magical" body which the poet seeks is the "subtle" or "spiritual" or "translucent" body of occidental mysticism, and the "diamond" body of oriental mysticism, and in psychoanalysis, the polymorphously perverse body of childhood.'[4] Fully connected with the undifferentiated body – and mind – of early childhood, Felix Krull remains throughout his life 'a child and dreamer' (VII, 315). This infantile realm is the wellspring of both Felix Krull's and Thomas Mann's narcissistic imagination and creativity. With his Hermetic celebration and transubstantiation of life as love and art, Felix Krull develops a cultural conception of love which encompasses the whole gamut from pure sexual energy to the spiritual realm of Christian *caritas*.[5] Love of self, love of others, and universal love, these are the Hermetic stages of self-realisation and self-intensification in a world Felix Krull sees originally and ultimately created and inspired by the cosmogonic powers of Eros. Given Felix's exultant drive to transcend the individual boundaries of body and mind, to reconnect with the quintessence of Eros and Logos, his personal memoirs mutate into a cultural anamnesis of truly anthropological dimensions. Within this larger context, his lifelong striving for 'the great, the whole, and the infinite' reveals itself as a longing for the Platonic Eros and his realm of eternal truth.

This dramatic return to Eros, ranging from pagan carnality to Platonic spirituality, is the great return of the culturally suppressed in Christian patriarchal civilisation. It marks a pervasive paradigm change which manifests itself in the ongoing sexual revolution and the radical transformation of ethics and aesthetics throughout Western civilisation. Thus, Felix Krull not only stands as a representative figure for Thomas Mann's multifaceted life and work, but his 'costume head' also reflects the cultural complexities of the twentieth century, its *belle époque* past and its postmodern future. To list only the latter's most salient features: its body cult, its preoccupation with sex, youth and beauty, the cultivation of narcissistic drives and androgynous fashions, our society's conspicuous consumption of wealth and its indulgence in a voyeuristic culture and entertainment industry, and last but not least, our New Age syncretic spirituality, which privileges pre-Christian, earth-centred mythologies. These *Zeitgeist* phenomena are all indications of the systematic disintegration of a patriarchal world and value-system, and, by the same token, powerful manifestations of the mythic resurrection of the Great Mother and her legendary Golden Age of affluence. Through her utopian matrix, Felix Krull gives birth to himself in his own ideal image. On a larger level, his Hermetic metamorphosis is also a sublime reflection of the American dream, or, to be more precise, a divine comedy about man's universal dream of being 'reborn'. For, more than ever before, (post)modern man is striving to overcome his limitations, be they sexual, social or spiritual, in other words to become reborn as a truly self-made (wo)man, hoping to realise all of his or her unlimited possibilities.

## NOTES

1 Hans Wysling, *Narzißmus und illusionäre Existenzform. Zu den 'Bekenntnissen des Hochstaplers Felix Krull'* (Berne and Munich: Francke, 1982).

2 Ibid., p.183.
3 Hélène Cixous and Cathérine Clément, *The Newly Born Woman* (Minneapolis: University of Minnesota Press, 1986), p. 13.
4 Norman O. Brown, *Life Against Death: The Psychoanalytical Meaning of History* (Middletown, CT: Wesleyan University Press, 1959), pp. 312–13.
5 His 'imitation of Goethe' also taught Mann that 'love' was the most frequent word in the work of his great Weimar model: see 'Goethe und die Demokratie', ix, 780.

## FURTHER READING

Beddow, Michael, 'Fiction and Meaning in Thomas Mann's *Felix Krull*', *Journal of European Studies* 10 (1980), 77–92

Nelson, Donald, *Portrait of the Artist as Hermes* (Chapel Hill: University of North Carolina Press, 1971)

Northcote-Bade, James, '*Der Tod in Venedig* and *Felix Krull*: The Effect of the Interruption in the Composition of Thomas Mann's *Felix Krull* Caused by *Der Tod in Venedig*', *Deutsche Vierteljahrsschrift* 52 (1978), 271–8

Rieckmann, Jens, ' "In deinem Atem bildet sich mein Wort." Thomas Mann, Franz Westermeier und *Die Bekenntnisse des Hochstaplers Felix Krull*', *Thomas Mann Jahrbuch* 10 (1997), 149–65

Steiner, George, 'Thomas Mann's *Felix Krull*', in his *Language and Silence* (London: Faber, 1967), pp. 297–307

Wysling, Hans, *Narzißmus und illusionäre Existenzform. Zu den 'Bekenntnissen des Hochstaplers Felix Krull'* (Berne and Munich: Francke, 1982)

# 14

## HINRICH SIEFKEN

# Mann as essayist

The perception of Thomas Mann's achievement as a writer and man of letters today rests largely on the relative popularity of his fiction, of his stories and some of his novels. That image has been slightly changed in recent years by the publication of his diaries and of some major new collections of letters, but Mann's prolific work as an essayist of both considerable substance and consummate artistry is little known. His non-fictional prose, written over the first half of this century and covering such subjects as his own life, the theatre (1908) and the German novel, sleep (1909), the artist and the man of letters (1913), the Great War, cosmopolitanism (1925), culture and socialism (1928), the cultural and intellectual climate of the Weimar Republic, many German and European writers and artists, democracy (1938), peace (1938), the problem of freedom and the Second World War (1940), and again major Russian and German figures like Dostoevsky (1946) and Chekhov (1954), Nietzsche (1947) and Schiller (1955) – this vast collection of carefully crafted argumentation is relatively little read. A new annotated German selection of Mann's essays arranged in chronological order in six substantial volumes, the best introduction to Mann the essayist available now, covers barely a third of the estimated six thousand pages of Mann's output.[1] The five volumes of non-fictional writings in the 1974 Fischer edition of Thomas Mann's works give a carefully crafted impression of the nature, range and wealth of his work as an essayist, but not a complete picture of Mann's major and minor essayistic efforts and their varying textual forms. A short introduction to this vast corpus of texts has to subsume them all under a loose definition of the term 'essay'.[2] It also has to explore possible reasons for the controversy surrounding many of them at the time of publication and for their limited influence today.

Neither Mann's life and public career as a major and representative German writer, honoured with the Nobel Prize for Literature in 1929, nor his artistic achievement and public status are intelligible without some understanding of the nature and significance of his essays, texts which originated as contributions to a continuous public debate conducted in newspapers, periodicals and magazines, by lectures and speeches to literary as well as political gatherings. It was a debate about the past, present and future of German tradition and culture in its European context, an increasingly fierce and bitter debate in which Mann participated, first in Germany and later from various countries in Europe and from exile in the USA. The search for reliable and inspiring authorities from the past who could serve as models for shaping the present and future resulted in claims and counter-claims in which quotations from and interpretations of the great writers and thinkers (as well as long-forgotten minor ones) were used as weapons. Centenary celebrations such as those of the Goethe year 1932 turned into public jousts for the true German tradition. In these public confrontations adaptations (and translations) of a particular essay often served Mann's purpose more than once. From exile he launched his own periodical, *Maß und Wert* [Measure and Value] (1937–40), with the intention of protecting what in his view had been the main characteristics and standards of genuine human dignity by testing their validity in the context of the present (XII, 802). Misleadingly for the modern reader, he called this technique of preserving the best from the past by exchanging it for the appropriate modern equivalent a 'conservative revolution'. In the same way he would speak for a while of a 'third realm' ('drittes Reich') in which true humanity would emerge as a synthesis between opposing material and spiritual claims. These examples should alert us to the difficulty of understanding the terms of Mann's discourse critically, but without undue prejudice.

Mann's essays are part of the turbulent political, social and cultural history of modern Germany. A few pointers to the way its changes affected him must suffice. Mann grew up in the Wilhelmine Empire and, although influenced by contemporary Western thinking and writing in his early years, sided patriotically, indeed chauvinistically, with Germany during the First World War in pieces like 'Thoughts in War' (1914) or *Frederick and the Grand Coalition* (1915). However, he gradually became convinced, after the abdication of the Emperor and despite the imposition of the Treaty of Versailles, that the young Weimar Republic had to be supported and protected. The patriotic conservative began to take the side of a liberal socialism by defending it from a Romantic position in 'On the German Republic' (1922). After the years of his increasingly vigorous and outspoken defence of a liberal and democratic republican position against the forces of the right, he suddenly found himself in exile in 1933 defending Wagner as a figure of sophisticated European modernism. Mann remained in Europe for a period, then moved to America and eventually returned to Europe, without ever settling in Germany again. Having broadcast his essays against Hitler for the BBC during the war years, from

October 1940 (*German Listeners!*, first published in full in 1945), Mann attempted in 1945 in a controversial essay, 'Germany and the Germans', to explain how Germany had turned into the Third Reich. In 1949, on the occasion of the Goethe bicentenary celebrations, he insisted that his 'Address in the Goethe Year of 1949' had to be heard not just in Frankfurt, in the Federal Republic, but also in Weimar, in the German Democratic Republic, and he thereby fell foul of the new political correctness of the Cold War and of McCarthyism in America. Throughout his life the essayist attracted controversy and fierce criticism, but kept returning to his self-imposed task, accepting its heavy demands on his time and energy and their consequences for the completion of his ambitious fictional projects.

Mann's involvement and intervention as essayist in the dramatic social and political changes of his lifetime was not an accident of history but born of a deep conviction. The point of departure was Mann's belief, first articulated in a short essay entitled 'Bilse and I' (1906) in defence of his bestselling first novel *Buddenbrooks*, that he was able to speak for many. Staggering early success had persuaded the young writer that the popularity of his writing gave it symbolic status. He spoke and wrote as the representative of many, even though at heart he was only articulating and explicating his own experiences. In that essay he insisted that, even though he had used details from the social reality of Lübeck, the resulting creation was not about Lübeck and its people but about himself and his vision: 'My work is never about you...but about me, about me' (x, 22). The popularity of his work was ample proof that such very personal writing, in which penetrating critical analysis and perfect artistic illusionism created a reality others could identify with, was representative of the experience of others. He then had to carry the responsibility of that burden – and he did not always carry it elegantly or easily. Mann's first major essay, the monster essay of the war years *Reflections of an Unpolitical Man* (1918), turned a bitter personal feud with his older, francophile brother Heinrich about the proper role of the writer and his task into a gigantic literary war effort. Piling quotation upon quotation as evidence, he took up arms as essayist ('Gedankendienst mit der Waffe') (xii, 9), ultimately for Imperial Germany and against France, for what he then saw as German culture threatened by the supposedly shallow civilisation of the West.

Soon, however, the essayist had to face the resentment of the readers he claimed to represent. They felt betrayed when the attitude he had taken and expressed seemed to change. When in 'On the German Republic' in 1922 he came out in support of the Weimar Republic as a particularly German version of a republic, he was attacked as a turncoat who had joined the un-German enemy, even though the arsenal for his arguments was as yet not radically different from that of the traditionalist right. As late as 1927 a reviewer complained that the second, slightly amended edition of the *Reflections of an Unpolitical Man* (1922) offered those who wanted to buy the anti-democratic version a sanitised democratic one.[3] The two entirely different versions of his speech of 1921, 'Goethe and Tolstoy' (which was turned into a book-length essay with the same title in 1925), both based on the same collection of notes and excerpts from two major popular biographies of these figures, demonstrate further how Mann adjusted his arguments to the cultural and political requirements of the day. In the later version he would consciously reject certain potentially chauvinistic notions about these great masters which he had entertained earlier but for which the time was no longer right. 'It is not the moment' (XI, 169) was the revealing phrase he used to signal his change of emphasis.[4]

One of the key points in the public debate concerned the very origin of human culture and artistic creation. Hailing Ricarda Huch in 1924, on her sixtieth birthday, as a model of a modern intellectual writer, Mann sided with those who advocated reason and analysis as mainsprings of literature against the powers of unconscious creativity. Indeed, Mann provocatively suggested that she might be more popular if she were less intelligent ('dümmer') and not the 'wondrously articulate empress in the realm of the conscious' (X, 429). It was her articulacy in the realm of conscious thought which made her the great writer ('Schriftstellerin') as which he greeted her. We should note the term he used to define her work; it was a particularly loaded word to German ears.

The divide between the European 'Schriftsteller' and the naively German 'Dichter' marked a disastrous ideological split in German culture. It also marked the divide between Mann's own conception of modern German art and of Weimar culture generally, and that which became the official creed of the National Socialist Third Reich. It would wreck the Section for Literature of the Prussian Academy of Arts in which both Mann and Ricarda Huch served, it threatened the livelihood of many artists and writers driven into exile, and caused untold human misery.[5] The front line between the opposing camps runs between the assumption that the author as inspired poet has no intellectual control over his or her creativity, which flows entirely from the rootedness in traditional national culture, and the assumption that with careful skill and control the author as writer, who knows the craft of writing and is familiar with the best of European culture and thought, consciously shapes the work. Again, the very words are signals – 'Dichter' or 'Schriftsteller'. To talk of 'Goethe's Career as a Writer', using the word 'Schriftsteller' as Mann did in 1932, was a programmatic provocation. It was carefully calculated, since Mann planned to claim Goethe as the true ideal of modern Germany because he transcended simple national limitations.

Mann's great Wagner essay of early 1933, 'The Suffering and Greatness of Richard Wagner', stressed the European sophistication of a German master 'whose nationalism was so thoroughly imbued with European artistry that it had become deeply unsuitable for German patriotic simplification' (IX, 423). This tribute eventually provoked such wrath, including a public protest by the city of Munich cast in the role of guardian of the orthodox German Wagner cult, that Mann did not dare return from his lecture tour abroad with that essay to his home in Munich.[6] The essayist paid dearly for these attempts born of personal conviction. He tried valiantly, but at the time in vain, to define and defend in a long series of public lectures and speeches the characteristics of German (and European) culture by exploring the work of some of its most famous exponents, such as Lessing, Goethe, Schiller, Nietzsche, Schopenhauer and Freud.

The conclusion Mann had drawn from his propulsion into a position of 'representation' was that he had to speak out for what he considered to be the best enlightened tradition of German culture and tradition. Combining such 'Schriftstellerei', such writing about the burning cultural issues of the day, with his 'Musik', the creation of art in fiction which transcends the limitations of the daily toil (XI, 714), was a Herculean adventure. (We notice the striking, slightly derogatory use of the word 'Schriftstellerei' suggesting the less permanent and less artistically ambitious nature of this work.) Conscious of the transient nature of essay-writing, Mann nevertheless responded enthusiastically to the 'task of the day' by restating his position again and again, using various opportunities, hoping that it might be, or become, a representative one. He would collect material from like-minded arguments by others, to enhance his authority. Even in exile he felt that he could speak for Germany, for Germany was where he was: 'wo ich bin, ist Deutschland'.[7] Furthermore, convinced of the continued relevance of these efforts at enlightenment, Mann collected some of them into volumes of essays with such titles as *Die Forderung des Tages* [The Day's Demand] (1930), *Bemühungen* [Endeavours] (1925), or *Rede und Antwort* [Address and Reply] (1922), which stressed that these were his best, subjective but representative attempts to respond to the ever-changing challenges of the time. There is more than a suggestion here, though, that the essays keep returning to a core of assumptions.

The interaction between the writer and the issues of the period is one reason for our difficulty in appreciating the work of the essayist. We require the original historical and social context of the essays in all its elusive detail, we have to read sympathetically yet critically the peculiar terminology, the linguistic manner and register of the period, and to grasp the nature of the essayist's response to it. All of this is often detectable only in brief allusions. A major difficulty, particularly as we approach the very core of the argument, is the highly abstract language of much of the discourse, operating freely, as it does, with nouns like 'Geist', 'Natur', 'Leben' and so on, which present a great challenge to any translator. Then there is the carefully crafted and complex rhetoric of the syntax. A short but striking example of these devices can be found in the brilliant and moving speech of 1932, 'The Trees in the Garden. A Speech for Pan-Europe' (XI, 869) which draws heavily on images from Mann's biblical fiction and culminates in a glorification of Goethe as the model of a man who, like Jacob, 'was blessed with the blessing down from heaven and with the blessing from the depth which lies below'. Goethe was someone who 'would have rejected the Romantic dualism of spirit and soul, of intellect and sensuality as unhealthy and hypochondriac'. The appeal to the authority of Goethe is an appeal to a paradigmatic attitude. Goethe knew 'like anyone who tells a story which deserves that name that his was a perception that thought in images whose sensuality he would not have liked to be called unintellectual. Art, that means life and spirit at the same time, it is the very life of life. Art is the spiritualisation of life, the belief that life needs the spirit' (XI, 869). The reader unfamiliar with the complex frame of references here, with the double blessing of Joseph, the famous lines by Goethe – 'Denn das Leben ist die Liebe, und des Lebens Leben Geist' ('For life is love, and the life of life is spirit') (G II, 75; quoted IX, 343) – and others, will miss the full significance of this passage. But even the various meanings of 'Geist', covering the whole range from reason, intellect and mind to spirit, even essence, force us to decode very carefully this mode of discourse in all its allusions so we may fully understand the message. The defence of a particular type of poetic writing turns into praise for a more perfect form of human existence in which an equilibrium is found between life in its passionate intensity and the demands of reason, and in which the essential human quality of love at its very heart is a gift of the spirit. Such philosophical, even theological reflections as a form of political discourse use a subjective code unfamiliar to most readers.

Moreover, we need to gauge accurately the degree of interdependency between the allusive argument of a particular piece written at a particular time, and the attitude of the essayist. Mann said quite explicitly in 1931 that his work as essayist served its time and its period, was 'Dienst an der Zeit' ('duty to the age'). It was, he said, driven by a sense of justice and fairness which continually urged him to attempt to keep the ship of state and of the common good on an even keel, invariably joining the weaker forces to sustain the equilibrium: 'Duty to the age . . . urges certain characters to move to the other side of the boat when it tilts towards one side' (XII, 653).[8] This presupposes that there has to be a reasonable balance between opposing forces in human culture and, as we have seen, that the time is not always right to stress more controversial aspects of a phenomenon. Much of the time Mann was trying to reinforce the forces of reason and control, of intelligent analysis and succinct formulation, against the strong tide of unquestioned traditional wisdom, irrationalism and over-confident emotionalism. Under different circumstances he might have seen all of these in a different light, always trying to keep a sense of natural balance. The essayist Mann, in quoting his supporters and opponents, and responding to his time, entered the ever-changing arena of cultural politics. Ideally, the reader ought to understand all the details of that route with its curious detours and the many different stages.

This may require a detailed understanding of the essayist's private code which he wants to share. It also involves a keen ear for the mocking language and the now dated concepts deployed by the essayist, for the resonances of words, an ability to pick up an allusion, the confidence to place a quotation – in short, a willingness to play the challenging games for which few readers were equipped at the time and even fewer will be equipped now, given the historical distance and the resulting detachment which gives a sharper profile to these devices. Using an annotated edition – without losing sight of the overall ease of the essayist's craft – is now an essential requirement for most readers.

The essayist Mann likes to dazzle the reader with sophistication and learning, sometimes playfully, but usually with serious intent. Such a display is often a carefully created illusion of learning based on excerpts from sources of various kinds – among them his own essays. Mann relies on significant detail located in a quotation, or a whole series of quotations, in a telling anecdote or piece of narrative, or in an incident which serves his purpose. What he needed was the intimacy with the subject thus created. He would then bring his own experience and judgement to bear on it. That would enable him to get under the skin and into the mind of the great and good, he had argued as early as 17 January 1906 in a letter to his brother Heinrich. The selective use of authorities, of 'Eideshelfer' ('compurgators') (XII, 11) for and against his case, results from this approach. It is a technique relatively easy to spot, yet invariably complex to understand. Nevertheless it was proudly proclaimed by the essayist as part of his artistry in 1918, when he explained his permanent need to quote as a sign of his immense gratitude for the benefit derived from comforting quotations.[9] The obverse is also true, however. Allusions are also a perfect vehicle for derision and censure, as for example the fierce passages (XII, 660–7) against a certain Rudolf Ibel in

'The Rebirth of Decency' (1931) who had attempted to quote Goethe against Mann's arguments in his 'German Address: An Appeal to Reason' (1930). Such passages are, in fact, an important reminder that the pose of Olympian detachment occasionally struck by Mann is much rarer than we are inclined to think. The cut and thrust of the battle over the cultural heritage and its rightful meaning generated much passion and bitterness.

The complex interaction between Mann's self-understanding and his chosen role as essayist to act as defender of the best German and European tradition often results in striking examples of identification with the apparently historical personalities. The best-known example is the charge of 'Kälte' (coldness), of detachment and emotional aloofness, which was levelled against Mann by critics near the turn of the century; it is a characteristic he then discovers in other artists and explores in his essays as well as his fiction. Relevant passages are to be found in 'Goethe and Tolstoy' (IX, 116, 119, 132), 'Speech on Lessing' (IX, 233), 'Goethe's Career as a Writer' (IX, 357), 'Nietzsche's Philosophy in the Light of our Experience' (IX, 708–9), 'Schopenhauer' (IX, 545) and elsewhere.

Similarly, the apparently abstract general issues of his essays are often very close to Mann's own interests and concepts. The essay on Lessing of 1929, for example, used one of Mann's most cherished notions, immensely influential in his fiction, that of the mythical archetype. Lessing becomes a model in whose footsteps modern man should follow, realising the obligation of the archetype to define an 'intellectual mode of life', a mode of living as a thinking individual, which has remained binding on later generations (IX, 229). This gives the essay a surprising urgency and immediacy, as if the battles of Lessing's life had to be fought again in a different guise by later generations. The essay closes with the striking statement that 'In the spirit of Lessing, and in his name, it is our task today to transcend any form of fascism and to reach the only true pact between reason and blood ['einem Bunde von Vernunft und Blut'] which would deserve the name of true human perfection ['Humanität']' (IX, 245).

The essay 'Freud's Position in the History of Modern Thought' of the same year, delivered as a speech to the students of the University of Munich, likewise defined for the young generation, 'who need to be reminded of this today' (X, 265), the contemporary significance of Freud. It lies in the proven need to dissolve impermanent forms of order by critical analysis (X, 280). The true revolution asserts itself as openness for the future by guiding us there through conscious understanding and discerning analysis of the past and the present (X, 265). The Freud Mann presents is primarily a great master and philosopher of human culture and history whose voice Germany, tempted by the claims of a reactionary past, will ignore at its peril. His teaching is 'one of the most important building blocks offered for the foundations of our common future, the home of a liberated and informed humanity' (x, 280).

These two examples illustrate the essayist's need to transcend his immediate subject in a way which renders it transparent in its relevance for the political and cultural situation in which he addresses his real or imaginary audience. Since Mann's model of individual and socio-political human existence is meant to be of general validity, even though he prefers to use German writers and thinkers to establish its relevance, all his essays have a tendency to generalise in the direction of an ideal. His essay 'Germany and Democracy' (1925) pointedly argued that even if it was futile to look to Goethe, Schopenhauer and Nietzsche, who shaped the German national consciousness, as teachers of democratic liberal thought, the Kantian concept of duty should enable Germany to grasp that its task was to serve democracy (otherwise Europe might be dead): 'the ability of the German soul to stretch itself beyond what is merely German, this heritage of the great Germans, who were always more than German, will prepare us for this service ['dies Vermächtnis großen Deutschtums, das immer ein Überdeutschtum war, wird uns zu solchem Dienst geschickt machen']' (XIII, 580). It became a central tenet of Mann's essays that the exemplary nature of all the truly great figures of tradition was their ability to look beyond the boundaries of superficial national characteristics and to recognise the human obligations of their paradigmatic role. As mediators between opposing and conflicting principles they represent different ways of reconciling them through 'the will to change the material world by the human spirit, the materialism of the spirit, which is a form of socialism' (IX, 704), as the Nietzsche essay puts it.

However, the essayist often finds his way into the subject-matter of his essay by discovering in it features familiar to him from self-observation and personal experience. The most striking example of this is the essay 'Brother Hitler' (1939) which demythologises Hitler by treating him as an inferior member of the family, as an unsuccessful artist who compensates for human shortcomings by seeking the attention of the whole world. The whole familiar pathology of the modern artist-figure can be brought to bear on the subject. Inevitably, one consequence of this very personal approach tends to be that Mann casts other figures to some extent in his own image, but the great gain may be the immediate contemporary relevance of the argument which would otherwise have appeared rather more remote and removed from the situation of the essayist.

The reader must remain conscious of the need to decode the essayist's carefully crafted, apparently general statements in order to grasp entirely the intimate interaction and the partial self-identification between the essayist and his subject. Reading the essay 'The Suffering and Greatness of Richard Wagner', one might be struck by a great series of such pointers. There are statements about Wagner's obsession with detail combined with the monumental nature ('großes Format') of his music (IX, 363); about the interlocking sequence in the production of individual works which form one cohesive whole (IX, 386); about a nervous constitution always working on the edge of exhaustion (IX, 387); about creating gigantic works by persistently piling up a few hours' work each day (IX, 388); about the pedantic order and bourgeois comfort of the surroundings in which he writes (IX, 410); and the resulting 'bourgeois neatness' ('bürgerliche Arbeitsakkuratesse') (IX, 411), reflected in the calligraphy of his manuscripts; about the gentle and masterly popular appeal ('Volkstümlichkeit') (IX, 415) of some of his music; about Wagner's discovery of Schopenhauer which is described in the words the young Thomas Mann had used for Thomas Buddenbrook's discovery of the philosopher (IX, 397, quoting I, 654). What Mann then attributes to Baudelaire, 'the joy of rediscovering himself in the artistic intentions of another' (IX, 423), defines an essential ingredient of the essayist's own technique here: the satisfaction of recognising, despite all the differences separating them, key characteristics of his own artistic attitude in a great master. As Mann had admitted in 'On the German Republic', this was a core assumption of his work as an essayist: even if he was not the equal of the great figures he chose, he claimed to belong to their family. 'I am no Goethe; but somehow I belong, distantly, just a little, as Adalbert Stifter put it, "to his family"' (IX, 816).

Since the publication of Mann's diaries with their revelations about his strong homoerotic inclinations, the reader has been able to respond with greater understanding to passages exploring, however subtly and, on the face of it, tentatively, male and female characteristics in some of the essays. For example, there is the digression on 'that field of the erotic in which the law of sexual polarity, thought generally valid, does not apply' in 'On the German Republic' (XI, 847–51). The general point emerging here is that the essayist's way of regarding and interpreting the subjects of his essays, and the concepts, the quotations, the language and the terminology he deploys, all act like filters which affect our perception as readers. The better we understand his technique, the more informed our critical insight into his work will be.

Naturally, Mann's artistic and political development over some fifty years as an essayist affects the character of his essays. He started with reflections on the nature of his own writing and his work as an artist, making the archer's bow and the musician's lyre the symbols of his work. The artist's irritable sensitivity responds, so he argued, to life's disturbing experiences with powerful vengeance, scoring bull's-eyes with his fierce, swift response of carefully chosen words which penetrate to the essence of the experience while giving it a brilliant aesthetic formulating: 'tief erkennen und schön gestalten' ('profound understanding and beautiful rendering') was the motto of 1906 (x, 19). The obsession with his own world makes the artist appear egotistical, but this obsession is a decisive element, giving formal shape to that limited experience which involved passionate involvement, painful insight and personal sacrifice ('Sweet Sleep', 1909; xi, 338). Writing about the novelist Fontane ('The Old Fontane'), Mann produced the helpful formula that the artist gives the world he writes about a voice but makes it speak in a tone very much his own (ix, 23). Detached from that world in an attitude of irony, he nevertheless feels a responsibility towards it. This results in Mann's definition of the writer's instinctive psychological reaction as one of 'interest' (ix, 33), in which affection and critical detachment, even 'love and hate' (xii, 846) fuse. The attitude of the writer generally, and of the essayist in particular, is neither one of complete devotion nor one of indifference. The true motivation is the need to understand. In order to understand, the essayist will not simply rely on his own originality and subjective reaction. He will be helped by finds, quotations, the opinions of others which he can make his own. What really matters is that penetrating, slightly malicious way of looking at the subject-matter designed to expose the prejudice or preconceived notions of his opponents.

From such self-reflection and defence of his own position in the early essays, Mann moved to a position where he claimed that the balance the artist has to strike between emotional attention and coldly critical analysis is in essence the problem of all human existence which is posed between the opposing forces of 'mind' ('Geist') and 'nature'. Mann had tabulated these forces in the notes for his unfinished essay 'Geist und Kunst' [Mind (or Intellect) and Art], which he had originally conceived as his personal equivalent to Schiller's great essay *On Naive and Sentimental Poetry* but was unable to write. We may have difficulty accepting all his assumptions about the opposing forces, but the central tenet is less controversial. At the core of all Mann's work as essayist is the firm conviction that the creative work of human beings, rightly interpreted, is driven by the same needs, desires and considered views in response to the challenges of human life in society and history, as those which shape human existence properly so called. The life of the great artist or thinker who rises to this task may be a model for later generations to follow by adapting it; it may be a myth to be reborn or a utopian ideal for the whole of humankind. The educational task of the essayist consists in asserting, interpreting, defending and proclaiming the validity of a core of related views which shape that ideal. In his own life a truly great artist, like Goethe, may even succeed, so Mann claimed, not just in proclaiming, but also in himself becoming, the transcendent 'Ideal der Deutschheit', an ideal of Germanness which acquires general human validity by ignoring national limitations. Testing this view in studies on many and varied topics became Mann's preoccupation as an essayist.

## NOTES

1 Thomas Mann, *Essays*, ed. Hermann Kurzke and S. Stachorski, 6 vols. (Frankfurt am Main: Fischer, 1993–1997). Quotations in this chapter are, however, from the 1974 edition of the collected works.
2 For further reading and more bibliographical information see Jürgen Eder, '*Allerlei Allotria'. Grundzüge und Quellen der Essayistik bei Thomas Mann* (Bonn: Bouvier, 1993), with excellent observations on the artistic characteristics deriving from Montaigne; the chapters by Rolf Gunter Renner and Hermann Kurzke in Helmut Koopmann (ed.), *Thomas-Mann-Handbuch* (Stuttgart: Kröner, 1990), pp. 629–706, and Hinrich Siefken, 'Der Essayist Thomas Mann', in H. L. Arnold (ed.), *Thomas Mann*, 2nd edn (Munich: Text und Kritik, 1982), pp. 132–47.
3 Cf. Klaus Schröter, *Thomas Mann im Urteil seiner Zeit. Dokumente 1891–1955* (Hamburg 1969), pp. 155–8.
4 See Herbert Lehnert and Eva Wessell, *Nihilismus der Menschenfreundlichkeit. Thomas Manns 'Wandlung' und sein Essay 'Goethe und Tolstoi'* (Frankfurt am Main: Klostermann, 1991), pp. 126–40; Clayton Koelb (ed.), *Thomas Mann's 'Goethe and Tolstoy'. Notes and Sources* (University, AL: The University of Alabama Press, 1984), pp. 9–16; Hinrich Siefken, *Thomas Mann: Goethe – "Ideal der Deutschheit". Wiederholte Spiegelungen 1893–1949* (Munich: Fink, 1981), pp. 97–100, 112–19.
5 See Inge Jens, *Dichter zwischen rechts und links. Die Geschichte der Sektion für Dichtkunst der Preußischen Akademie der Künste dargestellt nach den Dokumenten* (Munich: Piper, 1971).
6 See Hans Rudolf Vaget, 'Musik in München. Kontext und Vorgeschichte des "Protests der Richard-Wagner-Stadt München gegen Thomas Mann"', *Thomas Mann Jahrbuch* 7 (1994), 41–70.
7 'Tagebuchblätter' of April 1938. See Hinrich Siefken, 'Thomas Mann's essay *Bruder Hitler*', *German Life and Letters* 35 (1982), 168.
8 See Hinrich Siefken, 'Thomas Manns "Dienst an der Zeit" in den Jahren 1918–1933', *Thomas Mann Jahrbuch* 10 (1997), 167–85.
9 These claims, made in the preface to Mann's first major attempt at essay-writing, the *Reflections of an Unpolitical Man* (XII, 11), but long ignored, should be taken literally.

## FURTHER READING

Eder, Jürgen, '*Allerlei Allotria'. Grundzüge und Quellen der Essayistik bei Thomas Mann* (Bonn: Bouvier, 1993)
Koelb, Clayton (ed.), *Thomas Mann's 'Goethe and Tolstoy': Notes and Sources* (University, AL: The University of Alabama Press, 1984), pp. 9–16

Lehnert, Herbert, 'Thomas Mann in Exile 1933–1938', *Germanic Review* 38 (1963), 277–94

Siefken, Hinrich, 'Der Essayist Thomas Mann', in H. L. Arnold (ed.), *Thomas Mann*, 2nd edn (Munich: Text und Kritik, 1982), pp. 132–47

'Thomas Manns "Dienst an der Zeit" in den Jahren 1918–1933', *Thomas Mann Jahrbuch* 10 (1997), 167–85

# 15

T. J. REED

# Mann as diarist

A writer's diary can be a vehicle for self-examination, a record of reflection on the craft, a place for drafts and experiments, or itself a literary performance. The subjectivity of literature since the eighteenth century has made diaries both a key to the writer's private world and a substantive part of the work itself, in modern times virtually an independent genre. André Gide's *Journal* was designed to be just that, and he revised it for publication during his lifetime. Franz Kafka's diaries are a mixture of aperçus, sketches for works, and explorations (or doubts) of his calling to be a writer. Virginia Woolf's diary closely observes the creative process and registers the ebb and flow of her confidence. In the case of Thomas Mann, however, it was only in the early days that his diary was a means to literature, consciously worked on and needed for self-expression (letters to Otto Grautoff, 19 March 1896, 4 April and 21 July 1897). Later it was literary at most in patches and in passing, and intended mainly to be a matter-of-fact record of his daily life, in the most basic sense a 'Tage-Buch'.

This later phase is all we can be sure about, for although Mann appears to have kept a diary all his adult life, only parts survive. In 1896 he burnt the records he had made up to then, only to begin again at once; and in 1944–5 he burnt nearly all the pre-1933 diaries.[1] In 1950 again, he wondered whether to burn what he had written since 1933. The issue was his homosexuality, the secret of which he had guarded by previous burnings but had then gone on writing about, often in nostalgic reference back to the feelings of earlier days. Should he now dispose of this evidence too, or should he make it the means of belatedly coming out? He finally decided against destruction, and in 1952 packaged and sealed his notebooks down to the preceding year, inscribing the cover, in English: 'Daily notes 1933–1951 without literary value and not to be opened before twenty years after my death' (see diary, 5 June 1952). His daughter Erika sealed the last few notebooks in 1955.

Mann's verdict surely referred to the texture of the writing, which was meant originally for his eyes only and not consciously crafted. In later years much of it is verbless jottings, a skeletal account of the daily round. Style, however, is not the only kind of 'literary value'. What Mann had left was an unbroken run for the years from 1933 to his death in 1955, and also, unsignalled by his inscription, an erratic block covering the years 1918–21. These escaped the flames in 1944–5 because they documented the period he was at that point writing about in *Doctor Faustus*. The temporary need preserved in graphic form a particularly complex and intriguing phase of his life. Altogether there were thirty-two notebooks, which make up the ten volumes of *Tagebücher*, published over the two decades following the end of the embargo. Curiosity could never have let them rest.

The dates of the surviving diaries mean they are a record almost entirely of disturbed times: the political and social flux in the aftermath of Germany's defeat in 1918; the whole of Mann's exile from 1933, including the Second World War; and the Cold War. How the intimate record of an established writer's life in more tranquil times might have read – the period, say, from the success of *Buddenbrooks* in 1901 down to the outbreak of war in 1914, or the relatively stable middle years of the Weimar Republic culminating in the award of the Nobel Prize – we can only speculate. Even Mann's outwardly settled life in the forties and early fifties as an American citizen was only a thin crust over the anxieties of war and cold war, in both of which he was in different ways deeply implicated. Not until his last years in Switzerland, when the dual pressure of grand projects and political engagement eased, was there a return to something like tranquillity. But he now missed the commitment to demanding projects, though gloomily aware he no longer had the creative power to cope with them. *Felix Krull* seemed an unworthy occupation to the man who had written *Doctor Faustus*, and yet life without writing was unthinkable. The surprise success of *Krull* and the international celebration of his eightieth birthday boosted his morale, but he was already turning away from 'this strange dream of life that will soon be dreamt to its end' and echoing the verdict old Johann Buddenbrook murmured as he died: 'Kurios, kurios' (9 October 1954; cf. I, 72–3).

The discomfort of living through these turbulent times can, however, be put positively. Mann's diaries are a historical document – his historian son Golo called them 'ein Geschichtswerk', a work of history.[2] Mann's literary perceptiveness made him a shrewd observer of events, and his cultural experience gave him an understanding of German realities in exceptional depth.[3] A great deal of the interest lies not just in the substance but in the narrative perspective, the way a diary presents history. It cannot look back on a finished past as autobiography does; it can only register events as they happen and respond with hope or despondency, not knowing how the story will end. This gives special power and poignancy to a diary of the crucial years when Europe could have been plunged into a darkness that threatened to be millennial. As through other diaries of the time,[4] we relive the near-triumph of Nazism. We follow Hitler's repeated demands and diplomatic triumphs in the thirties, share the onlooker's helpless frustration at Western appeasement, feel the sickening blows of the Munich betrayal of Czechoslovakia and the Russo-German non-aggression pact, and on the individual human level the shock of suicides of colleagues and friends like Ernst Toller and Menno ter Braak – 'the wasteland is spreading', Mann quotes Nietzsche (1 October 1940). We watch the seemingly unstoppable German victories of the early forties, see the tide slowly turn in North Africa and at Stalingrad, and only breathe easy when it is firmly set. But we also witness the extraordinary resilience of morale through the darkest times, the 'irrational conviction that Hitler will not win' (18 April 1941), sometimes stated as a rash faith in the larger pattern of history: 'the democracies, as the secularised form of Christianity, are not yet ripe for overthrow by this false man-with-a-mission' (17 March 1940). Thomas Mann's faith is strengthened by the isolated figures of Roosevelt and Churchill, and eventually by the decisive facts, which he at once recognises as such, of Hitler's invasion of Russia and America's entry into the war. But by then we have amply felt what Mann calls 'the fear that evil may become universal, with no way out or refuge for the human mind' (22 May 1940), and have been reminded how complacent our sense of history normally is. The tension of a close-run historical thing and the thought of a counterfactual outcome make Mann's diaries of the thirties and forties, and to some extent of the Cold War years too, addictive reading.

This may seem strange, in a way, for they also contain vast amounts of banal detail. Yet these trivial elements complete the human picture by putting a real observer in the foreground. He recalls that the reason he persisted with his diary in the first shock of exile was precisely 'so as to record this history together with my everyday life' (8 February 1942).[5] Ordinary things have to go on: he cuts his nails while the German army is preparing its winter offensive on the Russian front (12/14 August 1941). 'The fate of the world is at stake. If one lives one's workaday life, it is only like the Londoners who come out of the cellar after the all-clear and queue for concert-tickets' (16 August 1940). So we are spared no aspect of the everyday: the names of callers and correspondents, social visits paid and received, magazines and books read (Mann goes back repeatedly and in genuine humility to the great novelists, Balzac, Tolstoy, Dostoevsky), music heard (mainly the eighteenth- and nineteenth-century classics, especially Wagner: he would gladly give 'all the music of Schönberg, Berg, Krenek and Leverkühn' for the opening scene of *Rheingold* (22 February 1948)), and films seen (Mann was an aesthetically undaunted cinema-goer). This last was perhaps his most American activity, in that strange intense world of transplanted German writers, composers, thinkers, actors and musicians. In Princeton he could have Einstein round to tea; in California he has supper with Schönberg[6] and gets Max Horkheimer to look after his house-plants when he is away from home, on one of those exhausting tours as a 'wandering preacher for democracy'. The exiled German geniuses, themselves a small piece of history, appear as everyday neighbours.

This mixture of the historic and the humdrum is then the setting in which Mann labours at projects of immense scale and complexity: the last two volumes of the Joseph tetralogy; the panorama of Goethe's social and intellectual world in *Lotte in Weimar*; the mythic-analytic confrontation with Nazism's cultural roots in *Doctor Faustus*. To a degree remarkable in a man often alleged to be self-centred, these grand creative undertakings remain unemphasised; their progress is regularly reported on, but the production of great literature every morning is almost taken for granted. In part Mann's work necessarily takes a back seat to contemporary history: while he reconstructs the land of the Pharaohs, modern armies are clashing there. It is hard to put artistic concerns before world crisis, even if his writing is directly or indirectly a response to it. There are moments when news of the war almost brings writing to a standstill: 'Deeply shaken and hardly able to work', he notes at the height of the London blitz (10 September 1940). More generally, though, the lack of expansiveness about his writing follows from the simple function his diary had: to 'hold on to the fleeting day . . . not so much in order to recall or re-read later as to render an account, to recapitulate, remain aware, and keep a controlling eye on things' (11 February 1934). Later we learn what the eye was meant to be controlling: 'Hold on to time! Use it!' (1 September 1938). The aim was self-organisation and self-justification in obedience to the Protestant work-ethic. In this sense, the production of literature was *not* taken for granted; it had to be wrested from the everyday, from every single day, and each entry had to confirm how far he had done that. It was an unremitting routine from which he was hardly ever free and never really wanted to be: 'Pottered in keeping with the festivity, but then worked at the chapter, wearing my new house-jacket' (25 December 1940).

Beyond the account of the daily stint and the circumstances in which it was achieved, there were the larger stints measured in years and achieved against the larger circumstance of exile: 'This morning I *completed "Joseph in Egypt"*, – a noteworthy date, when I think that work on this volume has accompanied the 3 years and nearly 6 months since we left Munich' (23 August 1936). Work on the Joseph novel had been a consolation and a link back to the old life when Mann's German world collapsed. It was now a measure of his exile, and of how well he had coped with it. Or again: 'Weather fine. At half-past eleven wrote the last words of *Doctor*

*Faustus*. Moved, certainly. Looking back. – Sunday 23 May 1943: "Began this morning writing 'Dr Faust.'" After which on the very next day I was working on a monthly German broadcast. Walked the length of Amalfi Drive. K. congratulated me. I recognise it is a moral achievement' (29 January 1947). This time, the high point is even more low-key. Where there was italic and an evening glass of champagne for the third part of the *Joseph* tetralogy, completion of *Doctor Faustus* is embedded in a suburban domesticity flatly evoked. There is no triumphal tone, just satisfaction at completing a long task while still meeting other deadlines. That 'monthly broadcast' was one of over fifty in the series *Deutsche Hörer!* [*Listen, Germany!*] beamed at Germany by the BBC: politically necessary, but taking time and energy away from his creative work. The diaries show the tension between these two commitments, to art and to political rhetoric, which may ultimately both serve the same humane cause, but make very different demands on the writer. The mood oscillates accordingly. On the one hand, 'I must turn away, turn away! Limit myself to personal and creative concerns. I need serenity and the consciousness of my special nature. I must not make hatred my business' (20 September 1938). On the other, 'Poor appetite, feeling sick. But a firmer state of mind today, serious and resolved to speak out in no uncertain terms in the name of the moral world and strike a blow at the vermin' (19 November 1937).[7] Others had no doubts. Mann quotes, without comment but plainly with satisfaction, his American publisher, Alfred Knopf: 'To all your other great qualities you add those of a great pamphleteer' (13 April 1940).

Mann's compulsion to 'account for and control' his writing activity did not involve saying much about the actual compositional process, much less conveying it in an exciting way. There is nothing remotely like the page of Kafka's diary which recounts the nocturnal genesis of *The Judgement*, filled with the excited awareness that he has broken new imaginative ground.[8] We always know of course what Mann's current project is, and he regularly notes which chapter he is engaged on. That, given the sheer size of his novels and the spans of time they took to write, is useful information. But the act of creation itself stays tantalisingly out of sight behind the sober daily summary. There is rarely much detail about how the day's writing went. Jottings like 'worked on the Nietzsche essay, eagerly' and 'On Nietzsche, desperately' (3 and 8 March 1947) are unusual, while his phrase for the early stages of *Doctor Faustus* – 'the first stormy run at it' (7 August 1943) – is quite exceptional. But then his relation with this novel *was* exceptional, sufficiently so to inspire a separate published account of its genesis, the 'novel of a novel'. Even then, the 'stormy run' is a retrospect on three months' work and seventy achieved pages, not an overflow of sudden emotion. Such excitement as the diaries convey comes rather from the effect his work-in-progress has on family members and friends when he reads the latest section: always a success, though writing the next day always seems to go less well as a consequence (24 February 1935). So at least we are allowed to be present at a work's earliest reception; also at Mann's worries about its coming public reception, especially in the case of *Doctor Faustus*, where alongside other forms of directness he has made ruthless use of old friends and acquaintances as models. They are 'victims of the cold gaze' (9 April 1947) and he is not sure how they will take it, especially across the already wide gulf between the émigré and those who stayed behind in Hitler's Germany – Emil Preetorius and Hans Reisiger (Sixtus Kridwiss and Rüdiger Schildknapp in the novel). Otherwise the diaries offer little insight into aesthetic issues, few signs of the writer casting around for the narrative scent, little reflection on problems of structure. The 1918–21 diaries are the richest seam. Working on *The Magic Mountain*, Mann wonders whether Hans Castorp should have Clawdia Chauchat now, or not till later, or perhaps not at all; he toys with the idea of having her never return to the sanatorium (9,11 and 26 April 1921); he reflects on how dated the novel now seems (12 April 1919) and on the 'problem of the ending' (14 October 1918), but does not spell out what that is – he is brooding rather than analysing. This volume also records Mann's political and existential disorientation, a significant aid to understanding his own *Bildung* process which went into the *Bildungsroman*.

The diaries were never consciously kept – in either sense of the word – so as to be source-material or support for his fiction, but on occasion they did serve those purposes. The 1918–21 diary both jogged his social memory and provided material for montage in *Doctor Faustus*. The unruly political meeting during the Munich *Räterepublik* is taken over direct into the novel; the chapter on the Kridwiss circle grows from a diary reminiscence.[9] At a more fundamental level than montage and memory, the perspective of a diary determines the very structure of *Doctor Faustus*. Unlike much fiction, the novel does not present Leverkühn's life as a complete story from the past, written in some unspecified interstice of time which by convention we do not enquire into. We see the narrative grow from the real date, 23 May 1943, on which both Zeitblom and Mann begin writing. It stays in step with an advancing present, marks the stages in Germany's defeat, and thus moves like a diary towards an ending not yet known, albeit foreseen with growing certainty. As in Mann's own diary, public events overshadow the narrator's private realm; only in the novel the public events and the life narrated are aspects of the same catastrophe.

There is another montage of diary material in Mann's last novel. The comic-erotic scene between Felix Krull and Diane Houpflé where the mature lady-writer declares her passion specifically for *young* men is taken over direct from Mann's paean to young *men*, confided to his diary when his tireless sexuality had one last sad fling of worship from afar (6 August 1950; VII, 446). Not for the first nor quite for the last time, Mann transposes homosexual into heterosexual feeling, giving his solemn enthusiasm a comic disguise. Disguise however was almost a thing of the past. The thing contained in those 'secret – *very* secret' writings (to Grautoff, 17 February 1896) burnt in 1896 for fear of chance discovery; the thing that could not be freely expressed in 1912 through *Death in Venice* for fear of destroying his career; the thing he was terrified the Nazis might use against him when his diaries were briefly in their hands ('an onslaught on the secrets of my life', 30 April 1933) – this central element of his inner life could perhaps now be revealed. There was a way and a timetable, and so close to death he had nothing to lose. At worst it was a threat to his posthumous reputation, and that was offset by a positive impulse to be known for what he really was. The reason for burning the old diaries became the reason for not burning the later ones.[10] He also now wanted to celebrate all the young men who had been the inspiration of particular times and works, 'a gallery no literary history will mention'; he lists them, from Armin Martens and Willri Timpe in his boyhood to Paul Ehrenberg in his early and Klaus Heuser in his later manhood (11 and 16 July 1950). After a particularly emotional – even, for once, 'literary' – half-page that combines his latest chaste passion with quotations from Michelangelo, on whom he is writing an essay, he wonders: 'Why am I writing all this? To destroy it in good time before my death? Or do I want the world to *know* me?' (25 Aug 1950). The next month, still in the toils of his late infatuation, he retains 'the idea at the back of my mind of burning all the diaries at some opportune moment' (15 September 1950). But another month on and he states his decision, in half jocular, half defiant tone: 'Carefree revelations then, so be it. Let the world know me, but only when everyone's dead' (13 Oct 1950).

The motif of 'the world knowing' is a quotation from Mann's favourite (also homosexual) poet August von Platen: 'The world shall know me now, so that it may forgive me.' That in turn echoes the saying that 'to understand is to forgive' ('tout comprendre, c'est tout pardonner'). Forgiveness cannot be meant literally, since the writer and his emotions have done no one any harm. Mann was not even confessing acts, only feelings: what the extant diaries record, and what they say or imply about episodes that figured in the lost diaries, makes plain that if Mann had a sexual 'past', it was as inhibited and unfulfilled as his present, its remembered high points a fleeting embrace or a kiss (24 January 1934; 20 February 1942). 'Forgiveness' can only be a metaphor for the world's willingness to accept human difference; and that starts another echo, of the even more ancient principle that nothing human is alien to us ('nihil humani a me alienum puto').[11] In that spirit, basic to a liberal culture, Mann's confession is a necessary and important part, though emphatically still only a part, of understanding the man and his work.

There was not much liberality, on any score, in the first response to his published diaries. Reviewers made much of the daily trivialities, ignoring the historical substance with which they were interwoven. They accused Mann of self-centredness, which is part of the definition of a diary. There were raised eyebrows at his psychological fragility in the early stages of exile, as if it was nothing much for a man of fifty-eight suddenly to lose the basis of life and work and be cast adrift in the world. They noted he was difficult to live with, forgetting that he had lamented the dehumanising effect of the literary profession since 1900. And they were unprepared for the 'revelation' of his homosexuality, which was really no more than a confirmation of what any observant reader of the works had guessed, and of what had been explicit in letters published back in the sixties (especially to Weber, 4 July 1920). It was a myopic response to selected facets of the diaries. Above all, it had lost sight of the contract we implicitly enter into when reading the modern literature of individuality. We accept what a writer chooses to tell us about himself, not as material to be used in evidence against him, but as an aspect of mankind embodied in him, which he has made productive and for which he speaks. The 'literary value' of Mann's diaries lies in their frank self-portrait of a distinctive individual under the pressure of his talent and his times.

## NOTES

1  See letter to Otto Grautoff, 17 February 1896; diary, 20 June 1944, 21 May 1945. The notebooks destroyed in these two batches in the forties must have been the 'fifty' (the number may be approximate) that Golo Mann rescued in 1933 from Munich, where they had briefly been in the hands of the Nazis. On a rough comparison with the text-to-time ratio of the surviving notebooks, fifty would correspond reasonably to the years 1896–1933. There is no pressing reason to assume that there was a fallow period or another burning.

2  Quoted by Inge Jens in the introduction to *Tagebücher 1953–55* (Frankfurt am Main: Fischer, 1995), p. xx.

3  For an example combining all these strengths, see 5 August 1934 on Hindenburg and Gerhart Hauptmann, Erasmus and Luther, Nazism and myth.

4  Notably Harold Nicolson's account of life in wartime Britain, *Diaries and Letters 1939–45* (London: Collins, 1967), and Jean Guéhenno's of life in occupied France, *Journal des années noires (1940–1944)* (Paris: Gallimard, 1947).

5  The words 'which I began again under the shock of exile' might mean that Mann had not kept a diary for some period immediately before March 1933, and would be the one piece of evidence for a break in the habit. More probably they mean that his keeping of a diary was interrupted by the European lecture-tour that turned into exile (in later years he commonly wrote up journeys on his return)

and that he 'began again' as soon as more pressing problems left him time to think of such things.

6 Even a brief verbless vignette can have character: 'Supper at Schönberg's. Hospitable welcome. Ill-behaved children. Excellent Viennese coffee. A lot with him about music' (27 August 1943).

7 It is noteworthy that the first of these two quotations figures as an 'appetiser' on the cover of the fourth volume of the *Tagebücher*. Thus even Mann's publisher emphasises the cliché of his political reluctance rather than the reality of his political engagement. Cf. above, 'Mann and History', p. 14 and note 12.

8 23 September 1912, in Franz Kafka, *Tagebücher*, ed. Hans-Gerd Koch, Michael Müller and Malcolm Pasley (Frankfurt am Main: Fischer, 1990), pp. 460–1, following the text of the story, pp. 442–60.

9 Unruly meeting: cf. diary, 10 and 13 December 1918, and *Doctor Faustus*, ch. 33 (VI, 453); Kridwiss circle: cf. diary, 15 April 1919, and *Doctor Faustus*, ch. 34 (cont.) (VI, 480–1). See also Peter de Mendelssohn, 'Dichtung und Wahrheit in den Tagebüchern Thomas Manns', *Ensemble: Internationales Jahrbuch für Literatur* 15 (1984), 7–28.

10 Hans Rudolf Vaget has argued that it was not the homosexual secret that made Mann burn his diaries in the forties, but what they contained of his political past – i.e. the national-conservative politics of 1914–21 – while the new diaries (post–1933) were consciously written for posterity; if sex had been the reason for burning, why was Mann again so frank in the diaries he went on writing? The answer is that he always kept open the option of destroying these too, as the entry of 25 August 1950 shows. When he chose not to do so, it was because of a changed situation: the prospect of death and the hope of humane understanding replaced the fear of social scandal. As for politics, certainly from the moment he went into exile Mann was keeping a conscious record – though not obviously for posterity, or he would never have considered burning this record too. But such political matter as the lost diaries might have contained could hardly have been more discrediting in liberal-democratic eyes than the published *Reflections of a Nonpolitical Man*. See Vaget, 'Confession and Camouflage: The Diaries of Thomas Mann', *Journal of English and Germanic Philology* 96 (1997), 567–90.

11 The 'tout comprendre' principle is relevant to the themes, and explicitly discussed in the text, of *Tonio Kröger*, *Death in Venice* and *Doctor Faustus*. The Latin line from Terence is an entry in Mann's earliest (literary) notebook. See *Notizbücher 1–6*, ed. Hans Wysling and Yvonne Schmidlin (Frankfurt am Main: Fischer, 1991), p. 24.

## FURTHER READING

Meyer, Martin, *Tagebuch und spätes Leid. Über Thomas Mann* (Munich: Hanser, 1999)

Vaget, Hans R., 'Confession and Camouflage: The Diaries of Thomas Mann', *Journal of English and Germanic Philology* 96 (1997), 567–90

# 16

TIMOTHY BUCK

# Mann in English

In 1921 Samuel Fischer, Thomas Mann's German publisher, and Alfred A. Knopf reached an agreement whereby Knopf would have exclusive rights for Mann's works in the USA. Mann, aware that his works would be known to a great many of his readers not in the German originals but in the English translations – that in effect the latter would constitute the works of Thomas Mann as far as the English-speaking world was concerned – was in no doubt about the importance of their being well translated: in a letter concerning *The Magic Mountain* he expressed his wish for 'a translation of a high artistic standard' ('eine künstlerisch hochwertige Übersetzung'). (He could not have foreseen that even greater importance would accrue to the English versions with the Nazi suppression of his works in Germany and his eventual exile in the USA.)

Although Helen Tracy Lowe-Porter (1877–1963) – 'die Lowe', as Mann would later call her – is widely known as Mann's authorised English translator, she was not his choice for the (as he saw it) crucial role of 'mediator' between himself and the English-speaking world. He was keen to have Herman George Scheffauer, an American man of letters who had translated one of his short stories for him, produce the English version of *The Magic Mountain*; and the negative reports that he had heard of the translation Lowe-Porter had made of *Buddenbrooks* (published 1924) made him unhappy about the suggestion that she would be a suitable translator for him. Knopf, who knew no German but had the right to choose the translator, disregarded Mann's misgivings and in 1925 took the fateful decision to appoint Lowe-Porter – a step that was supported by Martin Secker, who would be publishing *The Magic Mountain* in Britain; eventually Mann reluctantly acquiesced in the *fait accompli* (as he termed it). Lowe-Porter had won the prize, which she had so persistently sought, of being Mann's official translator, and over a period of two and a half decades – including a ten-year stint dedicated to the *Joseph* tetralogy – she would translate all of Mann's subsequent works of fiction except the last two (*Die Betrogene* [*The Black Swan*] and the complete version of *Felix Krull*).

By and large Lowe-Porter's translations were favourably received. In a full-page article on Mann in the *Times Literary Supplement* in 1951 she is praised as 'a devoted and very competent translator'; in 1958 Erich Heller saw the translation of Mann as 'an almost heroic literary venture, and its relative success a triumph of devoted labour'; thirty years later Nigel Hamilton eulogised her 'powers as a translator'.[1] All these verdicts are of a general nature, and it seems not unreasonable to suppose that they were based on general impressions, rather than on a close comparison of originals with translations, as is necessary in order to be able to form an opinion on the competence of a translator and the quality of a translation. Without such comparisons any critic is effectively in the same position as Forrest Reid, reviewing *Joseph in Egypt* for the *Spectator* in 1938: 'How closely Mrs Lowe-Porter's translation approaches to the original, I cannot tell, but it appears to have been carefully done.'

The novel idea that not everything *had* been carefully done in her translations emerged in an article by E. Koch-Emmery, who, focusing on how Mann's sentence structure fared in the translations, pointed out 'major discrepancies' between the originals and Lowe-Porter's versions.[2] And in 1970, in the introduction to his collection of newly translated stories by Thomas Mann, David Luke drew attention to serious errors in Lowe-Porter's translations.[3] In an attempt to establish a sound basis on which to form an assessment of these translations, I have examined extended random samples from four of them – *Buddenbrooks, The Magic Mountain, Joseph and his Brothers* and *Doctor Faustus*[4] – comparing them with the originals. These comparisons show that Lowe-Porter allowed herself a great deal of latitude, indeed licence, in translating Mann's works.

Mann and his official translator had, in fact, widely differing views as to what constitutes a good translation. According to a letter Mann wrote Lowe-Porter on 9 August 1926, a translation had to be as literal and accurate as the foreign language permitted, whereas for Lowe-Porter, as she wrote in her 'Translator's Note' accompanying *Buddenbrooks*: 'It was necessary to set oneself the bold task of transferring the spirit first and the letter so far as might be.' Koch-Emmery showed how, in the various novels, Lowe-Porter tended to ride roughshod over the letter of Mann's fastidiously crafted prose, upsetting the balance between the various parts of a sentence, shifting emphases, undermining the suspense the author might be building up, and so on. There is a good example in the very second paragraph of *Buddenbrooks*: where Mann's sentence begins gently to unfold its two main and three relative clauses, the translation uses three separate sentences which entirely lack the flow and rhythm of the original, packing all the action into the first so that the second and third make a purely static impression:

| | |
|---|---|
| Die Konsulin Buddenbrook, neben ihrer Schwiegermutter auf dem geradlinigen, weißlackierten und mit einem goldenen Löwenkopf verzierten Sofa, dessen Polster hellgelb überzogen waren, *warf einen Blick auf ihren Gatten*, der in einem Armsessel bei ihr saß, und *kam ihrer kleinen Tochter zu Hilfe*, die der Großvater am Fenster auf den Knien hielt. (I, 9) | Frau Consul Buddenbrook *shot a glance at her husband* and *came to the rescue of her little daughter*. She sat with her mother-in-law on a straight white-enamelled sofa with yellow cushions and a gilded lion's head at the top. The Consul was in his easy-chair beside her, and the child perched on her grandfather's knee in the window. (Part 1, Chapter 1; p. 3) |

Repeatedly, Lowe-Porter shies away from employing sentences containing a conjunction where Mann has one, preferring to use a co-ordinate clause or even to split up sentences. This entirely unnecessary practice alters the relationship between clauses and lays her open to the charge of impoverishing the style of the works concerned.

Her translations, especially that of *Buddenbrooks*, exhibit a great many omissions. Very often important descriptive adjectives or adverbs are dropped: thus, 'ergebene, fromme, fleißige' (devoted, pious, hardworking) Klothilde (*Buddenbrooks*) is deprived of all three adjectives in translation; Julchen leaps out at Tony from behind a tree 'zischend vor Wut' (hissing with rage) (*Buddenbrooks*), but the effect of the scene is somewhat diminished in the translation by the omission of a corresponding phrase; and while Frau Stöhr 'lachte maßlos und ordinär nach Herzenslust' (laughed inordinately and vulgarly to her heart's content) (*The Magic Mountain*), her *alter ego* in the translation merely 'laughed'. Oddly, Lowe-Porter frequently discards emotions expressed in the original *Buddenbrooks*; thus, 'Tony . . . war erstaunt, . . . zu finden' (was amazed to find) is reduced in the translation to 'Tony found'. Similarly, 'er betrachtete ihn etwas besorgt, als er ihn fragte . . .' (he looked at him somewhat anxiously as he asked him . . .) is emasculated into 'He said to him'. Even a notable comic variation on Mann's eyebrow leitmotif is suppressed: 'Die Treppe hinauf schritt er dem Konsul entgegen, indem er die Brauen hoch unter die Krempe seines grauen Huts erhob und sie dennoch zusammenzog' (He strode up the stairs towards the Consul, raising his eyebrows right up under the brim of his grey hat and nevertheless knitting them) – in Lowe-Porter's version the eyebrows remain unknit. With each such excision, of course, some more of the colour and flavour of Mann's work is lost.

No less dismaying – though unsurprising in view of 'the promise I made myself of never sending a translation [of a work by Mann] to the publisher unless I felt as though I had written the book myself' – are the additions Lowe-Porter made to Mann's texts. At one point in *Doctor Faustus*, for example, she presumes to insert her own interpretative comment: 'Es wäre doch noch schöner, meinten sie, wenn . . .' becomes 'It might be still finer, they *ironically* said, if . . .'. In *Joseph and his Brothers* the ruins of a great pyramid described as 'exhibiting proportions . . .' have an extra attribute added in the translation: 'are of a size *and pretentiousness* . . .'. In *Buddenbrooks* 'Tony' at one point becomes '*pert little* Tony', and we see Lowe-Porter succumb repeatedly to the 'creative author' within her, making a whole series of additions for which there is no basis in Mann's texts: 'turning her light eyes a little away, *that he might not see the bewilderment they expressed*', ' "How nice!" she *stammered again, with desperate finality*.' She even adds entire sentences, providing commentary and analysis where the author has seen no need; for example: '*The Frau Consul did not understand it all, but she got the general drift, and was glad.*'

The random samples reveal above all the extraordinary number of major, even catastrophic errors the translations contain, leading one to conclude that Knopf's chosen translator was simply not equipped with an understanding and a knowledge of German adequate to the task; cumulatively, they have the effect of completely undermining the authority of the translations. A small collection of examples is given here of the countless howlers that occur in the works sampled; often the wrong sense of a word is selected, sometimes words' meanings are simply guessed at – through false association with a homonym or similar-sounding word – and not infrequently Mann's syntax is misconstrued:

### Buddenbrooks

| | |
|---|---|
| *brieflich* (by mail) | 'quickly' |
| *Grundstück* (property) | 'ground floor' |
| *versiegen* (dry up, of tears) | 'be conquered' |
| *hie und da . . . konnte er den Versuch machen, sie auf seine Knie zu ziehen* (now and then . . . he managed to try and pull her onto his knees) | 'once he attempted to fall on his knees' |
| *wo geiht di dat!* (how are things?) | 'where are you going?'[5] |

### The Magic Mountain

| | |
|---|---|
| *Melone* (here: bowler hat) | 'melon' |
| *zerzaust* (dishevelled) | 'distracted' |
| *Papierschlangen* (streamers) | 'paper snakes' |

## Joseph and his Brothers

| | |
|---|---|
| *hegen* (keep (animals)) | 'honour' |
| *fauchen* (snarl) | 'purr' |
| *Wandel* (change) | 'wanderings' |
| *bestürzt* (dismayed) | 'in haste' |

## Doctor Faustus

| | |
|---|---|
| *Überangebot* (surfeit) | 'outbidding' |
| *Namensschild* (name-plate) | 'shield' |
| *Der Eindruck war schmerzlich . . . Aber ich vergaß ihn rasch* (The impression was painful... But I soon forgot it) | 'The impression was painful...but I quickly forgave him' |
| *daß mit den Trieben Propaganda gemacht wird* (that propaganda is being made out of the instincts) | 'along with the instincts, propaganda is made' |

Perhaps the most breathtaking example of Lowe-Porter's inadequate knowledge of German is her rendering in *The Magic Mountain* of 'Baiser' (meringue) as 'kiss': in her travesty of the scene concerned, Settembrini even imagines Frau Stöhr 'enjoying the kisses by yourself' (see III, 212 and Lowe-Porter's translation, pp. 150–1)!

Lowe-Porter's English is of an uneven quality, and can be unidiomatic, ungainly, ungrammatical, even incomprehensible. A few examples must suffice: 'most highly desirable' (*Doctor Faustus*), 'a young Slavic youth' (*The Magic Mountain*), 'whether he simply pretended the stay in Graz' (*Doctor Faustus*). A good many items are manifestly word-for-word translations from the German: 'instances there were only too many' (*The Magic Mountain*), 'always the one gave itself to be understood as substitute of the other' (*Doctor Faustus*), 'before his spiritual eye' (*Buddenbrooks*), 'he has come humanly near to her' (*Buddenbrooks*), 'that indeed gave you to think' (*The Magic Mountain*). *Doctor Faustus* posed special problems for the translator – as Mann had foreseen – and the at times intractable subject-matter led Lowe-Porter to produce English that is sometimes barely digestible, as illustrated by the following passage (the semi-colon incorrectly replaces a comma in Mann's text):

To a genuine sacrifice two valuations and qualitative ingredients belong: that of the thing and that of the sacrifice . . . But we have cases where the personal substance, let us say, was very rich in Germanness and quite involuntarily objectivated itself also as sacrifice; yet where acknowledgment of the folk-bond not only utterly failed [incorrect for: *fehlte* (was lacking)], but there was even a permanent and violent negation of it, so that the tragic sacrifice consisted precisely in the conflict between being and confession.   (Chapter 14; p. 124)

David Luke's new version of *Death in Venice* presents an opportunity to see Lowe-Porter's version in a different perspective. His stated and manifestly achieved aim is to translate more accurately than his American predecessor and to reflect, as far as possible, the story's elevated diction and the complexity of Mann's prose.

As far as Lowe-Porter's translation is concerned, her policy of aiming to re-create Mann's works in the spirit rather than the letter led to a version (1928) that at times bears only a loose relationship to the original. Let us begin with the carefully fashioned sentence structure, exemplified by the passage in which Aschenbach, waiting in Munich for his tram, looks across the street at the mortuary chapel. In the original, the main clause is followed by a clause introduced by the conjunction 'als' (when), which creates a new focus of interest and which only after three intervening phrases and a relative clause finally yields up its object: 'einen Mann' (a man). This build-up to the delayed object is reproduced by Luke, who broadly retains Mann's sentence structure, but Lowe-Porter, dispensing as so often with the conjunction, typically goes her own way:

|  | *Lowe-Porter* | *Luke* |
|---|---|---|
| Und der Wartende hatte während einiger Minuten eine ernste Zerstreuung darin gefunden, die Formeln abzulesen und sein geistiges Auge in ihrer durchscheinenden Mystik sich verlieren zu lassen, *als* er, aus seinen Träumereien zurückkehrend, im Portikus, oberhalb der beiden apokalyptischen Tiere, welche die Frei-treppe bewachen, *einen Mann* bemerkte, dessen nicht ganz gewöhnliche | Aschenbach beguiled some minutes of his waiting with reading these formulas and letting his mind's eye lose itself in their mystical meaning. He was brought back to reality by the sight of a man standing in the portico, above the two apocalyptic beasts that guarded the staircase, and something not quite usual in this man's appearance gave his thoughts a fresh turn.  (p. 4)[6] | The waiting Aschen-bach had already been engaged for some min-utes in the solemn pas-time of deciphering the words and letting his mind wander in con-templation of the mystic meaning that suffused them, *when* he noticed something that brought him back to reality: in the portico of the chapel, above the two apocalyptic beasts that guard the steps leading up to it, *a man* was standing, a man whose |

| Erscheinung seinen | slightly unusual appear- |
|---|---|
| Gedanken eine völlig | ance gave his thoughts |
| andere Richtung gab. | an altogether different |
| (VIII, 445) | turn. (p. 198)[7] |

As in the novels, Lowe-Porter's translation of individual sentences sometimes lacks the precision and clarity of the original. For example, 'So wußte und wollte denn der Verwirrte nichts anderes mehr, als den Gegenstand, der ihn entzündete, ohne Unterlaß zu verfolgen' – neatly rendered by Luke as 'So it was that in his state of distraction he could no longer think of anything or want anything except this ceaseless pursuit of the object that so inflamed him' – is very loosely (and inelegantly) conveyed by Lowe-Porter as: 'It came at last to this – that his frenzy left him capacity for nothing else but to pursue his flame.' The rhetorical force of a sentence such as 'Groß war sein Abscheu, groß seine Furcht' – Luke: 'Great was his loathing, great was his fear' – is entirely lost in Lowe-Porter's 'He trembled, he shrank.'

Failure to understand the German would seem to account for some mistranslations, but others, far from being involuntary errors, appear deliberately to overrule the author's meaning and substitute one of the translator's own choosing. For example, Aschenbach, delighting in the beauty of Tadzio's youthful frame, 'fand der Bewunderung, *der zarten Sinneslust* kein Ende', which is accurately rendered by Luke as 'there was no end to his wonder, *the delicate delight of his senses*' but diluted by Lowe-Porter into 'his admiration knew no bounds, *the delight of his eye* was unending': the important 'zart' (delicate) is lost, the total engagement of the senses narrowed to visual appreciation. Why did she make this change? One can only speculate as to the translator's motives, but one possibility is that she may have been trying to tone down the sensuality of '*zarte Sinneslust*'. She certainly appears to attempt to damp down the orgiastic excesses at the end of Aschenbach's wild dream: 'als ... grenzenlose Vermischung begann ... Und seine Seele kostete *Unzucht und Raserei* des Unterganges' becomes 'there now began ... an orgy of *promiscuous embraces* – and in his very soul he tasted the *bestial degradation* of his fall', expressing a moral stance at odds with the original and with Luke's faithfully unprudish 'as an orgy of *limitless coupling* ... began. And his very soul savoured the *lascivious delirium* of annihilation'. Another gratuitous alteration – this time an addition – is seen in a later paragraph:

| Und endlich lachte denn alles im | until at last they laughed in hotel, ter- |
|---|---|
| Garten und auf der Veranda, bis zu | race, and garden, down to the wait- |
| den Kellnern, Liftboys und Haus- | ers, lift-boys, and servants – *laughed* |
| dienern in den Türen. (VIII, 510) | *as though possessed.* (p. 65) |

Crucially, Lowe-Porter's rewriting of the novella shows Aschenbach and Tadzio, especially in their interaction with one another, in a somewhat different light. Mann's portrayal of Tadzio gives his face an expression 'von *holdem* und göttlichem Ernst' (Luke: 'of *sweet* and divine gravity'), and as he returns from a bathe his figure is described as '*vormännlich hold* und herb' (Luke: '*lovely* and austere *in its early masculinity*'). In erroneously rendering these two phrases as 'of *pure* and godlike serenity [*sic*]' and '*virginally pure* and austere' Lowe-Porter steers the reader into perceiving the youth as entirely innocent, non-erotic, free of the ambiguity that places him 'somewhere between innocence and a certain half-conscious sensuous coquetry' (Luke). It is difficult to avoid the impression that she was endeavouring to alter the content of the story. In the hotel foyer Tadzio is seen sitting with his family, a passive figure in Lowe-Porter's deviant rendering of 'Er saß, im Halbprofil gegen den Betrachtenden' (Luke: 'He was sitting, in semi-profile to Aschenbach's gaze'): 'The observer saw him in half profile'. This modification is significantly repeated in the scene next morning, when Tadzio, having exchanged a glance with Aschenbach the evening before, arrives late for breakfast and actively shows his awareness of Aschenbach's interest by turning his profile towards him ('und jetzt zumal, da er dem Schauenden sein genaues Profil zuwandte'); Lowe-Porter transfers the action to Aschenbach: 'and Aschenbach, sitting so that he could see him in profile'. And when Aschenbach's thoughts after his near-encounter with Tadzio on the way to the beach are conveyed, Lowe-Porter offers quite wild reinterpretations, rather than translations, of 'heilsame Ernüchterung' and (a key concept in the novella) 'Rausch' (consistently rendered by Luke as 'intoxication', whereas Lowe-Porter represents it variously as 'frenzy', 'bliss' and now 'illusion'):

|  | *Lowe-Porter* | *Luke* |
|---|---|---|
| Zu spät! dachte er in diesem Augenblick. Zu spät! Jedoch war es zu spät? Dieser Schritt, den zu tun er *versäumte*, er hätte sehr möglicherweise...zu *heilsamer Ernüchterung* geführt. Allein es war wohl an dem, daß der Alternde *die Ernüchterung nicht wollte*, daß *der Rausch* ihm zu teuer war. <br> (VIII, 494–95) | 'Too late! Too late!' he thought as he went by. But was it too late? This step he had *delayed* to take might so easily...have led to a *sane recovery from his folly*. But the truth may have been that the ageing man *did not want to be cured*, that his *illusion* was far too dear to him. (p. 50) | Too late! he thought at that moment. Too late! But was it too late? This step he had *failed* to take would very possibly have...led...to a *wholesome disenchantment*. But the fact now seemed to be that the ageing lover *no longer wished to be disenchanted*, that *the intoxication* was too precious to him. (p. 240) |

Later, when Aschenbach meets Tadzio and his family unexpectedly, the mention of an exchanged glance ('als sein Blick dem des Vermißten begegnete'; Luke: 'when his eyes met those of the returning absentee') is simply left out by Lowe-Porter. On the other hand, when one evening Aschenbach is relaxing in the hotel garden, she has the temerity to *invent* a glance not present in the original: 'while inwardly his whole being was rigid with the intensity of *the regard he bent on Tadzio,* leaning over the railing six paces off' ('während äußerste Aufmerksamkeit sein Inneres spannte; denn sechs Schritte von ihm lehnte Tadzio am Steingeländer'; Luke: 'while inwardly he was utterly engrossed; for six paces away Tadzio was leaning against the stone parapet'). Finally, in the penultimate paragraph of the story – the dying Aschenbach imagines that Tadzio is beckoning to him – Mann's authorised translator inexplicably omits the dramatic sentence: 'Und wie so oft, machte er sich auf, ihm zu folgen' (Luke: 'And as so often, he set out to follow him').

Mann himself was ambivalent about Lowe-Porter's translations. On the one hand, once she was engaged by Knopf he always supported her, answered her queries, encouraged and reassured her, praised her work in the most glowing terms, and publicly acknowledged his great indebtedness to her for the 'extraordinary achievement she has accomplished with the translation of all my books', as he wrote to *Time* (17 July 1944), pointing out that his literary standing in the USA and Britain owed much to his finding 'a translator of the devotion and linguistic talent of Mrs Helen Lowe-Porter'. (He was writing in order to rectify the unfortunate impression he had given in an interview with a *Time* reporter that he was not satisfied with his English translator.) On the other hand, Mann's praise, at least privately, was not always unreserved. For example, he qualified his approval for her *Doctor Faustus*: 'My relationship to the English language is not intimate enough for me to be justified in giving praise', he wrote to her (3 October 1948) – a less than wholly convincing reason, given his by then highly sophisticated command of English. And while in a letter to Agnes E. Meyer (15 October 1942) he is full of praise for the latest part of Lowe-Porter's translation of the *Joseph* saga (he pronounces it 'excellent'), the next sentence speaks volumes: 'After all ist sie doch wohl die beste Interpretin, die Knopf für mich finden konnte' (After all she is seemingly the best interpreter Knopf could find for me.)

The reservations that Mann felt about her work had mainly to do with his awareness (at variance with his public praise for her 'linguistic talent') of her imperfect knowledge of German, of which he was repeatedly reminded when looking through her translations in manuscript. In his diaries the name 'Mrs Lowe' not infrequently heralds pithy negative comments on the latest batch of work from her. In a letter to Mrs Hans Meisel (28 November 1939)

he sums up, frankly and with a certain fatalism, the mixed feelings he inevitably has about 'die Lowe':

> She has a superb command of her own language, English, but not such a good
> command of German, and that is what gives rise to the misunderstandings and
> inadequacies which I prefer not to look at, so as not to let my gratitude for the
> fact that Fate allotted me this translator dwindle away.

This sentence appears to provide the answer to the inevitable question: why
did Mann not press for a change of translator in view of all these deficiencies?
He was simply glad to have her – no doubt realising the difficulty of finding
someone else to take on his vast and difficult works of fiction. But there were
probably other factors too. As his diaries show, he led a fairly hectic life; it
must have been tempting to let the problem of the translations ride. And if
the translation process was interrupted, the consequent delays would have
affected the flow of dollar royalties on which he and his family depended
during their American exile. Moreover, the Knopfs would doubtless have
resisted the idea, given their strong personal commitment to Lowe-Porter
and their blind faith in her translating skills; Knopf's wife and colleague,
Blanche, was a staunch supporter. But above all, his feelings of friendship for
'die Lowe', outweighing his periodic – but private – outbursts of frustration
with her linguistic incompetence and slow progress, as well as the frequent
social interaction between the Manns, the Lowes and the Knopfs, would have
made it virtually impossible to advocate the step which professionalism and
his international standing as an author demanded, but which would have
seemed to her like an incomprehensible stab in the back, especially as he had
always been so lavish in his praise for her work.

It was an issue that Mann must have been loath to confront; although
the alternative to facing it – that is, condoning the continued production of
debased English versions of his works – must have been hard to bear for
one so concerned with the quality of those translations. He was, however,
able to console himself with the thought that his German-speaking literary
friends already read his works in German, and that ultimately he would be
judged on the basis of his German originals.

In the series of grossly distorted and artistically diminished versions on
which, to this day, most English-speakers' perception of Mann's work is
based,[8] the loss, not only of accuracy but also of quality, is inestimable and
largely unrecognised. The botching of the authorised English translations
of Mann arose as the result of a powerful publisher's fiat bringing about
the mismatch of an author of world stature with an ambitious, startlingly
underqualified translator, who plainly did not know her own limitations.

Once Mann had brought the severe criticisms that had been made of her treatment of *Buddenbrooks* to Knopf's attention, they should have been looked into by someone competent to do so; apparently they were not, an omission that was discourteous to Mann and crucial in helping Helen Lowe-Porter to gain, as Mann's translator, the fame she desired – even a kind of 'immortality', as predicted by her friends. The losers have been, and remain, Thomas Mann and (unwittingly) his English-speaking readers the world over.

The publication by Knopf of a new translation of *Buddenbrooks* by the American John E. Woods in 1993, followed two years later by his version of *The Magic Mountain*, gave rise to hopes that Mann's novels might at last become available to English speakers in a more acceptable form.[9]

In various ways Woods's translations represent a considerable improvement on Lowe-Porter's. They are written in a modern idiom free of the irksome archaisms ('wherein', 'thither', 'betimes', etc.) in which Lowe-Porter so frequently indulges; there is an absence of eccentric English; the approach to sentence structure is sensible, and shows Lowe-Porter's syntactical aberrations to be quite unnecessary. Above all, greater precision is manifested in the rendering of individual sentences; in the following examples from Chapter 4 of *The Magic Mountain* (III, 139–63) Lowe-Porter's rendering is wrong, Woods's correct:

| | *Lowe-Porter* | *Woods* |
|---|---|---|
| männliche Entschlossenheit | the settled convictions of the mature man | manly resolve |
| Sie sprach *des langen und breiten* von ihrem Papa | She spoke *at random* of her papa | She spoke *at great length* about her papa |
| der Wulstlippige | the youth with the voluptuous lips | the thick-lipped lad |
| etwas Anderes, *Erschütterndes*, was er *neulich* gesehen hatte | something else, something which gave him *a sudden thrill* | something else that had *shaken* him when he had noticed it *recently* |

Unfortunately, the improvement that the Woods translations represent is only relative; they too fall short of the high artistic standard requested by Mann back in 1925. A close scrutiny of the early chapters of the two novels concerned reveals that Knopf have once again employed a translator whose knowledge of German appears inadequate to the task, and who is capable of careless errors. Some examples:

### Buddenbrooks

| | |
|---|---|
| *abgewandt* (turned away) | 'turned toward' |
| *weiß* (white) | 'wide' |
| *Madame Buddenbrook ... sah ihr kichernd in den Schoß* (Madame Buddenbrook ... looked down at her [daughter-in-law's] lap with a giggle) | 'Madame Buddenbrook ... giggling as she spoke into her own lap' |
| *leichtsinnig* (thoughtless) | 'licentious' |
| *das Wesen ... dem sie das Leben schenkte* (the creature to whom she had given life) | 'the child she had paid for with her life' |
| *dergleichen kann sich wiederholen* (that sort of thing can happen again) | 'that sort of thing cannot be repeated' |
| *miteinander verbunden* (connected) | 'separated' |

### The Magic Mountain

| | |
|---|---|
| *die Wendung ..., die ihn auf irgendeine Weise beklemmend und seltsam anmutete* (the phrase ... which somehow struck him as oppressive and strange) | 'the phrase ... which ... somehow made him feel anxious and queer' |
| *Wenn du was vorstellen willst hier in der Stadt* (If you want to be somebody in this town) | 'If you fancy living a nice life here in the city' |
| *und verweilte lange vor einem Herrenmodegeschäft, um festzustellen, daß die Auslage durchaus auf der Höhe sei* (and lingered for a long time outside a gentleman's outfitters to see if the window display was up-to-date) | 'he lingered awhile outside a men's clothing store, just to make sure that his own wardrobe was up to snuff' |
| *Mit einem Kopfnicken begrüßte die Nachzüglerin ihre* | 'Her tablemates greeted the latecomer with nods' |

*Tischgesellschaft* (The latecomer
   greeted her table companions
   with a nod)

Even decades after his death, the saga of the English translations of Mann has
failed to find a satisfactory conclusion; the consequences of the agreement
reached between Samuel Fischer and Alfred A. Knopf remain with us. Leaving aside Luke's faithful renderings of the stories, essentially two Thomas
Manns continue to circulate in the English-speaking world: the German originals, read by academics and some students of German, and the Lowe-Porter
'adaptations into English' – now supplemented by the two flawed contributions from Woods – which, unbeknown to the English-speaking reader,
constitute a different, a pseudo-Mann. It is a deplorable situation, for which
no remedy is in sight.[10]

## NOTES

1 Erich Heller, *The Ironic German: A Study of Thomas Mann* (London: Secker
   & Warburg, 1958), p. 31; Nigel Hamilton, *The Brothers Mann: The Lives of
   Heinrich and Thomas Mann 1871–1950 and 1875–1955* (London: Secker
   & Warburg, 1978), p. 350.
2 'Thomas Mann in English Translation', *German Life and Letters* 6 (1952–3),
   275–84.
3 *Tonio Kröger and Other Stories*, trans. David Luke (New York: Bantam Books,
   1970), republished, with the addition of *Death in Venice*, in 1988 as *Death in
   Venice and Other Stories*. Republished by Penguin in 1993 as *Selected Stories*,
   this collection should not be confused with H. T. Lowe-Porter's *Death in Venice*,
   published separately by Penguin.
4 Quotations from the Lowe-Porter translations are from the following editions:
   *Buddenbrooks* (London: Secker & Warburg, 1942); *The Magic Mountain*
   (London: Secker & Warburg, 1960); *Joseph and his Brothers* (London: Secker
   & Warburg, 1956); and *Doctor Faustus*, Everyman's Library 80 (London:
   D. Campbell, 1992).
5 It is quite clear that Lowe-Porter simply guessed, with disastrous results, the
   meaning of those parts of the passages in Low German dialect that she did not
   understand.
6 References are to *Death in Venice* (Harmondsworth: Penguin, 1955).
7 References are to *Selected Stories* (Harmondsworth: Penguin, 1993).
8 The Lowe-Porter translations, originally published in Great Britain by Secker
   & Warburg, are now published in paperback by Minerva.
9 *Buddenbrooks: The Decline of a Family*, trans. John E. Woods (New York: Knopf,
   1993; London: Everyman's Library, 1994); *The Magic Mountain*, trans. John
   E. Woods (New York: Knopf, 1995).
10 The author and editor thank the editors of the *Modern Language Review* for
   permission to reuse some material that first appeared there in vols. 91 (1996) and
   92 (1997).

# FURTHER READING

Berlin, Jeffrey B., 'On the Making of *The Magic Mountain*: The Unpublished Correspondence of Thomas Mann, Alfred A. Knopf, and H. T. Lowe-Porter', *Seminar* 28 (1992), 283–320

Buck, Timothy, 'Loyalty and Licence: Thomas Mann's Fiction in English Translation', *Modern Language Review* 91 (1996), 898–921

'Retranslating Mann: a Fresh Attempt on *The Magic Mountain*', *Modern Language Review*, 92 (1997), 656–9

Buck, Timothy, George S. Miller, Bernard Ashbrook, and Peter Newmark, 'Thomas Mann', in Olive Classe (ed.), *Encyclopedia of Literary Translation into English*, 2 vols. (London and Chicago: Fitzroy Dearborn, 2000), pp. 901–10

Koch-Emmery, E., 'Thomas Mann in English Translation', *German Life and Letters* 6 (1952–3), 275–84

Lubich, Frederick A., 'Thomas Mann's Sexual Politics – Lost in Translation', *Comparative Literature Studies* 31 (1994), 107–27

Thirlwall, John C., *In Another Language: A Record of the Thirty-Year Relationship between Thomas Mann and his English Translator, Helen Tracy Lowe-Porter* (New York: Knopf, 1966); contains H. T. Lowe-Porter's essay 'On Translating Thomas Mann'

# SELECTED BIBLIOGRAPHY

*Works by Thomas Mann*

In German, Mann's collected works are available in *Gesammelte Werke*, 12 vols. (Frankfurt am Main: Fischer, 1960), reissued with an additional volume in 1974. Paperback editions of the whole set and of individual works are readily available.

The *Tagebücher* are published in ten carefully annotated volumes, ed. Peter de Mendelssohn (vols. i–v) and Inge Jens (vols. vi–x) (Frankfurt am Main: Fischer, 1979–95).

There is also an annotated edition of the essays, including some items missing from the *Gesammelte Werke*: Thomas Mann, *Essays,* ed. Hermann Kurzke and S. Stachorski, 6 vols. (Frankfurt am Main: Fischer, 1993–7).

Mann's writings on Wagner have recently been collected and annotated in *Im Schatten Wagners: Thomas Mann über Richard Wagner: Texte und Zeugnisse 1895–1955,* ed. Hans R. Vaget (Frankfurt am Main: Fischer, 1999).

The basic collection of letters is Thomas Mann, *Briefe,* ed. Erika Mann, 3 vols. (Frankfurt am Main: Fischer, 1962–5), with annotations; it has been supplemented by many editions of correspondence between Mann and other individuals, including his brother Heinrich; his publisher Gottfried Berman-Fischer; the mythographer Karl Kerényi; Hermann Hesse; his youthful friend Otto Grautoff; his American patroness Agnes Meyer; and many others.

A complete, 58-volume annotated edition of Mann's literary works, essays, diaries and letters, the 'Grosse kommentierte Frankfurt am Mainer Ausgabe', is being prepared for Fischer by Eckhard Heftrich, Hermann Kurzke, T. J. Reed, Thomas Sprecher, Hans R. Vaget and Ruprecht Wimmer, in collaboration with the Thomas Mann Archive in Zürich.

Thomas Mann's works are readily available in English translations by H. T. Lowe-Porter, most recently republished by Minerva; but see the critique of these translations in chapter 16 above. See also the following:

*Buddenbrooks: The Decline of a Family*, trans. John E. Woods (New York: Knopf, 1993; London: Everyman's Library, 1994)
*The Magic Mountain*, trans. John E. Woods (New York: Knopf, 1995)
*Death in Venice and Other Stories*, trans. with introduction by David Luke (London: Vintage, 1998). Includes David Luke's translations of 'Little Herr Friedemann',

'The Joker', 'The Road to the Churchyard', 'Gladius Dei', 'Tristan', and 'Tonio Kröger', with a fifty-page introductory essay including a list of Lowe-Porter's mistakes.

*Death in Venice, Tonio Kröger, and Other Writings*, ed. Frederick A. Lubich, with a foreword by Harold Bloom (New York: Continuum, 1999). Includes translations by David Luke of 'Tonio Kröger', 'Tristan', and *Death in Venice*.

'The Blood of the Volsungs', trans. Ritchie Robertson, in *The German-Jewish Dialogue: An Anthology of Literary Texts, 1749–1993*, ed. Ritchie Robertson, World's Classics (Oxford: Oxford University Press, 1999)

Selected essays, translated by H. T. Lowe-Porter, are available as *Essays of Three Decades* (London: Secker & Warburg, 1947) and *Last Essays* (London: Secker & Warburg, 1959). Mann's major essay on Wagner is available in English as *Thomas Mann: Pro and Contra Wagner*, trans. Allan Blunden, ed. Erich Heller (London: Faber, 1985). Mann's longest non-fictional work has been translated as: *Reflections of a Nonpolitical Man*, trans. Walter D. Morris (New York: Ungar, 1983).

Selections from Mann's diaries are available in English in *Diaries 1918–1939* (London: Deutsch, 1983).

Selections from Mann's correspondence available in English include:

*Letters of Thomas Mann, 1889–1955*, trans. Richard and Clara Winston (London: Secker & Warburg, 1970; Berkeley: University of California Press, 1990), based on Erika Mann's three-volume edition

*Mythology and Humanism: The Correspondence of Thomas Mann and Karl Kerényi*, trans. Alexander Gelley (Ithaca and London: Cornell University Press, 1975)

*The Hesse–Mann Letters: The Correspondence of Hermann Hesse and Thomas Mann, 1910–55* (London: Peter Owen, 1976)

*Letters of Heinrich and Thomas Mann, 1900–1949*, trans. Don Reneau (Berkeley: University of California Press, 1998)

*Secondary literature*

There are numerous introductory studies in German. They range from the encyclopaedic *Thomas-Mann-Handbuch*, ed. Helmut Koopmann (2nd edn, Stuttgart: Kröner, 1995), to the booklets on some individual texts, including *Mario und der Zauberer*, in the series 'Erläuterungen und Dokumente' (Stuttgart: Reclam). A recent series of handy paperbacks, 'Selbstkommentare' (Frankfurt am Main: Fischer), collects Mann's own statements about various works, including, so far, *Buddenbrooks*, *Der Zauberberg*, *Doktor Faustus*, and *Lotte in Weimar*. They supplement the volumes on Thomas Mann in the series *Dichter über ihre Dichtungen*, ed. Hans Wysling (Munich: Heimeran, 1975–82).

The reader reliant on English sources should turn to two books by contributors to this volume. One is T. J. Reed's *Thomas Mann: The Uses of Tradition* (Oxford: Clarendon Press, 1974), reissued in 1996 with a new chapter defending Mann against those critics who took the publication of the diaries as an occasion to denigrate him. This has established itself as the central study of Mann in any language. The other is the collection of essays entitled *Thomas Mann*, ed. Michael Minden, in the series 'Modern Literatures in Perspective' (London and New York: Longman, 1995), which begins with a survey of Mann's changing reputation, then reprints various comments on Mann by his contemporaries, followed by a series of essays written during the past thirty years on Mann as a public figure and on *Buddenbrooks*, *The Magic Mountain* and *Doctor Faustus*. A number of these essays have been specially translated from German.

The following is a list of further studies of Mann, mainly in English but with a few particularly important items in German. Studies focused on individual texts are listed at the end of the appropriate chapter.

## Biography

Bürgin, Hans, and Hans-Otto Mayer, *Thomas Mann: Eine Chronik seines Lebens* (Frankfurt am Main: Fischer, 1965)
Hamilton, Nigel, *The Brothers Mann: The Lives of Heinrich and Thomas Mann, 1871–1950 and 1875–1955* (London: Secker & Warburg, 1978)
Hayman, Ronald, *Thomas Mann: A Biography* (London: Bloomsbury, 1996)
Heilbut, Anthony, *Thomas Mann: Eros and Literature* (London: Macmillan, 1996)
Kurzke, Hermann, *Thomas Mann: Das Leben als Kunstwerk* (Munich: Beck, 1999)
Mendelssohn, Peter de, *Der Zauberer: Das Leben von Thomas Mann*, vol. I (Frankfurt am Main: Fischer, 1975); vol. II (Frankfurt am Main: Fischer, 1992)
Prater, Donald A., *Thomas Mann: A Life* (Oxford: Clarendon Press, 1995)
Winston, Richard, *Thomas Mann: The Making of an Artist, 1875–1911* (London: Constable, 1982)
Wysling, Hans, and Yvonne Schmidlin (eds.), *Thomas Mann: Ein Leben in Bildern* (Zürich: Artemis, 1974)

## Collections of essays

Bloom, Harold (ed.), *Thomas Mann* (New York: Chelsea, 1986)
Ezergailis, Inta M. (ed.), *Critical Essays on Thomas Mann* (Boston: Hall, 1988)
Hansen, Volkmar (ed.), *Interpretationen: Thomas Mann, Romane und Erzählungen* (Stuttgart: Reclam, 1993)
Neider, Charles (ed.), *The Stature of Thomas Mann* (New York: New Directions, 1947)

## General studies

Apter, T. E., *Thomas Mann: The Devil's Advocate* (London: Macmillan, 1978)
Dierks, Manfred, *Studien zu Mythos und Psychologie bei Thomas Mann* (Berne: Francke, 1972)
Elsaghe, Yahya, *Die imaginäre Nation: Thomas Mann und das 'Deutsche'* (Munich: Fink, 2000)
Feuerlicht, Ignace, *Thomas Mann und die Grenzen des Ich* (Heidelberg: Winter, 1966)
Goldman, Harvey, *Max Weber and Thomas Mann: Calling and the Shaping of the Self* (Berkeley: University of California Press, 1988)

Heller, Erich, *The Ironic German: A Study of Thomas Mann* (London: Secker &
  Warburg, 1958)
Kurzke, Hermann, *Thomas Mann: Epoche, Werk, Wirkung* (Munich: Beck, 1985)
Lukács, Georg, *Essays on Thomas Mann*, trans. Stanley Mitchell (London: Merlin
  Press, 1964)
Marcus, Judith, *Georg Lukács and Thomas Mann: A Study in the Sociology of Lit-
  erature* (Amherst: University of Massachusetts Press, 1987)
Swales, Martin, *A Students' Guide to Thomas Mann* (London: Heinemann, 1980)
Travers, Martin, *Thomas Mann* (Basingstoke: Macmillan, 1992)

# INDEX

Numbers in bold type indicate a sustained discussion of the subject.